THE AUTHORITY OF INFLUENCE

GENDERING ASIA

A Series on Gender Intersections

Gendering Asia is a well-established and exciting series addressing the ways in which power and constructions of gender, sex, sexuality and the body intersect with one another and pervade contemporary Asian societies. The series invites discussion of how people shape their identities as females or males and, at the same time, become shaped by the very societies in which they live. The series is concerned with the region as a whole in order to capture the wide range of understandings and practices that are found in East, Southeast and South Asian societies with respect to gendered roles and relations in various social, political, religious, and economic contexts. As a multidisciplinary series, *Gendering Asia* explores theoretical, empirical and methodological issues in the social sciences.

Series Editors: Wil Burghoorn, Gothenburg University; Cecilia Milwertz, NIAS; and Helle Rydstrøm, Lund University (contact details at: http://www.niaspress.dk).

NIAS Press is the autonomous publishing arm of NIAS – Nordic Institute of Asian Studies, a research institute located at the University of Copenhagen. NIAS is partially funded by the governments of Denmark, Finland, Iceland, Norway and Sweden via the Nordic Council of Ministers, and works to encourage and support Asian studies in the Nordic countries. In so doing, NIAS has been publishing books since 1969, with more than two hundred titles produced in the past few years.

UNIVERSITY OF COPENHAGEN

Nordic Council of Ministers

The AUTHORITY
Women and Power in Burmese History
of INFLUENCE

Jessica Harriden

Nordic Institute of Asian Studies
Gendering Asia series, no. 7

First published in 2012 by NIAS Press
NIAS – Nordic Institute of Asian Studies
Leifsgade 33, 2300 Copenhagen S, Denmark
Tel: +45 3532 9501 • Fax: +45 3532 9549
E-mail: books@nias.ku.dk • Online: www.niaspress.dk

British Library Cataloguing in Publication Data
Harriden, Jessica.
   The authority of influence : women and power in Burmese
   history. -- (Gendering Asia ; 7)
      1. Women--Burma--Social conditions. 2. Women--Burma--
   History. 3. Power (Social sciences)--Sex differences--
   Burma.
   I. Title II. Series
   305.4'09591-dc22

      ISBN: 978-87-7694-088-1 (hbk)
      ISBN: 978-87-7694-089-8 (pbk)

Typesetting by NIAS Press
Printed in in the United Kingdom by Marston Digital

Cover photograph: Burmese *longyi* (© the author).

Contents

Map

Figures

Preface

One of the challenges in seeking to provide a 'long view' of gender-power relations in Burmese history is how to tell a complex story, or multiple stories, in one short volume. Given the broad scope of this study – to examine women's access to social, economic and political power over an extended historical period – it is not possible to examine all the available sources. I made the decision to limit the discussion of some issues, and to exclude some others, in the interests of developing clear and balanced chapters.

As a modern historian, I have relied on the works of established scholars of classical and pre-modern Burmese history who are well versed in the material of these earlier periods. Most Burma historians will be familiar with the political influence of queens and the arguments put forward about women's relatively 'high' social status and economic influence in pre-colonial society. What I have tried to do in this book is to show how and why the gender-power relations that characterised pre-colonial Burma have persisted into the present. While Burmese society has undergone dramatic transformation and upheaval during the last 125 years, in many respects women's relationship to power remains little different from what it was centuries ago. This book is as much about the lives of Burmese women today as it is about women who lived in the distant past.

As I write this preface, there is much uncertainty and debate about how the political, social and economic landscape of Burma may – or may not – be changing. Political and economic analysts, foreign diplomats and NGO workers are well aware of the complexities of Burma's myriad problems at the elite policy-making level and 'on the ground'. An appreciation of the historical roles and status of women will be helpful for anyone seeking to contextualise the current situation of Burmese women. For the benefit of non-Burmese and non-academic readers, I have tried to include references to English-language sources and translations of Burmese texts which are (for the most part) readily accessible.

In the process of researching and writing this book, I have received generous support from both institutions and individuals. This work was published with the assistance of a grant from the Australian Academy of the Humanities. As a PhD student, I received two academic scholarships from the University of Queensland, an Australian Postgraduate Award and a Graduate Student Research Travel Award, which enabled me to conduct archival and ethnographic research in Burma, Thailand and London. I wish to thank the staff of the Oriental and India Office Collections (British Library), the School of Oriental and African Studies Library (University of London), the Universities' Historical Research Centre Library (Yangon University) and the Universities' Central Library (Yangon University). I extend special thanks to the staff of the Social Sciences and Humanities Library and the School of History, Philosophy, Religion and Classics at the University of Queensland for their support and assistance.

I am forever indebted to my family for their unconditional love and support, endless patience and good humour. My parents, El and Peter, welcomed me back home when I returned from London with no money and kept me (relatively) sane while I finished writing my thesis. Allison, Shannon and Ben reminded me to live it up once in a while. My grandparents, John and Maria (Omi and Opa), have always offered unwavering love and support. Sadly, Opa passed away before he had a chance to see the book in its final form. Tara supplied endless cups of tea and laughs while I was revising the manuscript for publication. I am also deeply grateful to Norm and Jeannie for taking the time to read and comment on the final draft. Many friends have sustained me during the long research and writing process, but I would like to extend particular thanks to Lana, Rebecca, Josie, Lara, Jane, Kirsty, Louise, Jess, Joan and Majella.

I am deeply indebted to the many Burmese who generously shared their knowledge and experiences with me during my time in Burma and Thailand. Many people who agreed to speak to me did so at great personal risk, often to discuss painful experiences of suffering and loss. I would like to thank them all for sharing their stories. In particular, I extend my heartfelt appreciation to members of the Women's League of Burma, Burmese Women's Union, Kachin Women's Association Thailand and Social Action for Women for their assistance and hospitality while I was conducting interviews in Thailand.

I am most grateful to scholars who reviewed various versions of the text and offered constructive criticism and thoughtful suggestions, especially Barbara Andaya, Andrew Selth, Gustaaf Houtman, Bénédicte Brac de la Perrière and one anonymous reviewer. Special thanks to those who granted permission to use their photographs and illustrations, including Brenden Allen, Gillian Fletcher, Harn Lay, Bertil Lintner and Noel Singer.

I extend my deepest gratitude to my PhD advisers for their generous support and invaluable insights. Robert Cribb suggested that a study of women and power in Burmese history would make an interesting thesis topic and also drew the map of Burma. Bob Elson spurred me on with the judicious and alternate application of pressure and praise. But I would never have begun, let alone finished, this book without the guidance and support of Martin Stuart-Fox, who first introduced me to Southeast Asian history. Martin and Bob have gone above and beyond their role as supervisors, guiding me through the publication process and (re)reading countless drafts. Finally, my heartfelt thanks go to Gerald Jackson, Wil Burghoorn and the staff at NIAS Press. This book would never have come to fruition without their support.

Abbreviations

ABFSU	All Burma Federation of Student Unions
ABSDF	All Burma Students' Democratic Front
ACWC	ASEAN Commission on the Promotion and Protection of the Rights of Women and Children
AFPFL	Anti-Fascist People's Freedom League
ASEAN	Association of Southeast Asian Nations
BIA	Burma Independence Army
BLOM	British Library Oriental Manuscript
BRC	Burma Relief Centre
BSPP	Burma Socialist Programme Party
BWU	Burmese Women's Union
CEDAW	Convention on the Elimination of All Forms of Discrimination Against Women
CPB	Communist Party of Burma
GCBA	General Council of Burmese Associations
GONGO	Government-Organised Non-Governmental Organisation
IDP	internally displaced person
ILO	International Labour Organization
INGO	international non-governmental organisation
IOR	India Office Records
KIO	Kachin Independence Organisation
KMT	Kuomintang; Chinese nationalist army
KNDO	Karen National Defence Organisation
KNU	Karen National Union

KNWO	Karenni National Women's Organization
KWA	Kachin Women's Association
KWAT	Kachin Women's Association Thailand
KWHRO	Kuki Women's Human Rights Organization
KWO	Karen Women's Organization
LWO	Lahu Women's Organization
MI/MIS	Military Intelligence Service
MMCWA	Myanmar Maternal and Child Welfare Association
MNCWA	Myanmar National Committee for Women's Affairs
MWAF	Myanmar Women's Affairs Federation
MWEA	Myanmar Women's Entrepreneurial Association
MWO	Mon Women's Organization
NGO	non-governmental organisation
NLD	National League for Democracy
NLD–LA	National League for Democracy Liberated Area
NUP	National Unity Party
PWO	Palaung Women's Union
PWU	Pa-O Women's Union
RWU	Rakhaing Women's Union
SAW	Social Action for Women
SHRF	Shan Human Rights Foundation
SLORC	State Law and Order Restoration Council
SPDC	State Peace and Development Council
SSA	Shan State Army
SWAN	Shan Women's Action Network
TDWU	Tavoy District Women's Union
TWU	Tavoy Women's Union
UN	United Nations
UNHCR	United Nations High Commission on Refugees
UNICEF	United Nations International Children's Emergency Fund

US/USA	United States of America
USDA	Union Solidarity and Development Association
USDP	Union Solidarity and Development Party
WEAVE	Women's Education for Advancement and Empowerment
WLB	Women's League of Burma
WRWAB	Women's Rights and Welfare Association of Burma
YMBA	Young Men's Buddhist Association

Map of Burma

INDIA

CHINA

KACHIN
STATE

SAGAING
DIVISION

Shwebo

Sagaing Mandalay

CHIN
STATE

Bagan
(Pagan)

MANDALAY
DIVISION

SHAN
STATE

LAOS

Chauk

Mrauk-U

MAGWAY
DIVISION

Naypyitaw

RAKHINE
STATE

KAYAH
STATE

Prome (Pye)

BAGO
DIVISION

Bago (Pegu)

AYEYARWARDY
DIVISION

Yangon

KAYIN
STATE

YANGON
DIVISION

Mawlamyaing

MON
STATE

THAILAND

N

Dawei

300 kilometres

TANINTHARYI
DIVISION

International
boundaries

State/Division
boundaries

RBC

Introduction: Engendering Burmese History

A history of gender equality?

'*M*yanmar women have enjoyed equal rights with Myanmar men since time immemorial.'[1] This assertion of gender equality has become the unofficial slogan of the Myanmar Women's Affairs Federation (MWAF), the largest women's organisation in the Union of Myanmar, or Burma, as the country is more commonly known.[2] Yet there is overwhelming evidence that Burmese women have fewer opportunities to exercise political, economic and social power than men. The country's most prominent female political leader, Daw Aung San Suu Kyi, was released from her latest period of detention in November 2010, but she faces the prospect of rearrest if her popularity or political activities are deemed too threatening by the authorities. Days before her release, the military-backed Union Solidarity and Development Party (USDP) won the vast majority of seats in the country's first general election since 1990. Only 20 women were elected to the 659-seat national parliament. Burma's latest Constitution, enacted in 2008 following a controversial referendum held in the aftermath of Cyclone Nargis, reserves one quarter of legislative seats for the military, a predominantly male institution. From 1962 to March 2011, many Burmese suffered under the hands of a series of brutal military dictatorships, but women were (and remain) particularly vulnerable to

---

1   Dr Daw Khin Aye Win and Daw Zin Zin Naing, 'The role of Myanmar women in building a nation', in Myanmar Women's Affairs Federation, *Papers presented in honour of Myanmar Women's Day, 3 July 2005* (Yangon: [U Kyi Win at] Universities Press, 2005), 23.

2   The State Law and Order Restoration Council (SLORC) officially renamed the country 'Myanmar' in 1989, although Burmese opposition groups and some countries and international organisations reject this name change. For the sake of consistency, I will refer to the country as 'Burma' throughout this book. 'Burmese' conventionally refers both to the collectivity of peoples living in contemporary Burma (including Burmans, Shans, Karens, and so on) and to the language and culture of the predominant Burman ethnic group.

1

the damaging effects of extreme poverty and state-sponsored violence. Traditional cultural attitudes condoning discrimination against women, coupled with low levels of government spending on education and health, have also impeded women's opportunities for social and economic advancement.

Was this the kind of 'equality' that Burmese women 'enjoyed' in the past? Not according to British colonial administrator, Harold Fielding Hall, who observed one hundred years ago that Burmese women 'assumed a freedom unknown elsewhere. They knew no limits but their own disinclination'. Yet he went on to state that women needed to surrender their power if Burma was to make progress in the modern world, since 'it is the mark of rising nations that men control and women are not seen.'[3] Looking further back into Burma's pre-colonial history, we find evidence of powerful queens who dominated kings and their courts, even though the prevailing social system accorded women a lower status than men. It appears, then, that at least some Burmese women exercised power in the past, even if few do so today. This book endeavours to explain how they lost that power, and what attempts some women have made to recover it.

The 'gender gap' in Burmese history

The past two decades have seen growing scholarly interest in the experiences and contributions of women in Southeast Asian societies. While anthropologists, social scientists and feminist scholars have led the way in this regard, historians have also begun to examine the significance of women's activities and influence in Southeast Asian history. In the introduction to *Other pasts: women, gender and history in early modern Southeast Asia*, Barbara Watson Andaya observed that traditional historiography focused on inter-state diplomacy, political leadership and warfare – spheres of political and military action in which men played the dominant roles – which effectively marginalised women as subjects of historical enquiry.[4] When historians did mention women, they were usually represented as subservient, passive subjects with little or no

---

3   H. Fielding [Hall], *A people at school* (London: Macmillan, 1906), 260, 268.

4   Barbara Watson Andaya, 'Introduction', in Barbara Watson Andaya (ed.), *Other pasts: women, gender and history in early modern Southeast Asia* (Honolulu: Center for Southeast Asian Studies, University of Hawai'i at Manoa, 2000), 2.

political agency. For example, in an article on elite women of the Ava period (1365–1555), Burmese historian Tun Aung Chain concluded that women were 'always used and manipulated, the tools and pawns of the statecraft of the age.'[5] Occasionally, however, historians described Burmese queens as influential and even aggressive political actors who used 'sorcery' and 'sexual wiles' to control and manipulate kings and royal officials.[6] Traditional historiography has struggled to reconcile these contrasting images of Burmese women, usually relegating the latter to an obscure footnote in an otherwise male-dominated history. But is this representation accurate, or do traditional approaches overlook evidence of female power because of preconceived ideas about the pre-eminence of male power? Can a 'gendered' approach – one that actively seeks out female as well as male voices – provide a more comprehensive account of power relations in Burmese history?

In a recent survey of literature on women and gender in Southeast Asia, Andaya lamented that Burmese history remained 'understudied'.[7] Mi Mi Khaing's *The world of Burmese women*, published in 1984, remains a standard text.[8] Recent unpublished research examines women's religious, socio-economic and political roles in classical Pagan,[9] Queen Supayalat's influence in late-nineteenth century Konbaung politics,[10] and female participation in the nationalist struggle against British colonial rule.[11] Tharaphi Than's doctoral thesis explores the political and social experiences and influence of female writers, soldiers and prostitutes

---

5   Tun Aung Chain (Mingyinyo), 'Women in the statecraft of the Awa kingdom (1365–1555)', in *Essays given to Than Tun on his 75th birthday: studies in Myanma history, volume 1* (Yangon: Than Tun Diamond Jubilee Publication Committee, 1999), 107–20.

6   Arthur Purves Phayre, *History of Burma, including Burma proper, Pegu, Taungu, Tenasserim, and Arakan: from the earliest time to the end of the first war with British India*, second edition (London: Susil Gupta, 1967), 250–51, 260; Daw Khin Khin Ma, 'Myanmar queens in historical and literary texts', in *Texts and Contexts in Southeast Asia, Part III, Proceedings of the Texts and Contexts in Southeast Asia Conference, 12–14 December 2001* (Yangon: Universities Historical Research Centre, 2003), 197–204.

7   Barbara Watson Andaya, 'State of the field: studying women and gender in Southeast Asia', *International Journal of Asian Studies* 4, 1 (2007): 126.

8   Mi Mi Khaing, *The world of Burmese women* (London: Zed Books, 1984).

9   Pyone Yin, 'Women in the Bagan period' (MRes thesis, University of Yangon, 2001).

10 May Pwint Khaing, 'The role of Queen Supayalat during King Thibaw's reign' (MRes thesis, University of Yangon, 2001).

11 Naing Naing Maw, 'The role of Myanmar women in the nationalist movement (1906–1942)' (MA thesis, University of Yangon, 1999).

between 1942 and 1962.[12] Chie Ikeya has contributed several important publications which focus on how representations of Burmese women in the popular press reflected wider debates about gender, modernisation and nationalism in colonial Burma.[13] While the above studies all examine aspects of female agency and influence in Burmese society, they focus on discrete historical periods: none delve further into the past or examine more recent social, economic and political developments in order to assess how women's roles and status have changed over time (or conversely, how they have *not* changed).

This book aims to assess the nature, scope and limitations of female power from pre-colonial times to the present day. Such an approach is particularly pertinent when we consider that many historians have asserted that women had a relatively favourable economic position and social status in 'traditional' Southeast Asia, even though few women attained positions of authority in formal political and religious institutions.[14] We must be cautious about accepting 'traditional' gender roles at face value, however. The cultural construction of gender-power relations is an ongoing process that involves men and women negotiating, questioning and challenging prevailing ideas, institutions and practices in order to make sense of their lives and further their interests in specific social, economic and political contexts. Although it was exceptional for Burmese women to hold high political office, and impossible for them to become monks, many women found alternative ways to exercise political and religious influence. Queens used their familial connections to male rulers to enhance their political power at court. Women also performed important religious roles as merit-makers, nuns and spirit mediums. During the last one hundred years alone, Burma has under-

---

12 Tharaphi Than, 'Writers, fighters and prostitutes: women and Burma's modernity, 1942–1962' (PhD thesis, University of London, School of Oriental and African Studies, 2010).

13 Chie Ikeya, 'Gender, history and modernity: representing women in twentieth century colonial Burma' (PhD thesis, Cornell University, 2006); 'The "traditional" high status of women in Burma: a historical reconsideration', *Journal of Burma Studies* 10 (2005/2006): 51–81; 'The modern Burmese woman and the politics of fashion in Burma', *Journal of Asian Studies* 67,4 (November 2008): 1277–308; *Refiguring women, colonialism and modernity in Burma* (Honolulu: University of Hawai'i Press, 2011).

14 Georges Coedès, *Histoire ancienne des états hindouisés d'Extrême-Orient* (Hanoi: Imprimerie d'Extrême-Orient, 1944), 7–10; D. G. E. Hall, *A history of South-East Asia* (London: Macmillan, 1964), 3; Anthony Reid, *Southeast Asia in the age of commerce 1450–1680. Vol. 1: The land below the winds* (New Haven; London: Yale University Press, 1988), 162–65.

gone tremendous social, economic and political upheaval. Despite facing many challenges as a result of colonialism, civil war and military rule, women have emerged as some of the country's most influential political activists and social commentators.

A methodology for restoring Burmese women to history

How can we introduce a gendered perspective to Burmese history? The obvious place to begin is with the existing source material, which I have re-examined in order to show where and why female voices have been omitted, overlooked and occasionally embellished in traditional historical accounts. This task is not as difficult as it may be for others studying societies where women were 'hidden away' or otherwise excluded from public life. In any given historical period, Burmese women were 'there' – participating in religious rituals, engaging in commerce and taking an active interest in political affairs. The more important question is why Burma historians, and the Burmese themselves, accorded less importance and prestige to women's roles than men's roles. To answer this question, I have drawn on other disciplinary approaches that emphasise the legitimacy and agency of certain groups over others, namely feminist, anthropological and social science discourses on power.

Concepts of 'power' are neither universal nor fixed, but are constantly being constructed, contested and negotiated by men and women in different historical circumstances. Maila Stivens has warned against accepting uncritically Western discourses of power that privilege men's exercise of authority in formal political institutions, but ignore the contribution of women's political behaviour and influence in informal contexts.[15] In this book, I use a broad definition of 'power' that acknowledges the importance of women's informal political, religious and economic activities within the household and in the local community. Most Burmese readily acknowledge that women have always exercised considerable influence over their husbands and other male family members in the 'private' realm of the household, even while they deferred to men's authority in public. This book will explore the important concept of 'family' in Burmese political culture, and consider how women's influ-

---

15 Maila Stivens, 'Why gender matters in Southeast Asian politics', in Maila Stivens (ed.), *Why gender matters in Southeast Asian politics* (Clayton, Vic.: Centre of Southeast Asian Studies, Monash University, 1991), 9–24.

ence within the domestic realm could and often did extend to the public political domain. Political power derived from a complex network of social relationships that was strengthened through kinship, marriage and other 'familial' ties such as those formed between patrons and their clients. In pre-colonial Burma, queens could enhance their power by negotiating marriage alliances with ruling families. Under military rule, the wives and daughters of senior generals played an important role in facilitating military patronage networks. Familial connections were also crucial in establishing the legitimacy of female nationalists, insurgents and politicians, including Aung San Suu Kyi.

Our understanding of Burmese political culture owes much to the pioneering work of Lucian Pye, who eschewed universalistic theories of political behaviour in favour of more comparative and contextual interpretations. Pye argued that, in Burmese culture, '[c]onsiderations of power and status so permeate even social relationships that life tends to become highly politicised. The fact that Buddhism is a central feature of Burmese life makes the quest for power more subtle and more indirect.'[16] In the 1970s and 1980s, a number of researchers sought to demonstrate that Buddhist concepts shaped notions of gender relations in Southeast Asian societies and legitimised social hierarchies in which men exercised power over women.[17] This study will consider how localised Burmese concepts naturalising gender differences were conflated with 'Buddhist' values and practices to assert men's spiritual superiority, which effectively prevented most women from attaining prominent positions in formal religious and political institutions associated with power, authority and prestige.

Other scholars have argued that Southeast Asian concepts of bilateralism diffused distinctions of hierarchy in gender relationships and

---

16   Lucian W. Pye, *Politics, personality and nation building: Burma's search for identity* (New Haven; London: Yale University Press, 1962), 146.

17   A. Thomas Kirsh, 'Economy, polity, and religion in Thailand', in G. William Skinner and A. Thomas Kirsch (eds.), *Change and persistence in Thai society: essays in honour of Lauriston Sharp* (Ithaca; London: Cornell University Press, 1975), 172–96; Melford E. Spiro, 'Gender hierarchy in Burma: cultural, social, and psychological dimensions', in Barbara Diane Miller (ed.), *Sex and gender hierarchies* (Cambridge; New York; Oakleigh, Vic.: Cambridge University Press, 1993), 316–33; Khin Thitsa, 'Nuns, mediums and prostitutes in Chiengmai: a study of some marginal categories of women', in C. W. Watson (ed.), *Women and development in South-East Asia* (Canterbury: Center of South-East Asian Studies, University of Kent at Canterbury, 1983), 4–45.

allowed for alternative paradigms of power and prestige.[18] Seen in this light, women's informal religious and political activities were highly valued as complementing men's formal religious and political roles. Western preconceptions about the pre-eminence of political leadership and physical strength as markers of 'power' has led to the assumption that power can only be exercised by those who hold senior positions in formal bureaucratic and military organisations. In the West, the power of the individual in office stems largely from the power of the office itself, rather than the personal qualities of the office holder. The Burmese, however, tend to place as much emphasis on the personal and moral qualities of their political leaders.

Many Burmese words associated with 'power' include a moral dimension. The vast majority of Burmese Buddhists believe that men possess *hpoun* ('glory'), an innate spiritual superiority acquired through accumulated merit, which enables them to assume positions of formal political authority (*ana*). Women, by contrast, are generally excluded from such positions (and discouraged from seeking them) because they do not possess *hpoun*. While *ana* is a morally ambiguous term, *awza* ('influence') is inherently positive. People with *awza* – those who are recognised for their charisma, wisdom and high morality – can exercise considerable political influence even if they do not hold any formal political office. Gustaaf Houtman has convincingly argued that Aung San Suu Kyi's power is largely a function of her *awza*, her moral and spiritual strength, which many Burmese recognise in spite of the fact that she has never been a member of parliament.[19] The above studies, which will be explored in greater detail in the following chapters, provide a useful starting point for examining the relationship between women and power in Burmese history.

---

18 Wazir Jaham Karim (ed.), *'Male' and 'female' in developing Southeast Asia* (Oxford; Washington: Berg Publishers, 1995), esp. chapters 1 and 2; Charles F. Keyes, 'Mother or mistress but never a monk: Buddhist notions of female gender in rural Thailand', *American Ethnologist* 11, 2 (May 1984): 223–41.

19 Gustaaf Houtman, *Mental culture in Burmese crisis politics: Aung San Suu Kyi and the National League for Democracy* (Tokyo: Institute for the Study of Languages and Cultures of Asia and Africa, Tokyo University of Foreign Studies, 1999), esp. 157–76. Aung San Suu Kyi plans to contest a seat in by-elections scheduled for April 2012, which may see her assume parliamentary office for the first time.

Challenges for researchers – availability and reliability of sources

The lack of historical research on Burmese women reflects both the considerable difficulties of conducting research inside Burma and the nature of available source materials. Challenges for researchers include how to locate relevant primary sources – many of which are not only rare or out-of-print, but housed in various private, archival and library collections in Burma, England and elsewhere. Under military rule, Burmese authorities were notoriously suspicious of foreigners (particularly Westerners), making it extremely difficult for non-Burmese scholars to conduct research inside the country. In Yangon (Rangoon), the Universities' Historical Research Centre (UHRC) Library and the Universities' Central Library collections are severely under-resourced and contain little scholarly material covering the post-1962 period, in particular. Among these collections, however, are many useful English and Burmese-language newspapers, journals and monographs as well as unpublished theses and manuscripts. Officially sanctioned publications can be purchased from government bookstores, but it is often more fruitful (if time-consuming) to trawl through the many second-hand bookstalls that line the streets of downtown Yangon in search of rare and out-of-print books. I was also fortunate to gain access to several extensive and well-preserved private library collections, although the owners requested anonymity in order to avoid persecution by the authorities.

Existing source materials pose significant challenges for researchers interested in women's history. Our knowledge about the lives of women in pre-colonial Burma is based on lithic inscriptions recording dedications to Buddhist establishments and various written texts including royal chronicles, court records, Buddhist commentaries, literary works and the customary law codes (*dhammathats*). Most scholars have relied heavily on epigraphic evidence to reconstruct the history of early Burma.[20] Although stone inscriptions tend to record formulaic statements about Buddhist values and ideals, they can also shed light

---

20 Useful epigraphic sources include Government of Burma, *List of inscriptions found in Burma*, compiled and edited by Charles Duroiselle (Rangoon: Superintendent Government Printing, 1921); G. H. Luce and Pe Maung Tin (eds.), *Inscriptions of Burma*, 6 volumes (Rangoon: Oriental Studies Publications, University of Rangoon, 1933–56). Pe Maung Tin also wrote the seminal article, 'Women in the inscriptions of Pagan', which was originally published in the *Journal of the Burma Research Society* in 1935. See Burma Research Society, Fiftieth Anniversary Publications No. 2, Selections of articles from the *Journal of the Burma Research Society* (History and Literature) (Rangoon, 1960), 411–21.

on the economic, social and religious roles of female donors and other women. Royal chronicles are generally regarded as less reliable historical records, since they often describe events that occurred hundreds of years earlier and are peppered with authorial biases, discrepancies with regards to dates, persons and events, and the combination of mythical and real events. Moreover, chroniclers focused on recording the 'grand narratives' of Buddhism, kingship and political struggles between male rulers, so effectively marginalising women's roles as important historical actors. Recent gender-based research has demonstrated, however, that a re-examination of courtly narratives can shed light on female agency in pre-modern Southeast Asian polities.[21]

Michael Aung-Thwin and others have shown that chronicles and literary sources can reveal important cultural 'statements' including conceptions of power and gender.[22] Such texts often present an idealised version of femininity to which women were expected to conform. The *Hmannan yazawin* or the 'Glass Palace Chronicle of the kings of Burma' was compiled in 1821 at a time when King Bagyidaw's relatives and ministers were greatly concerned about the chief queen's influence over the king and his court.[23] While the *Hmannan* may not always faithfully describe how the royal women of Pagan acted and thought centuries earlier, it does provide us with an insight into how nineteenth century (male) elites viewed women's roles at a crucial period in Burmese history.

---

21 Ruzy Hashim, 'Bringing Tun Kudu out of the shadows: interdisciplinary approaches to understanding the female presence in the Serajah Melayu', in Andaya (ed.), *Other pasts: women, gender and history in early modern Southeast Asia*, 105–24.

22 Michael Aung-Thwin, 'Prophecies, omens and dialogue: tools of the trade in Myanmar historiography', in D. Wyatt and A. Woodside (eds.), *Moral order and the question of social change: essays on Southeast Asian thought* (New Haven: Yale University Southeast Asian Studies, 1982), 78–103; John N. Miksic, 'Heroes and heroines in Bagan-period Myanmar and early classic Indonesia', in Universities Historical Research Centre, *Views and Visions, Part I, Proceedings of the Views and Visions Conference, 18–20 December 2000* (Yangon: Universities Historical Research Centre, 2001), 58–71; Thet Htoot, 'The nature of the Burmese chronicles', in D.G.E. Hall (ed.), *Historians of Southeast Asia* (Oxford: Oxford University Press, 1961), 50–62; Maung Htin Aung, *Burmese history before 1287: a defence of the chronicles* (Oxford: The Asoka Society; London: [Distributed by] Luzac, 1970), 2.

23 The *Hmannan* was based on U Kala's *Maha yazawindawgyi* ('The great royal chronicle'), which was compiled in the early eighteenth century. See U Kala, *Maha yazawindawgyi* [The great royal chronicle], edited by Pe Maung Tin, Saya Pwa and Saya U Khin Soe, 3 volumes (Yangon: Hanthawaddy Press, 1960–61). Gordon Luce and Pe Maung Tin translated parts 3, 4 and 5 of the *Hmannan* (which relate the history of Pagan) into English in 1923. See *The Glass Palace Chronicle of the kings of Burma*, translated by Pe Maung Tin and G. H. Luce (London: Oxford University Press, 1923; Rangoon: Rangoon University Press, 1960).

Similarly, the *Konbaungzet maha yazawindawgyi* ('Great royal chronicle of the Konbaung Dynasty')[24] reveals the attitudes of male elites towards powerful queens of the latter Konbaung period, who were blamed for the loss of Burmese sovereignty in the late nineteenth century. I have re-examined these chronicles in order to reveal female voices (where they exist) and to show how these sources both reflected contemporary attitudes towards women and influenced future generations' conceptualisations of appropriate female roles and behaviour.

Male British and Burmese elites were equally concerned with evaluating and proscribing female roles and behaviour in colonial Burma (1886–1948). British merchants, official envoys and residents described their encounters with and impressions of Burmese women in personal journals and records of diplomatic missions.[25] Archival records documenting the colonial administration of Burma, many of which are housed in the India Office Records at the British Library in London, reveal that British attitudes towards Burmese women were highly ambivalent. Christian colonial elites associated the relative social freedom of Burmese women with 'loose' morality, and regarded education primarily as a means of instilling European ideals of domesticity and subservience in the indigenous female population. Burmese nationalists referred to women's 'traditional' high status in order to strengthen their claims to independence from colonial rule, but they also criticised women who married or associated with foreigners on the grounds that this weakened the 'purity' of the Burmese 'race' (*amyo*) and culture.[26]

One of the by-products of colonial education was an increase in the number of newspaper and magazine articles and literary works authored

---

24   Tin (of Mandalay), *Konbaungzet maha yazawindawgyi* [Great royal chronicle of the Konbaung Dynasty], 3 volumes (Yangon: Ledimandaing, 1967–68). Originally published in 1908, this chronicle comprised the narrative of the Glass Palace Chronicle (1752–1854) and U Tin's own account of the reigns of Mindon (1853–78) and Thibaw (1878–85) and the latter's exile.

25   Hiram Cox, *Journal of a residence in the Burmhan empire*, with an introduction by D.G.E. Hall ([Farnborough]: Gregg International, 1971); Michael Symes, *An account of an embassy to the Kingdom of Ava, sent by the Governor-General of India in the year 1795* (London: W. Blumer and Co., 1800; republished Westmead, Farnborough, Hants., England: Gregg International Publishers Limited, 1969); Michael Symes, *Journal of his second embassy to the Court of Ava in 1802*, edited with an introduction and notes by D.G.E. Hall (London: Allen & Unwin, 1955); Gwendolen Trench Gascoigne, *Among pagodas and fair ladies: an account of a tour through Burma* (London: A. D. Innes, 1896); Harold Fielding Hall, *The soul of a people*, second edition (London: Macmillan, 1898).

26   Ikeya also makes this point in 'The "traditional" high status of women in Burma', 60, 63–75.

and, in some cases, published by Burmese women. The late colonial period saw the emergence of some of Burma's most celebrated female journalists, publishers and novelists, who highlighted women's experiences of colonialism, nationalism and modernity in their writings.[27] Several biographies shed light on the lives of Burma's ethnic minority women during the first turbulent decade of independence. In *The white umbrella*, Canadian journalist Patricia Elliot recounts the life of Sao Hearn Hkam, an elite Shan nationalist who served as a member of parliament in U Nu's government and went on to play a leading role in the Shan insurgency following the 1962 military coup.[28] Other firsthand accounts by Karen, Kachin, Mon and Shan women describe how their experiences of discrimination by the predominantly Burman *tatmadaw* (armed forces) prompted them to become involved in ethnic nationalist organisations.[29] These sources are particularly useful for scholars seeking to understand Burma's long history of inter-ethnic conflict from a gendered perspective.

The imposition of military rule following General Ne Win's 1962 coup severely impeded the ability of scholars to conduct research in Burma. Most government records and statistics remain either unavailable to the public, incomplete or inaccurate, which makes it extremely difficult to obtain reliable information concerning women's access to education, health and social welfare services, employment opportunities and formal political processes.[30] Indigenous scholars are subjected to strict censorship laws: even prominent historians like Daw Ni Ni Myint, who was once married to Ne Win, are unable to publish anything that could be construed as critical of the government and its policies. In

---

27 The prime example is Ma Ma Lay, *Mon ywe mahu* [Not out of hate] (Yangon: Shumawa, 1955). For an English translation, see Ma Ma Lay, *Not out of hate: a novel of Burma*, edited by William H. Frederick; translated by Margaret Aung-Thwin; introduced by Anna Allott; afterword by Robert E. Vore; Monographs in International Studies, Southeast Asia Series, No. 88 (Athens, Ohio: Ohio University Center for International Studies, 1991). See also Khin Myo Chit, *Colourful Burma*, volume 2 ([Rangoon, Burma]: Daw Tin Aye [for] Paper Stationery Printed Matter and Photographic Stores Trade Corporation, BE 2500 [1988]).

28 Patricia Elliot, *The white umbrella* (Bangkok: Post Books, 1999).

29 Altsean Burma, *Burma: voices of women in the struggle* (1998), *Burma – women's voices for change* (June 2002), and *Burma – women's voices together* (2003). All published by Altsean Burma, edited by the Thanakha Team (Bangkok: Alternative ASEAN Network on Burma).

30 The government's Central Statistical Organization periodically publishes a *Statistical profile of children and women in Myanmar*, which contains some statistical data on women's formal political representation and access to education, health and social welfare services as well as limited information on female prisoners.

The status of Myanmar women, Ni Ni Myint reiterated the official view that 'throughout Myanmar history women have enjoyed equal rights with men', before proceeding to discuss women's status in the areas of education, health, employment, law and the family.[31] Significantly, there is no chapter on women's participation in politics. Ni Ni Myint cites government statistics which reveal that less than one percent of senior government positions are held by women. Yet she concludes that women simply 'prefer' to enter other professions, ignoring overwhelming evidence that military rule reinforced male-dominated power structures and effectively excluded women from positions of political authority.

As a foreigner interested in studying 'women' and 'power', my own efforts to conduct research in Burma had to be carefully negotiated because of the regime's hostility towards Aung San Suu Kyi, whose popularity and influence has endured despite the (former) military government's repeated attempts to silence her and her supporters.[32] Aung San Suu Kyi's political career is well documented in primary and secondary sources.[33] Yet scholars have paid surprisingly little attention to the role that Aung San Suu Kyi's gender has played in debates about her effectiveness as a political leader, or considered how her high profile has influenced the development of both state-sponsored and expatriate Burmese women's organisations.

There is a need to understand how Burmese women exercised power in the past, as men and women negotiate the boundaries of gender-power relations in modern Burma. The recent proliferation of women's organisations inside Burma and along its borders has been ac-

---

31   Ni Ni Myint, *The status of Myanmar women* ([Kitakyushu], Japan: Kitakyushu Forum on Asian Women; [Yangon], Myanmar: Universities Historical Research Centre, September 2002).

32   The military government's views about Aung San Suu Kyi were evident in scathing personal attacks frequently published in the state-controlled press, notably *The New Light of Myanmar*.

33   Aung San Suu Kyi, *Freedom from fear and other writings*, foreword by Vaclav Havel, edited and introduced by Michael Aris (Harmondsworth: Penguin Books, 1991) (2nd edition published in London: Penguin, 1995); Aung San Suu Kyi with Alan Clements, U Kyi Maung, U Tin U, *The voice of hope: Aung San Suu Kyi conversations with Alan Clements*, with contributions by U Kyi Maung and U Tin U (New York: Seven Stories Press, 1997); Ang Chin Geok, *Aung San Suu Kyi: towards a new freedom* (Sydney: Prentice Hall, 1998); Bertil Lintner, *Aung San Suu Kyi and Burma's unfinished renaissance*, Working Paper 64 (Clayton, Vic.: Centre of Southeast Asian Studies, Monash University, 1990); Josef Silvertstein, 'The idea of freedom in Burma and the political thought of Daw Aung San Suu Kyi', *Pacific Affairs* 69, 2 (Summer 1996): 211–28.

companied by various pronouncements and recommendations aimed at 'empowering' women, but different women's organisations can have vastly divergent views about what 'empowerment' entails. For expatriate women's organisations, it involves increasing women's participation in political decision-making and leadership within the exiled democratic movement and in Burmese society as a whole. Many expatriate women's organisations are closely aligned with male-led opposition and ethnic nationalist organisations, but the feminist goals of the former often conflict with the male-dominated power structures of the latter. State-sanctioned women's organisations are predominantly concerned with mobilising women in support of the government rather than any genuine desire to promote gender equality. Although organisations like the MWAF are nominally led by the wives of senior government leaders, policies and programs are ultimately directed by their husbands and so reinforce male power in Burmese society.

The political influence of state-sponsored women's organisations is much debated in Burmese news media abroad, but within the state-controlled press they are mentioned mainly in self-congratulatory pieces on the opening of schools, health clinics and beauty pageants. I have referred extensively to UN and international human rights organisations' reports in order to provide a more comprehensive analysis of the Burmese government's implementation of the Convention on the Elimination of All Forms of Discrimination Against Women (CEDAW). Expatriate news services frequently report on human rights abuses and other forms of discrimination against women, but some reports betray a strong political bias and must be treated with caution.[34] Regional human rights groups such as Altsean Burma also publish regular reports on the status of Burmese women, but the most extensive literature on violence and other forms of discrimination against women is produced by expatriate Burmese women's organisations. Many of their reports are available online at www.womenofburma.org.

I have supplemented this material with my own interviews, conducted with Burmese women during two research trips to Burma and Thailand in November 2003–January 2004 and June–July 2005 as well

---

34 Expatriate news organisations include *The Irrawaddy* (a Thai-based print and online publication) and the *Democratic Voice of Burma* (a Norwegian-based news organisation and radio station) among others.

as subsequent email correspondence. Interviewees included members of state-sanctioned women's organisations and expatriate women's and human rights organisations in Yangon, Mandalay, Bangkok, Chiang Mai, Mae Sot and Mae Hong Son. Despite the potentially controversial and sensitive nature of the issues discussed, most interviewees were eager to share their personal experiences and views on women's status and access to power. This was true even in cases where women had been imprisoned or been subjected to other forms of violence including military rape. Members of state-sanctioned women's organisations were (understandably) reluctant to criticise the government in any way, while opposition activists were more critical of the (former) military regime and its policies and sometimes their male colleagues in the exiled democratic movement. In most cases, interviewees' names have been withheld to ensure their anonymity. While it is impossible to describe the experiences of *all* Burmese women in *every* historical period, by analysing a wide range of sources I hope to provide a nuanced, comprehensive study of female power in Burmese history in the following chapters.

Chapter outline

Chapter 1 explains how Burmese concepts of power and gender have informed men and women's social roles and behaviours. Notions of power emphasising male spiritual superiority enabled men to assume positions of authority in formal political and religious institutions. Yet many cultural beliefs and practices also affirmed women's important roles within the family and in the household-oriented economy, which were highly valued as complementing men's more prominent roles in public office. This chapter examines the concept of 'family' in Burmese political culture and explores how some women were able to gain political influence through their familial relationships with powerful men.

Chapter 2 discusses how the development of the Burmese polity as a form of extended family network supported and strengthened by female royal lineages, marriage alliances and client-patron relationships enabled some women to exercise social, economic and political influence in classical and pre-modern Burma. Chapter 3 undertakes a closer examination of female power in the Konbaung era (1752–1855), and considers how powerful queens overtly challenged men's authority during a crucial period when the Burmese state was threatened by internal

14

power struggles and British economic, military and political aggression. Historical representations of these women had important implications for Burmese and British conceptualisations of 'appropriate' female behaviour in the colonial period.

Chapter 4 explores the impact of colonialism and nationalism on women's roles and status during the first half of the twentieth century. Access to formal education opened up new economic and social opportunities for women, but educated women who embraced modern lifestyles and took up paid employment outside the home often faced criticism for forsaking Burmese tradition and culture. Women performed important roles in the anti-colonial struggle, but prevailing cultural attitudes prevented most female nationalists from seeking or attaining positions of political leadership. The first decade of independence was marked by political factionalism, ethnic separatism, civil unrest and increasing militarisation, which impeded efforts to rebuild the nation's economic and social institutions. The focus on power struggles between male political and military leaders effectively limited most women's political activism to supporting roles, although a few elite women gained prominence as members of parliament and underground insurgent organisations. These issues are discussed in chapter 5.

Chapter 6 analyses the devastating impact of military rule on women between 1962 and 1988. Under Ne Win's leadership, the military elite assumed control over the country's political, economic and social institutions. Women bore the worst effects of military rule including extreme poverty, social control, increasing violence and political oppression. Chapter 7 is concerned with explaining how one woman, Aung San Suu Kyi, rapidly rose to prominence as the leader of Burma's pro-democracy movement at the height of the mass anti-government demonstrations in 1988. This chapter analyses the sources of Aung San Suu Kyi's power and considers why her high profile has not translated into a significant increase in women's power within the democratic movement.

Chapter 8 considers whether there was any improvement in women's lives under the State Law and Order Restoration Council (SLORC) (1988–97) and the State Peace and Development Council (SPDC) (1997–March 2011). Since the early 1990s, the state has allowed – and, in some cases, directed – the establishment of several organisations with the declared aims of promoting women's advancement. Since the government has consistently claimed that women have the same rights as men, it is valid to ask what motivated its new-found interest in women's issues, what purposes these organisations actually served, and whether they offered any new avenues of power for women.

In chapter 9, the focus moves outside Burma to discuss how expatriate Burmese women began to question traditionalist ideas about gender roles that limited women's participation in political leadership and decision-making processes. In their efforts to achieve equality with men, these women have to overcome patriarchal attitudes and deep-rooted stereotypes to show that they can play an equal role in bringing about peace and democratic reform in Burma. The final chapter draws together the main themes of the book in order to explain how Burmese women have been disempowered and considers what prospects there are for improvement of their position in the future.

1

The Ambiguous Status of Women in Burmese Society

*I*n order to examine the nature, scope and limitations of female power in Burmese history, we first need to understand how the Burmese have viewed themselves, their society and the world around them. This chapter seeks to discern regular threads underlying diverse Burmese worldviews, which shaped men's and women's everyday behaviour. Worldviews are constructed through upbringing, formal education, socialisation and life experience, and are both individual and shared – to the extent to which ideas are held in common. All forms of social interaction, including gender relations, are interpreted and evaluated through this process of conceptualisation. Worldview refers both to conceptions of how the social world *is* constituted (in a material and descriptive sense) and how it *should be* constituted (in an ideal and prescriptive sense). At times, then, we might expect to find discrepancies between the *ideal* roles and behaviours ascribed to women and the *actual* roles and behaviour of women in their everyday lives. Faced with the circumstances of life, women will be expected by most Burmese to act in a certain way and most will, but not all.

This chapter will consider how various influences shaped both Burmese notions of gender relations and conceptions of how power should legitimately be exercised. Depending on one's definition of 'power', it is possible to deny, undermine, reveal or reify women's agency and influence in society. Traditional Western conceptualisations of power have tended to focus on the authority exercised by people who hold senior positions in formal political, military and religious institutions. The patriarchal, hierarchical nature of Burmese institutions meant that most women were excluded from exercising power in this sense. Localised understandings of power were also conflated with Buddhist and Brahmanic concepts to assert men's spiritual superiority and authority over women in public, formal contexts. Yet other indigenous concepts of power emphasised the importance of leaders' personal qualities and charisma, which allowed some women to assert moral authority and influence even while they were denied access to formal political or religious office. Patriarchal social hierarchies were also 'softened' by the bilateral nature of kinship relationships, which enabled women to exercise social, economic and even political influence through informal, familial networks.

Defining power and its forms

Put simply, power is the capacity to bring about intended consequences in the behaviour of others. Sociologists have demonstrated that power relations are embedded in all social relationships. Talcott Parsons defined social power as a specific mechanism of social interaction operating in the political subsystem of society, which enables some people to exercise control over others in order to attain collective goals.[1] He also observed that there are qualitative differences between forms of social interaction and that people can have personalised and formally detached relationships based on the roles they play. Thus, he distinguished between 'expressive' and 'instrumental' systems of social interaction, where the former would include families while the latter would include bureaucracies.[2] In *The sources of social power*, Michael Mann applied sociological theory in a detailed historical analysis of power.[3] Mann defined power as the ability to pursue and attain goals through the mastery of one's environment; social power, more specifically, refers to mastery exercised over other people. In order to attain their goals, humans set up networks of socio-spatial organisation. Mann identified four such

---

1 Talcott Parsons and Edward A. Shils, 'The social system', in Talcott Parsons and Edward A. Shils (eds.), *Toward a general theory of action* (New York: Harper & Row, 1962), 202; Talcott Parsons, *Structure and process in modern societies* (Glencoe, Illinois: Free Press, 1960), 181.

2 Parsons and Shils, 'The social system', 209–18. See also Talcott Parsons, *The social system* (Glencoe, Illinois: Free Press, 1951).

3 Michael Mann, *The sources of social power. Vol. 1. A history of power from the beginning to A.D. 1760* (Cambridge: Cambridge University Press, 1986); *The sources of social power. Vol. 2. The rise of classes and nation-states, 1760–1914* (Cambridge: Cambridge University Press, 1993).

networks – ideological, economic, military and political – as the main sources of social power.[4]

Let me briefly consider how the first three of these sources of social power operated in the Burmese context. Ideological power is an important form of social power in religiously centred cultures because religion prescribes the means of organising social relations. These influence how institutions of power are constructed, in particular the forms of economic and political regulation they provide. Buddhist ideology played a crucial role in the development of Burmese socio-political organisation and continues today to inform conceptions of how power should legitimately be exercised in Burmese society. Although Buddhism did not create social and gender hierarchies, Burmese notions of male spiritual superiority were often conceptualised in 'Buddhist' terms, which reinforced the belief that such hierarchies were entirely natural. Yet many Buddhist texts and rituals also celebrated women's maternal roles and virtuous qualities, which allowed women to exercise influence in a more egalitarian way within their families and communities. The personalised nature of power relationships in Burmese culture enabled women with familial connections to powerful men to extend their influence well into the formal political arena.

Economically, women maintained a degree of independence in Burmese society until the introduction of the Western capitalist system under colonial rule marginalised women's traditional economic roles, which were centred on small-scale agriculture, trading and industry, especially weaving and textile manufacture. Following the 1962 coup, economic power became concentrated in the hands of those with close connections to the military elite. Women's control over household finances was increasingly perceived as a burden, rather than a privilege, as they struggled to provide for their families in the face of soaring commodity prices and low wages. Military leaders' efforts to control the population through the suppression of civil society and tolerance of state-sanctioned violence turned out to be particularly detrimental to women. Many women became active participants in the democratic movement, both within Burma itself and abroad, in response to military oppression. Ideological, economic and military power will be discussed

---

4   Mann, *The sources of social power. Vol. 1*, 1–33. These four networks are commonly known as the 'IEMP model' of social power.

in greater detail below and in the following chapters, but let us now turn to Mann's fourth source of social power – political power.

Mann defined political power in terms of the state and its institutions. This narrow definition assumes that political power can only be possessed by people who hold an official position in a governmental or related organisation, and does not take into account the negotiated relationship between state and non-state actors. We need to consider the relationships between men (who hold political office) and women (who do not) as negotiated power relationships themselves. This kind of analysis requires a broader, more inclusive definition of political power that can accommodate these relationships – one that recognises informal power exercised by women within their families and local communities as functioning alongside the more visible formal power exercised by (predominantly male) government officials.

The Burmese have always placed great emphasis on personalised as well as institutional forms of power, status and prestige. Lucian Pye and Gustaaf Houtman have analysed two Buddhist concepts of power – *ana* and *awza* – in order to explain how institutional and personalised forms of power function in modern Burmese political culture.[5] *Ana* refers to 'authority' or centralised power that is public and attributable, whereas *awza* or 'influence' is personalised power that is inferred and attributed indirectly. The military's institutional power is characterised by *ana*-style authority; it is less effective than *awza* in that it is not 'popular'. By contrast, Aung San Suu Kyi has no official authority or *ana*, although this may change if she is elected as a member of parliament. Nevertheless, she possesses great *awza* in terms of her personal charisma, and her spiritual and ethical approach to leadership forms a crucial element in the moral power invested in her by others.[6] Aung San Suu Kyi's *awza* functions in much the same way as Max Weber's 'charismatic authority' in that it is regarded by her supporters as a 'supernatural' gift that makes her a 'natural' leader.[7]

---

5   Pye, *Politics, personality, and nation building*, 148–50; Houtman, *Mental culture in Burmese crisis politics*, 160–76. Although the concepts *ana* and *awza* are commonly used to describe post-1962 Burmese politics, they were also used to explain the power of monarchs and spirits in pre-colonial Burma.

6   Houtman, *Mental culture in Burmese crisis politics*, 282–86.

7   Max Weber, *Economy and society: an outline of interpretive sociology*, edited by Guenther Roth and Claus Wittich (New York: Bedminster Press, 1968), III, 1113–17.

Benedict Anderson proposed that the Javanese conceive power as 'concrete, homogenous, constant in total quantity, and without inherent moral implications'.[8] Is Anderson's framework more useful than Mann's for explaining how power operates in Burmese society? Like the Javanese, the Burmese view power as a concrete, creative energy. Many Burmese believe in an innate spiritual quality, known as *hpoun* ('glory'), which resides in the physical body of all male humans. Anderson's second principle presumes that the power possessed by one person is essentially the same as that possessed by another. Yet many Burmese believe that women cannot possess *hpoun* – they can only hope to be reborn as men with *hpoun*. The third principle relates to the idea that the total sum of power in the universe remains constant, although the distribution of power may vary. Anderson and others have employed the concept of 'mandala' to explain how political boundaries in pre-modern Southeast Asian polities contracted and expanded in response to the relative strength of neighbouring polities. In other respects, however, Anderson's concept of constant power sits uncomfortably with the Buddhist notions of impermanence that inform Burmese power relationships. This brings us to Anderson's fourth principle – that power has no inherent moral implications. Some Burmese believe that possession of *hpoun* is self-legitimising: 'Simply by virtue of possessing power, one has demonstrated that one has acquired considerable merit in past lives. Thus the question of moral legitimacy does not arise.'[9] While this statement would seem to support Anderson's theory, other types of power recognised by the Burmese include a moral dimension. Although *ana* is morally ambiguous, *awza* has an inherently positive value. Thus, Anderson's model can only partially explain how power operates in Burmese society.

The role of gender is conspicuously absent in Mann's and Anderson's analyses of power, which makes their models inadequate for scholars interested in women's history. Traditional analyses of power present a gendered discourse in which authority is seen as a hierarchical and male-dominated relationship. This patriarchal view of power does not adequately explain male–female relationships, however, because all power relationships have to be negotiated and negotiation is never one way.

8   Benedict R. O'G. Anderson, 'The idea of power in Javanese culture', in *Language and power: exploring political cultures in Indonesia* (Ithaca; London: Cornell University Press, 1990), 23.

9   Min Zin, 'The power of hpoun', *The Irrawaddy* 9, 9 (December 2001).

Recent anthropological and sociological research has demonstrated that the bilateral nature of social relationships in Southeast Asian societies diffused gender hierarchies and allowed men and women to exercise influence and power in different social, economic and political contexts.[10] A better understanding of indigenous ideas about the complementarity of gender roles and the significance of kinship relationships can enhance our ability to recognise women's informal power within the Burmese family.

Theravada Buddhism as a source of ideological power

The above has been by way of a theoretical introduction. I will turn now to the central role that Theravada Buddhism has played in Burmese society, and consider how Buddhist concepts have informed Burmese notions of power relations with implications for the ways in which gender roles were constructed, interpreted and negotiated by men and women. The importance of Theravada Buddhism as a source of ideological power in Burmese society must not be underestimated. Since its formal adoption by Burmese rulers in the eleventh century, Buddhist concepts and values have significantly conditioned how men and women interpret their societal roles and interaction, not to mention the wider relationships between communities and centres of political and economic power.[11] Of the current Burmese population of around 59 million, nearly 90 per cent are Buddhist, and Buddhist notions are still very much a part of modern Burmese culture.[12]

---

10   Shelley Errington, 'Recasting sex, gender, and power: a theoretical and regional overview', in Jane Monnig Atkinson and Shelley Errington (eds.), *Power and difference: gender in island Southeast Asia* (Stanford: Stanford University Press, 1990), 1–58; Wazir Jaham Karim, 'Bilateralism and gender in Southeast Asia', in Karim (ed.), *'Male' and 'female' in developing Southeast Asia*, 35–74.

11   Insofar as it concerns relations between men and women, Buddhism is hardly different from other world religions that gradually extended their influence into Southeast Asian societies as a result of expanding international trade and diplomacy, military conquests, and religious conversions. Barbara Watson Andaya provides a useful overview of how the expansion of world religions affected women's roles and status in early-modern Southeast Asian societies in *The flaming womb: repositioning women in early modern Southeast Asia* (Honolulu: University of Hawai'i Press, 2006), 70–103.

12   According to government figures, 89 per cent of the current population of 58.6 million are Buddhist; 5 per cent are Christians, 4 per cent are Muslims, and the rest are Hindus or Animists. See 'Selected basic ASEAN indicators', http://www.aseansec.org/stat/Table1. pdf, accessed on 23 March 2011; United Nations General Assembly, Human Rights Council, Working Group on the Universal Periodic Review, 'National report submitted in accordance with paragraph 15(a) of the annex to Human Rights Council resolution

It must be stressed, however, that Buddhist conceptions of power, like traditional Western analyses of power, do not totally explain the variety of relationships between men and women. The adoption and interpretation of Buddhist ideology, texts and rituals was negotiated by Burmese men and women, and by elites and non-elites, to suit local political, economic and social conditions. Although Buddhist concepts were progressively assimilated at all levels of Burmese society, influencing notions of gender roles and how power should be exercised, they did not necessarily override other indigenous concepts of gender and power. While some of these indigenous concepts emphasised men's superiority and authority over women in formal political and religious contexts, others emphasised the complementary, bilateral nature of social relationships in which women's familial and economic roles were both influential and highly valued.

Contrasting images of women in Buddhist and Burmese literature

An examination of Burmese Buddhist literature and beliefs reveals tensions between positive and negative portrayals of women and femininity, which influenced the development of gender roles and stereotypes in Burmese Buddhist society. On the one hand, women's maternal role and nurturing qualities were praised; on the other hand, women were denigrated as greedy, undisciplined temptresses. Buddhist canonical literature explicitly states that women are as capable of men as attaining *nibbana* (Enlightenment) and many Buddhist texts recount stories of devout women who gained *arahantship*[13] and generally performed good deeds supportive of the *sangha*. Female benefactors and renunciants demonstrated virtuous qualities such as compassion, charity, chastity and self-sacrifice. Burmese Buddhists would have been familiar with stories about devout women including Prince Siddhartha's maternal aunt

---

5/1. Myanmar', A/HRC/WG.6/10/MMR/1, 10 November 2010. These government estimates are not entirely accurate or free from manipulation, however. There has been no official census in Burma since 1983, and the last countrywide census was conducted in 1931. Furthermore, the government has deliberately exaggerated the (already very high) proportion of Buddhists in Burma in order to promote its vision of a unified (Buddhist) state and to marginalise its political opponents in the ethnic opposition, many of whom are Christians. Similarly, the official number of Muslims is grossly underestimated due to the government's refusal to recognise 750,000 Rohingyas as Burmese citizens.

13 In the Theravada tradition, an *aharant* ('worthy one') is an enlightened being who has attained *nibbana*.

and foster mother, Maha Pajapati Gotami, and wife, Princess Yasodhara, who dedicated themselves to following the Buddha and were among the first women to become fully ordained *bhikkhuni* (female Buddhist monastics).[14] The *bhikkhuni* lineage disappeared sometime after the thirteenth century, but the argument that women can no longer become female monks is justified in terms of a historically broken ordination lineage rather than women's inherent unsuitability to monastic life. Burmese Buddhist nuns continued to be ordained as *thilashin* ('owners of virtue'), although they were no longer formally recognised as members of the *sangha*. The status of *thilashin* will be discussed in greater detail below.

Although some Buddhist texts assert that men and women are equally capable of spiritual growth and attaining Enlightenment, others describe women as spiritually inferior beings who threaten to tempt men away from that very path. The following extracts from the Jataka (stories of the Buddha's previous lives) depict women as passionate, lustful and deceitful creatures:

Kaṇḍina-Jātaka:
Cursed be the dart of love that works men pain!
Cursed be the land where women rule supreme!
And cursed the fool that bows to woman's sway![15]

Anṇḍabhūta-Jātaka:
'Tis nature's law that rivers wind;
Trees grow of wood by law of kind;
And, given opportunity;
All women work iniquity.

A sex composed of wickedness and guile,
Unknowable, uncertain as the path
Of fishes in the water – womankind
Hold truth for falsehood, falsehood for the truth!

---

14 After her husband died, Gotami led a large group of women to the Buddha and asked to be ordained into the *sangha*. Although the Buddha initially refused her request, he acknowledged that Gotami had been of great service to him and that women had the same spiritual potential as men and were able to attain *arahant*ship. The Buddha eventually granted her request and Gotami, Yasodhara and the other women were ordained as *bhikkhuni* and admitted to the *sangha*.

15 Cited in E. B. Cowell (ed.), *The Jātaka: or stories of the Buddha's former births* (London: Published for the Pali Text Society by Luzac & Co., 1957), I, 43.

As greedily as cows seek pastures new,
Women, unsated, yearn for mate on mate.
As sand unstable, cruel as the snake,
Women know all things; naught from them is hid![16]

Contrasting images of women were also evident in Burmese literary sources and legal texts, where certain passages reflected Buddhist as well as Brahmanic influences. The *Lokanīti*, a treatise on the nature of the world thought to have been written sometime around the eleventh century or later, was taught in most monastic schools and included behavioural guidelines for women. The author described a 'good' woman as one who showed 'devotedness to her husband' and respected him 'like a slave'.[17] Other anthologies of maxims and moral stories described women as being more intelligent and industrious than men, but also emphasised women's excessively greedy and lustful natures. The author of the *Dhammanīti* claimed that women have an 'appetite that is twice that of men, their intelligence four times, their assiduity six times, and their [sexual] desires eight times', and concluded that 'If each woman had eight husbands ... she is indeed not satisfied'.[18] Burmese customary law codes (*dhammathats*), which overall presented a relatively egalitarian view of gender relations, also included passages that suggested women were spiritually inferior to men.[19] The *Manugye dhammathat* relates a good wife's thoughts about her husband: '[B]eing a man, Buddhahood is within his reach, while I, being a woman, shall have to strive hard to be first re-born as a man.'[20]

References to women's maternal role in Buddhist literature also revealed the ambiguous social and religious position of women. Mothers

---

16 *Ibid.*, I, 155.

17 Cited in James Gray, *Ancient proverbs and maxims from Burmese sources* (Trübner & Co Ltd, 1886) (reprint London: Routledge, 2000, 2001), 22–24.

18 Cited in *Ibid.*, 71–72.

19 The *dhammathats* were based on the Indian laws of Manu and were probably introduced to Burma before the tenth century and later became law throughout the Burman and Mon polities sometime between the eleventh and sixteenth centuries. For an English translation of the *dhammathats*, see U Gaung, *Translation of a digest of the Burmese Buddhist law concerning inheritance and marriages: being a collection of texts from thirty-six dhammathats*, 2 volumes (Rangoon: Government Printing, Burma, 1902-09). See also Vicentius Sangermano, *A description of the Burmese empire*, compiled chiefly from Burmese documents by Father Sangermano; translated from his manuscript by William Tandy; with a preface and note by John Jardine (London; Santiago de Compostela: Susil Gupta, 1966), 121–76.

20 U Gaung, *Translation of a digest of the Burmese Buddhist law*, II, 123.

were often portrayed as wise, compassionate and giving to the point of self-sacrifice. Women's nurturing qualities were affirmed in the fifth book of the *Vinaya-Pataka* ('Book of Discipline'), which describes the Buddha's respect for his aunt and foster mother, Maha Pajapati Gotami, who nursed the Buddha (then Prince Siddhartha) when he was a child. Yet the 'five forms of female suffering' – menstruation, pregnancy, childbirth, separation from parents, and service to one's husband – reinforced the belief that women must have accumulated bad karma in previous lives.[21] As mothers, women were thought to have a particular attachment to the family which prevented them from achieving the detachment necessary for Enlightenment and precluded them from attaining the same spiritual status as men. Mi Mi Khaing asserted that, 'For us [women] it is no less than a glorious truth to recall that the greatest concentration, clear thought, and enlightenment was attained by the Buddha as a man who had discarded his family ties ruthlessly. So there is no doubt in our minds. Spiritually, a man is higher than a woman.'[22] Thus, while women were often portrayed positively as generous, compassionate and loyal wives and mothers, femininity was also strongly associated with excessive sexual desire, suffering and attachment to worldly concerns. Although the images of womanhood described above did not necessarily reflect the actual lived experiences of Burmese women, they nonetheless informed the social construction of gender roles and stereotypes which were often disadvantageous to women.

The influence of *hpoun* on gender-power relations

Localised Burmese notions of power were often conflated with Buddhist concepts which legitimised the traditional social hierarchy in which men were accorded greater power and prestige than women. Specifically, men's possession of *hpoun* made them 'spiritually higher' than women.[23]

---

21 Hiroko Kawanami, 'Can women be celibate? Sexuality and abstinence in Theravada Buddhism', in Elisa Jane Sobo and Sandra Bell (eds.), *Celibacy, culture and society: the anthropology of sexual abstinence* (Madison, Wisconsin: The University of Wisconsin Press, 2001), 145.

22 Mi Mi Khaing, 'The Burmese woman', *The Nation* (Rangoon), 4 June 1961.

23 Melford Spiro, *Kinship and marriage in Burma: a cultural and psychodynamic analysis* (Berkeley: University of California Press, 1977), 259; Mi Mi Khaing, *Burmese family* (Bloomington: Indiana University Press, 1962), 48. Although Spiro and Mi Mi Khaing argue that men alone possess *hpoun*, others assert that women can possess *hpoun*, though not to the same extent as men. See Ni Ni Myint, *The status of Myanmar women*, 65.

If spiritual power was considered in terms of being closer to or more distant from Enlightenment, then male superiority was evident in the fact that only men could become monks and the assertion that Buddhahood was only attainable in a lifetime as a man. The highest status in Burmese socio-religious organisation was reserved for the *sangha* and monks or *hpoungyi* who were endowed with 'great *hpoun*'. Hpoun was closely associated with karma (*kan*) – the natural law of moral cause and effect – because *hpoun* was acquired through past acts of merit. Respected monks were referred to as *hpoun-(k)gan* because they possessed 'strong and effective karma'.

Belief in karma and rebirth provided a further explanation for individual fortune and social status in Buddhist Burmese society. Karma reinforced social hierarchy, for everyone was born into the social situation they deserved. Hierarchical categories of relative merit were linked to the wider social organisation and power relations. In pre-colonial Burma, socio-political power was accorded in descending order from the monarch, government, aristocracy and peasantry.[24] Men were accorded higher status than women because they had accrued more merit in their past lives, although women born into elite families were believed to have superior karma to lower-class men and women. While women were not necessarily excluded from acquiring *hpoun*, most were unable to attain the spiritual authority and influence associated with men, monks in particular. Even in modern Burma, belief in *hpoun* and its influence on gender-power relations is evident in everyday social interaction between the two sexes. Wives serve their husbands first at mealtimes and walk behind them in public, being careful not to touch the man's right shoulder where his *hpoun* resides. At public gatherings, men are seated on chairs up front while women sit behind them on the floor. Women cannot ride on the roofs of buses and trucks, which would place them physically higher than the men inside the vehicles.

Although belief in karma reinforced social hierarchies, Buddhism also emphasised the temporary, fluid nature of power relationships,

---

24 Although the *sangha* was deemed separate to secular society, in reality it was intimately connected to the wider social, political and economic order. The monarch was the principal patron of the *sangha* and kings often patronised particular orders or individual monks. Rulers also periodically sought to 'purify' or reform the *sangha* in order to prevent the institution from becoming too powerful and to regain control over land and labour.

as impermanence (*anicca*) was one of the three 'signs of being'.[25] Both men and women had the ability to improve their karma, and thereby their social status, by engaging in merit-making activities. Women from all social classes actively participated in Buddhist rituals and made considerable donations to the *sangha* in order to improve their karma. A woman's *dana* ('generosity', Pali *dāna*) was highly valued by men, since her meritorious deeds would be shared among family members and would also benefit the wider community. We can see then, the limitations of appealing to the dichotomy of male superiority/female inferiority to explain all the varieties of relationships between men and women. Buddhism informed a variety of roles for women, some of which were more highly esteemed than others. Although women rarely held positions of authority in formal religious and political institutions, they performed important religious, economic and social roles in their families and communities which enabled them to exercise influence in Burmese society.

The religious position of women in Burmese society

Burmese Buddhist women have always taken an active part in religious life as donors, merit-makers and renunciants. Inscriptions from the Pagan era (1044–1287) reveal that respected senior nuns performed Buddhist rites for royalty and other members of the community. Women were also generous supporters of the *sangha* and dedicated land, silver and their own labour to serve Buddhist establishments.[26] After the *bhikkhuni* disappeared, Buddhist women continued to be ordained as *thilashin* and there are more than 30,000 practising *thilashin* in Burma today. Although the present *sangha* consists of male monks (*bhikkhu*) and novices (*thamanei*) only, Sayadaw U Pandita, one of Burma's most renowned Buddhist teachers, has stated that this does not mean that women are spiritually inferior to men:

> If a woman wants to renounce the world, it is still possible to enter a monastery. Though strictly speaking it is not possible to become a bhikkhuni according to the original Vinaya rules of discipline for the Sangha, it is nonetheless still possible to become a bhikkhu or a bhik-

---

25   The other 'signs of being' are the inevitability of suffering (*dukkha*) and the non-existence of a permanent self or soul (*anatta*).

26   See chapter 2 for a detailed discussion of women's generosity towards the *sangha*.

khuni according to the suttas, the Buddha's discourses. For this, the only requirement is a sincere practice to purify one's mind according to the Noble Eightfold Path. There is no loss of privileges in this form of bhikkhu-hood: in fact, it may be more appropriate for our times. If everyone simply becomes a bhikkhu, there will be no problems, no inequality.[27]

In reality, however, *thilashin* have always occupied an ambivalent religious position in Burmese society. Although most women become *thilashin* in order to accumulate merit, other factors may influence their decision to renounce the worldly life including the wish to avoid suffering associated with marriage and motherhood as well as overcome economic hardship resulting from the death of family members or illness. Generally speaking, *ngyebyu* nuns who enter the monastic life at an early age are regarded as more spiritually accomplished than *tawdwet* nuns who are usually older women who have been married or widowed. Most *ngyebyu* nuns are unmarried virgins who are believed to be 'purer' and more disciplined than sexually experienced women. *Ngyebyu* nuns are also known as 'scholarly' nuns because they have spent many years studying Buddhist scriptures.[28]

Formal educational opportunities for Buddhist nuns and laywomen were extremely limited in pre-colonial Burma because most teachers (who were predominantly monks) did not prioritise female education. A few senior nuns instructed female members of royal families on moral conduct, but most women were unable to attain knowledge of Buddhist scriptures and rituals and therefore had little religious influence in the wider community. Female education in general became more acceptable during the colonial period, and the Buddhist revival led by U Nu's post-independence government saw an increase in the number of nunneries and educational opportunities available to female monastics. Improved access to education has enabled *thilashin* to enhance their social and religious status in modern Burma. *Thilashin* who undertake studies in Buddhist scriptures and Pali can sit the state ecclesiastical exams and be-

---

27 Sayadaw U Pandita, *In this very life: the liberation teachings of the Buddha*, foreword by Joseph Goldstein; edited by Kate Wheeler (Somerville, MA: Wisdom Publications, 1992), 130–31.

28 *Ngebyu* nuns are 'ones who are young and pure', whereas *tawdwet* nuns are 'ones who have left the forest'. Hiroko Kawanami, 'Patterns of renunciation: the changing world of Buddhist nuns', in Ellison Banks Findly (ed.), *Women's Buddhism, Buddhism's women: tradition, revision, renewal* (Somerville, MA: Wisdom Publications, 2000), 159–54.

come *dhammasariya* ('Teachers of the Dhamma'). Celebrated *thilashin* who possess great charisma and spiritual knowledge are able to attract powerful benefactors and larger donations than the average monk, but they are also regarded as exceptional women.[29] Nuns are rarely invited to officiate at formal religious ceremonies because they are considered to have lower status than monks, although many nuns offer counselling and support to the laity in informal settings.

Nuns, like monks, are respected by lay Burmese Buddhists who believe they must have *parami* ('virtue', 'integrity') in order to endure the harshness of monastic life. In many respects, however, *thilashin* face more hardships than male monastics. Hiroko Kawanami has pointed out that membership of the *sangha* endows monks with institutional authority, whereas *thilashin* must rely on their individual spiritual achievements and the reputation of their nunneries in order to secure sufficient donations for their daily needs. Monks remain entirely dependent on the laity to provide them with food and other basic necessities, whereas most *thilashin* can handle money and are expected to cook and look after themselves. While this may be interpreted as a sign of nuns' independence, in reality most *thilashin* receive fewer and smaller donations than monks and so often struggle to make ends meet.[30]

Many Burmese also look down upon *thilashin* because they do not conform to the feminine ideal, which centres on women's domestic roles as wife and mother.[31] This negative attitude towards *thilashin* was recognised by British visitors to Burma in the late eighteenth and early nineteenth centuries. In 1795, the British envoy Michael Symes noted that while a few 'venerable dames' (older *thilashin*) were accorded 'some portion of respect' by the Burmese, many nunneries had been abolished because they were 'injurious to the population'.[32] Another British traveller observed that older nuns were permitted to reside in monastery buildings only because their age made them less 'dangerous to the cold

---

29   Hiroko Kawanami, 'Monastic economy and interactions with society: the case of Buddhist nuns in Burma/Myanmar' (Lancaster University: unpublished discussion paper, 2007), 9.

30   *Ibid.*, 4-14.

31   Penny Van Esterik, 'Lay women in Theravada Buddhism', in Penny Van Esterik (ed.), *Women of Southeast Asia* (De Kalb, Illinois: Center for Southeast Asian Studies, Northern Illinois University, 1996), 42-61; Kawanami, 'Can women be celibate?', 143.

32   Symes, *An account of an embassy to the Kingdom of Ava*, 213.

professors of celibacy [Buddhist monks] within the walls.'[33] These accounts reflected the popular belief that a woman's primary function was to raise children (and thus increase the human resources available to the state), and that the very existence of female ascetics threatened to reduce the power of the *sangha*. Even in modern Burmese society, monks' celibacy is seen as a sign of their spiritual superiority, whereas *thilashin* are often pitied or denigrated because they have renounced their traditional familial roles.[34] Thus, the social position of Buddhist nuns is highly ambivalent in Burma, as it is in other parts of Asia and the West.

Women's roles in animist practices and rituals

Animist beliefs play a vital role in the everyday lives of many Burmese, and the syncretic nature of religious practices is evident in the fact that Buddhists, Christians and Muslims pay homage to various spirits (*nats*) on a regular basis. *Nat* shrines are a common sight in and around Burmese homes, teashops, temples, parks and many other locations where spirits are believed to reside. Women usually take responsibility for ensuring that household *nat* shrines are well maintained and make offerings to the *nats* on behalf of the family. In some forms of animism practised by villagers in Karen State, married women are regarded as the spiritual heads of the household who – together with their married daughters – assume responsibility for worshipping the spirits, which binds the family and spirits together. Significantly, only married women and their married daughters are believed to capable of binding the family and spirits successfully; single women and men do not have this power. Mothers are entrusted with passing on spiritual knowledge to their daughters and women also take a leading role in organising animist ceremonies before and after the annual harvest.[35]

Throughout Burma, women perform important religious roles as spirit mediums. The term *nat* refers to a diverse range of beings including Hindu divinities (*deiwa*) as well as local nature and territory spirits,

---

33 Captain James Low, 'History of Tenasserim', *Journal of the Royal Asiatic Society* 3 (1836): 330.

34 Kawanami, 'Can women be celibate?', 143; Kawanami, 'Monastic economy', 9.

35 Karen Human Rights Group, *Dignity in the shadow of oppression: the abuse and agency of Karen women under militarisation* ([Thailand]: Karen Human Rights Group, November 2006), 17–18.

many of which are female.[36] Some *nats* are spirits of humans, both male and female, who died a tragic or violent death. These powerful spirits, who can protect but also potentially harm the living, must be worshipped or pacified through ritual offerings. In order to legitimise their control over local populations and to integrate Buddhist and local animist belief systems, Pagan rulers developed a pantheon of thirty-seven *nats*, ten of whom were female representations of wives, consorts, daughters, mothers and servants of male rulers. King Anawrahta (1044–77) designated Shwezigon Pagoda as the official abode of these *nats*, who served as spirit agents of the state as well as ancestral and territorial guardians.[37] In modern Burma, state officials continue to patronise the shrines of territorial *nats* to assert their political authority over citizens, particularly in ethnic minority areas.[38]

In modern Burma the main ritual manifestation of the *nat* cult is spirit possession, which is performed by mediums who interpret the *nats'* will. Spirit mediums, whether female or male, are believed to have been 'seduced' by the *nats* and are commonly known as *nat kadaw* or *nat* 'wives'.[39] The initiation of new spirit mediums takes the form of a ritual marriage between the medium and the *nat*; once mediums have undergone a period of training, they are able to control the possessing spirit. *Nat kadaw* perform at local festivals (*nat pwe*) in which members of the population make offerings to propitiate the *nats* and appeal to the *nats* to resolve grievances via the spirit mediums. Mediums' power and prestige are determined by the size and status of their client base and disciples. Senior *nat kadaw* take on followers or disciples who are trained in particular schools of possession. Depending on their skills

---

36   Alexandra de Mersan, 'A new place for Mra Swan Dewi: Changes in spirit cults in Arakan (Rakhine) State', *Asian Ethnology* 68, 2 (2009): 307–32. De Mersan notes that many Arakanese believe that cities and other important physical territories are controlled by female spirits. These spirits were originally 'powers of the soil', but were later raised to the status of 'Lady' or 'Queen' of the particular territory.

37   A. J. Day, 'Ties that (un)bind: families and states in premodern Southeast Asia', *Journal of Asian Studies* 55, 2 (1996): 389.

38   De Mersan, 'A new place for Mra Swan Dewi', 321–25.

39   Many *nat kadaws* are transsexual or 'effeminate' men who are believed to be able to embody both male and female *nats* more effectively than heterosexual men or women.

and experience, spirit mediums are granted titles such as 'minister' and 'queen' that reflect their position within the professional hierarchy.[40]

Female spirit mediums are respected by many Burmese for their spiritual knowledge and skills, and thereby gain social power and prestige. Yet women's influence as spirit mediums has also been undermined because of ambivalent feelings about *nat* worship among the Burmese as well as the 'base' nature of many ritual ceremonies. Although many Burmese consult *nats*, educated people from urban areas often dismiss *nat* worship as a form of superstition associated with uneducated villagers. Burmese authorities no longer condone spirit cults, even though many government officials worship *nats* either as individuals or on behalf of the state. Ritual performances associated with *nat* worship often involve the excessive consumption of alcohol and other 'immodest' behaviour. Many Burmese believe that it is women's inherent weaknesses – such as their passionate, undisciplined natures – that makes it possible for spirits to possess them in the first place.[41]

The social and religious standing of *thilashin* and *nat kadaw* is therefore highly ambiguous. *Thilashin* are admired for their religious dedication and ability to renounce the world as well as their spiritual knowledge. In order to pursue the path towards Enlightenment, however, they must reject the ideal of womanhood which revolves around the roles of wife and mother. Although Buddhist nuns are arguably more independent than monks, they rarely attain the same levels of religious authority and influence. Female spirit mediums perform important roles as ritual specialists who have the power to interpret the will of the *nats*, but their status is compromised since they are believed to have been 'seduced' by the *nats* as a result of their inherently weak natures.

Women's roles within the traditional family

Traditional gender relationships within the Burmese family were based on perceived differences between the two sexes, buttressed by patriarchal notions of power and the principle of regard for *hpoun*, which emphasised male superiority and female inferiority. Fathers and husbands

---

40 For more detailed discussion on the roles and status of spirit mediums, see Bénédicte Brac de la Perrière, '"Nat's wives" or 'children of nats': from spirit possession to transmission among the ritual specialists of the Cult of the Thirty-Seven Lords', *Asian Ethnology* 68, 2 (2009): 283–305.

41 Kawanami, 'Can women be celibate?', 144.

were considered to be the 'natural' heads of the household due to their spiritual superiority as well as their role as the main breadwinners, and were the ones to whom all other family members had to defer. Women were taught to respect their sons as masters and their husbands as gods (*'Thaa goh thakin; liin goh phaya'*). A woman's status within the family was centred on her role as wife and mother. There was a strong social expectation that women should marry and that the ideal relationship between husband and wife was one of male supremacy and female subservience. The Indian Laws of Manu, upon which much of Burmese customary law is based, describe a wife who is like a servant as the best of seven types of wife (a wife could also be like a murderer, a thief, a tyrant, a mother, a sister or a friend).[42] Men preferred to marry younger women, who accorded them greater respect due to their age and who could bear them more children. The older husband was encouraged to exercise authority over his younger wife much as a father would over his daughter or an (elder) brother would over his sister.[43]

The ambiguity of women's position within the family becomes apparent when we consider the role of the mother in Burmese Buddhist culture, which overall had a positive value. The Burmese word for 'family' is *mithazu* ('mother-child-group') and parents are called *mi-ba* ('mother-father'), in which 'mother' comes first. Both parents were due high respect in Burmese culture, but the mother was to be honoured before the father. Merit-making activities reinforced the positive image of woman as mother and nurturer. Perhaps believing that they required more merit in order to be reborn as men, women became the primary supporters of the *sangha*, often donating food and clothing for entire monasteries. In the last analysis, the *sangha* was also dependent

---

42 The seven types of wives are also described in the *Rajadhammasangaha* ('Treatise on the Compassionate Disposition of Righteous Government'), which was composed by the influential minister U Hpo Hlaing and presented to King Thibaw (1878-85) upon his ascent to the throne. The *Rajadhammasangaha* reflected Hpo Hlaing's views about how power should be exercised and was probably intended as a (not so subtle) criticism of Thibaw's wife, Queen Supayalat, who dominated her husband and his court. Supayalat's involvement in state political and military affairs will be discussed in chapter 3. See Hpo Hlaing, Yaw Mingyi U (Wetmasut Myoza Wungyi), *Rajadhammasangaha*, edited by U Htin Fatt (Maung Htin) (Rangoon: Sape U Publishing House, 1979). Euan Bagshawe's English translation, published in 2004, is available at http://burmalibrary.org/docs/ THE_RAJADHAMMASANGAHA.pdf.

43 Daw Sein Sein, 'The position of women in Hinyana Buddhist countries (Burma, Ceylon and Thailand)' (MA thesis, University of London, 1958), 24–25.

on women for its membership, and the 'life debt' that boys owed to their mothers for bringing them into the world and raising them was acknowledged in the *shinbyu* novitiation ceremony that all Burmese Buddhist boys undergo.

While marriage and motherhood were upheld as the ideal roles for Burmese females, it should be noted that many women did not marry or have children. Spinsterhood did not necessarily imply a reduction in social status; in fact, spinsters (known as *apyogyi* or 'big virgins') were generally respected for their ability to resist sexual temptation. Because they did not have husbands or children, spinsters often had greater social and economic independence than married women and mothers who were tied to a life of domesticity. In modern Burma, many single women pursue professional careers and have more time and resources to donate to the *sangha* and practise meditation, which enhances their religious status.[44]

Women's historically 'high' social status and economic value

Women performed important and highly valued roles in the traditional household-oriented economy, where the sexual division of labour reflected popular beliefs about gender and power. In the predominantly agrarian-based rural economy, men performed physically demanding tasks including ploughing, metalworking and woodworking as well as formal political and religious roles. Women were involved in the transplanting and harvesting of rice, vegetable-growing, raising small livestock, food preparation, weaving and market trading. They were also responsible for child-rearing as well as the majority of household work, which included management of finances. Women's reproductive role was highly valued in a society where power was measured largely in terms of control over human resources, rather than control over territory for its own sake. The more children a woman had, the more family members there were to perform household chores and labour and thereby contribute towards the family's well-being. Women's high economic value was enhanced by matrilocal residence patterns, where husbands resided with their wives' parents for the first year (or more) after marriage. During this period, the new husband was expected to assist his in-laws in the fields and in other tasks.

---

44 Kawanami, 'Can women be celibate?', 146.

Post-marital matrilocal residence created a levelling mechanism which potentially diffused the husband's formal authority over his wife. The husband left the security of his parents' home and moved in with his wife's parents, who as heads of the household could exercise authority over their son-in-law and ensure that he treated their daughter well. The wife also avoided interpersonal tensions associated with moving into the home of her husband's parents, such as conflict with her mother-in-law over the distribution of household work.[45] Although older married daughters eventually moved out of the parental home and established their own households, the youngest daughter usually resided permanently with her parents and cared for them until they died. While this may have restricted the daughter's personal autonomy, she was compensated financially since she not only received a share of the household income while her parents were alive but also inherited the parental home upon their death.[46] These kinship support networks and economic incentives therefore enhanced women's position within the household.

Some scholars have argued that women's involvement in economic activities was actually conditioned by Buddhist strictures against worldly attachment, which devalued women's economic roles and the position of women in general.[47] Traditional female tasks such as managing finances were viewed as potentially demeritorious acts. Monks adhered to a precept to abstain from handling money and other 'polluting substances', so nuns and laywomen were required to buy food and make offerings to monks. Conversely, sexual differentiation in the division of labour could also indicate a complementary view of gender roles, rather than one focused on a male–female hierarchy of spiritual superiority and inferiority. Ni Ni Myint cites popular sayings such as 'When a husband carries the bundle on his shoulder, a wife carries a bundle on her head' as evidence

---

45 Spiro, *Kinship and marriage in Burma*, 123–24.

46 *Ibid.*, 137.

47 A. Thomas Kirsch, 'Buddhism, sex roles, and the Thai economy', in Penny Van Esterik (ed.), *Women of Southeast Asia* (De Kalb, Illinois: Center for Southeast Asian Studies, Northern Illinois University, 1996), 21–22; Kirsch, 'Economy, polity, and religion in Thailand', 172–96. Similarly, Ward Keeler has argued that women's economic roles were devalued in Javanese society. As spiritually inferior beings, women were less likely to succeed in ascetic practices associated with (male) power, and so were given control over household finances and other (less prestigious) material matters instead. See Ward Keeler, 'Speaking of gender in Java', in Jane Monnig Atkinson and Shelley Errington (eds.), *Power and difference: gender in Southeast Asia* (Stanford: Stanford University Press, 1990), 127–52.

that men and women performed different, but equally valued, economic roles in pre-colonial Burma.[48] British colonial administrators interpreted Burmese women's economic activity as evidence of 'high' social status. Harold Fielding Hall noted that

> almost every woman has some occupation besides her own [familial] duties. In the higher classes she will have property of her own to manage; in the lower classes she will have some trade. I cannot find that in Burma there have ever been certain occupations told off for women in which they may work, and others tabooed to them. As there is no caste for the men, so there is no caste for the women. They have been free to try their hands at anything they thought they could excel in, without any fear of public opinion.[49]

Even the American Baptist missionary Henry Park Cochrane, who described the sexual division of labour as decidedly unequal – with women bearing the main burden – conceded that

> the Burmese woman holds a higher place than is enjoyed by her sisters in any other Oriental land .... The Bazaar is almost wholly run by the women, each having her own stall and keeping her own accounts in her head .... While Mohammedan and Hindu women are shut up in harems and zenanas, the Burmese women walk the streets with head erect, puffing their huge cheroots without the slightest thought of being the 'weaker vessel'.[50]

In his seminal work, *Southeast Asia in the Age of Commerce,* social historian Anthony Reid pointed to women's social and economic independence as one of the defining characteristics of pre-colonial Southeast Asian societies.[51] Reid never claimed, however, that men and women had equal status; he argued only that women enjoyed a position closer to equality in Southeast Asia than they did in China or India. In fact, Reid found that men and women did not usually compete directly in religious, political, social or economic spheres, so 'it could not be said

---

48   Ni Ni Myint, *The status of Myanmar women,* 39.

49   Fielding, *The soul of a people,* 215.

50   Henry Park Cochrane *Among the Burmans: a record of fifteen years of work and its fruitage* (New York: Fleming H. Revell Co., c.1904), 55.

51   Reid, *Southeast Asia in the age of commerce 1450–1680, Vol. 1,* 162–65. See also Anthony Reid, 'Female roles in pre-colonial Southeast Asia', *Modern Asian Studies* 22, 3 (1988): 629–45.

that women were equal to men'.[52] The decline in women's economic power began during the colonial period, when increasing competition from British, Indian and Chinese businessmen effectively limited the scope of women's traditional economic activities and entrepreneurial opportunities to household purchase and small-scale trading.

Reid and others have convincingly argued that the sexual division of labour in Southeast Asian societies reflected the bilateral nature of gender relationships, in which men and women traditionally performed different roles in distinct spheres – women in the private domain of the household economy and men in the public domain of the state.[53] Fielding Hall would undoubtedly have agreed with this view:

> [The Burmese woman] has a very keen idea of what things she can do best, and what things she should leave to her husband …. She knows that the reason women are not supposed to interfere in public affairs is because their minds and bodies are not fitted for them …. She knows that she can do certain business as well as or better than her husband, and she does it. There is nothing more remarkable than the way in which she makes a division of these matters in which she can act for herself, and those in which, if she act at all, it is for her husband.[54]

Seen in this light, women's economic roles were highly valued because they contributed to the family's well-being without usurping men's authority as head of the household.

It is worth noting at this point that Orientalist discourses on gender and power were evident in colonial accounts about the 'high' status of Burmese women. Although British authorities admired Burmese women's economic abilities and initiative, they were also concerned about what they regarded as the excessive social freedom of the indigenous female population. In the colonialists' view, Burmese women's 'immodest' dress, the relative ease with which they could initiate divorce, and their poor child-rearing skills made them prime candidates for 'civilising' projects. Fielding Hall regarded the Burmese as too 'feminine' (read: weak)

---

52 Reid, 'Female roles in pre-colonial Southeast Asia', 629.

53 *Ibid.*, 629–45; Reid, *Southeast Asia in the age of commerce 1450–1680, Vol. 1*, 146–63; Keyes, 'Mother or mistress but never a monk', 223–41; Karim, 'Bilateralism and gender in Southeast Asia', 35–74.

54 Fielding, *The soul of a people*, 218–19.

and believed that Burmese society needed to become more 'masculine' in order to progress and modernise.[55]

Criticism of the 'autonomy thesis'

Other scholars reject the argument of a relatively 'high' status for Burmese women because the fact that some women enjoyed economic and social freedom does not compensate for women's relative absence from positions of power in government and other offices associated with prestige and authority.[56] Burmese political systems grew out of cultural understandings of family roles and relationships, which assumed that power relationships were naturally patriarchal and hierarchical. The widespread belief in male spiritual superiority effectively prevented most women from seeking or attaining high political office. Despite the important role of women within the family, the unequal division of labour and responsibilities within the household meant that women had fewer educational, vocational and social opportunities than men.

Traditionally, the Burmese lived in large households with extended families and daughters were expected to help their mothers care for their siblings and older relatives, even if this meant sacrificing their own needs and desires. In pre-colonial Burma, formal education was provided by the *sangha* for boys only, although some girls were enrolled in lay schools 'superintended by women' as early as the 1830s.[57] There were more opportunities for females to gain a formal education under the colonial administration, but even then young women were usually encouraged to enter 'appropriate' professions like nursing and teaching. Traditional cultural ascription to women of social roles and behaviours was perhaps the greatest barrier to overcome for women who aspired to become politically active. Women who chose to be involved in politics

---

55 Fielding, *A people at school*, 268.

56 Maureen Aung-Thwin, 'Burma: a disenfranchised prime minister, the myth of equality, women from heaven', *Ms* (July/August 1991): 18–21; Janell Mills, 'Militarism, civil war and women's status: a Burma case study', in Louise Edwards and Mina Roces (eds.), *Women in Asia: tradition, modernity and globalisation* (St Leonards: Allen & Unwin, 2000), 265–90.

57 Low, 'History of Tenasserim', 330. Although Low claimed that many girls could read and write, census data suggests that female literacy rates were low in pre-colonial Burma, and only began to increase significantly after 1910. The number of literate females aged five years and over increased from 7 per cent in 1911 to 11.2 per cent in 1921, then to 16.5 per cent in 1931. See Census Commissioner of India, *Census of India, 1931: Part One, Report*, Vol. 11, *Burma* (Rangoon: Office of the Superintendent Government Printing and Stationery, 1933), 170.

risked being looked down on as selfish creatures who neglected their familial duties.[58] Yet many Burmese defended the lack of female participation in formal politics with assertions that women were always able to exercise political influence, albeit indirectly, from within the family.

Gender and the exercise of political power

We have seen that traditional discourses of power focus on men's authority in formal political institutions but largely ignore women's political behaviour and influence in informal contexts. Gender historians have argued that we need to consider the family as a social system itself comprising gendered, rather than patriarchal, relations of power. In order to understand how political power operated in pre-colonial Southeast Asia, Barbara Andaya has suggested that we need to focus less on 'kingdoms' and instead consider how these societies were actually 'cultural-economic unities comprised of a web of kinship-infused relationships'.[59] In other words, Southeast Asian polities were like extended families connected both by blood and marriage and by ties of obligation and loyalty. This enabled some elite women to influence political decision-making through their relationships to men in power, even though most women were excluded from directly participating in affairs of state.

Mina Roces coined the term 'kinship politics' to explain how political power in post-war Philippines was gendered, rather than male-dominated.[60] Power was traditionally held by the kinship alliance group and women with kinship or marriage ties to men in power viewed themselves as sharing in that power. Women's extended kinship networks also enabled them to broker marriage alliances, settle disputes, and negotiate relationships with Spanish missionaries in the pre-modern Philippines.[61] The concept of 'kinship politics' can also help to explain the way female power operated in Burmese society. The complementary nature of

58   Khin Myo Chit, *Colourful Burma*, 5–12; Brenda Belak, *Gathering strength: women from Burma on their rights* (Chiang Mai: Images Asia, 2002), 256.

59   Barbara Watson Andaya, *To live as brothers: Southeast Sumatra in the seventeenth and eighteenth centuries* (Honolulu: University of Hawai'i Press, 1993), 213. See also the introduction to Watson Andaya (ed.), *Other pasts*, 21; Day, 'Ties that (un)bind', 384–409.

60   Mina Roces, *Women, power, and kinship politics: female power in post-war Philippines* (Westport, Connecticut: Praeger, 1998).

61   Peter Schreurs, *Caraga Antigua, 1521–1910: the hispanization and christianization of Agusan, Surigao, and East Davao*, second edition (Manila: Republic of the Philippines, National Commission for Culture and the Arts, National Historical Institute, [2000]), 125, 127.

male–female relationships was entirely compatible with the notion of 'the politics of partnership', where power was exercised most effectively through kinship networks in which women were active participants. In pre-colonial Burma, the understanding that power was shared by the king and his chief queen was expressed in familial descriptions of the royal couple as mother and father of the people.[62] As mothers of kings and future kings, queens performed crucial political roles in establishing and legitimising a king's rule and that of his successive heirs. Kings were therefore indebted to their mothers and accorded them great status, wealth and respect. Royal women also successfully negotiated marriage alliances with ruling families and built up extensive patronage networks to maintain and enhance their political power.[63]

In the wider community, women could participate in decision-making together with their husbands or on their behalf. Although political offices were typically open to males only, some female *thugyi* (hereditary chiefs) assumed responsibility for local administration, acting jointly with their husbands or solely as widows or household heads. Colonial authors observed that many women were active, if not autonomous, political actors who ably assisted their husbands and male family members in performing official duties. Fielding Hall described how the wife of one village headman organised the pursuit, capture and arrest of a group of armed robbers who had stolen the village cattle in her husband's absence:

> Everything was done as well and as successfully as if [her husband] Saw Ka himself had been present. But if it had not been for the accident of Saw Ka's sudden reappearance, I should probably never have known that this exploit was due to the wife. For she was acting for her husband, and she would not have been pleased that her name should appear.[64]

Women therefore took a keen interest in official matters, but preferred to exercise influence through their husbands' names so as not to threaten men's authority.

---

62   Pyone Yin, 'Women in the Bagan period', 12; William J. Koenig, *The early Burmese polity, 1752–1819: politics, administration and social organization in the early Kon-baung period* (Ann Arbor: Center for South and Southeast Asian Studies, The University of Michigan, 1990), 167.

63   These issues will be discussed in greater detail in chapters 2 and 3.

64   H. Fielding [Hall], 'Burmese women', ([Burma], unpublished mimeograph, [19--]), 30.

During the struggle against colonial rule, wives and female relatives of male nationalist leaders were actively involved in the independence movement, though usually in supporting roles. Similarly, when parliamentary democracy was established following independence, wives of male politicians ably supported their husbands and, in several cases, assumed their husbands' political roles when the latter were assassinated or arrested, because they considered it their duty to carry on their husbands' work. While few women held official positions of authority under military rule, most Burmese believe that women with close ties to the military exercised considerable political and economic influence.[65]

Elite women who exercised power through the practice of 'kinship politics' were not usually considered threatening to political stability because they were unlikely to challenge the status quo, preferring to influence their male relatives behind the scenes in order not to threaten their public image of power. These women generally accepted that their proper role was working alongside men to improve the lot of their families and communities, secure in the knowledge that influencing or manipulating men in private would be more fruitful than diminishing their public authority. Although women were able to exercise influence over their husbands and other male relatives indirectly, overt displays of female power were considered illegitimate, immoral and, potentially, dangerous to men.

Male ambivalence about female power: the ideology of the dangerous female

Many Burmese believed that a woman could weaken a man's *hpoun*, and thereby his spiritual power, in order to establish her influence over him.[66] Burmese historical and literary sources often portrayed women as immoral and sexually promiscuous beings who threatened to usurp men's 'natural' authority. Female sexuality was deemed particularly dangerous to men, who were powerless to resist female temptresses and their seductive ways, and so were distracted from the path to Enlightenment. The *dhammathats* list 40 'blandishments' that women might use in

---

65 Louise Williams, *Wives, mistresses and matriarchs: Asian women today* (London: Phoenix Press, 2001), 186–87.

66 Spiro, *Kinship and marriage in Burma*, 264–71.

their attempts to seduce or manipulate men.[67] Stories of 'henpecked husbands' were common among all social classes. In *The citizen of Burma*, Po Ka claimed that '[a]mong his boon companions at the toddy tope the young villager may, when chaffed by his friends, deny that he is under "petticoat government", but when he gets home he becomes her obedient slave.'[68]

Men's fear of female power was particularly evident in the negative portrayal of queens who dominated kings and their courts. The most infamous of these women was Queen Supayalat, the wife of King Thibaw, the last ruler of the Konbaung dynasty in the late nineteenth century. To this day, many Burmese believe that Supayalat's influence over her weak-willed husband and her inappropriate interference in state affairs ultimately caused the downfall of the Burmese monarchy and loss of independence. Although Ni Ni Myint has convincingly argued that Supalayat was actually motivated both by a passionate love for Thibaw and an intense desire to protect Burmese sovereignty in the face of British military aggression,[69] the widespread belief that Supayalat used her power inappropriately reinforced the view that women should not be involved in politics.

Even in modern Burmese society, female sexual organs are considered polluting and everyday social practices reveal how men are careful to protect their *hpoun* from potentially 'contaminating' substances like menstrual blood.[70] Men and women do not bathe in the same water, and women's skirts and undergarments are washed and dried separately. The belief that men's power is potentially weakened by their proximity to dangerous women is evident in the state-sponsored media's attacks on Aung San Suu Kyi's male colleagues in the National League for Democracy (NLD). *New Light of Myanmar* reports have described male NLD members as 'those who skipped out bending under the

---

67   U Gaung, *Translation of a digest of the Burmese Buddhist law*, II, 20.

68   U Po Ka, *The citizen of Burma* (Rangoon: British Burma Press, 1914), 67.

69   Ni Ni Myint, 'Queen Supayalat', in Myanmar Historical Commission, Ministry of Education, Union of Myanmar, *Selected writings of Ni Ni Myint: member of the Myanmar Historical Commission* (Yangon: U Kyi Win, Manager (02384) at the Universities Press, 2004), 80–96.

70   Many world religions promoted the belief that female sexual organs and menstruation were polluting, and ultimately threatened men's power, and examples of 'dangerous females' were common in other Southeast Asian societies besides Burma. See Andaya, *The flaming womb*, esp. 72, 88, 197, 199–200, 204.

skirt-hanging clothesline', implying that they have been emasculated by their female leader.[71] In 2007, the Thai-based Lanna Action for Burma group launched a 'Panties for Peace' campaign in which activists were encouraged to send women's underwear to Burmese embassies in response to the military's crackdown against protesting monks. Campaign organisers urged women 'to take away the power of the military junta by sending your knickers to Burmese embassies which is a culturally insulting gesture of protest'.[72] Although this campaign attracted considerable media attention in the West, many Burmese opposition activists were reluctant to support such radical political action, suggesting that belief in the importance of protecting male *hpoun* remains widespread.

On 12 February 2011, many Burmese were shocked by newspaper reports and televised images of SPDC Chairman General Than Shwe and other senior military leaders dressed in women's *acheik* when greeting female members of parliament at a state dinner.[73] Expatriate Burmese news media claimed that the generals' unusual cross-dressing was an intentional act of superstition, known as *yadaya*, designed to undermine Aung San Suu Kyi's influence and reverse her karma.[74] Many Burmese believe that military leaders perform *yadaya* in order to change the future predicted by astrology or omens.[75] In this case, the generals allegedly hoped to reverse astrologers' predictions that a woman (Aung San Suu Kyi) would one day rule Burma by dressing like women.

Negative portrayals of female power in the media suggest that many Burmese are still reluctant to judge powerful women on their individual merit. Women who have initially gained political prominence through their connections to powerful men have often struggled to assert power in their own right. An article published in the *Far Eastern Economic Review* in August 1993 encapsulated this dilemma with the wry observation that a woman's political success was determined by the ability 'to

---

71   'Very sorry – in the Tawgyi', *New Light of Myanmar*, 4 June 1996.

72   Panties for Peace website: http://www.pantiesforpeace.info/, accessed on 22 May 2009.

73   An *acheik* is a sarong worn by women at weddings and other formal occasions.

74   Wai Moe, 'Than Shwe skirts the issue', *The Irrawaddy*, 17 February 2011.

75   For a discussion of another *yadaya* ritual allegedly performed by former SPDC Secretary 1 Khin Nyunt, see Keiko Tosa, 'The chicken and the scorpion: rumour, counternarratives, and the political uses of Buddhism', in Monique Skidmore (ed.), *Burma at the turn of the 21*[st] *century* (Honolulu: University of Hawai'i Press, 2005), 165–66.

choose one's father carefully, or a husband likely to be assassinated.'[76] Burma's state-controlled media launched numerous propaganda campaigns in an effort to undermine Aung San Suu Kyi's political credibility, portraying her either as a power hungry individual who feeds off her late father Aung San's reputation as an independence hero, or as the widow of a foreigner who is merely a 'puppet' of Western 'neo-colonialists'.[77] Identification with Aung San and the support of Western governments undoubtedly enhanced Aung San Suu Kyi's political legitimacy in the eyes of many Burmese and non-Burmese. Yet those deny her political influence in her own right ignore the fact that her popularity stems largely from her promotion of Buddhist ideals of non-violence, compassion and loving-kindness, which provide her with moral power that stands in stark contrast to the morally corrupt power of the (former) military leadership.

The construction of a 'Burmese' identity: implications for women's power

How the Burmese think about themselves as individuals belonging to a community, and how they think about others, have an important influence on power relations. The construction of 'Burmese' identity is an ongoing, complex process, since it involves creating a sense of commonality and unity among a population of nearly 60 million people with diverse religious, ethnic, linguistic and cultural backgrounds. One way to create a common national identity has been to distinguish 'Burmese' from 'non-Burmese'. The idea that all Burmese need to protect themselves and their traditions from 'undesirable' foreign influences has not just encouraged xenophobia, it has also slowed the processes of modernisation, which elsewhere have opened up new opportunities for women to adopt new roles and exercise power. Furthermore, the conceptualisation of 'Burmese' identity has been spearheaded by male Burman elites who, consciously or unconsciously, determined that to be 'Burmese' was to be 'Burman' and thus condoned – and, in some cases, encouraged – discrimination against non-Burmans.

---

76 Frank Ching, 'Asia's women leaders depend on parents' or husbands' fame,' *Far Eastern Economic Review* 156, 38 (19 August 1993): 28.

77 See, for example, Myo Chit, 'Let's tell the truth', *New Light of Myanmar*, 30 May–5 June 1996; Pauk Sa, 'What do you think? The ugly American', *Kyemon*, 14 October 1996.

Historically, Burmese elites have held deep suspicions about foreigners, which reflected the fragility of rulers' weak institutionalised power. Mandala polities were inherently unstable: a ruler's power was strongest at the centre of the mandala and weakest at its boundaries, which expanded and contracted as neighbouring polities fought for dominance over territory and resources. Rulers negotiated marriage alliances and built up extensive patronage networks to strengthen their power bases, but the practice of royal polygamy produced large extended families and numerous potential rivals to the throne, resulting in frequent succession disputes and internal rebellions. Male rulers' fear of losing their power to outsiders was further heightened by the idea that women, as the weaker sex, were particularly susceptible to foreign influences that represented a serious threat to the political, economic and cultural integrity of the state.[78] Marriage alliances were important tools of statecraft that symbolised the tributary power relationships between a ruler and his subjects, but male elites were careful to preserve the royal lineage against external influences by discouraging intermarriage with 'foreign' (*kala*) women.[79] Burman rulers also looked down on other indigenous ethnic groups whom they regarded as 'uncivilised', and preferred to marry other Burmans.[80]

Commoners were not subject to the same restrictions as royalty and the majority of Burmese women were relatively free to choose their marriage partners and consort with foreigners. In their early contacts with the Burmese, European traders and envoys observed that Burmese women could enhance their social, economic and even political status by entering into relationships with wealthy foreign men.[81] Women's sexual freedom was severely curtailed, however, following the British colonisa-

---

78 Maureen Aung-Thwin, 'Foreigners and females in Burmese eyes', in J. J. Brandon (ed.), *Burma/Myanmar towards the twenty-first century: dynamics of continuity and change* (Bangkok: Open Society Institute, Thai Studies Section, 1997), 35–44.

79 During the Pagan era, Burman elites looked down on or felt threatened by Indian (*kula* or *kala*) women: see *The Glass Palace Chronicle*, 105. The word *kala* can also mean 'foreigners', including the British and Europeans in general. During the twentieth century, the term came to refer mainly to Indians, while the word *bo* (which is associated with the military ranking of a general) was used to denote 'British' or 'European'.

80 Koenig, *The early Burmese polity*, 38.

81 Justin Corfield and Ian Morson (eds.), *British Sea-Captain Alexander Hamilton's A new account of the East Indies (17ᵗʰ–18ᵗʰ century)* (Lewiston; Queenstown; Lampeter: The Edwin Mellen Press, 2001), 360; Symes, *An account of an embassy to the Kingdom of Ava*, 72–73, 217–18; Cox, *Journal of a residence in the Burmhan empire*, 319–21.

tion of Burma in the late nineteenth century. Colonial elites discouraged sexual unions between British officers and Burmese women in an effort to distance themselves from the indigenous population and maintain colonial prestige. At the same time, nationalist ideology emphasised the importance of protecting 'Burmese' racial and cultural purity, and women who married foreigners (particularly Indian Muslims) faced criticism for relinquishing traditional cultural values and undermining national unity.[82] By entrusting women with maintaining Burma's cultural integrity, nationalist leaders appeared to empower women with responsibility for preserving valued traditions and safeguarding future generations of Burmese against undesirable foreign influences. Yet women were also expected to accept restrictions on their behaviour for the sake of the national interest, which effectively limited their access to positions of power and decision-making in most fields, including politics.

Following the 1962 coup, successive military governments' isolationist policies reinforced the notion that women needed to be 'protected' from undesirable foreign influences. Draconian state slogans exhorting citizens to 'crush all internal and external enemies of the state' reveal that military leaders were deeply concerned about domestic as well as foreign threats to their power. Women involved in the political opposition were specifically targeted by authorities and continue even now to face intimidation, arrest and imprisonment. The generals' fear of losing power also inhibited their ability to engage in political dialogue with Aung San Suu Kyi. From the early 1990s onwards, the SLORC-SPDC regime attempted to counter Aung San Suu Kyi's influence and improve its international image through the establishment of mass women's organisations that ostensibly aimed to promote women's advancement. Yet military/government elites remain reluctant to allow women any substantial role in political processes at the national, state, or local level. State-sanctioned women's organisations have served primarily to mobi-

---

82   These issues are neatly summarised in two articles by Chie Ikeya, 'The "traditional" high status of women in Burma', 66–75 and 'The modern Burmese woman and the politics of fashion in Burma', 1299–301. See also Ma Khin Mar Mar Kyi, 'Race, gender and sexuality in the reconstruction of politics in 20th century Burma/Myanmar', in David S. Mathieson and R. J. May (eds.), *The illusion of progress: the political economy of reform in Burma/ Myanmar* (Adelaide: Crawford House Publishing, 2004), 255–57. Further discussion of intermarriages between Burmese Buddhist women and non-Burmese/non-Buddhist men is provided in chapter 4.

lise members in support of the central government, despite the fact that its policies of forced relocation, requisition of labour and military rape have oppressed women, particularly those living in conflict zones and ethnic minority areas.

Female political activists face many challenges, one of which is changing community perceptions of their capabilities. Within the democratic movement, many political organisations are male-dominated with centralised power structures, making it difficult for women to participate equally in decision-making and leadership. For many Burmese women living in exile, exposure to new ideas about gender equality, feminism and human rights has prompted them to question and, ultimately, challenge prevailing cultural beliefs and power structures that keep women in subordinate positions. These women have formed their own grassroots organisations with explicitly political aims to empower women and promote female leadership in their local communities, the exiled democratic movement and, ultimately, all spheres of Burmese society.

Conclusions

The way in which Burmese women viewed themselves, and they way in which they were viewed by Burmese men, had an enormous influence on all aspects of religious, political, social and cultural life. On the one hand, cultural constraints on women's roles and behaviour prevented them from attaining power in the same ways as men. The construction of hierarchical gender relationships based on popular notions of male superiority and female inferiority was reflected in socio-political structures and institutions that reinforced male images of power. The clearly demarcated roles for men and women in traditional Burmese society were based on perceived gender differences buttressed by patriarchal notions of power including the principle of *hpoun*. As the spiritually superior sex, men were considered to be the 'natural' heads of the family and household. Boys also had more opportunities to gain formal education than girls. Men, therefore, were more favourably positioned than women to assume leadership roles in political, religious and military institutions that were associated with power and prestige. On the other hand, cultural practices that affirmed women's maternal and domestic roles allowed women to exercise influence within the family and to negotiate alternative paths to social power through their familial relationships with powerful men. Although women were expected to submit to male authority, they made important decisions concerning the well-being of their family members and often had sole control over the household finances. Women also made significant contributions to the *sangha* through the donation of money and gifts and the presentation of their sons as novices, which was acknowledged in Buddhist rituals and ceremonies. In recent years, even in isolationist Burma, traditional concepts of gender and power have been challenged by the forces of modernisation and globalisation, bringing with them alternative views about the role of women. More women have begun to question and challenge prevailing notions of acceptable female roles and behaviour in Burmese society. In doing so, they are bringing about changes in the dominant Burmese worldview that will allow more avenues for women to seek power.

2

Religion, Royalty, Marriage and Motherhood: Images of Female Power in Classical and Pre-Modern Burma[1]

*I*t is impossible to condense the history of the past two millennia into one volume, let alone a single chapter. For this reason, as the title of this chapter suggests, I have chosen to focus on some of the more prominent themes and images relating to notions of womanhood and femininity that emerge through an examination of selected source materials covering the period up to the mid-eighteenth century. While the resulting narrative may be incomplete, I hope to draw attention to some aspects of female power in classical and pre-modern Burmese polities. The rise of Theravada Buddhism provided women with opportunities to accumulate merit and display their material wealth and status, but Buddhist images and rituals also promoted the notion of an 'ideal' female that emphasised the generative, nurturing function of women to the exclusion of other roles. It is conceivable that women embraced Buddhism partly because the affirmation of their maternal roles actually enhanced their influence within the family. The development of Burmese political organisation as a form of extended family network enabled elite women to exercise significant political influence through

---

1   This chapter focuses on Pyu, Mon and Burman polities. Pyu sites in the central and northern regions of modern-day Burma date from around 200BC to 900CE. Archaeological and epigraphic evidence reveals that Mon peoples inhabited parts of Lower Burma from the third century or earlier. Until recently, most Burma historians took this to mean that a Mon 'civilisation' existed in Lower Burma from an early date. Michael Aung-Thwin has convincingly argued, however, that there was no major Mon polity until the late thirteenth century: see Michael A. Aung-Thwin, *The mists of Rāmañña: the legend that was Lower Burma* (Honolulu: University of Hawai'i Press, 2005). The major Burman polities are conventionally periodised as the Pagan Dynasty (1044–1287), Ava Dynasty (1364–1555), First Toungoo Dynasty (*circa* 1486–1599) and Restored Toungoo Dynasty (1597–1752). The Konbaung Dynasty (1752–1885) will be discussed in chapter 3.

their relationships with powerful men. As Burmese polities evolved and expanded, the struggles for economic, social and political dominance among elites, and the increase in social mobility among the lower classes, reveal that women were vitally concerned about maintaining and enhancing their power and status.

Before we explore these issues, a word about the source materials is in order. Our knowledge of early Burmese society is based on archaeological and epigraphic sources including sculptures, artefacts, relief images and votive tablets recording donatory inscriptions. From around the fifteenth century onwards, various literary texts were also inscribed on palm leaf in 'book' form. Chronicle accounts were usually written many years after the events they describe took place, so we might expect to find discrepancies regarding dates, persons and events in these sources. The personal views and political motives of authors and their patrons, as well as cultural traditions, influenced the topics chroniclers, poets and dramatists wrote about and the meanings they imposed. Omissions, embellishments and the combination of real, semi-fictional and mythological characters permeate many texts. While the sources may not accurately reflect the realities of women's lived experiences, they are of interest for other reasons. Specifically, these historical representations of women influenced the cultural construction of gender roles which had important implications for women's ability to exercise social power in the more recent past.

Early religious practices and the rise of Theravada Buddhism

Although we know very little about the lives of women in early Burmese polities, they clearly took an active interest in spiritual matters. Religious practices in Pyu society were highly syncretic and incorporated animist, Hindu and Buddhist influences. Ritual goods such as bronze 'mother-goddess' figures indicate animist practices, but the symbolism of these artefacts remains unclear. Examples found in the Samon Valley appear to be female figures with raised circles around the chest and belly, which could be associated with fertility rituals. Some figures have multiple 'breasts' and 'wombs', however, so this theory is speculative.[2] Many

---

2   Pamela Gutman and Bob Hudson, 'The archaeology of Burma (Myanmar) from the Neolithic to Pagan', in Ian Glover and Peter Bellwood (eds.), *Southeast Asia: from prehistory to history* (London; New York: RoutledgeCurzon, 2004), 149–76; Elizabeth Moore, 'Bronze and Iron Age sites in Upper Myanmar: Chindwin, Samon and Pyu', *SOAS Bulletin of Burma Research* 1, 1 (Spring 2003): 24–39.

sculptures include a mixture of Theravadin, Mahayanist and Hindu images. Inscriptions reveal that elite women performed important roles as religious benefactors either on their own or together with their husbands. Pali inscriptions found in Sri Ksetra (dated to the fourth century CE) record that a wealthy woman, Bodhisiri of Nagarjunakonda, made significant donations to the *sangha*.[3] Excavations in the village of Kalagangon uncovered Hindu images as well as a hollow reliquary casket depicting four Buddha images (dated to the late fifth or sixth century CE). The inscription mentions the donors' names as Sri Prabhu Varman and Sri Prabhu Devi, where 'Varman' suggests a Pallava influence.[4]

Although various religious influences were evident in Pyu society, the bulk of sculptures and inscriptions indicate that the Theravada tradition gained prominence from an early date.[5] Chinese texts dating from the third century describe the Pyu ('P'iao') as Buddhists. The *Man Shu*, compiled by Fan Cho in the ninth century, records that the Pyu 'reverence the Law of the Buddha'. The following passage from this text also indicates that elite Pyu women possessed significant wealth and high status:

> The women on the top of their heads make a high coiffure, adorned with gold, silver and real pearls. They wear for show blue skirts of *p'o-lo* (silk cotton?) and throw about them pieces of gauze-silk. When walking, they always hold fans. Women of noble family will have three persons, or five persons at their side, all holding fans.[6]

The Mon would have been familiar with Buddhism through their contact with Indian and Sinhalese culture, but other religious traditions were also evident in Lower Burma. An undated inscription recounts that a stone statue of a standing Buddha near Hpa-an was carved by a queen

---

3   Janice Stargardt, 'The great silver reliquary from Sri Ksetra: the oldest Buddhist art in Burma and one of the world's oldest Pali inscriptions', in M. J. Klokke and K. R. van Kooij (eds.), *Fruits of inspiration: studies in honour of Prof. J. G. de Casparis, retired Professor of the early history and archaeology of South and Southeast Asia at the University of Leiden, the Netherlands, on the occasion of his 85th birthday* (Groningen: Egbert Forsten, 2001), 508.

4   G. H. Luce, *Phases of Pre-Pagan Burma* (Oxford: Oxford University Press, 1985), 137; Elizabeth Moore, 'Interpreting Pyu material culture: royal chronologies and finger-marked bricks', *Myanmar Historical Research Journal* 13 (June 2004): 17.

5   G. H. Luce, 'The ancient Pyu', *Journal of the Burma Research Society*, 27, 3 (1937): 239–53.

6   Fan Cho, *The Man Shu: Book of the Southern barbarians*, translated by Gordon H. Luce, edited by Giok-Po Oey, Data Paper Number 44 (Ithaca: Southeast Asia Program, Department of Far Eastern Studies, Cornell University, December 1961), 90–91.

of Martaban who struggled against the rising tide of Hinduism.[7] One eighteenth century Mon chronicle describes how Tissaraja (1043–57), the 'heretic' (Hindu) king of Pegu, persecuted Buddhists and destroyed Buddha images. Upon hearing that a devout maiden, Bhadradevi, had restored the images and worshipped them, the king ordered her execution, but found that she could not be killed:

> By virtue of the spirit of loving kindness in the maiden when King Tissarājā made the elephants trample [her], they dared not trample; when they made the fire it would not burn [her]; killing her she did not die; destroying her she was not destroyed; the king had to throw down his pride, humble his heart, and follow the leading of the maiden. He had to turn again to a sense of the benefits of the religion, had he not?[8]

When Bhadradevi performed a miracle by creating Buddha images which then flew up to the heavens, the king was persuaded to convert to Buddhism, and raised her to the position of chief queen.[9] Michael Aung-Thwin has dismissed this story as an 'origin myth' in which the 'devout maiden' resembles the fifteenth century Mon queen, Bana Thau (known as Shin Saw Bu in Burmese).[10] Nonetheless, this account suggests that later chroniclers recognised that women could exert influence over powerful men.

During the eleventh century, the Burman rulers of Pagan in central Burma established authority over Lower Burma, which facilitated growing cultural exchange with the Theravada stronghold of Sri Lanka. Theravada Buddhism gradually came to predominate as Pagan rulers sought to 'purify' religious practices and consolidate their authority over the region. Royal patronage raised the status of Theravada Buddhism and promoted its influence among ordinary people, including women. Before we consider why Buddhism attracted female supporters, it is pertinent to provide a brief overview of women's roles and status in Pagan society.

---

7   Maung Htin Aung, *A history of Burma* (New York; London: Columbia University Press, 1967), 27. According to Michael Aung-Thwin, the earliest date for this inscription is 1176CE: Aung-Thwin, *The mists of Rāmañña*, 61.

8   R. Halliday, 'Slapat rājāwan datow smin ron: a history of kings, with text, translation, and notes', *Journal of the Burma Research Society* 13, 1&2 (1923): 66–67.

9   Godfrey Eric Harvey, *History of Burma: from the earliest times to 10 March, 1824, the beginning of the English conquest* (London: Frank Cass & Co. Ltd., 1967), 7–9.

10   Aung-Thwin, *The mists of Rāmañña*, 97–99. Bana Thau's career is discussed later in this chapter.

Women's roles and status in Pagan society

Michael Aung-Thwin described Pagan during the eleventh and twelfth centuries as 'the center of a bustling, thriving, dynamic kingdom' with a population of around two million.[11] Women's roles and status in Pagan society were determined by their class as much as their gender. Class distinctions were based on differences of birth, wealth and profession, although these divisions were less rigid than those found in other Asian societies, such as India. The ruling class comprised members of the royal family and high-ranking officials, who gained power and status from their family lineage, titles and appanages. Commoners were organised into four main categories: *asañ* were unbonded people who earned their livelihood through private business; *kwyan-tō* were people in the royal service; *kwyan* were people bonded to private individuals; and *purā kwyan* were those dedicated to Buddhist establishments.[12]

Queens and other high-ranking women (including princesses, royal relatives, wives of high officials and maids of honour) performed a range of duties in the service of the king and his court. Although the highest ministerial offices (*amat*) were reserved for men, women were appointed as *sūkri* – lower-level administrative officials who ruled over individual provinces (*kliy sūkri*) and villages (*rwā sūkri*). Educated women were also appointed as royal secretaries (*atwanre*) and clerks (*cākhīpuil, cātawkhī*). The king and other senior members of the court would have entrusted these women with sensitive information, which would have given them considerable power and influence. Women were also responsible for important economic matters including supervision of the royal granaries (*kyī sañ*). Aside from these administrative and financial responsibilities, women also performed more 'feminine' duties such as fanning the king and offering him betel leaves and nuts. Accomplished female singers, musicians and dancers also entertained the members of the court.[13]

Although socio-economic status varied within the *asañ* class, some women – including wives and daughters of rich agriculturalists, artisans,

---

11   Michael Aung-Thwin, *Pagan: the origins of modern Burma* (Honolulu: University of Hawai'i Press, 1985), 115.

12   For a more detailed discussion of these four commoner groups, see Aung-Thwin, *Pagan*, 74–91.

13   Pe Maung Tin, 'Women in the inscriptions of Pagan', 412–13.

professionals and traders – would have lived comfortably and had a measure of economic independence. These women evidently were concerned with preserving their wealth, since they frequently acted as witnesses in legal disputes regarding inheritance and property matters such as the ownership of land and *kwyan*.[14] We can assume that these women were respected and influential individuals in Pagan society, since the *dhammathats* prescribed that legal witnesses should be people who are 'just, pious, and religious, who give alms, and do good works'.[15] Inscriptions also mention female elders (*sankrī*) and assistant elders (*sanlyan*) of social groups (*san*) who would have exercised considerable influence and authority in their communities.[16]

Women performed important roles in the agrarian-based economy, as agriculturalists involved in transplanting and harvesting rice, growing and selling fruits and vegetables, weaving cloth and preparing food for monks, and maintaining the extensive temple buildings which included monasteries, libraries and schools. Female singers, musicians and dancers would have performed at festivals and other community gatherings. Inscriptions mention female cowherders (*ācī*), oil sellers (*chi sañ*), spinners (*khrañ nay sañ*), weavers (*kī sañ*), and musicians (*pantyā*) among other professions.[17] Women were probably paid less than men for performing the same labour, however. Vincentius Sangermano noted that daily labour wages were set at 'a quarter or the eighth part of a [*klyap*] for women, and twice as much for a man'.[18] The tendency for people to live in groups according to their occupation and ethnicity also had important implications for their socio-economic status. Occupations were usually hereditary, which made it difficult for men and women to change professions or relocate to more prosperous areas when employ-

---

14 *Ibid.*, 420–21.

15 This quote is taken from the 'Abstract of the Burmese code entitled Damasat; or The Golden Rule', Vincentius Sangermano's edited version of the twelfth-century *Dhammavilasa Dhammathat*. See Sangermano, *A description of the Burmese empire*, 275. Sangermano was an Italian missionary who resided in Burma between 1782 and 1808.

16 Pe Maung Tin, 'Women in the inscriptions of Pagan', 414–16.

17 G. H. Luce, 'Note on the peoples of Burma in the 12th–13th century A.D.', *Journal of the Burma Research Society* 42, 1 (June 1959): 68, 71–73. The suffix *sañ* describes one's occupation.

18 'Abstract of the Burmese code entitled Damasat; or The Golden Rule', in Sangermano, *A description of the Burmese empire*, 276. A *klyap* was equivalent to one *tical* or approximately a half ounce of silver.

ment opportunities were scarce.[19] Social mobility was therefore limited, particularly for members of the *kwyan* classes.

Kwyan is often glossed as 'slave', but this term did not necessarily imply a reduction in one's socio-economic status. In practice, 'kwyanship' (to use Aung-Thwin's term) denoted the obligation and relationship formed between a client and his or her patron. Some people voluntarily became *kwyan* to gain social and economic security; others became *kwyan* involuntarily through debt, war or birth.[20] Inscriptions record the names of thousands of male and female *kwyan*, many of whom were dedicated not just as families but in groups according to occupation and ethnicity. *Kwyan* performed a range of services depending on their skills and the needs of their patrons. In return for their labour, *kwyan* were provided with sufficient food, clothing, tools and land. When Queen Saw dedicated *kwyan* to a monastery in 1291, she instructed the monks to treat them well.[21] In three inscriptions dated 1227, 1235 and 1249, around ten per cent of the *kwyan* mentioned were literate (*cātat*), one quarter of whom were female. The percentage of literate women among the free population was probably considerably higher.[22] Members of the elite voluntarily dedicated themselves and their children to Buddhist establishments, which suggests that they did not lose social status by becoming *purā kwyan*. In fact, some people who became *purā kwyan* stood to benefit economically as well as spiritually since they were exempt from crown service and taxation payments.[23] Women were therefore actively involved in the social and economic life of Pagan, and were among the most dedicated supporters of the *sangha*.

Examples of female piety, wealth and status in Pagan

The expansion of Theravada Buddhism coincided with the gradual disappearance of the *bhikkhuni*. Pagan inscriptions mention the names of several female ascetics who had the same titles as senior monks, such as *Shkiñ* ('Lord'), indicating that these women were accorded high respect

---

19 Aung-Thwin, *Pagan*, 112–14.

20 *Ibid.*, 75–79.

21 Than Tun, 'Social life in Burma 1044–1287', in Paul Strachan (ed.), *Essays on the history and Buddhism of Burma by Professor Than Tun* (Whiting Bay: Kiscadale Publications, 1988), 54.

22 *Ibid.*, 56.

23 Aung-Thwin, *Pagan*, 86.

and religious status. Several inscriptions mention the head of a nunnery, Ui Chi Taw, who recited the *paritta* at a pagoda built by Princess Acaw Lat in 1261. Ui Chi Taw would have been 83 years old at the time, and would likely have been accorded the same honour as a monk by virtue of her age and spiritual attainment. Pe Maung Tin suggests that Ui Chi Taw was most likely a *bhikkhuni*, despite her lay name.[24] Although the *bhikkhuni* later disappeared altogether, the formal exclusion of females from the *sangha* did not prevent women from participating in Buddhist rituals and accruing merit. In fact, the Theravadin emphasis on *dana* ('generosity') as a principal means of accumulating merit may have enhanced the status of devout laywomen (*upasika*). Women from all social classes participated in merit-making activities by practising *dana*. Elite women – including royalty and wealthy members of the *asañ* class – gained merit and social prestige by building monasteries and temples, and through the dedication of silver, land and slaves to existing Buddhist establishments. Lower class women could also earn merit by making smaller donations of food, drink, clothing and flowers to the *sangha*.

Donatory inscriptions reveal that women desired to attain not only spiritual Enlightenment, but also material wealth and personal qualities that would enhance their power and status in this life. Since men were considered to be further along the path to Enlightenment, it was common for women to express a desire to be reborn as a man or a *nat* (spirit). One senior queen, Phwā Jaw (Pwazaw), hoped to be reborn as a man or spirit with great power and influence:

> When I become [a man], I wish to have happiness, luxury and wealth, better than the average person; when I become a *nat*, I wish to have the appearance and radiance of excellence and dominion (and) I wish to have long life, to be free from illness, have a good appearance, melodic of voice, good figure, to be loved and respected by all men and gods. I wish to have, in terms of animate things, such things as elephants and horses. I wish to be great in *phun* [glory], dominion, (have a large) retinue, reputation; whenever I am born, I wish to be fully equipped with *danā* [gift-giving], precepts, faith, wisdom, nobility, which are virtues, and know not a bit of

---

24   *Paritta* refers to the Buddhist ritual formula invoking protection. According to Than Tun, seven *bhikkhuni* recited the *paritta* on this occasion, whereas Pe Maung Tin claimed that Uim Chi Taw was the only female present alongside seven other male dignitaries. See Than Tun, 'Religion in Burma 1000–1300', in Paul Strachan (ed.), *Essays on the history and Buddhism of Burma by Professor Than Tun*, 33; Pe Maung Tin, 'Women in the inscriptions of Pagan', 414.

misery. At the end, having enjoyed bliss as man and *nat*, I wish the state of *arahant*ship which is noble, having internalized the doctrine of release and the tranquil and serene peace of *nibbāna*.[25]

Phwā Jaw was a key member of the royal family who had already amassed considerable material wealth as well as social and political clout. She lived through the reigns of six kings who lavished her with expensive gifts including land, slaves and palanquins befitting her high status. Her prayer would thus seem to express a formulaic acceptance of gender-based spiritual hierarchies and a desire to increase her already significant wealth and status, rather than dissatisfaction with her life.

Like men, women could become wealthy through birth, marriage, inheritance or business or any combination of these factors. The right family connections could enhance a woman's economic, social and political power, and kinship and marital ties were duly recorded in donors' inscriptions. Female donors did not usually record their own names, preferring to address themselves indirectly through their connections with male relatives. Any relationship with royalty was also recorded: for example, 'the King's wife, Kramcan's daughter', 'the queen's mother, Sinkasū's wife', and 'the King Cañsū's daughter, Phyakkasu's wife'.[26] Although these naming traditions suggest that a woman's status was usually determined by her relationship and proximity to men in power, there are several instances where women of high rank, including some single women, mentioned their own names, contrary to usual practice.[27] These women evidently were extremely wealthy and powerful in their own right, as their reputations apparently did not depend on their male connections.

The relationship between husband and wife would appear to have been relatively egalitarian in Pagan society, although polygamy was widely practised among the elite and may have created unequal power relationships between men and women. While a man could have more than one wife, a woman could not have more than one husband. The *dhammathats* relating to marriage, property and inheritance upheld women's right to work and control their own finances, although lesser

25 Cited in Aung-Thwin, *Pagan*, 41. The original inscription can be found in G. H. Luce and Pe Maung Tin (eds.), *Selections from the inscriptions of Pagan* (Rangoon: British Burma Press, 1928), 103–04.

26 Pe Maung Tin, 'Women in the inscriptions of Pagan', 417.

27 *Ibid.*, 416–18.

wives, concubines and women of 'ill fame' including dancing girls and prostitutes had fewer property and legal rights.[28] Generally, property earned or accumulated during marriage was jointly owned by both husband and wife. In 1231, a rich woman called Ui Kram Kyan San and her husband recorded that 'these slaves that we – the loving couple – have agreed to dedicate are not the inheritance begotten from our parents nor from our ancestors of seven generations. They are entirely the product of our labour.'[29]

Although the husband was recognised as the leader of the household, upon his death the wife inherited the major portion of his estate including farmland and slaves. In 1228, one widow, the wife of San Phiyon, recorded that, 'As my husband died when I was above twenty, I enjoyed the services of those slaves of my husband and I enjoyed the produce of those cultivable lands of my husband.'[30] Extremely powerful women could dispose of their wealth as they saw fit. Princess Acaw Lat, the daughter of King Uzana (1249–54) by his chief queen, left this record in 1270: 'I did not dedicate these *kwyan* to the Three Gems [the Buddha, the *Dhamma* and the *Sangha*]; I did not give them to my relatives .... When I am dead, let them go to where the grass is tender and the water clear.'[31] Aside from demonstrating this princess's power in denying wealth to her natural heirs, this inscription suggests that *kwyan* were treated with compassion by their owners and donors, who gained merit by freeing them.

Buddhist images and practices affirming women's maternal roles

Women's merit-making activities took the form of public dedications and rituals which affirmed women's generous, compassionate natures. Buddhist symbolism also promoted a positive image of woman as mother and nurturer. The image of a woman nursing a child was the quintessential symbol both of motherhood and Buddhist loving-kindness (*metta*) and compassion (*karuna*), and featured prominently in Burmese temple art and architecture, including the sixteenth-century

---

28 U Gaung, *Translation of a digest of the Burmese Buddhist law*; Sangermano, *A description of the Burmese empire*, 221–76.

29 Than Tun, 'The legal system in Burma 1000–1300', in Paul Strachan (ed.), *Essays on the history and Buddhism of Burma by Professor Than Tun*, 81.

30 *Ibid.*, 80.

31 Cited in Aung-Thwin, *Pagan*, 83.

Anoma Buddha image in Mrauk U, the ancient capital of Arakan.[32] The mother–son bond also formed a direct link with the *sangha*. When a boy entered a monastery as a novice, the merit accrued to his mother for her selflessness in giving birth and nurturing him. Even in modern Burma, the *shinbyu* ceremony is believed to confer greater merit than any other form of *dana*. A son's debt to his mother is considered so great that the *shinbyu* can repay her only for the milk consumed from one of her breasts.[33]

The symbolic role of the wet-nurse as the epitome of generosity is evident in stories describing the devotion of the Buddha's maternal aunt and foster mother, Maha Pajapati Gotami, who had nursed Prince Siddhartha when he was a child. The Burmese believed that children owed a life-long debt to the women who raised and nurtured them, and royal wet-nurses were respected and rewarded for their generosity and self-sacrifice.[34] Upon ascending the throne in 1236, King Kyazwa (1234–49) presented gifts to his step-mother, who had raised him: 'I knew not my mother. My step-mother nourished me so that I grew up. My step-mother is my mother.' To repay this debt, Kyazwa built his step-mother a house and gave her a family of slaves and fields, which she later donated as a monastery.[35] Another Pagan ruler, King Narathihapade (1254–87), gave land, slaves and cows to his wet-nurse 'as the price of the milk I drank'.[36] Wet-nurses and their relatives were not only rewarded financially; some were also promoted to positions of political power. King Anawrahta (1044–77) chose a Mon lady of noble birth as a wet-nurse for his son, Sawlu. When Sawlu became king (1077–84),

---

32 Barbara Watson Andaya, 'Localising the universal: women, motherhood and the appeal of early Theravāda Buddhism', *Journal of Southeast Asian Studies* 33, 1 (February 2002): 22–23.

33 Melford Spiro, *Buddhism and society: a great tradition and its Burmese vicissitudes* (New York; London: Harper and Row, 1972), 234; Andaya, 'Localising the universal', 8.

34 The concept of 'milk-debt' was found elsewhere in Southeast Asia. In Indonesia, Islamic law reinforced indigenous beliefs that there was a special bond between a 'milk-mother' and the children she nursed, and between 'milk-siblings' who were fed by the same woman. See Andaya, *The flaming womb*, 129.

35 Pe Maung Tin, 'Women in the inscriptions of Pagan', 418–19; Than Tun, 'History of Burma 1000–1300', in Paul Strachan (ed.), *Essays on the history and Buddhism of Burma by Professor Than Tun*, 16.

36 Narathihapade's predecessor had made the same offer and had also given Ui Pon San an umbrella and a golden palanquin with a painted awning and bells attached to the rear of the awning. See Pe Maung Tin, 'Women in the inscriptions of Pagan', 414; Than Tun, 'History of Burma 1000–1300', 19.

he appointed her son as the governor of Pegu.[37] We can see, then, that Buddhist practices emphasising the importance of *dana* celebrated women's maternal qualities, which enabled women to enhance their social status and, in some cases, political power through their sons.

The mother–son bond had an important function in practical politics, which allowed women to exercise power over and through their sons. In his study of families and states in pre-modern Southeast Asia, Tony Day suggested that scholars should focus less on the notion of male dominance in families and more on how a man's notion of power would have been shaped by his love and respect for his mother who was powerful in her own right.[38] In the case of Burma, historical sources point to the mothers of kings as exemplars of female piety and generosity. Given the importance of conceptualisations of kinship in the development of Burmese socio-political organisation, the royal mother was also well-positioned to exercise significant social and political power.

The political roles and influence of royal women

Women were important political actors in classical and pre-modern Burmese polities, where socio-political organisation was based on kin or kin-like relationships between a king and his queens, princes, princesses, advisers and subjects.[39] The king's power rested on a variety of factors including birth and karma. Male rulers sought to legitimise their power by emphasising both these attributes, which were inextricably related since a king was born into the royal family by virtue of his karma in past lives. The importance given to birth meant that women, as mothers of kings and future kings, played a crucial role in establishing and legitimising a king's rule and that of his successive heirs. A Burmese king considered himself to be a Buddha-in-the-making and was addressed as *purā*, 'The Exalted One', used to denote the Buddha himself.[40] Kings often used the symbolism of motherhood to emphasise their Buddhist credentials, which suggests that the role of the mother was held in high esteem. Chroniclers described the ideal kings' 'maternal' relationship with their subjects, as showing kindness and compassion towards their

---

37 Htin Aung, *A history of Burma*, 38.

38 Day, 'Ties that (un)bind', 389.

39 Aung-Thwin, *Pagan*, 129.

40 Than Tun, 'Religion in Burma 1000–1300', 27.

own 'womb-children'.[41] Queens were called *ami purā*, the female counterpart of the male *purā*. The prefix *ami* or *mi* has several meanings, one of which is 'mother'. The primary role of the queen as a royal mother was therefore reflected in her title. The chief queen represented the epitome of motherhood.

A king could have several queens and numerous concubines, but the chief queen was the most powerful, in theory if not always in practice. Also known as the 'southern' queen, the chief queen alone was crowned together with the king and participated with him in building the kingdom. The idea that power and authority were shared by the royal couple was expressed in familial descriptions of the king and chief queen as father and mother of the people.[42] The chief queen was sometimes referred to as *man nhama tō*, literally 'the king's royal younger sister'. During the Pagan period, it was common for the chief queen to be a half-sister or close cousin of the king. Aung-Thwin suggests that this pattern of royal marriage symbolised the ideal relationship of the king and chief queen as one of siblings protecting the throne.[43] The brother–sister relationship was also emphasised in post-Pagan chronicles, which referred to a mythical royal ancestor named Mahāsammata (Maha Thamada), the 'first elected king of this world cycle'.[44] In the Maha Thamada or 'Sakyan line' origin story, early Burmese kings married their sisters to ensure the purity of the royal lineage. In the nineteenth century, the compilers of the *Glass Palace Chronicle* revised earlier chronicles in order to emphasise the importance of the female royal lineage in ensuring the continuity of the succession.[45] The chief queen's primary political role was to provide the link between successive generations of royalty. The eldest son of the king and chief queen was the heir apparent (*einshemin*); their eldest daughter was the *tabindaing* or 'Princess of the Solitary Post',

---

41   *The Glass Palace Chronicle*, 20–24.

42   Pyone Yin, 'Women in the Bagan period', 12; Koenig, *The early Burmese polity*, 167.

43   Aung-Thwin, *Pagan*, 154. Tun Aung Chain notes that royal marriages between half-brother and half-sister were rare in the Ava kingdoms, although they did occur. See Tun Aung Chain, 'Women in the statecraft of the Awa kingdom', 112.

44   Royal chronicles also referred to another mythical ancestor of Burmese kings known as *Pyu-saw-hti*, the child of the solar king and a female *naga* (serpent). See G. H. Luce, 'Old Kyaukse and the coming of the Burmans', *Journal of the Burma Research Society* 42, 1 (June 1959): 90.

45   Koenig, *The early Burmese polity*, 86–87.

whose union with a Sakyan prince would ensure the purity of the royal lineage.[46]

Queens performed an important political function by legitimising the king's rule and ensuring political stability, and did not necessarily lose their power and status when a new king ascended the throne. In fact, the new monarch relied on his connection to the queens of his predecessors in order to enhance his own power. Rulers often married their predecessors' queens to strengthen their claims to the throne. At the beginning of the Pagan dynasty, a Mon noble lady, Hkin U, became queen to three successive monarchs – Anawrahta (1044–77), Sawlu (1077–84) and Kyanzittha (1084–1111). If the new king was not the *einshemin*, the rightful heir apparent, he might marry his predecessor's chief queen in order to enhance his legitimacy. Narathihapade (1254–87) married the chief queen of his late father King Uzana because his own mother was of low birth.[47] The founding ruler of a dynasty could also marry the queen of a predecessor to assert his power and emphasise the continuity of the royal lineage. King Thadominbya (1364–67), who founded the Ava dynasty, married Saw Onmar, who was of the royal lineage of Pagan.[48]

Power struggles and social mobility in mandala polities

Scholars have used the concept of 'mandala' to draw attention, metaphorically, to the nature and relations of power in pre-modern Southeast Asian polities.[49] Unlike modern states, whose administrative control reaches to defined frontiers, the extent of political power in pre-modern societies diminished with distance from the centre and boundaries shifted as neighbouring mandalas sought to strengthen their relative positions. A ruler's power and influence in these societies depended less on the acquisition of territory for its own sake than on the control over human resources for the purposes of taxation (through tribute) or

---

46 Aung-Thwin, *Pagan*, 153.

47 *Ibid.*, 158; Than Tun, 'History of Burma 1000–1300', 19. Narathihapade's mother was a turner's daughter who became one of Uzana's concubines. Narathihapade was only raised to the throne because the chief minister had taken a dislike to the *einshemin*.

48 Tun Aung Chain, 'Women in the statecraft of the Awa kingdom', 113–14.

49 Michael Aung-Thwin notes that the structure of the Pagan court was based on the Hindu–Buddhist principle of four cardinal points protecting a centre, suggesting that the Burmese perceived the kingdom as a mandala. The queens, princes and ministers resided in the eastern, southern, northern and western parts of the palace, surrounding the king's throne at the centre. See Aung-Thwin, *Pagan*, 164.

conscription. As rulers sought to increase their power through marriage alliances and the extension of patronage networks, proximity to the king became more ambiguous and political rivalries increased as the members of the court sought to maintain and enhance their status.

The Pagan court had initially privileged those who were born or married into the royal family, but it soon introduced ranks and titles which reflected people's positions in the court hierarchy. As the royal family grew larger, the title of *ami purā* was used to distinguish a 'queen' from a 'concubine', rather than kin from non-kin.[50] As a result, women with kinship ties to the king lost some of the exclusive status they had once enjoyed. The prayer of one lady provides us with an insight into the power struggles between women at the Pagan court: 'May the queens and ladies-in-waiting ... look at one another with eyes of love, without one speck of anger or cloying.'[51] This shift in the composition of the court resulted in greater social mobility, which enabled some women of non-royal birth to gain access to influential positions. Such mobility was possibly made easier in the absence of a rigid class system, although commoners were still considered inferior to those with royal or elite backgrounds.

A woman of low birth who became a concubine or lesser wife of the king could increase her status in several ways: she could bear him a son (and potential heir), she could possess rare beauty and become a favourite, or she could provide him with dedicated service. Women who possessed these attributes and won the king's praise could exercise considerable influence over palace affairs. King Narapatisithu (1173–1210) probably had many queens although only six of them are recorded in inscriptions. Among them, the most influential queen was Caw Mrakan Sañ. Although she was not the chief queen, her son, Nadaungmya (1210–34), was named his successor.[52] The chronicles tell us that she was a gardener's daughter who was favoured for her beauty, but moreover for her dedication to the king, which was demonstrated when she cured the king's whitlow by keeping his finger in her mouth until the tumour burst.[53] As a reward for her sacrifice, the king made her son heir

---

50   *Ibid.*, 134.
51   Pe Maung Tin, 'Women in the inscriptions of Pagan', 419.
52   Than Tun, 'History of Burma 1000–1300', 13.
53   *The Glass Palace Chronicle*, 141.

to the throne, despite the fact that he had several other sons who could have claimed equal right to it.

The chronicles contain cautionary tales about the dangers of criticising the mother of the king, regardless of her birth. When Narathihapade's influential chief minister Yazathingyan insulted the king's mother for being of low birth, he was sent into exile for questioning the king's legitimacy.[54] Similarly, it could be dangerous to insult the mother of a prince because the strong bond between mother and son sometimes overrode their loyalty to the king. The chronicles relate the story of one of Narathihapade's lesser queens, Shinmauk, who was insulted when her son Thihathu was given a pig's hind trotters to eat. When she switched them with the front trotters that had been given to another queen's son, the king teased Shinmauk and Thihathu by calling them 'Stealer of pig's trotters' and 'son of a stealer of pig's trotters'. Thihathu's brother Uzana warned Narathihapade that 'These twain, mother and son, will certainly assail my lord the king, if they may.'[55] Thihathu would later poison Narathihapade in an act of revenge. Aside from demonstrating the strength of the mother–son bond, these examples reveal the symbiotic nature of power relationships at court. To gain power and influence, the queen depended on her son's ability to become king, while the prince relied on his mother's ability to persuade the king and ministers to place him on the throne.

As Burmese mandalas expanded, it became increasingly difficult for rulers to subdue the rebellions that arose as multiple princes, queens, ministers, officials and clients struggled to gain dominance. The problem of maintaining effective authority in outer-lying areas was compounded by weakness at the centre, which was periodically subjected to succession disputes. The increase in royal marriage and concubinage led to a proliferation of princes and, in the absence of a firm principle of succession, various members of the royal family, supported by court factions, contested each succession.[56] This pattern continued up to the beginning

---

54 Narathihapade's mother was a turner's daughter who became one of King Uzana's concubines. See *The Glass Palace Chronicle*, 160–61.

55 *Ibid.*, 170.

56 Tun Aung Chain has discussed the challenges this presented to the rulers of Martaban in the thirteenth and fourteenth centuries: Tun Aung Chain, 'Pegu in politics and trade, ninth to seventeenth centuries', in Sunait Chutintaranond and Chris Baker (eds.), *Recalling local pasts: autonomous history in Southeast Asia* (Chiang Mai: Silkworm Books, 2002), 25–52.

of the Restored Toungoo dynasty, when Nyaunggyan Min (1597–1606) and his successors reorganised the 'classical' state structure by appointing non-relatives to regional posts, forcing princes to reside at court and positioning crown service units (*amhudan*) close to the capital.[57] Even then, rival queens, princes and ministers continued to extend their own patronage networks and to form alliances in order to enhance their power.[58] In the next chapter, we shall see how powerful Konbaung queens used their familial and ministerial connections to exert influence over kings and their courts with devastating consequences for the Burmese.

Female agency in royal marriage alliances

Marriage alliances formed a crucial element of statecraft in mandala societies as they concerned the reorganisation of socio-political relationships and, more specifically, the relationships between men and women. Male rulers relied on their female relatives to help them establish, maintain and strengthen political relationships by entering into marriage alliances with other male rulers and elites. In doing so, these women became parties to political contracts designed to ensure loyalty, tribute and friendship between a king and his clients and allies. An analysis of female agency in marriage alliances can provide further insights into women's exercise of political power.

Traditional historiography has tended to regard royal marriage relations as a male-dominated arena, in which women were mere items to be exchanged between kings and other powerful men. This tendency is not surprising, given that historical sources such as royal chronicles emphasised the power relationships between male elites. Several Burmese historians have argued that women were regarded as mere 'ornaments' and 'pawns' to be used by men. Maung Htin Aung noted that victorious Pyu kings would often take the wives of their defeated enemies as part of the spoils of war.[59] Daw Khin Khin Ma claimed that royal women were exchanged as gifts between kings as if they were no more than mere objects.[60] In an article exploring the nature of royal marriage alliances

---

57 Day, 'Ties that (un)bind', 398.

58 Victor B. Lieberman, *Burmese administrative cycles: anarchy and conquest, c. 1580–1760* (Princeton, N.J.: Princeton University Press, 1984), 139–98.

59 Htin Aung, *A history of Burma*, 93–98.

60 Khin Khin Ma, 'Myanmar queens in historical and literary texts', 197.

during the Ava period, Tun Aung Chain concluded that elite women were 'used and manipulated, the tools and pawns of the statecraft of the age'.[61] One might argue that Burmese historians' analyses reflected their own cultural assumptions about women's limited political agency, but Western historians have expressed similar views.[62] The implication one draws from these studies is that Burmese women had little or no power in determining whom they married.

In the revised edition of *History, culture and region in Southeast Asian perspectives*, O. W. Wolters encouraged scholars to adopt a more inclusive, gender-based approach to the study of mandala history.[63] Yet few scholars have considered how women, in negotiating, accepting or rejecting marriage contracts, actively participated in the politics of mandala societies. It is possible, however, to read accounts of marriage alliances as testimonies to female influence in pre-modern Southeast Asian societies.[64] Elite women – including queens, princesses and wives of high officials – were as concerned with the achievement of status and power as were men. It is entirely probable that these influential women would have been involved in negotiating and approving marriage alliances in an effort to preserve and promote their own status and that of their relatives and favourites. Marriage alliances were often used to resolve court crises or to prevent war with neighbouring polities, and the men and women involved were therefore positioned at the centre of major political power struggles. Since marriage relationships were crucial to the maintenance of royal legitimacy and dynastic stability, a woman's actions – her compliance or defiance – could affect the outcome of major political events.

Burmese rulers often sought to resolve power struggles over territory and the right to rule through marriage alliances. Chronicles described how royal women actively negotiated their own marriage alliances in order to restore peaceful relations with male rulers. *The Glass Palace*

---

61 Tun Aung Chain, 'Women in the statecraft of the Awa kingdom', 116.

62 For example, Victor Lieberman has described how political alliances between Shan federations were cemented by gifts of women to the overlord's harem. See Victor B. Lieberman, *Strange parallels: Southeast Asia in global context, c. 800–1830, Volume 1: Integration on the Mainland* (Cambridge: Cambridge University Press, 2003), 124.

63 O. W. Wolters, *History, culture, and region in Southeast Asian perspectives*, revised edition (Ithaca, New York: Southeast Asian Program, Cornell University in cooperation with The Institute of Southeast Asian Studies, Singapore, 1999), 165.

64 See Ruzy Hashim's alternative reading of female power in royal marriage alliances in fifteenth-century Malaka: Hashim, 'Bringing Tun Kudu out of the shadows', 105–24.

Chronicle relates the story of a Pyu queen, known as Nanhkan, who married Prince Mahathambaw of Sri Ksetra in the hope that their alliance would ensure peace and prosperity throughout the country. The queen had already defeated the Kanyans in battle and won a struggle for the throne against her brother.[65] The brother-in-law of the Tagaung king suggested she marry his nephew, Prince Mahathambaw: 'Make him king over your country, and let him rule, order, and unite you.' The queen reportedly accepted this advice, saying 'I am a woman. The country will be peaceful and prosperous only when one with might and authority quells the rising of our enemies.'[66] This account suggests that women were expected to marry and defer to their husbands' 'natural' authority. Although *The Glass Palace Chronicle* was compiled in the nineteenth century, the fact that there were only two ruling queens in Burmese history suggests that women generally accepted that it was inappropriate for them to rule.[67]

Women could also refuse to enter or honour marriage contracts that were arranged on their behalf. *The Glass Palace Chronicle* states that the widows of King Naratheinkha of Pagan (1170–73) appealed to their brother-in-law and Naratheinkha's successor, Narapatisithu (1173–1210), to be allowed to remain in his service rather than offered in marriage to one of the king's ministers. The queens asserted their royal birth and marital status to strengthen their case: 'O king, are we women known to covet so many husbands? We have done no sin. We are not mere sisters-in-law. We are all daughters of thine aunts, Chit-on and Eindawthi. We are all wives of a king.'[68] Narapatisithu listened to their appeals and offered his minister the daughter of a great nobleman instead. When the minister refused the king's offer, Narapatisithu killed him for his insolence. Than Tun questioned the historical ac-

---

65 Kanyans were the people living in the seven hill-tracks beginning with Thantwe. Nanhkan founded a village at Thagya-in and lived there with her army, while her brother moved out to Hpo-u with his army. See *The Glass Palace Chronicle*, 12–13.

66 *Ibid*. The queen subsequently made Mahathambawa king.

67 The peculiar circumstances that led Bana Thau (Shin Saw Bu) (1453–72) to ascend the throne at Pegu and Dagon are discussed below. Another queen, Kuvera(mi), reportedly ruled over Arakan for seven years in the early fourth century. See E. H. Johnston, 'Some Sanskrit inscriptions of Arakan', in Vladimir Braginsky (ed.), *Classical civilisations of South East Asia: an anthology of articles published in The Bulletin of SOAS* (London: RoutledgeCurzon, 2002), 161, 173.

68 *The Glass Palace Chronicle*, 138–39.

curacy of this account, claiming that there was no king on the Pagan throne between 1165 and 1174, but Michael Aung-Thwin notes that Naratheinkha reigned from 1170 until his death in 1173.[69] In any case, the above episode demonstrates that later chroniclers were aware of female agency in marriage negotiations. Royal women were concerned about maintaining their status and calculated the propriety of elite marriage relationships carefully. It would have been inappropriate for senior queens of a king to be married even to a high member of the nobility.

Beliefs about the appropriateness of royal marriage alliances appeared to be closely related to indigenous concepts of ethnicity and race.[70] Chronicle accounts suggest that the ethnic Burmans of Pagan looked down on or felt threatened by the influence of 'foreign' (*kala*) women over the king and his court.[71] Kyanzittha's ministers advised him against marrying his daughter to the prince of Pateikkara for fear that Pagan would become 'nought but a Kala country'.[72] One of Alaungsithu's (1111–67) wives, the daughter of the king of Pateikkara, was so influential as to be allowed to sit by the king's side on the royal couch. The king's eldest son was so incensed by this that he exclaimed, 'Shall this Kala wench abide on the couch in my presence, before all the ministers and councillors?'[73] Such women were perceived as a threat to men's authority because of their racial or ethnic identity as well as their gender. Intermarriage between ethnically Burman rulers and *kala* women could potentially lead to the subjugation of the former to 'foreign' powers. The notion that any woman, let alone a foreigner, would have greater influence over the king than the princes and ministers would also upset the traditional gendered hierarchies of power in which the exercise of political power was (in theory) an exclusively male domain. Male ambivalence towards inter-racial marriages may also have reflected a desire

---

69   Than Tun, 'History of Burma 1000–1300', 12; Aung-Thwin, *Pagan*, 22, 156–57.

70   It should be noted, however, that concepts of racial and ethnic identity were not necessarily fixed or discrete political or cultural categories in pre-colonial Burma. Personal and regional loyalties were often more important factors in determining political allegiance. For a discussion on these issues, see Victor B. Lieberman, 'Ethnic politics in eighteenth-century Burma', *Modern Asian Studies* 12, 3 (1978): 455–82.

71   The Burmese term *kala* derives from the Pali or Sanskrit word *kula* ('family', 'caste') and usually referred to Indians. See Luce, 'Notes on the peoples of Burma in the 12th–13th century A.D.', 70.

72   *The Glass Palace Chronicle*, 105.

73   *Ibid.*, 126.

on the part of the elite to preserve the cultural and racial 'purity' of the royal lineage.

At the height of the Pagan dynasty, kings rarely faced external threats to their power and royal intermarriage with non-Burman women was uncommon. During the fifteenth and sixteenth centuries, however, the Burman rulers of Ava sought to legitimise and extend their authority by forging marriage alliances with ruling families from neighbouring Shan, Mon and Arakanese polities.[74] Marriage alliances between Mon and Ava elites carried the implication of equality, whereas relationships with Shan princes were established with lesser princesses of the Ava kingdom.[75] When Viharadevi, daughter of the Mon King Razadarit (1384–1422), was offered as a gift to King Thihathu of Ava (1422–26), she was accorded the status of a queen. Viharadevi was already a widow when she was given away in marriage, first by her brother to King Thihathu, then by Thihathu's successor Kale Kyetaungnyo (1426–27) to Tarahpyu, Lord of Pakhan, and finally to King Mohnyin Thado (1427–40). Although Viharadevi may have accepted her situation initially, and actually remained in Ava for seven years, she eventually escaped with the help of two Mon monks and returned to Hanthawaddy (Pegu).

Female rule as the exception to the rule: a case study of Bana Thau (1453–72)

In 1453, Viharadevi was crowned as ruler of Pegu. Popularly known as Bana Thau (in Mon) or Shin Saw Bu (in Burmese), she was the only woman to rule over a major Burmese polity.[76] A queen's prominent status

---

74 Michael Aung-Thwin, *Myth and history in the historiography of early Burma: paradigms, primary sources, and prejudices* (Athens: Ohio University, Center for International Studies, 1998), 134, 199n; Tun Aung Chain, 'Women in the statecraft of the Awa kingdom', 108.

75 Tun Aung Chain, 'Women in the statecraft of the Awa kingdom', 114–15.

76 There is some debate among scholars as to whether Bana Thau reigned alone or together with her former tutor and son-in-law Dhammazedi. Some scholars believe that Bana Thau reigned at Pegu for seven years (1453–60) and then retired to Dagon (Rangoon), allowing Dhammazedi to ascend the throne: Robert Halliday, *The Mons of Burma and Thailand, Volume 2: Selected articles*, edited with a foreword and photographs by Christian Bauer (Bangkok: White Lotus, 2000), 101; Noel F. Singer, 'The golden relics of Bana Thau', *Arts of Asia* 22, 5 (September–October 1992): 81. Emmanuel Guillon argues that Bana Thau continued to rule over Dagon until her death in 1472: Emmanuel Guillon, *The Mons: a civilisation of Southeast Asia*, translated and edited by James V. Di Crocco (Bangkok: The Siam Society under Royal Patronage, 1999), 170–72. For other theories about the length and nature of Bana Thau's rule, see See Saya Thein, 'Shin Sawbu', *Journal of the Burma Research Society* 1, 2 (December 1911): 10–12; Htin Aung, *A history of Burma*, 98–100.

Figure 2.1: Idealised portrait of Bana Thau (Shin Saw Bu). Reproduced by permission of Noel F. Singer and *Arts of Asia*.

was usually determined by her union with the king, and female monarchy was also contrary to Buddhist notions of statecraft. Emmanuel Guillon has argued, however, that Mon rulers who were given the title Baña ('crown prince') actually ruled in the name of the queen mother, even though each was in his time nominally the reigning monarch.[77] Viharadevi would have exercised considerable power behind the scenes, playing the role of conciliator between her male relatives before the crown was passed to her by general consensus. Her ascent to the throne was made possible only when no male relatives of King Razadarit were left to rule.

---

77   Guillon, *The Mons*, 160, 170–72.

Anthony Reid has shown that other Southeast Asian polities participating most fully in the expanding commerce of the region were not infrequently governed by women.[78] Southeast Asian women were recognised for their economic abilities and Bana Thau's reputation as a successful ruler was based largely on her achievements in this area. Her reign was characterised by economic prosperity as she presided over the emergence of Pegu as an important centre of maritime trade: '[merchants] from distant towns arrived in great numbers, unusual wearing apparel became abundant, and the people had fine clothes and prospered exceedingly.'[79] Bana Thau also exchanged Buddhist missions with Ceylon and paid particular attention to the Shwedagon Pagoda, enlarging the platform, laying paving stones and offering a bronze bell weighing 1700 viss (2720 kg) as well as her weight in gold (25 viss, 40kg), the latter being used to gild the pagoda.[80] Thus, Bana Thau's political legitimacy was based on her royal lineage, economic prowess and piety, which were classic attributes of a Burmese ruler.

While Bana Thau was a successful ruler according to contemporary notions of (male) leadership, chroniclers highlighted her 'feminine' qualities (or lack thereof). The *Maha yazawin* implies that the future Bana Thau took her two monk tutors as lovers when she was still married to King Thihathu: 'The wily princess managed to arrange a love intrigue with the two yahans, and by their aid succeeded in escaping to Rangoon, where in no great time she was placed on the throne.'[81] This account suggests that Viharadevi used her cunning and sexuality to secure political power. Viharadevi was 60 years old when she was became ruler of Pegu, and an episode in the *Thaton-nwe Chronicle* describes how the queen faced criticism because she was well past child-bearing age.[82] When the queen's guards ordered an old man to make way for the royal palanquin, he protested, 'I must get out of the way, must I? I am an old fool, am I? I am not so old that I could not get a child, which is more

---

78   Reid, *Southeast Asia in the age of commerce 1450–1680, Volume 1*, 163–70; Reid, 'Female roles in pre-colonial Southeast Asia', 640.

79   This excerpt from the Mon chronicle, *Mon yazawin*, is cited in Lieberman, *Burmese administrative cycles*, 26.

80   Tun Aung Chain, 'Pegu in politics and trade, ninth to seventeenth centuries', 41–42.

81   Cited in Htin Aung, *A history of Burma*, 100.

82   She had three children from her first marriage: a son, who died in 1450, and two daughters.

than your old queen could do!' The queen reportedly accepted this rebuke and thereafter referred to herself as Bana Thau ('Old Queen').[83] This account highlights the prevailing notion that a queen's status was dependent upon her ability to bear children and a potential (male) heir. Bana Thau later retired to Dagon after arranging for her younger daughter to marry her former monk teacher, Pitakahara, who ascended the Pegu throne as King Dhammazedi (1472–92). Even after she moved to Dagon, Bana Thau probably continued to exercise considerable political influence as Dhammazedi's mother-in-law.[84]

Image of the evil, scheming queen

Women who used their sexuality to enhance their power at court were often condemned for their involvement in palace intrigues. Bana Thau's contemporary Shin Bo Me provides a striking example of a woman who used marriage alliances aggressively to enhance her own position and power. Shin Bo Me held great influence at the court of Ava as the queen of five successive kings. Initially promoted to queen by her uncle King Minkhaung I (1401–22), she was also made queen by Minkhaung's son and successor Thihathu. Shin Bo Me became jealous when Thihathu gave greater favour to Viharadevi and conspired with the *sawbwa*[85] of Onbaung (Hsipaw), Sao Loi Hsan Hpa, to bring about Thihathu's death. Shin Bo Me had promised Sao Loi Hsan Hpa that they would marry and jointly rule Ava, but after Thihathu was executed (in 1426) his young son, Minhlange, was placed on the throne. Shin Bo Me poisoned Minhlange so that her lover, Kale Kyetaungnyo could become king. Kyaytaungnyo was driven out by Mohnyin Thado, who finally 'tamed' Shin Bo Me and made her his junior queen.[86]

---

83   Cited in Harvey, *History of Burma*, 117. See also Saya Thein, 'Shin Sawbu', 11, Singer, 'The golden relics of Bana Thau', 81.

84   In 1855, a Pali dedicatory scroll was discovered near Shwedagon Pagoda, which described how the 'Lord of Kings' performed *puja* before the hair of a rajadevi. Although the king and rajadevi were not identified by name, Noel Singer suggests that they were Dhammazedi and Bana Thau, noting that the king would have been indebted to his mother-in-law. See Singer, 'The golden relics of Bana Thau', 84; Colonel Sykes, 'Account of some Golden relics discovered at Rangoon, and exhibited at a Meeting of the Society on the 6th June, 1857, by permission of the Court of Directors of the East India Company', *Journal of the Royal Asiatic Society of Great Britain & Ireland* 17 (1860): 298–308.

85   A *sawbwa* (*saopha* in Shan) was a Shan hereditary ruler.

86   Khin Khin Mar, 'Myanmar queens in historical and literary texts', 198–99, 202; U Sai Aung Tun, 'Shan-Myanmar relations as found in the Hsipaw Chronicle', in Universities Historical

Shin Bo Me was portrayed by chroniclers and historians as an arche-typal dangerous woman whose interference in the affairs of the kingdom caused political instability and disrupted the royal succession. The im-age of the 'evil, scheming queen' was a common trope used in Burmese and other Southeast Asian chronicles, which served to denigrate women who did not conform to idealised understandings of femininity.[87] Such women were generally characterised by their dominant personalities and aggressive sexuality that threatened to undermine male authority and prowess. By plotting to install their favourites on the throne, these women entered the male domain of politics, thereby upsetting the 'natu-ral' order. It was common for new kings to eliminate potential rivals by imprisoning or executing their male relatives and other aspirants to the throne. Such purges were considered necessary to maintain political sta-bility, when ordered by the king, but it was unacceptable for a queen to do the same. Shin Bo Me had no children, and her willingness to kill an innocent child (the boy-king Minhlange) further demonstrated her lack of maternal spirit. Another episode highlights Shin Bo Me's lack of re-spect for male authority. On one occasion when the Venerable Tet Thay asked Minkhaung to donate the royal textile tax, the king replied that he would first need to consult the queen. When the monk questioned whether a woman should govern a king, Shin Bo Me was outraged and reportedly said that, had the monk been a layman, she would have killed him instantly.[88] By insulting a respected member of the *sangha*, Shin Bo Me only enhanced her reputation as an evil woman. Significantly, this account also reveals that the king sought the queen's advice about important matters.

'Feminine' attributes as a source of women's power

While it was not acceptable for women to dominate men in public, queens and other senior women of the court often advised the king on a range of matters behind the scenes. In the private context of the royal family and household, women's 'feminine' qualities were highly valued as

---

Research Centre, *Texts and Contexts in Southeast Asia, Part III, Proceedings of the Texts and Contexts in Southeast Asia Conference, 12–14 December 2001* (Yangon: Universities Historical Research Centre, 2003), 255–56; Htin Aung, *A history of Burma*, 93–94.

87   For a comparative study of the fifteenth-century Lao queen Maha Thevi, see Martin Stuart-Fox, 'Who was Maha Thevi?', *Journal of the Siam Society* 81, 1 (1993): 103–08.

88   Khin Khin Mar, 'Myanmar queens in historical and literary texts', 199.

they provided a supportive and steadying influence on the king. In times of great stress or conflict, a queen's advice could uplift the king's spirits or soothe his fiery temper. Women therefore had the ability to affect the outcome of important political events. The chronicles recount several episodes in which Queen Saw gave wise counsel to her husband, King Narathihapade, on a range of political, military and personal matters. It should be noted here that the Queen Saw mentioned in the chronicles is actually an amalgam of at least two historical persons.[89] While the Queen Saw of the chronicles is a semi-fictional character, she nonetheless serves an important role in affirming the 'ideal' female behaviour that all women were encouraged to emulate.

The chronicles recount that Queen Saw advised the king on important political and military matters. In one instance, she suggested he recall the chief minister from exile to deal with a revolt at Martaban. Narathihapade also asked her whether he should (re)appoint his general Tharepyissapate as mayor of the inner palace after the latter failed to attack Macchagiri.[90] Queen Saw sought to protect the ladies of the palace from incurring the king's wrath. When a young handmaiden accidentally sneezed in the king's presence, the queen counselled him to control his anger. She also removed nearby weapons when the king slept, as he was liable to wake suddenly and strike his handmaidens with whatever was close to hand.[91] Queen Saw's influence was also seen in the events leading up to and immediately following the fall of Pagan in 1287. When Narathihapade faced defeat at the hands of the invading Chinese army and retreated to Bassein, she comforted him: 'Not even the universal monarch, King Mandhata ... is free from rise and fall, separations, and the breach of death.'[92] When the king considered returning to Pagan, she warned Narathihapade that his son, Thihathu, intended to overthrow him. When Thihathu brought poisoned food to his father the king, Queen Saw convinced Narathihapade to accept defeat and death with dignity: '[I]t is nobler for thee to eat of the poisoned dish and die, than

---

89 Donatory inscriptions mention at least two Queen Saws. One Queen Saw was the mother of Singhapati and Tryaphyā who dedicated land, gardens and slaves to a pagoda in 1241. Another Queen Saw, mother of Rājasura, dedicated slaves to a monastery in 1292. See Than Tun, 'Social life in Burma 1044–1287', 54.

90 *The Glass Palace Chronicle*, 161, 164.

91 *Ibid.*, 167–69.

92 *Ibid.*, 177.

to meet a fearful death with thy blood gushing red at point of sword and lance and weapon.'[93] Narathihapade accepted these final words of advice and ate the poisoned food.

Following Narathihapade's death, Queen Saw continued to exert an influence over his successors as the dowager queen. When Narathihapade's son, Kyawzwa (1287–1300), yielded to the Tatars at Tagaung and agreed to paid annual tribute to the Emperor, Queen Saw, believing that his actions were not in the best interests of the kingdom, plotted with 'three princely brothers' to overthrow Kyawzwa and place his younger son, Saw Hnit, on the throne. In 1312, she allowed the youngest brother, Thihathu, to establish a palace at Pinya and install his throne, thereby effectively declaring him the rightful king.[94] Despite the fact that her actions contributed to the downfall of the Pagan dynasty, Queen Saw's influence over political events is portrayed more positively than that of Shin Bo Me, possibly because the former remained loyal to her husband and people while the latter sought power and glory for her own gain. Shin Bo Me was the archetypal 'evil, scheming queen', whereas Queen Saw was the epitome of the caring, loyal wife.

Female archetypes in popular Burmese art and literature

Although the above discussion focuses on queens, whose lives were very different from those of lower-class women in many respects, all women shared important experiences. Nearly every mature woman could relate to the experience of being a wife and mother, regardless of whether she was a queen or a peasant.[95] As lower-class women sought to improve their social status, they would have modelled their behaviour on that of the elite. Moreover, ordinary women and men would have been exposed to (and influenced by) the expanding body of literature that spread throughout the population, particularly from the fifteenth century onwards. These texts often contained cultural 'statements' about power and gender – typically through portrayals of 'good' and 'evil' characters – that

---

93 *Ibid.*, 179.

94 Harvey, *History of Burma*, 75–79; Htin Aung, *A history of Burma*, 72–77. Following other colonial scholars, Harvey refers to the three brothers as 'Shan'. Michael Aung Thwin has repudiated this 'myth' and the related belief that the subsequent Ava period was a 'Shan period'. See Aung-Thwin, *Myth and history in the historiography of early Burma*, 121–43.

95 Nuns may be a notable exception in this regard, although many nuns were older women or widows who had been wives and mothers before taking their vows.

served as models of behaviour for living men and women to emulate or repudiate.[96]

Jataka stories, poetry and dramatic works were important vehicles for disseminating ideas among the population, literate and non-literate alike, and successive generations of women would have been socialised to conform to the 'ideal female' identified in these narratives of exemplary social behaviour. Jataka scenes were depicted in stone sculptures and terracotta plaques in and around Buddhist temples in Thaton in lower Burma as early as the eleventh century. In Pagan temples, Jataka images were accompanied by glosses in Pali and vernacular scripts from the early twelfth century onwards. The Jataka were also studied in monasteries, and monks would have woven these stories into their public discourses. The popularity of the last ten Jataka of Mahanipata, also known as the 'Great Ten Jataka', was evident in their prominence in the temples of Pagan. The Vessantara Jataka – which describes how Prince Vessantara gave up all of his possessions, including his wife Maddi and their children, in order to progress towards Enlightenment – must have resonated with many women. Plaques lining the walls of the Ananda temple depict Maddi's desperate search for her children and the family's eventual happy reunion.[97] Even today, many Burmese still regard Maddi, Mahamaya, Canda and Thambula as the 'four ideal wives' from the Jataka who epitomised loyalty to their husbands.[98]

Major themes from the Jataka were evident in various forms of popular literature which first appeared in 'book' form (inscribed on palm leaf) in the fifteenth century. Among the most popular literary genres were *pyo*, poems written in four-syllable lines with various rhyming schemes, which often incorporated and embellished themes from the Jataka. The *Kogan Pyo*, composed in 1523 by the monk Shin Maha Ratthasara, was based on the Hatthipala Jataka. It relates the story of King Esukari's

---

96 See, for example, Aung-Thwin, 'Prophecies, omens and dialogue', 78, 85; Miksic, 'Heroes and heroines in Bagan-period Myanmar and early classic Indonesia', 58–71.

97 Charles Duroiselle (ed.), *Epigraphia Birmanica: being lithic and other inscriptions of Burma* (Rangoon: Superintendent, Government Printing Office, 1919–36), vol. II, part 1, pp. 130–32; vol. II, part 2, plates 351–60, 377.

98 Khin Aye, 'The role of Jātakas in Myanmar literature', in Universities Historical Research Centre, *Views and Visions, Part I, Proceedings of the Views and Visions Conference, 18–20 December 2000* (Yangon: Universities Historical Research Centre, 2001), 112. Mahamaya, Canda and Thambula feature in the Khandahala Jataka (J. 542), Canda-Kumara Jataka (J. 485) and Thambula Jataka (J. 519).

Brahmin chaplain, whose sons refuse the crown and instead embrace the monastic life. Grieving the loss of his sons, the chaplain joins them in the forest and is followed by his wife, the king, the queen and eventually all the people. In the *Kogan Pyo*, the chaplain's wife is described as a weeping mother who mourns the loss of her sons and the husband whom she regarded as her master. Eventually, she decides to follow their example and renounce the world.[99] One verse describes how the Brahmin encounters a poor woman with seven sons who is unable to identify their father(s), and so makes the excuse that a tree spirit gave them to her out of pity. The author describes her 'words of deceit and cunning indeed'.[100] Shin Maha Ratthasara captures the human nature of the characters, but also points to social obligations and models of behaviour for men and women. The virtuous Brahmin's wife dutifully follows her husband into the forest, while the poor woman with many sons (and no husband) must conceal her shame.

The *yadu* was another poetic form popular in the sixteenth and seventeenth centuries. One well-known *yadu*, 'Victory Land of Golden Yun', was composed in 1583 by Queen Hsinbyushinme, daughter of Thado Dhammaraja and niece of King Bayinnaung (1551–81). Hsinbyushinme's husband, Nawrahtaminsaw, was appointed King of Chiang Mai in 1578. Hsinbyushinme accompanied her husband to Chiang Mai, but the couple endured long periods of separation while Nawrahtaminsaw was away on various military campaigns. In the 'Victory Land of Golden Yun', Hsinbyushinme describes the natural beauty surrounding Chiang Mai and expresses her sorrow at being unable to enjoy these delights with her husband:

> Victory Land of Golden Yun, our home
> thronged pleasantly like paradise.
> the clear moving waters flow incessantly,
> the forests teem with singing birds, the breezes replace the sere leaves
> as buds peep and petals spread ....
> Yet my love is not here to enjoy;
> I in loneliness watch the delights

---

99 Shin Maha Ratthasara, *Catudhammasara Kogan Pyo*, edited by Daw Khin Saw (Rangoon: Buddha Sasana Council, 1959), v. 174–233.

100 *Ibid.*, v. 8. For an English translation of this verse and other excerpts from the *Kogan Pyo*, see John Okell, '"Translation" and "embellishment" in an early Burmese *Jātaka* poem', *Journal of the Royal Asiatic Society* 3/4 (October 1967): 137.

in this season of diverse scents
in Yun City created by you, lord,
and await your return
topmost of the royal lineage of the sun ....
Since my lion-hearted husband marched to war
I guarded my mind and kneeling
before Buddha's representative images
of Phra Kaew, Phra Sing, golden Maha Ceti
and the famous Phra Suthep,
images as bright as the sun
on western hill-top beyond the city, and within,
with reverence I say my prayers,
rising glory of the lineage of the Sun.[101]

While the above examples extol wives' devotion and loyalty to their husbands, other literary sources depict women as bewitching or lustful creatures who threatened to undermine men's authority and power. The *Ummadanti Pyo*, based on the Jataka of the same name, was written by the Konbaung court poet U Shun in 1848. It relates the story of King Sivi, who was bewitched by the beauty of Ummadanti, the wife of the commander-in-chief. The king's uncontrollable passion for Ummadanti drove him to madness, leading the people to consult astrologers and physicians in an effort to cure his illness.[102] Perhaps the most negative portrayal of women was found in the popular *Paduma Pyazat* ('Paduma Play'), written by the renowned court dramatist and poet U Pon Nya who served under kings Tharrawaddy, Pagan and Mindon in the mid-nineteenth century.[103] The plot is based on the Paduma Jataka, in which the king banishes his seven sons and their consorts out of fear that they might rebel against him. While in the forest, the brothers' hunger leads them to kill and eat six of the women, but the eldest prince Paduma manages to save his consort. The couple then encounter a thief whose limbs have been amputated as punishment for his crimes. The princess becomes infatuated with the grotesque thief and tries to kill the prince

---

101 Cited in Ni Ni Myint, '"Victory Land of Golden Yun" – A queen and her poem', in Myanmar Historical Commission, Ministry of Education, Union of Myanmar, *Selected writings of Ni Ni Myint: member of the Myanmar Historical Commission* (Yangon: U Kyi Win, Manager (02384) at the Universities Press, 2004), 20–21.

102 Maha Minhla Mingaunggyaw, *Ummadantī Pyo* (Yangon: Burma Research Society, 1964).

103 *Paduma* was written in 1855, although it was not published until 1927. U Pon Nya, *Paduma Pyazat*, Buddha's birth story no. 193 (Rangoon, 1927).

by pushing him off a cliff.[104] Paduma reflects that women's insatiable sexual desire will lead them to

> ... kill their rightful husbands the moment they want a new lover. Their lust blinds them. As the tongue of a snake, their cunning, their desires, their behaviour, are double-tipped. They receive all, just as a roaring fire receives all rubbish. They will love even men as low as dogs and pigs. One is more certain of one's ability to drink up all the waters of the ocean, than of the faithfulness of one's wife. My lords, I have lost faith in all women, but I should have known better than to have had such faith at all.[105]

U Pon Nya's criticisms were directed against the junior queens who allegedly engaged in illicit affairs and deception. Htin Aung notes that, when the play was first performed, the royal women protested so much that King Mindon ordered U Pon Nya to write another play highlighting women's virtues. U Pon Nya subsequently wrote *Waythadaya*, his version of the Vessantara Jataka, which praised Maddi's love for her husband and children.[106]

The influence of royal women at the Konbaung court will be discussed in the next chapter. I mention the *Ummadanti Pyo* and *Paduma Pyazat* here to show how popular literary forms portrayed contrasting images of women – as loyal, caring wives ('good' women) or lustful, deceiving temptresses ('evil' women) – which influenced the development of gender roles and stereotypes in Burmese society. Literary representations of females and femininity did not necessarily reflect the actual lived experiences of women, and the extent to which ordinary men and women believed that these portrayals were accurate is also open to question. Nonetheless, the fact that these sources remained popular many years later suggests that they probably had a socialising influence over successive generations of Burmese.

---

104 Unbeknownst to the princess, Paduma survives and finds his way back to the capital, where he eventually becomes king. The princess and the thief later arrive in the capital and Paduma, upon recognising them, orders them to be imprisoned. He later commutes their execution sentence and sends them into exile.

105 Quoted in Maung Htin Aung, *Burmese drama: a study, with translations, of Burmese plays* (London: Oxford University Press, 1937), 231.

106 *Ibid.*, 77, 94.

Conclusions

Although females rarely attained positions of formal political power in classical and pre-modern Burmese society, women's influence within the family was enhanced through the practise of *dana* as a form of shared merit-making and the positive portrayal of maternal qualities in Buddhist texts and rituals. The development of the Burmese mandala polity as a form of extended family network supported and strengthened by female royal lineages, marriage alliances and client–patron relationships enabled elite women to exercise significant political influence through their familial connections to male rulers. Gender–power relations were reciprocal and interdependent in nature. Kings relied on their familial connections to royal women to legitimise their rule, while royal women used their relationships with male rulers and elites to maintain and strengthen their own positions at court. Although non-royal women had limited opportunities to improve their economic and social circumstances, the expansion of the royal court enabled some lower-class women to enhance their status and influence through their relationships with powerful men.

By the mid-eighteenth century, at the beginning of the Konbaung era, the image of the 'ideal' woman as a supportive wife and mother was firmly rooted in the Burmese collective consciousness. Konbaung chroniclers and future generations of Burmese would subsequently record (and judge) the deeds of powerful women in terms of how closely they conformed to this ideal. In reality, this did not prevent women with strong personalities, knowledge and skill from exercising significant economic, social and political influence through their relationships with powerful men. But, as we shall see, women who overtly challenged men's authority were criticised by male elites for undermining political stability at a time when the integrity of the Burmese state was threatened by external as well as internal forces.

3

Powerful Women of the Konbaung Dynasty

*T*he Konbaung period (1752–1885) marks a watershed in Burmese history. It began with the promise of wealth and prosperity and ended with the demise of the Burmese monarchy and the imposition of British colonial rule. During the early Konbaung era, women exercised significant economic influence as cultural power-brokers between European and Burmese men. Queens and other royal women continued to exercise considerable influence over kings and the court from behind the scenes. During the latter part of the dynasty, however, women's status declined as increasing indebtedness and economic hardship forced many poor women into slavery. Ambitious queens dominated kings and the court at a time when the Burmese state was seriously weakened by internal succession disputes and British political, economic and military aggression. As Burmese rulers struggled to maintain their hold on power, there was a tendency for male elites to blame these queens for interfering in the traditionally male sphere of political and military affairs, rather than criticise kings for their own shortcomings. Negative portrayals of powerful women influenced chroniclers, historians, and later generations of Burmese by reinforcing cultural beliefs that held that women should not be involved in politics.

The foundation of the Konbaung state

During the first half of the seventeenth century, Restored Toungoo rulers introduced administrative reforms that significantly altered the power relationships between kings, members of the royal family and court officials. The king's relatives were required to live in the capital and the appanage system was changed to prevent them from directly administering provincial areas where they could amass large followings and financial and military resources in order to challenge the king's power. At the same time, the development of royal–ministerial factions and patronage networks enabled senior councillors of the *Hluttaw* and the *Byedaik* to increase their influence over the king and court.[1] During the first half of the eighteenth century, intense factional politics considerably weakened the military and administrative capacity of the central authority and defections, banditry and rebellion spread throughout the country. In 1752, rebel leaders from Pegu invaded the capital and captured King Mahadhammaraza Dipadi (1733–52), which signalled the end of the Restored Toungoo dynasty.[2]

In the ensuing power vacuum, a charismatic Burman named U Aung Zeiya (later known as Alaungpaya) from Mokhsobo (Shwebo) in upper Burma organised the local population under his control into service groups and drove the southern forces from upper Burma before carrying the war into the delta, and then to Pegu. When Pegu fell to Alaungpaya's forces in May 1757, he became the undisputed king of Burma and founder of the Konbaung dynasty. Although his hereditary claims to authority were weak, Alaungpaya quickly build up a network of loyal followers whom he appointed to key administrative and military positions. 'Alaungpaya' means 'Embryo Buddha', and the king styled himself as a *cakkavatti* ('Universal Monarch') who would restore order and prosperity following a period of oppression and turmoil.[3] Successive Konbaung rulers sought to emulate this Buddhist ideal of kingship in order to combat internal rebellions and external threats to their power from neighbouring polities and European nations. The expansionist aims of early Konbaung rulers and the rise in commercial activity throughout the region brought the Burmese into closer contact with the British colonial government in India and the East India Company. The increase in commercial and diplomatic relations between the two countries allowed some Burmese women to extend their economic and political influence, since women were heavily involved in localised trade and performed important roles as power-brokers at the royal court.

---

1 Koenig, *The Burmese polity*, 7–12; Lieberman, *Burmese administrative cycles*, esp. chapters 2–3. The *Hluttaw* was the key administrative body for the affairs of state throughout the kingdom, and was headed by a council of ministers called *wungyis*. The *Byedaik* was the department responsible for the administration of the inner palace and the king's personal affairs; senior ministers of the *Byedaik* were called *atwinwuns*.

2 Lieberman, *Burmese administrative cycles*, chapter 4.

3 *Ibid.*, 229–50; Koenig, *The Burmese polity*, 71–79. The Burmese term for *cakkavatti* is *setkyamin*.

'Connubial commerce' in Konbaung society

From the sixteenth century onwards, European missionaries, private merchants and government officials increasingly visited and resided in Burma, sometimes for extended periods. As these Europeans recorded their early impressions of Burmese society, many were struck by the relatively high level of freedom and status enjoyed by Burmese women (compared to women in South Asia, but also in Europe).[4] They were particularly impressed by women's economic activity and ability. Burmese women who entered into commercial and sexual relationships with European men acted as important cultural power-brokers, both facilitating and benefiting from the increasing trade and diplomatic relations between European and Burmese elites.

The Burmese invaded and annexed Arakan in 1784, which brought the western border of the country right up to the edge of British India. In 1795, the British sent an envoy to the Court of Ava in an attempt to defuse tensions over the issue of the Arakan border and to negotiate a commercial treaty with the Burmese. During his seven-month stay in the country, Captain Michael Symes observed that 'women ... manage the most important mercantile concerns of their husbands' and described how the governor's wife undertook daily inspections of Rangoon's shipyards and oversaw the construction of her husband's barge. Symes also reported that 'connubial commerce' (temporary marriages) between Burmese women and foreign traders was widely accepted and encouraged by Burmese and Europeans alike.[5] Konbaung rulers accepted these temporary marriages because they were concerned with increasing the population; any children born of such unions were claimed as Burmese subjects.[6] Aside from the sensual pleasures and comfort that female companionship offered, European traders also benefited from the local knowledge and contacts of their Burmese wives. The Scottish sea captain and trader, Alexander Hamilton, observed in the early eighteenth

---

4   See, for instance, John Jardine, 'Introduction', in Sangermano, *A description of the Burmese empire*, xviii–xix.

5   Symes, *An account of an embassy to the Kingdom of Ava*, 72–73, 217–18. There is evidence that temporary marriages between European traders and Burmese women were common from the sixteenth century or earlier. See D. G. E. Hall, *Early English intercourse with Burma 1578–1743*, second edition (London: Frank Cass & Co. Ltd, 1968), 100–01.

6   Symes, *An account of an embassy to the Kingdom of Ava*, 72–73, 329.

century that Burmese women successfully managed their foreign husbands' economic enterprises:

> [I]f their Husbands have any Goods to sell, they set up a Shop and sell them by Retail, to a much better Account than they could be sold for by Wholesale, and some of them carry a Cargo of Goods to the inland Towns, and barter for Goods proper for the foreign Markets that their Husbands are bound to, and generally bring fair Accounts of their Negotiations.[7]

Burmese women who married European traders stood to gain not only economic and social status, but also political influence by acting as intermediaries between their European husbands, Burmese merchants and the royal court. Captain Hiram Cox, who was sent to Rangoon as the British representative in 1796, described the political power exercised by these women in his journal. When seeking an audience with the king, Cox sought assistance from the Portuguese *shahbandar*[8] of Rangoon and his Burmese wife, who was considered to be the principal mediator between foreigners and the court of Ava. Together the couple arranged for foreigners like Cox (and Burmese too) to obtain an audience with influential members of the royal family.[9]

Hamilton noted that Burmese women were 'very fond of marrying with Europeans' because they benefited both economically and socially from such unions. Marriage contracts were usually formalised through the exchange of gifts: the husband presented money, jewellery and clothing to his wife; in return, she offered him sexual intimacy. Husbands were also required to support their wives with a monthly payment if they had to leave the country. Both husband and wife were expected to remain faithful for the duration of the marriage, but divorce was easily obtained by mutual consent. A divorced woman suffered no loss of status; rather, her prospects of remarriage were enhanced because it was assumed she had gained both wealth and knowledge through her previous marriage. Thus, Hamilton observed, '[S]he is never the worse, but rather the better lookt on, that she has been married to several European husbands.'[10]

---

7   Cited in Corfield and Morson (eds.), *British Sea-Captain Alexander Hamilton's A new account of the East Indies*, 360.

8   The *shahbandar* was the master-attendant of the harbour.

9   Cox, *Journal of a residence in the Burmhan empire*, 319–21.

10   Cited in Corfield and Morson (eds.), *British Sea-Captain Alexander Hamilton's A new account of the East Indies*, 360.

British attitudes towards Burmese women became more ambivalent following the gradual annexation of Burma during the nineteenth century. As British officials and merchants extended their control over Lower Burma, they no longer required Burmese women's assistance to engage in trade. Moreover, British assumptions of racial, sexual and religious superiority affected their attitudes towards Burmese women. Although sexual relationships between British men and Burmese women were common throughout the Konbaung period, the men tended to regard these women as concubines, rather than wives.[11] Following the complete annexation of Burma in 1886, colonial administrators actively discouraged sexual relationships between British officers and Burmese women in an effort to maintain colonial prestige and authority.[12]

Impact of commercialisation and taxation on women's socio-economic status

Although women were excluded from the highest levels of state administration, some held authoritative positions at the local administrative level. *Sittans* (records of inquiry) from the early Konbaung era mention female *thugyi* ('big people'), local hereditary chiefs who were responsible for administering *myo* (districts or townships) or *ywa* (villages) either jointly with their husbands or solely as widows or chief householders. These positions of authority were sometimes inherited through the maternal line.[13] Mi Ein, the *thugyima* of Myei-thin-dwin village, explained that 'My great-grandmother Má Nyeìn Tha had charge of this village. When she was no more, my grand-mother Mí San had charge. When she was no more, my mother Mí Wei had charge. As she is no more, I have had charge from (the year) 1119 (1757) until now [1765].' *Thugyi* were responsible for maintaining records of revenue including state taxes, and *sittans* reveal that women collected monies from concessions such as fishing grounds, toll stations and ferries. As astute traders, women facilitated patron–client relationships by acting as important intermediaries

---

11   See, for example, correspondence in 'Sir Charles Bernard's letters.' MSS Eur D 912 ff. 58, 67–68. Bernard served as Chief Commissioner of Lower Burma from 1880 to 1887.

12   Colonial authorities' ambivalent attitudes towards Burmese women is discussed in greater detail in chapter 4.

13   Frank N. Trager and William J. Koenig with the assistance of Yi Yi, *Burmese sit-tàns, 1764–1826: records of rural life and administration*, translations by William J. Koenig (Tucson: University of Arizona Press, 1979), 64, 175–76, 214, 253, 255–58, 343.

between producers and consumers, and benefited financially through their role as taxation agents. In Talok *myo*, Mi Win Tha collected tax from hereditary weavers to submit as crown revenue and retained half of the overage herself.[14] The 1803 *sittan* of Mek-hkaya *myo* records that a woman, Mi Zan Hpyu, was the *myo's* hereditary tax collector. As her commission, Mi Zan Hpyu received

> 1 *kyat* from purchaser and vendor per load of tea; 1 *kyat* of silver each from purchaser and vendor per *viss* of silver of value of goods sold by weight or measure; 1 *mù* of silver per pack animal, and 1 *pè* every third bazaar on the sale of small articles.[15]

Although some women benefited from acting as local brokers and state agents in collecting revenue, poor families without official connections bore the brunt of increased tax demands. Local industries in which there was considerable female involvement attracted specific taxes. In Salei *myo*, for instance, weaving looms were levied at a fixed rate of one hundred cubits of white cloth and a packet of tea.[16] Female traders were required to pay at toll stations when transporting goods to market; taxes were also deducted from the wages of women porters and labourers in the salt tracts of the Irrawaddy Delta.[17] In Prome, the wives of crown cavalry servicemen were required to make fruit jam and dye 150 lengths of cloth for submission to the local court each year.[18] At any time, households could also be requisitioned for other forms of state support including the donation of oil and food 'to the extent of their generosity'.[19] In the predominantly agrarian economy, poor cultivators increasingly relied on moneylenders to finance loans, and cumulative debt became more burdensome as a result of high interest rates. In the 1860s, King Mindon introduced the *thathameda* tax, which was set at ten per cent of household income and was intended to replace all other taxes; 'destitute' families were to be exempt from taxation. As local of-

---

14   Trager and Koenig, *Burmese sit-tàns*, 341.

15   *Ibid.*, 354. See also J. S. Furnivall, 'Matriarchal vestiges in Burma', *Journal of the Burma Research Society* 1, 1 (1911): 21; John White, *A voyage to Cochin China*, introduced by Milton Osborne (London: Longman, Hurst, Rees, Orme, Brown and Green, 1824; reprinted in Kuala Lumpur; New York: Oxford University Press, 1972), 245–46.

16   Trager and Koenig, *Burmese sit-tàns*, 322–23.

17   *Ibid.*, 132, 200; White, *A voyage to Cochin China*, 261.

18   Trager and Koenig, *Burmese sit-tàns*, 137–38.

19   *Ibid.*, 113, 120.

ficials continued to exact other fees and payments from the populations under their jurisdiction, however, the *thathameda* tax would have constituted an additional economic burden on many women as managers of household finances.[20]

Elite women may have benefited economically and socially from the upswing in commercial activity and contact with foreign traders, but lower-class women increasingly became vulnerable to poverty and servitude.[21] During the late seventeenth century, the increasing commercialisation of the economy allowed non-royal patrons to form their own private entourages of debt-slaves, and many poor families were forced to sell their children into slavery to repay their debts. Although Restored Toungoo rulers issued royal edicts prohibiting this practice, Symes found that many families still sold their daughters to debt creditors in the late eighteenth century.[22] Many of these girls were sold on by creditors into domestic service and/or prostitution. Symes mentioned that there was an entire village of prostitutes known as Mima-Shun-Rua, which suggests that these women were segregated from and ostracised by the rest of society.[23] In the report of his 1855 mission to Ava, Captain Henry Yule described another prostitute's quarter in Sagyeen-wa on the Irrawaddy, and observed that '[T]he women themselves have no share in the produce of their wretched traffic, but are often beaten by the old woman in whose immediate charge they are, when their pains do not come up to her expectations.'[24]

Women's ability to gain socioeconomic power and influence therefore depended on a range of factors including their marital status, family

20 Thant Myint-U, *The making of modern Burma* (New York: Cambridge University Press, 2001), 118–25; Andaya, The flaming womb, 140–41.

21 For a comparative study of the decline in women's status in Southeast Asia during this period, see Barbara Watson Andaya, 'From temporary wife to prostitute: sexuality and economic change in early modern Southeast Asia', *Journal of Women's History* 9, 4 (Winter 1998): 11–34.

22 Than Tun (ed.), *The Royal Orders of Burma, A.D. 1598–1888*, edited with an introduction, notes and summary in English of each order by Than Tun (Kyoto: Center for Southeast Asian Studies, Kyoto University, 1983–90), II, 28; Symes, *An account of an embassy to the Kingdom of Ava*, 216–17.

23 Symes, *An account of an embassy to the Kingdom of Ava*, 216, 205. 'Mima-Shun-Rua' literally means 'village of concubines'.

24 Henry Yule (comp.), *A narrative of the mission to the Court of Ava in 1855; together with The journal of Arthur Phayre, Envoy to the Court of Ava*, and additional illustrations by Colesworthy Grant and Linnaeus Tripe; with an introduction by Hugh Tinker (London, 1857; reprinted in Kuala Lumpur; London; New York: Oxford University Press, 1968), 161.

connections, class and relative position in patron–client networks. Elite women were able to enhance their economic and social power through their involvement in influential patronage networks as mediators between local and foreign traders, and between European officials and the Burmese court. At the local level, female administrative officials who exercised authority as *myothugyi* and taxation agents were able to profit by exacting concessions on local trade. The majority of lower-class women, however, were particularly vulnerable to the effects of increased taxation and high interest rates. The main beneficiaries of the taxation system were the immediate members of the royal family, including queens and princesses who acquired substantial income through the appanage system, as we shall see below.

The power and influence of royal women at the Konbaung court

Women of the royal family and the chief queen, in particular, were extremely powerful figures at the Konbaung court. As the principal consort of the king and mother of the heir apparent, the chief queen could exercise significant political influence. Alaungpaya often left the capital for extended periods to conduct various military campaigns. Although the crown prince was nominally in charge of the administration during the king's absences, Alaungpaya asked his chief queen, Me Yun San, to oversee his governorship. The king apparently believed that the chief queen's diplomatic skills and gentle nature made her a more able administrator than the crown prince. One royal order dated 1 January 1760 states that 'Alaungmintaya's Chief Queen would be extremely kind and generous. These are indeed the good qualities of a good administrator and she is expected to help her son in the government so that there would be nothing like an oppressive rule.'[25] As the queen's son, the crown prince would also have been expected to respect his mother's authority.

Europeans who resided in Burma during Bodawpaya's reign (1782–1819) remarked on the chief queen's involvement in political matters. Symes recalled how the chief queen, Me Lun Me, together with the crown prince, had persuaded Bodawpaya to admit the British embassy following an incident on the Arakanese border. He noted that the queen had a calming influence on the king and 'frequently soothed the wildest paroxysms

---

25   Than Tun (ed.), *The Royal Orders of Burma*, III, 63–64.

[sic] of his rage.'[26] Me Lun Me was also the principal intermediary between Europeans and the king. Cox's Burmese contacts advised him against directly approaching Bodawpaya with a request and recommended that he send gifts to Me Lun Me instead: '[Y]ou should endeavour to conciliate the queen to your interest, by sending her something curious.'[27] Alaungpaya's and Bodawpaya's chief queens' exercise of political power was tolerated by the Burmese because it occurred, for the most part, behind the scenes. The queens did not openly challenge men's authority; rather, they worked in cooperation with the crown prince and male ministers of the court.

Below the chief queen there were up to three senior queens who were accorded precedence on the basis of their location in the palace: they were known as the northern queen, the middle queen and the western queen. In cases where the chief queen had no son, the king would usually choose a son of another principal queen as his heir. For this reason, these queens played important political roles in the matter of royal succession. King Singu (1776–82) instituted the rank of western queen after his three principal queens failed to bear him sons.[28] As we shall see below, King Mindon's (1853–78) middle queen became involved in the power struggle for the throne when Mindon failed to nominate an heir.

During Bodawpaya's reign, the number of queens increased significantly. In addition to the four principal queens, second and third ranks of queens were created. The two queens of the second rank – the queen of the south apartment and the queen of the north apartment with the golden lining – resided in the palace and had a higher status than the third rank of queens, known as *myoza* queens, who were given titles according to their appanages.[29] These lesser queens were recruited from official families and William Koenig suggests that they were actually concubines who were given the title of queen to ensure their families

---

26 Symes, *An account of an embassy to the Kingdom of Ava*, 307–08; Symes, *Journal of his second embassy to the Court of Ava in 1802*, 172–73. As Me Lun Me had no sons; the crown prince was the eldest son of Bodawpaya's second queen Me Lun Thu.

27 Cox, *Journal of a residence in the Burmhan empire*, 115.

28 Singu's chief queen and middle queen both gave birth to daughters, but the middle queen's daughter died in infancy. Singu ordered the execution of his first north queen before she could conceive. When he elevated the middle queen to the northern palace, he appointed her two younger sisters as middle and western queens respectively. See Koenig, *The Burmese polity*, pp. 203–04; Yi Yi, 'Life at the Burmese court under the Konbaung kings', *Journal of the Burma Research Society* 44, 1 (June 1961): 88.

29 A *myoza* (literally 'eater of the *myo*') was a person who was assigned the crown's share of the *myo*'s revenue.

remained loyal to the king.[30] Whereas Restored Toungoo rulers concentrated their appanages in the central zone to prevent princely uprisings, early Konbaung rulers extended the appanage system throughout the realm.[31] By raising his concubines to the status of queens, Bodawpaya hoped to extend his control over the resources of the outlying provinces, since revenue was traditionally submitted to the *myoza*. Conversely, the king was obliged to extend the appanage system because the royal family had grown so large. The term *myoza* literally means 'to eat the *myo*' and Vincentius Sangermano observed that Bodawpaya's numerous wives, concubines and children 'swallowed up all the riches of the land; the cities, villages, and lakes'.[32] The *myoza* system therefore enhanced the economic power of queens, including the chief queen, to whom a number of specific taxes including silver and produce were payable.[33] The system was open to massive abuse and Mindon would later allocate salaries to members of the royal family and officials in order to alleviate the tax burden on the poor.[34]

Power relations between royal women and official families

Throughout the Konbaung period, there is evidence of extensive marriage connections and patronage relations between royal and official families. If a particular queen was favoured by the king, her male relatives were rewarded with important roles in the administration. Alaungpaya's chief queen and northern queen were from elite families in neighbouring towns and Alaungpaya appointed many of their relatives to key administrative posts.[35] If a queen fell out of the king's favour, however, her male relatives would also be punished. Singu's northern queen, Ma Min Aung, was the daughter of the general Maha Thiha Thura, who was appointed *athi wungyi*.[36] Symes described Ma Min Aung as a young queen 'endowed with virtue, beauty, and accomplishments' but noted that

---

30 Koenig, *The Burmese polity*, 167.

31 Lieberman, *Burmese administrative cycles*, 78–81; Koenig, *The Burmese polity*, 123–26.

32 Sangermano, *A description of the Burmese empire*, 83.

33 Trager and Koenig, *Burmese sit-tàns*, 75 and 143–44.

34 Thant Myint-U, *The making of modern Burma*, 121.

35 Koenig, *The Burmese polity*, 190–91.

36 Maha Thiha Thura was one of the original followers of Alaungpaya. An *athi wun* was an officer responsible for administering the *athi* sector of the population. *Athi* were free citizens who were not enrolled in a crown service unit.

Singu, who was of a jealous and irrational disposition, often accused her of infidelity.[37] Singu eventually divorced Ma Min Aung and stripped her father of his office. Both were sent into exile, and Ma Min Aung was later drowned on Singu's orders.[38] Thus, the status and fortunes of queens and male officials from the same family were often inextricably linked.

Male officials often used their connections with women of the royal court to enhance their own power and position. Some senior ministers married into the royal family, while lower level officials placed their daughters or other female relatives in the royal harem, where they might become favourites of the king.[39] As the number of females at the court increased, queens sought to use their influence over the king to increase their own power and promote their male relatives to positions of authority. The process had to be sensitively managed, however, for the king's male relatives and advisers could easily feel threatened by ambitious queens who intruded too far into the traditionally male-dominated political arena and openly challenged their power. During Bagyidaw's reign (1819–37), the powerful chief queen, Nanmadaw Me Nu, and her brother dominated the king, which brought them into conflict with the princes and male ministers.

Queen Me Nu's influence at Bagyidaw's court (1819–37)

Me Nu's family reportedly came from Palagon village, where her father was a gaoler and her mother worked in the market.[40] The future king Bagyidaw met Me Nu when he was crown prince and made her one of his concubines. When he proposed to marry Me Nu, the ministers protested that she was of low birth until the crown prince convinced them that she possessed qualities of unrivalled influence and greatness.[41]

---

37 Symes, *An account of an embassy to the Kingdom of Ava*, 51.

38 Tin (of Mandalay), *Konbaungzet maha yazawindawgyi* [Great royal chronicle of the Konbaung Dynasty], 3 volumes (Yangon: Ledimandaing, 1967–68), I, 515. According to William Koenig, one late Konbaung source suggests that Singu suspected the northern queen was plotting to overthrow him: see Koenig, *The Burmese polity*, 295n.

39 Koenig, *The Burmese polity*, 150–51; Ma Kyan, 'King Mindon's councillors', *Journal of the Burma Research Society* 44, 1 (June 1961): 43–60; Myo Myint, 'The politics of survival in Burma: diplomacy and statecraft in the reign of King Mindon, 1853–1878' (PhD thesis, Cornell University, 1987), 123–24.

40 Albert Fytche, *Burma past and present, with personal reminiscences of the country* (London: C. Kegan Paul, 1878), 201.

41 *Ibid.*, 32.

Their marriage also created tensions within the royal family. The Prome prince bore a long-standing hatred towards Me Nu after his daughter, the crown prince's first wife, died in 1811 (reportedly out of mortification due to Me Nu's elevation to the position of wife).[42] Me Nu apparently tried to suffocate another wife, the Padaung princess, but she was rescued by Prince Tharrawaddy, the crown prince's brother.[43] In 1819, the crown prince ascended the throne as King Bagyidaw and made Me Nu his chief queen; her brother Maung Oh was also rewarded, raised to the position of Myoza of Salin.

Me Nu was the king's closest and most powerful adviser – her influence over Bagyidaw was so great that his relatives attributed her power to 'sorcery'.[44] The Salin Myoza was equally hated for his cruelty, arrogance and insatiable desire for power. Bagyidaw's uncles, the Taungoo and Prome princes, were imprisoned and later killed, apparently on the orders of Me Nu and her brother, though it was common for new kings to eliminate potential rivals in this manner.[45] Me Nu desired either to make her brother heir to the throne or to dominate the heir apparent, Bagyidaw's son by his deceased first queen, by marrying him to her only daughter. Both proposals were unacceptable to the king's relatives, who feared the loss of their own power as well as the damaging effects of such a succession on the 'purity' of the royal lineage.[46] Together with her brother, Me Nu also built up an extensive patronage network throughout the realm, appointing loyal followers to key posts both at court and in the outer-lying provinces.

As Me Nu and the Salin Myoza gained ascendancy at court, a power struggle developed between them and Bagyidaw's brother, Prince Tharrawaddy, a senior army commander who was widely respected. In

---

42   'A historical memorandum of royal relations of Burmah hunters family from beginning to present 1228 AD 1866. Collected from Burma history and various parts – best corrected by various prince and Queen and old officials of this Burmah.' Yadanabhoom (Mandalay) 4th December 1866. BLOM OR 3470 ff. 11–12. Hereafter cited as 'BLOM OR 3470'.

43   R. R. Langham-Carter, 'Queen Me Nu and her family at Palangon', *Journal of the Burma Research Society* 19, 2 (1929): 32.

44   Yule, *A narrative of the mission to the Court of Ava*, 223–24; Fytche, *Burma past and present*, 201–02; Phayre, *History of Burma*, 250.

45   BLOM OR 3470 ff. 11–12. The *Konbaungzet mahayazawindawgi* only implies that the Taungoo prince was executed. See Tin, *Konbaungzet maha yazawindawgyi*, II, 226.

46   Fytche, *Burma past and present*, 202. See also Oliver B. Pollack, *Empires in collision: Anglo–Burmese relations in the mid-nineteenth century* (Westport; London: Greenwood Press, 1979), 16.

January 1824, war broke out between the Burmese and the British following a series of rebellions and border disputes. Prince Tharrawaddy recommended negotiating for peace, but Me Nu and her brother encouraged the king to continue fighting even when Rangoon fell to the British.[47] When the British troops were within 50 miles of the then capital Ava, Bagyidaw was forced to concede defeat. Under the Treaty of Yandabo signed on 24 February 1826, the Burmese lost not only Assam and Manipur, but also the maritime provinces of Arakan and Tenasserim. In addition, the Burmese were required to pay reparations of one hundred lakhs of rupees (one million pounds sterling).[48]

Bagyidaw became afflicted by depression after the treaty was concluded and, in 1831, a regency was appointed because the king was no longer considered fit to attend to state affairs. Tharrawaddy was to preside over the regency council, but Me Nu and her brother conspired to arrest him on the pretext that he was plotting to overthrow the king. In February 1837, the Salin Myoza ordered the arrest of the influential Pagan princess, sister of Tharrawaddy and Bagyidaw, on the charge of hoarding arms. Tharrawaddy advised the princess to surrender, before withdrawing to Shwebo himself.[49] Following a successful revolt against the royal forces controlled by the Salin Myoza, Tharrawaddy assumed the throne in order to rescue Bagyidaw from the influence of the chief queen and her brother.[50] He demanded that Me Nu be separated from Bagyidaw, and several ministers who supported the queen were arrested on charges of corruption.[51] Most scholars agree that Me Nu and her brother were executed, although Burmese historian Khin Khin Ma claims that Tharrawaddy's daughter, Setkya Dewi, convinced him to allow Me Nu to live with Bagyidaw in a specially built palace.[52]

Me Nu has been portrayed by chroniclers and historians as the archetypal evil, scheming queen whose personal lust for power and

---

47   Yule, *A narrative of the mission to the Court of Ava*, 224; Phayre, *History of Burma*, 250–51.

48   Maung Htin Aung, *The stricken peacock: Anglo–Burmese relations, 1752–1948* (The Hague: Martinus Nijhoff, 1965), 30–31.

49   Tin, *Konbaungzet maha yazawindawgyi*, II, 490–93; 'Henry Burney to Government of India, 3 March 1837, IPP/194/35', in Walter Sadgun Desai, *History of the British residency in Burma, 1826–1840* (Rangoon: University of Rangoon, 1939), 235.

50   Tin, *Konbaungzet maha yazawindawgyi*, II, 542.

51   *Maulmain Chronicle*, 2 December 1837.

52   Khin Khin Ma, 'Myanmar queens in historical and literary texts', 201.

interference in political and military affairs had disastrous consequences for the Burmese.[53] Several scholars have described her as an evil ancestress of two other powerful queens, Hsinbyumashin and Supayalat, who seemed to inherit her taste for power with fateful results for the country (as we shall see below).[54] Me Nu was willing to go to any length to remove potential rivals in order to enhance her own power at court, and threatened to weaken the royal lineage by manipulating the succession to strengthen her authority. She was regarded as having a sinister influence over the king, and persuaded Bagyidaw to wage the first of three unsuccessful wars against the British. The Yandabo treaty was not only humiliating for the Burmese; they also lost two important coastal provinces to the British, who were intent on exploiting the commercial value of the region. Diplomatic relations between the two countries steadily deteriorated after the war and Bagyidaw's successors struggled to retain their hold on power in the face of increasing British economic, military and political aggression.[55] Me Nu was not the only influential queen during this period of upheaval, however. Queen Setkya Dewi's skill as an astrologer allowed her to play a key role in determining political and military strategies during the reigns of Bagyidaw's successors, Tharrawaddy (1837–46) and Mindon (1853–78).

Setkya Dewi's influence over Tharrawaddy and Mindon

Setkya Dewi was the eldest daughter of Tharrawaddy and his chief queen and the half-sister of Tharrawaddy's successors, Pagan and Mindon. Well educated and particularly skilled in making astrological calculations and predictions, Setkya Dewi was much admired at court and exercised great influence over her father the king. In 1837, she had prophesied that Tharrawaddy's revolt against Bagyidaw would be successful.[56] Tharrawaddy moved to Amarapura the same year but, at Setkya Dewi's suggestion, did not consecrate the new capital until 1840.

---

53 Tin, *Konbaungzet maha yazawindawgyi*, II, 490–93; Ni Ni Myint, 'Queen Supayalat', 81–82; Harvey, *History of Burma*, 294–95.

54 Khin Khin Ma, 'Myanmar queens in historical and literary texts', 200–01; Langham-Carter, 'Queen Me Nu', 35.

55 For an account of the failure of Burmese–British diplomatic relations, see Htin Aung, *The stricken peacock*.

56 D. G. E. Hall (ed.), *The Dalhousie-Phayre correspondence, 1852–56* (London: Oxford University Press, 1932), 63; Myo Myint, 'The politics of survival in Burma', 125–26.

The king also granted Setkya Dewi the right to pardon anyone who had been sentenced to death, which potentially allowed her to overrule his decision.[57] By pardoning criminals in this manner, Setkya Dewi exemplified the Buddhist ideals of compassion and loving-kindness.

During the early 1840s, Tharrawaddy's psychological well-being deteriorated. Burmese historian Htin Aung has argued that the king was driven to melancholia by the shame of the Yandabo treaty and the realisation that he did not have adequate military resources to defeat the British.[58] Internal political intrigues also played heavily on the king's mind. Since assuming the throne, Tharrawaddy had amassed over 100 wives and concubines whose sons vied for his position. British contemporaries believed that Tharrawaddy's health problems were exacerbated by the sexually promiscuous behaviour of his queens, several of whom were expelled from the palace for taking other lovers.[59] The Pagan prince, who was the heir apparent, moved to secure his power by convincing Tharrawaddy that his favourite wife, the western queen, was plotting to overthrow him. The queen was executed, but Tharrawaddy reportedly never recovered from the shock of her (apparent) betrayal and went insane.[60] These events seemed to support the widespread belief that the royal women's infidelities were damaging to the king's prestige and power. Tharrawaddy died in November 1846 and the Pagan prince ascended the throne. Setkya Dewi managed to avoid persecution, possibly because Pagan did not consider his unmarried half-sister to be a threat to his power, though she would later play a key role in the uprising against him.

Following a minor dispute between British merchants and the Governor of Rangoon in 1851, the Governor-General of India, Lord Dalhousie, issued a harsh ultimatum to the Burmese and began making preparations for war.[61] The Second Anglo–Burmese War broke out in 1852 and proved disastrous for the Burmese. In January 1853, the British annexed the province of Pegu including the ports of Rangoon,

---

57 Khin Khin Ma, 'Myanmar queens in historical and literary texts', 201.

58 Htin Aung, *The stricken peacock*, 40.

59 *Maulmain Chronicle*, 28 April 1841; Yule, *A narrative of the mission to the Court of Ava*, 228.

60 Yule, *A narrative of a mission to the Court of Ava*, xxxiii, 229; Htin Aung, *A history of Burma*, 223.

61 Htin Aung, *The stricken peacock*, 41–51; Dorothy Woodman, *The making of Burma* (London: The Cresset Press, 1962), 122–44.

Bassein and Martaban, and renamed it Lower Burma. The war was unpopular and provoked a revolt at the Burmese court led by Pagan's younger half-brother, Prince Mindon. Setkya Dewi encouraged Mindon to revolt, saying 'Pagan's reign is already at an end, in accordance with his horoscope. According to your fortunes, if you personally raise the standard of revolt from Shwebo you will be successful.'[62] Mindon subsequently gained the throne and made Setkya Dewi his chief queen, partly out of respect for her advice. Setkya Dewi was the half-sister of both Mindon and Pagan, so Mindon may also have sought to placate Pagan's supporters by appointing her as his chief queen. Mindon also would have wished to avoid the same fate as Bagyidaw, who had chosen a non-royal woman as his chief queen (Me Nu), and consequently struggled to overcome factional strife at court.[63] The power relationship between the new king and chief queen was therefore reciprocal: Mindon gained legitimacy by marrying Setkya Dewi, and Setkya Dewi's status was elevated by becoming Mindon's chief queen.

Setkya Dewi was 40 years old when she married Mindon and bore him no children, but she possessed other 'feminine' qualities that made up for her inability to produce an heir. Her wise counsel calmed the king, who was troubled by the problem of the royal succession amid persistent rumours that the British were encouraging princes to rebel against him.[64] In 1866, when the Myingun and Padein princes rose up in rebellion against Mindon, Setkya Dewi persuaded him to hold on to the throne, ensuring that she maintained her own position and power in the process.[65] Mindon's position was considerably weakened by the British annexation of Lower Burma, but his failure to curb the power struggles between his numerous queens and sons posed the most immediate threat to political stability during the latter years of his reign.

Mindon's queens and the problem of the royal succession

Mindon was renowned for his healthy sexual appetite and had at least 40 queens, 50 sons and 56 daughters. Stories about the 'pleasure apart-

---

62   Cited in Myo Myint, 'The politics of survival in Burma', 123–24.

63   *Ibid.*, 81.

64   Khin Khin Ma, 'Myanmar queens in historical and literary texts', 202; Htin Aung, *The stricken peacock*, 59.

65   Myo Myint, 'The politics of survival in Burma', 64, 82.

ment' at Mindon's court remained popular over one hundred years later.[66] None of Mindon's four principal queens bore him a son, however, which posed problems in terms of securing a peaceful and stable succession. Mindon had initially named his younger brother, Prince Kanaung, as the heir apparent, but when the latter was killed during the 1866 rebellion, the king was reluctant to name another successor. When Albert Fytche visited the royal court in 1867, Mindon told him that he wished to avoid the 'the fearful anarchy and civil war previously wrought in his own country by the children of former kings by different mothers scrambling for the inheritance.'[67] Mindon's queens played a central role in these power struggles as they sought to enhance their own status and that of their relatives and favourites.[68] Mindon's senior ministers and other male elites were determined, however, to limit the queens' influence over the king and his court.

Power struggles and sexual intrigues at Mindon's court

Mindon's senior councillors were anxious to preserve their power and avoid a repeat of the past – when Me Nu and her brother had dominated Bagyidaw's court – and frequently warned him that if the queens' relatives interfered with state affairs it would be detrimental to the country. The councillors were also critical of the queens' influence over the king, particularly where ministerial matters were concerned. On one occasion when Mindon appointed two provincial governors at his queens' request, the Pakhan Wungyi complained that the queens had encroached upon the ministers' rights to make such appointments. Mindon eventually gave in to the Pakhan Wungyi, who was one of his most trusted and influential advisers.[69] In 1873, the powerful *atwinwun*, Hpo Hlaing, criticised Mindon for favouring officials who offered their daughters to him. A furious Mindon threatened to execute Hpo Haing with a spear, before backing down and leaving the room.[70] Ironically,

---

66 Chit Sein Lwin, *Konbaungkhit saungkyamyaing hmattan* [Notes on the Pleasure Apartment in the Konbaung Period] (Yangon: Kyonpyaw Sarpay, 1967).

67 Fytche, *Burma past and present*, 235.

68 Following the princely rebellion, the British compiled a comprehensive memorandum containing detailed information about Mindon's queens and their relative power bases. See BLOM OR 3470.

69 Yule, *A narrative of the mission to the court of Ava*, 102; Ma Kyan, 'King Mindon's councillors', 55.

70 See Maung Htin's introduction to Hpo Hlaing's *Rajadhammasangaha*, 56.

several senior ministers had gained prominence through their connections with Mindon's queens. Hpo Hlaing owed his own position
to Setkya Dewi, who had suggested that he serve Mindon during the
revolt against Pagan. Following his outstanding service, Mindon had appointed Hpo Hlaing to the position of *atwinwun*. Two of Mindon's lesser
queens were the daughters of the Laungshe and Yenangyaung *wungyis*.[71]
Despite these marriage and patronage ties, the ministers did not tolerate
any attempts by the queens to challenge their authority.

Other members of the male elite expressed dissatisfaction about
what they considered to be the dangerous influence and inappropriate
behaviour of the women of the court. The Bhamo Sayadaw, head of
the renowned Bhamo monastery, was highly offended when Mindon
asked a Buddhist nun named Mai Kin to instruct his queens on moral
conduct and religious principles. The monk declared that the 'king
must take me as a rebel or perhaps he wants to instruct me in the way of
ascetics. Tell him that a man who lives between the hills does not need
instruction from a man who lives between the thighs of women.'[72] The
Sayadaw believed the king to be held under the (carnal) influence of his
queens and may have been angered by Mindon's many sexual relationships, which were inconsistent with his Buddhist beliefs (though not,
importantly, with his duty to produce an heir). It is also likely that the
Bhamo Sayadaw objected to the appointment because Mai Kin was the
sister of his rival, the Shangalagyun Sayadaw, who was a member of the
ecclesiastical council and a favourite of the king.

Male elites were concerned that the 'immoral' behaviour of some
royal women posed a threat to the stability of the state, which was already
under pressure due to succession disputes and uneasy relations with the
British. Royal women were expected to be exemplars of modesty; any
promiscuous behaviour on their part would reflect badly on the king,
since it would appear that he had lost his authority and sexual prowess.
Despite these expectations, at least two of Mindon's lesser queens were
expelled from the palace for engaging in romantic intrigues. U Pon Nya's
Paduma Pyazat ('Paduma Play') served as a warning to the women of the
court, but also to the king, since it recounted the tale of a woman whose

---

71   BLOM OR 3470; Myo Myint, 'The politics of survival in Burma', 123–24, 128; Ma Kyan,
     'King Mindon's councillors', 55.

72   Cited in Myo Myint, 'The politics of survival in Burma', 151.

excessive lust led her to attempt to kill her husband (read: the king).[73] It was not always women who were unfaithful, however. One of the most well-known *bawle* ('plaintive songs') from this period – which remains popular today – was composed by Princess Hlaing Hteik-hkaung Tin, who described the infidelities of her husband, Mindon's younger brother Prince Kanaung. The princess contrasts the early days of their courtship, when the prince promised never to leave her for another, with the painful realities of married life as she waits for her husband to return to their bedchamber at three o'clock in the morning: 'Trusting your love, I put myself entirely in your hands. But you take your pleasure elsewhere, avoiding me, and your face is troubled, clouded with anger. Why should this be so?'[74] In practice, men's promiscuity was seen as a sign of their virility and authority, whereas the women of the court were expected to remain sexually pure, modest and subservient.

Supayalat – the last queen of Burma

In October 1877, Mindon fell seriously ill with dysentery and the senior ministers met to discuss the royal succession. Their preference was to appoint a young prince who could be easily controlled; this would allow the ministers to consolidate their power and introduce a limited monarchy along European lines. Unable to reach consensus on a particular prince, they turned to Queen Hsinbyumashin for support. Hsinbyumashin was the most senior queen, Setkya Dewi having died a few years earlier, and she seized the opportunity to increase her power at court. She desired to marry one or all of her three daughters – Supayagyi, Supayalat and Supayahtwe – to Prince Thibaw and place him on the throne. The son of Mindon and one of his lesser queens (the Laungshe Queen), Thibaw was young and inexperienced, and Hsinbyumashin believed that she could manipulate him and her daughters, and thereby assume power in the palace.[75] Mindon's councillors, including the powerful chief minister Kinwun Mingyi, approved her choice for entirely different reasons. Following Mindon's death, Hsinbyumashin and

---

73   For an English translation of *Paduma Pyazat*, see Htin Aung, *Burmese drama*, appendix V.

74   Cited in U Hla Pe, *Burma: literature, historiography, scholarship, language, life and Buddhism* (Singapore: Institute of Southeast Asian Studies, 1985), 15–16.

75   Ni Ni Myint, 'Queen Supayalat', 82; Ni Ni Myint, *Burma's struggle against British imperialism 1885–1895*, second edition (Rangoon: The Universities Press, 1985), 16; May Pwint Khaing, 'The role of Queen Supayalat during King Thibaw's reign', 14.

Figure 3.1: Supayagyi, Supayalat and Thibaw, circa 1885 (© The British Library Board, all rights reserved, 26/09/2011, photo 312/(73)).

the Kinwun Mingyi announced Thibaw's enthronement as king on 2 October 1878.[76] Supayagyi and Supayalat were anointed as Thibaw's queens, but although Supayagyi was named chief queen, the ambitious Supayalat immediately set about dominating Thibaw and his court, thus thwarting her mother's own plans for power.

Ni Ni Myint has suggested that Supayalat must have shared the same 'genetic structure' as Hsinbyumashin, implying that the daughter inherited her mother's desire for power.[77] Supayalat's ambition certainly seemed to equal, if not surpass, that of her mother and also her grandmother, Queen Me Nu. The new queen immediately set about removing from power any person whom she considered to be a threat. Supayalat was jealous of other women in the palace, fearing that the king might be more attracted to them than he was to her. Thibaw's marriage to Supayagyi reportedly was never consummated, which may have been due to Supayalat's influence. Thibaw was also fond of the *tabindaing* princess, Selin Supaya, but she chose to enter a nunnery

---

76 Tin, *Konbaungzet maha yazawindawgyi*, III, 440.

77 Ni Ni Myint, 'Queen Supayalat', 82.

rather than marry him, which neutralised any threat she may have posed to Supayalat.[78] At Supayalat's request, Thibaw issued an order stating that she was to dress his hair every morning in his chamber. In this way, the queen sought to prevent other women from sharing the king's bed. She also prohibited maids of honour from wearing revealing clothes and ordered some of the prettier courtiers to leave the palace and return to their homes.[79] Supayalat was thereby able to exercise her authority over the women of the court.

In his fictionalised account of Supayalat's life, *Thibaw's Queen*, Harold Fielding Hall described how the queen's strong personality inspired either admiration or fear in all who met her:

> She was not beautiful but she was a queen. Women far more beautiful than she faded before her into nothingness. And her eyes … like pools of deep brown water, so large, so wonderful, but with a flame deep down in them that made one fear. She always cared for herself to make herself admired, her manners to those she loved were as the charm of a magician. And her voice was as clear as a silver gong thrilling across the evening waters where all is still. No one ever did but one of two things: they either loved her forever or hated her as men hate and fear death. For she was very proud and very fierce, and when she hated she never forgave. There were two things that she could not abide: any attempt to wean the king from her, or any insult to his dignity. Whenever she heard that any woman was trying to come between her and the king she became like a mad thing; there was nothing she would not do. When any one tried to reduce the king's power or glory she would never allow it. Easier would death be than suffer such things.[80]

Thibaw's Queen reads like a romantic novel, possibly because it was drawn largely from the observations of one of Supayalat's young, devoted handmaidens. Both Fielding Hall and Ni Ni Myint describe Supayalat's 'love' for Thibaw,[81] which makes her less admirable qualities – such as

---

78 Selin Supaya was the daughter of the Linbin Queen, one of Mindon's lesser queens. Shway Yoe [Sir James George Scott], *The Burman: his life and notions*, with an introduction by John K. Musgrave (New York: W. W. Norton & Company, 1963), 453–54. See also Tin (of Pagan), *Myanma min okchokpon sadan* [Documents relating to the administration of Burmese Kings], 5 volumes (Rangoon, 1931–33), II, 251.

79 Ni Ni Myint, 'Queen Supayalat', 85–86.

80 H. Fielding Hall, *Thibaw's queen* (London; New York: Harper and Brothers, 1899), esp. 46–47, 98–99.

81 *Ibid.*, 43; Ni Ni Myint, 'Queen Supayalat', 85.

her jealousy and violent temper – seem more understandable if not excusable. The notion that Supayalat 'loved' her husband also makes her appear more acceptably 'feminine' than if she was acting out of sheer lust for power. It is far more likely, however, that Supayalat was determined to preserve her own power through that of her husband.

By monopolising Thibaw's attention, Supayalat went against palace tradition, which held that kings were entitled to have many queens and consorts, and effectively instituted the practice of royal monogamy. Regardless of what the queen's intentions were, this seemed like a sensible way to avoid the succession problem that had plagued Thibaw's father, Mindon, due to his large number of wives, concubines and sons. We might expect the king's ministers to oppose Supayalat's attempts to eliminate the practice of royal polygamy, which traditionally had provided them with a means of gaining influence at court. It is somewhat surprising, however, to find their sentiments echoed by British Christians like the colonial administrator Sir James George Scott:

> Thibaw Min could not be otherwise than miserable. The harridan queen kept him in most humble subjection. Hitherto every king of Burma had had at least four chief queens ... but Supayalat persisted in remaining sole controller of the royal heart ... Such an unusual state of things, such a disgrace as a woman's slave for a king, had never befallen any country before.[82]

Scott's main concern seemed to be that Supayalat's influence over the king weakened his authority and upset the 'traditional' gendered hierarchies of power (male/female, master/slave). Thibaw and Supayalat had only five children: a son born in 1879, who died of smallpox in 1880, and four daughters. Thibaw's legitimacy as a ruler was already weak and he compared poorly with the virile Mindon who fathered several children a year. Supayalat not only failed to have another son, she also prevented the king from fathering an heir by another wife, thereby threatening the continuation of the royal lineage. When Thibaw's close friend, the Myoza of Yanaung, suggested he take more wives – which would not only strengthen the king's ties with ruling families but also potentially reduce Supayalat's influence – she ordered his execution.[83]

---

82 Shway Yoe, *The Burman: his life and notions*, 457. Scott wrote under the Burmese pseudonym Shway Yoe.

83 Thant Myint-U, *The making of modern Burma*, 162–63. See also F. Tennyson Jesse, *The lacquer lady* (London: William Heinemann Ltd., 1929), which was based partly on interviews with surviving courtiers.

Thant Myint-U further suggests that Thibaw's failure to marry relatives of influential *sawbwa*s played a role in Shan uprisings which further weakened the already vulnerable state.[84]

Supayalat against the ministers

In other respects, Supayalat had a 'traditional' view of kingship and resented what she perceived to be encroachment on royal prerogative by the ministers. Shortly after Thibaw's accession, the administrative system was restructured and fourteen ministries were instituted. The new king was presented with a compendium of essays entitled *Rajadhammasangaha* ('Treatise on the Compassionate Disposition of Righteous Government'). Hpo Hlaing, the author of the *Rajadhammasangaha*, described it as a 'book of the proper behaviour for Kings and other high officers of government'.[85] In reality, the *Rajadhammasangaha* was intended to instruct Thibaw in the cabinet arrangements that would now bind him. Significantly, the ministers proposed that the king and queen should be allowed access to treasury funds only with the approval of Hpo Hlaing himself (who was then Finance Minister).[86] Hpo Hlaing disapproved of the king's and queen's lavish expenditure on frivolous entertainment, especially when there was growing unrest among the population due to the government's taxation policies. Supayalat strongly opposed the ministers' attempts to limit royal control over decision-making and spending, in particular. In *Thibaw's Queen*, Supayalat makes an impassioned speech to Thibaw denouncing the administrative reforms that would effectively reduce him to a mere puppet:

> Do you know all that is going on about you? Do you understand what is happening? You think you are king, but is it so? I think not, but that the ministers are really the kings. They have divided the kingdom. Each has taken to himself part of what is yours. See how, one minister is in charge of the river and all boat business. All that concerns these subjects comes to him, and he passes orders. As far as these go he is king. And one minister is over the revenue, and another over the foreign affairs, and another over justice, and another over war. So is the kingdom divided up. You are king but in name. Let us stop all this.[87]

---

84 Thant Myint-U, *The making of modern Burma*, 171.

85 See Maung Htin's preface in Yaw Mingyi U Hpo Hlaing, *Rajadhammasangaha*, 70.

86 *Ibid.*, 78–79; Tin, *Myanma min okchokpon sadan*, II, 241–46.

87 This is Fielding Hall's reconstruction: *Thibaw's queen*, 54–55.

In the face of fierce opposition from Supalayat, the restructured administrative departments never functioned as the ministers had intended, and key ministries including warfare and revenue remained effectively under royal control.[88]

Supayalat's influence was crucial in the dismissal and imprisonment of several of Mindon's most trusted and capable senior ministers including Hpo Hlaing, who died not long after his arrest. The dismissed ministers were replaced with new officials who obeyed the king and queen. Supayalat also kept a close eye on her mother and elder sister, Hsinbyumashin and Supayagyi, by placing them in a single residence under her supervision.[89] Several coronation ceremonies were held between 1880 and 1882 in which both Thibaw and Supalayat assumed new royal titles.[90] These public rituals were intended to demonstrate Thibaw and Supayalat's absolute authority as king and queen, while simultaneously signalling the decline in influence of the ministers and Hsinbyumashin. By eroding the power basis of the male ministers and the queen mother, Supayalat sought to remove her political rivals, but the king and queen soon faced new challenges. The government struggled to raise revenue and regularise taxation and a lottery system which was introduced in an effort to resolve the state's economic problems actually resulted in an increase in gambling, corruption and poverty.[91]

War, exile and annexation

Meanwhile, the British were looking for an excuse to extend their control over upper Burma. At the beginning of Thibaw's reign, over 40 princes and princesses who had been held captive since Mindon's illness had been put to death. The British held Supayalat and Hsinbyumashin responsible for the royal massacres and most Burmese also maintained Thibaw's innocence. James George Scott claimed that Thibaw initially refused to kill his relatives, but was eventually worn down by the two

---

88 Tin, *Myanma min okchokpon sadan*, II, 241–46. See also Maung Htin's biographical preface of the *Rajadhammasangaha*, 79; Thant Myint-U, *The making of modern Burma*, 163.

89 Tin, *Konbaungzet maha yazawindawgyi*, III, 512, 535. During Mindon's reign, Supayalat had acted as an informer at her mother's royal apartments.

90 *Ibid.*, III, 571, 574.

91 Tin, *Myanma min okchokpon sadan*, II, 224; May Pwint Khaing, 'The role of Queen Supayalat during King Thibaw's reign', 40; Thant Myint-U, *The making of modern Burma*, 166. The lottery system was abolished in 1880.

queens. After the massacres, he fell more and more under the 'malign influence of the termagant queen [Supayalat]'.[92] British designs on commercial expansion, the resurgence of Anglo–French rivalry in the region, and political instability in upper Burma led the British to pursue military intervention. In 1885, the British government lodged a formal protest against the *Hluttaw's* decision ordering the Bombay Burma Trading Corporation, a British timber firm, to pay compensation to Burmese foresters and the king. The British sent an ultimatum to the Burmese in October containing the following demands: that a British representative must be allowed to settle the dispute against the trading corporation; that a permanent British Resident must be established at Mandalay together with an armed guard; that Mandalay must conduct foreign relations only with British permission; and that Mandalay must allow the British to conduct trade with China through Burmese territory. The Burmese were to accept these demands by 10 November or face war.[93]

Thibaw and his ministers, along with Supayalat and Hsinbyumashin, sat in council to consider the British demands and determine a course of action. The council was divided into two factions, one in favour of war and one against. The fact that Hsinbyumashin and Supayalat led the two factions at this crucial moment in Burmese history demonstrates that they exercised great influence over state affairs. Hsinbyumashin and the Kinwun Mingyi appealed for peace and moderation, believing that a conciliatory response could prevent or at least delay the outbreak of war.[94] Supayalat and the Taingda Mingyi refused to accept the British conditions and argued that the Burmese must be prepared to fight.[95] The council eventually decided to draft a conciliatory reply to the British in the hope that further negotiations would take place, but by this stage the British course of action had been set and no Burmese response could have prevented war. British troops entered upper Burma on 11 November and advanced steadily northwards. On 27 November, the British forces reached Sagaing near Mandalay and the Burmese were forced to surrender. Thibaw, Supayalat and their daughters were sent

---

92   Shway Yoe, *The Burman: his life and notions*, 457.

93   For a pro-Burmese account of these events, see Htin Aung *The stricken peacock*, 79–89.

94   Ni Ni Myint, 'Queen Supayalat', 88; Htin Aung, *The stricken peacock*, 88–89.

95   May Pwint Khaing, 'The role of Queen Supayalat during King Thibaw's reign', 55.

into exile in India and the whole of Burma (with the exception of the Shan states) was declared a province of British India on 1 March 1886.

Despite the fact that there was little she could have done to prevent war, Supayalat's determination to fight the British confirmed the widespread belief that it was dangerous to allow women to become involved in political and military affairs. In *Thibaw's Queen*, Fielding Hall wrote that Supalayat collapsed when the British troops entered the royal palace, crying 'It is I – I alone – the queen that have brought destruction to the king my husband and my people.'[96] Many Burmese also blamed Supayalat for dominating Thibaw and ignoring the wise counsel of his ministers, thus bringing about the end of the Konbaung dynasty, the monarchy she held so dear, and the country's independence. In the 1914 publication, *The citizen of Burma*, U Po Ka wrote:

> We have no better proof of the evils brought about by the interference of the women than the fact that the fall of the Burmese empire and the deportation of the last king was brought about by the conduct of the queen whom even the lord of white elephants with his unlimited authority could not control.[97]

Supayalat's reputation improved somewhat when she became a figurehead for Burmese nationalists, who were willing to overlook her faults in their desire to see Burma restored to its former independence and glory. Thibaw died in December 1916, and Supayalat was allowed to return to Burma in 1919, despite British fears that this would lend support to nationalists who were strongly advocating the restoration of Burmese rule.[98] In September 1925, a group of nationalists demanded that Supayalat be accorded 'such treatment as is befitting her position as the Chief Queen of Burma',[99] but as she died two months later the threat that she posed to the British never materialised.[100] Nonetheless, the British government

---

96   Fielding Hall, *Thibaw's queen*, 286–87.

97   Po Ka, *The citizen of Burma*, 73.

98   'Government of India, Finance Department, Pensions and Gratuities, No. 458 of 1920, To The Right Honourable Edwin Montagu, His Majesty's Secretary of State for India, Simla, the 30th September 1920.' IOR/L/PS/10/641 ff. 94, 100.

99   'Extract from official report of the Legislative Assembly debates, 7 September 1925.' IOR/L/PS/10/641 ff. 63, 64.

100 Ni Ni Myint, 'Queen Supayalat', 89.

contributed 20,000 rupees towards her funeral expenses in order to prevent further nationalist agitation.[101]

In the years following her death, Supayalat was portrayed negatively by British and Burmese writers alike. An obituary published in the London *Daily Telegraph* on 25 November 1925 described her as Thibaw's 'jezebel of a consort' and 'a person of evil memories'.[102] According to an article published in *The Irrawaddy* more than 80 years later, the name Supayalat continues to evoke in most Burmese minds the image of a ruthless woman corrupted by her desire for absolute power.[103] Supayalat was undoubtedly an ambitious queen who exercised great influence over Thibaw and effectively curtailed the power of other members of the royal court. It is unclear, however, whether she was motivated by a personal desire for power or a desire to protect the king (or both). The main criticism levelled at Supayalat was her failure to conform to the 'feminine' ideal. She ruthlessly eliminated her personal and political rivals and monopolised the king's attention, even when she failed to produce a male heir. Most of all, she was condemned for overtly challenging the male ministers of Thibaw's court and intervening in political and military matters with fateful results.

Conclusions

The three Konbaung queens who were viewed negatively both by their contemporaries and by the majority of historians – Me Nu, Hsinbyu-mashin and Supayalat – were perceived to have acted like men as they sought to gain power and influence through their unfeminine, ruthless and war-like behaviour. At the same time, they used their 'feminine wiles' – sexuality, scheming and sorcery – to dominate their husbands, thereby threatening the traditional male power base of princes and ministers. When the integrity of the Burmese state was threatened by internal and external forces, such as princely uprisings and British imperialist aggression, these queens were criticised by male elites for their inappropriate use of power. Chroniclers and historians subsequently portrayed these women as 'evil queens' whose 'interference' in the male domains of political and military affairs brought about the downfall of

---

101 'Burma: – treatment of the Family of ex-King Thebaw.' IOR/L/PS/10/641 ff. 41–42.

102 'Obituary: Ex-Queen Supiyawlat of Burmah', *Daily Telegraph*, 25 November 1925.

103 Khin Maung Soe, 'The tragic queen', *The Irrawaddy*, February 2007.

the Konbaung dynasty and the loss of Burmese independence. These negative portrayals have had a lasting effect on how subsequent generations of Burmese perceived women's roles, reinforcing the view that women should not be involved in politics and leadership roles more generally, just when a new nationalist struggle for independence was shaping up. Although women increasingly became politically active as the Burmese nationalist movement gained momentum in the early part of the twentieth century, most limited their participation to providing support for their male colleagues.

4

The Impact of Colonialism and Nationalism on Women

*F*ollowing their victory against the Burmese in the Third Anglo–Burmese War in 1885, the British set about extending their control over the entire country. Under colonial rule, Burmese political, economic and social structures evolved into far more complex systems, creating new opportunities in administration, trade, industry and agriculture, which attracted (mainly male) British, Indian and Chinese immigrants to the country. Colonial administrator and scholar John S. Furnivall described the heterogeneous society that resulted from the combination of immigrant and indigenous peoples as a 'plural society' in which the various groups 'mix but do not combine'.[1] The emergence of the plural society had huge implications for power relations as these groups struggled for social, economic and political dominance.

Foreigners rapidly gained control over the local administration and economy, leaving the Burmese to compete for subordinate positions in the colonial hierarchy. Women's traditional economic roles, which centred on small-scale trade, industry and agriculture, came under threat due to increased competition from Indian and Chinese traders and labourers. The colonial education system provided opportunities for women to improve their employment prospects, but colonial elites and many Burmese regarded female education primarily as a means of preparing girls for marriage and motherhood. Young women were therefore encouraged to enter 'appropriate' occupations that would not interfere with their domestic responsibilities. Women who sought paid employment outside the home and adopted 'modern' dress and behaviours challenged prevailing gender norms at a time when many

---

1   J. S. Furnivall, *Colonial policy and practice: a comparative study of Burma and Netherlands India* (New York: New York University Press, 1956), 304.

Burmese were struggling to reconcile their desire to embrace modernity with the goal of preserving traditional values and culture. The increase in inter-racial marriages between indigenous women and immigrant men also stimulated vigorous debates about the importance of protecting women's traditional marital rights and maintaining the purity of the Burmese 'race', culture and religion.[2]

Increasing Burmese resentment towards their colonial rulers contributed to an emerging sense of national consciousness from the beginning of the twentieth century onwards. During the 1920s and 1930s, educated women were among the most prominent and influential nationalists who advocated greater participation of women in political and public life. Many women joined nationalist organisations and participated in disobedience campaigns and strike actions to protest against colonial rule, but for the most part they performed supporting roles under the leadership of male nationalists. In their desire to preserve traditional Burmese culture from foreign influences and to restore independence from colonial rule, nationalists largely overlooked the fact that indigenous conceptions of gender limited women's ability to seek more prominent political roles.

British ambivalence towards Burmese women

From the outset, colonial elites had ambivalent attitudes towards Burmese women. On the one hand, they openly admired women's industriousness and intelligence, particularly in business matters; Burmese men were viewed as lazy and apathetic in comparison. Sir James George Scott claimed that Burmese women were 'emphatically and without dispute from any corner, the better half of the race'.[3] On the other hand, the British considered female independence and influence to be the mark of an uncivilised and backward society. A modern nation was to be a

---

2   Colonial authorities and Burmese nationalists conceptualised 'race' in terms of ethnicity and country of origin. All indigenous peoples, regardless of ethnicity, were considered to be 'Burmese' including Burmans, Karens, Shans, Mons, Kachins, Chins and so on. Burmese cohesion was weakened, however, by religious and cultural differences as well as long-standing tensions between the Burman majority and ethnic minority groups, which were exacerbated by colonial 'divide and rule' policies. Burmese nationalists regarded non-indigenous peoples, including the British colonialists, Indians and Chinese immigrants, and some Eurasians and Anglo-Burmese as 'non-Burmese' aliens. The terms 'Eurasian' and 'Anglo-Burmese' refer to people of mixed European and Burmese descent. The majority of Eurasians and Anglo-Burmese had Burmese mothers and European or British fathers.

3   Sir J. George Scott, 'The position of women in Burma', *The Sociological Review: Journal of the Sociological Society* 6, 2 (April 1913): 146.

masculine nation: '[I]t is the mark of rising nations that men control and women are not seen.'[4] It was widely acknowledged that women exercised considerable power over men in the private realm of the household, if not in public. Scott marvelled at the way in which women 'rule the household without seeming to exercise any authority' and claimed that there were 'very few Burman husbands that would close any deal or venture or any speculation without first consulting their wives.'[5] Harold Fielding described Burmese men as being like 'boys still in the nursery … under women's governance.'[6] He also observed that the average Burmese woman displayed a keen interest in and knowledge of public affairs, and that

> … her desire and power of influencing them is great. But she learnt long ago that the best way to act is through and by her husband, and that his strength and his name are her bucklers in the fight. Thus women are never openly concerned in any political matters.[7]

Women's ability to influence official matters was partly a function of traditional Burmese political culture, in which power was exercised through personal relationships. To gain the patronage of the husband, it was entirely natural to approach the wife. The impersonal, modern bureaucratic system that developed under colonial rule represented a significant departure from the traditional political system based on personalised forms of authority.[8] Although many women continued to exercise influence over their husbands within the family, the colonial concept of a modern, masculine nation relied on the exaltation of male authority and power structures and constrained women's political roles.

Colonial ambivalence towards Burmese women could also be seen in negative portrayals of women as sexually promiscuous, manipulating temptresses. A common theme in colonial literary sources was the belief that women's sexuality gave them power over men, who were unable to resist their beauty and charms.[9] In the account of her travels through

---

4   Fielding, *A people at school*, 268.

5   Scott, 'The position of women in Burma', 140, 145.

6   Fielding, *A people at school*, 27.

7   Fielding, 'Burmese women', 23–24.

8   For instance, the British abolished the position of *myothugyi*, which prevented local hereditary officials from acting as mediators between state officials and the general population.

9   Fielding, *The soul of a people*, 196–204; Scott, 'The position of women in Burma', 140.

Burma in the late nineteenth century, Gwendolyn Trench Gascoigne referred to Burmese women as 'bewitching little dames' who used their sexuality to control men: 'I can well believe a henpecked husband is not quite an unknown quantity in Burma.'[10] George Orwell, who served in the Indian Imperial Police during the 1920s, wrote disparagingly about Burmese women in his novel, *Burmese Days*. Orwell describes Ma Hla May, the Burmese mistress of the British official John Flory, as a 'grotesquely beautiful' woman who loves the 'idle concubine's life'. Flory rejects Ma Hla May after he meets and falls in love with a young English woman, Elizabeth Lackersteen. Ma Hla May wants to continue to live as a *bo kadaw*, a white man's wife, and she continues to torment and blackmail Flory. When Ma Hla May causes a scene outside the church, screaming and tearing at her clothes, Flory is publicly disgraced and eventually commits suicide.[11]

Underlying these negative portrayals was the belief that women's social freedom and influence over men threatened to undermine colonial power and prestige. In order to maintain their sense of superiority, the male colonial elite took deliberate measures to distance themselves from the native population. Although it was common for British men to take Burmese wives or mistresses prior to annexation, the colonial government actively discouraged British officers from entering into sexual relationships with Burmese women. In his report to the White Cross Society in 1894, Sir Alexander Mackenzie stated that 'an officer, openly living with a Burmese mistress, not only degrades himself as an English gentleman, but lowers the prestige of the English name'.[12] Government memorandums warning British officers about the evils of taking Burmese wives or mistresses endorsed the view that women's perceived and actual influence over men would harm the reputation of the colonial administration.[13] The influx of British women following World War One may have limited the number of open sexual relationships between British men and Burmese women, as it did in other colonial societies in

---

10 Trench Gascoigne, *Among pagodas and fair ladies*, 47.

11 George Orwell, *Burmese days* (London: The Camelot Press, 1935).

12 *Times of India*, 15 December 1894, p. 9, cited in 'Parliamentary Notice, Session 1895, House of Commons.' IOR/L/PJ/6/391 File 269.

13 'Confidential memorandum from the Chief Secretary to the Government of Burma to the Secretary to the Government of India, Home Department, dated Rangoon, 24 January 1903. (G.B.C.P.O. – No 562, Chief Secy., 26–1–1903 – 35).' IOR/L/PJ/6/629 File 517.

Southeast Asia.[14] Even so, immigrants comprised only five per cent of the total female population in 1931, which meant that relations between foreign men and indigenous women continued.[15]

Between 1891 and 1931, the total 'Eurasian' population grew from 7,132 to 19,200.[16] Eurasians occupied a highly ambivalent position in colonial society. Their innate 'Burmese-ness' meant that Eurasians were denied the high status enjoyed by Europeans, but colonial elites also believed that Eurasian children should be 'Europeanised' to prevent them from falling (further) under undesirable indigenous influences.[17] The belief that Burmese women were incapable of caring for their own children led colonial authorities to forcibly remove many Eurasian children from their Burmese mothers.[18] In her memoirs, Maureen Baird-Murray, the daughter of an Irishman and Burmese woman, describes how she was sent to an English convent school at age seven where she was 'to be turned into a reasonably acceptable European.'[19] Although children who received a Western education had a better chance of securing employment than the average Burmese, girls were trained primarily to become better wives and mothers (as we shall see below). Concepts of racial purity also influenced Burmese nationalists, who sought to prevent Burmese Buddhist women from entering into sexual unions with non-Burmese, non-Buddhist men.

The effect of intermarriage with Asians on Burmese women's status

Colonial rulers were less concerned about regulating marriages between Asian immigrants and Burmese women, since these unions did not affect colonial prestige. Marriages between Burmese women and Indian and

---

14 John G. Butcher, *The British in Malaya, 1880–1941: the social history of a European community in colonial Southeast Asia* (Kuala Lumpur; New York: Oxford University Press, 1979), 134–47.

15 For a breakdown of population statistics by race and gender based on 1921 and 1931 census data, see Ikeya, *Refiguring women, colonialism, and modernity in Burma*, 22.

16 *Ibid.* See also *Census of India, 1931*, 230–32; John Clement Koop, *The Eurasian population in Burma* (New Haven: Yale University, Southeast Asian Studies, 1960), 22.

17 Penny Edwards, 'On home ground: settling land and domesticating difference in the "non-settler" colonies of Burma and Cambodia', *Journal of Colonialism and Colonial History* 4, 3 (Winter 2003) (electronic resource).

18 Penny Edwards, 'Half-caste: staging race in British Burma', *Postcolonial Studies* 5, 3 (November 2002): 292–93.

19 Maureen Baird-Murray, *A world overturned: memoirs of a Burmese childhood, 1933–1947* (Brooklyn: Interlink Books, 1998), 146–47.

Chinese immigrants became increasingly common in colonial society.[20] The prevalence of such unions alarmed Burmese nationalist leaders like U May Oung, who claimed that many Burmese women were 'impelled [to marry foreigners] … out of poverty'.[21] Nationalists expressed concern that Burmese Buddhist women who married non-Burmese, non-Buddhist men were denied their traditional divorce, property and inheritance rights.

Colonial authorities were not particularly sympathetic to the nationalists' arguments, possibly because they believed that Burmese customary laws relating to marriage and inheritance matters gave women too much power and influence. Under Burmese customary law, divorce could be obtained by mutual consent, wives and husbands had an equal share in any property acquired during marriage, and widows and children of both sexes had inheritance rights. British women had no property inheritance rights at that time. Fielding Hall believed that the Burmese laws should be 'modified' because 'it is no good for a man to be feminised'.[22] Although customary marriage laws were left largely intact, when there was a conflict between Burmese Buddhist law and Hindu or Islamic law, the colonial courts usually gave precedence to the latter codes. The Special Marriage Act of 1872 granted Buddhist women who married non-Buddhists the status of wife and their children legitimacy, but women had to renounce their rights under Burmese customary law.[23]

During the 1920s and 1930s, nationalists actively campaigned for the protection of women's customary marital and inheritance rights and discouraged inter-racial marriages, especially unions between Burmese Buddhist women and Indian Muslim men.[24] Ironically, the nationalist focus on protecting the purity of the Burmese *amyo* ('race')[25] actually had the effect of constraining women's behaviour. A woman's patriotism

---

20 According to the 1931 census, 80 per cent of immigrants were South Asian, 15 per cent were Chinese, and the remainder were Europeans or others. The vast majority of South Asian and Chinese immigrants were men. See *Census of India, 1931*, 60–63.

21 May Oung, *Leading cases on Buddhist law* (Rangoon, 1914), 14.

22 Fielding, *A people at school*, 261.

23 Dr Maung Maung, *Law and custom in Burma and the Burmese family* (The Hague: Martinus Nijhoff, 1963), 69–70.

24 See, for example, Daw Mya Sein's comments at the Burma Round Table Conference, in Government of Burma, *Burma Round Table Conference, 27th November 1931–12th January 1932: Proceedings* (Rangoon: Superintendent, Government Printing and Stationery, 1932), 54–55.

25 *Amyo* can also refer to ancestors, kin, religion and culture.

was dependent upon her having a Burmese spouse and women who had relationships and children with foreigners were criticised in the press for polluting their race, religion and culture. One article published in *Seq-Than* ('Ten Million') in November 1938 blamed Burmese women who took Indian husbands for destroying the 'purity' of the Burmese 'race':

> You Burmese women who fail to safeguard your own race, after you have married an Indian[,] your daughter whom you have begotten by such a tie takes an Indian as her husband. As for your son, he becomes a half-caste and tries to get a pure Burmese woman. Not only you but your future generation also is those who are responsible for the ruination of the race.[26]

The public condemnation of Indo-Burmese marriages needs to be considered in light of the wider socioeconomic context in which Burmese men had lost not only their women, but also key economic roles to Indians. Colonial administrators preferred to employ Indians as civil servants, police and labourers, and Indian merchants and moneylenders were more competitive than their Burmese counterparts in local markets.

Loss of women's traditional economic roles and status

The years following annexation up to World War One were marked by rapid agricultural and commercial expansion, which transformed the indigenous subsistence economy into a commercial colonial economy dependent on the import of consumer goods and the export of cash crops and raw materials. Although Burmese women's entrepreneurial ability and initiative gave them a measure of economic power in the traditional, subsistence-oriented society, they lacked the necessary commercial experience and Western education to enable them to compete successfully in the export-oriented plural society whose economy was increasingly dominated by Indian and Chinese moneylenders and traders.

Colonial policy designed to encourage free enterprise facilitated the rapid expansion and modernisation of rice production during the last quarter of the nineteenth century. Burmese women, who traditionally participated in most aspects of rice cultivation, increasingly had to compete for work with Indian and Chinese labourers who were willing to accept low wages. Poor Burmese rice cultivators who lacked capital

---

26 Cited in Ikeya, *Reconfiguring women, colonialism, and modernity in Burma*, 135. See also Pu Gale, *Kabya pyatthana* [The half-caste problem] (Yangon: Kyi Pwa Yei, 1939), 126.

to gain landholder and occupancy rights were obliged to borrow from Indian moneylenders (*chettiars*) at high interest rates. Those who were unable to repay their debts either had to leave their homes or were reduced to the status of renter-tenants. By the early 1930s, nearly half of the agricultural land in the delta was effectively in the hands of the *chettiars*.[27] Aside from rice production, many women produced hand-made textiles, which they sold in local bazaars, street stalls, or door-to-door. The demand for locally-made textiles fell as cheap, machine-made fabrics were increasingly imported from Britain and India. Burmese women bought foreign-made, imported textiles and sold them, but for marginal profits. The indigenous weaving industry suffered as a result, although early nationalists encouraged women to wear traditional hand-woven *htamein* (skirts) and *eingyi* (blouses).[28] Many women who lost their land and livelihoods were eager to support the nationalists, who urged men and women to purchase goods made locally and boycott foreign-made products.

Faced with new economic pressures through penetration of their traditional local markets, women increasingly entered the paid workforce. While some found employment locally as hired labourers for foreign businessmen and landowners, others were forced to leave their homes and families to find work in cities and large towns. The decline in women's traditional economic roles and status was accompanied by an increasing sense of social displacement and cultural degeneration as women were separated from their families and communities. The fraying of traditional gender roles, which might otherwise have allowed an increase in women's economic power, was offset by the strong belief that women's primary role was as wife and mother. The introduction of formal education for females expanded women's employment opportunities, but mainly in 'appropriate' professions, which only served to reinforce gender differences.

---

27 R. E. Elson, *The end of the peasantry in Southeast Asia: a social and economic history of peasant livelihood, 1800–1990s* (Houndmills, Basingstoke, Hampshire: Macmillan Press; New York: St. Martin's Press, 1997), 134–36.

28 Chie Ikeya notes that young women increasingly preferred to wear modern, Westernised dress, which prompted public debates about women's morality and dedication to nationalism, particularly during the 1930s and 1940s. See Ikeya, *Refiguring women, colonialism, and modernity in Burma*, especially chapters 4 and 6.

Female education under colonial rule: opportunities and limitations

Before the mid-nineteenth century, monastery schools administered by the *sangha* had provided the only means of gaining a formal education and were exclusively for boys. Christian missionaries established the first school for girls in Burma in 1827, and British authorities introduced co-educational schools in Lower Burma in 1868. By 1869, around 5,000 students were enrolled in 340 lay schools, around one quarter of whom were female, but attendance was intermittent and educational standards were less rigorous than those applied in monastic schools.[29] During the first half of the twentieth century, it gradually became more socially acceptable for girls to attain a formal education, which offered the best means of economic and social advancement in colonial society. Furnivall described the growth of female education as the most 'outstanding feature of progress under British rule'.[30] Between 1910 and 1931, there was remarkable growth in the overall number of female students enrolled in educational institutions: primary enrolments increased from 53,291 to 136,550; secondary enrolments from 17,280 to 74,849; and tertiary enrolments from 17 to 178.[31] The majority of girls completed primary level education only, however.[32] In 1913, the Burmese scholar and advocate of colonial education Taw Sein Ko lamented that the vast majority

---

29 Juliane Schober, 'Colonial knowledge and Buddhist education in Burma', in Ian Harris (ed.), *Buddhism, power and political order* (London; New York: Routledge, 2007), 57.

30 J. S. Furnivall, 'Planning for national education', 9 September 1951, p. 6. MSS Eur D 1066/5.

31 For a comparative list of male/female enrolments at all education levels between 1900 and 1931, compiled from 1921 and 1931 census data, see Ikeya, 'Gender, history and modernity', 72. In neighbouring Thailand, which was never brought under direct colonial rule, female school enrolments also increased dramatically after Thai authorities introduced educational reforms in an effort to modernise. After formal education for women was introduced in 1901, the number of female students rose from 11,400 in 1904 to 232,120 in 1925. See Tamara Loos, 'The politics of women's suffrage in Thailand', in Louise Edwards and Mina Roces (eds.), *Women's suffrage in Asia: gender, nationalism and democracy* (London; New York: Routledge, 2004), 183.

32 Furnivall, 'Planning for national education', 6. The same pattern prevailed in other Southeast Asian countries including Thailand and Indonesia. In Thailand, only 70 women were enrolled at Bangkok's Chulalongkorn University by 1925: Loos, 'The politics of women's suffrage in Thailand', 183. Islamic practices including female seclusion and child marriage led many Indonesian Muslims to withdraw their daughters from school once they reached puberty. See Jean Gelman Taylor, *The social world of Batavia: European and Eurasian in Dutch Asia* (Madison, Wis.: University of Wisconsin Press, 1983), 163–66; Saskia Wieringa, 'Aborted feminism in Indonesia: a history of Indonesian socialist feminism', in Saskia Wieringa (ed.), *Women's struggles and strategies* (Aldershot, Hants, England; Brookfield, Vt.: Gower, c1988), 71–73. Even within the Indonesian women's movement, views on female education varied considerably. See Kongres Perempuan Indonesia, *The*

of Burmese considered girls' education 'unnecessary'.[33] Women who worked in urban bazaars required basic literacy and numeracy skills only, and formal education was of limited value to female agriculturalists living in rural areas. Many parents did not prioritise girls' education due to social expectations about appropriate gender roles in which men were the primary breadwinners and women were the home-makers. Once married, a woman would be supported by her husband and only needed to work to supplement his income.

The ability to increase one's employment prospects and social status depended largely on the type of school a child attended. Vernacular schools provided basic Burmese-language instruction in reading, writing and arithmetic. Anglo-Vernacular schools offered more subjects and, although most instruction was still in Burmese, English was taught as a second language. The vast majority of girls attended Vernacular or Anglo-Vernacular schools and so had little or no prospect of gaining a university education, which required a good knowledge of English. Only wealthy families could afford to send their daughters to elite European (English) schools. Girls who went on to study at university increasingly gained professional qualifications and employment in the fields of education, medicine, law, journalism and public administration, but the proportion of women in these professions remained low.

Advocates of female education stressed its potential to improve family relationships as well as the welfare of the country as a whole. Christian missionaries and colonial authorities viewed schools as vehicles for instilling Eurocentric conceptions of femininity and domesticity in Burmese girls.[34] Concerned about the high infant mortality rate, which they attributed to poor hygiene and lack of child-rearing skills, government officials regarded education primarily as a means to instruct Burmese women on how to take better care of their children. In 1914, Po Ka, a Burmese official in the Judicial Service, asserted that

> A woman's sphere of activity is her home. It may be well for the race if she is better educated and taught to take better care of her children; for

first Indonesian Women's Congress of 1928, translated and with an introduction by Susan Blackburn (Clayton, Vic.: Monash University, 2007), 15, 45, 58, 63–64, 69–71, 79–83.

33 Taw Sein Ko, *Burmese sketches* (Rangoon: British Burma Press, 1913), 224.

34 Tinzar Lwyn, 'Stories of gender and ethnicity: discourses of colonialism and resistance in Burma', *The Australian Journal of Anthropology* 5, 1&2 (1994): 60–85; Ikeya, 'Gender, history and modernity', 89–92.

then we have some hope that there will be a material reduction in the death rate of infants in Burma, which at present is too horrible to contemplate. With the advance of education she will undoubtedly become more *womanly* [my emphasis].[35]

Many Burmese Buddhists also believed that education played an important role in preparing young girls for marriage and motherhood. In an essay read before the Rangoon College Buddhist Association in December 1913, female student Ma Hta claimed that education provided new opportunities for women who had previously been considered fit only for 'domestic work and other drudgery', but she also stressed the importance of educating women so that they may become better wives and mothers.[36]

The prominent writer and nationalist Daw Khin Myo Chit argued that colonial education had a constraining, rather than a liberating, effect on women. She claimed that most girls who gained a 'modern education' were 'groomed to be good wives and mothers and nothing else'.[37] Mi Mi Khaing agreed that the 'modern classes' saw their daughters' education as a means of increasing their value on the 'marriage market'.[38] Many parents who sent their daughters to high school and university did so in the hope that they would attract wealthy suitors and marry into the officer class, which was associated with prestige and influence. Once they had completed higher education, young women were directed by relatives and teachers towards professions that suited their 'natural' maternal, nurturing abilities such as nursing and teaching.[39] Furthermore, women often felt obliged to give up their jobs once they were married due to the strong social expectation that a 'good' wife stayed at home and cared for

---

35 Po Ka, *The citizen of Burma*, 73.

36 Ma Hta, *The education of women in Burma* (Rangoon: The Rangoon College Buddhist Association, 1914), 3–4, 8. This view was widespread in other Southeast Asian countries and, indeed, throughout Europe and the 'West' in general.

37 Khin Myo Chit, *Colourful Burma*, 5, 8.

38 Mi Mi Khaing, *Burmese family*, 93.

39 In other Southeast Asian countries, too, women were expected to observe cultural norms about gender-appropriate roles and seek 'suitable' employment only. In Thailand, for instance, educational policy makers warned that 'although women are allowed to study as much as men they must be taught to be women and to be aware that they will always be women.' This quote, taken from an article written by Prince Chayanat and published in the women's journal *Satriniphon* in October 1914, is cited in Loos, 'The politics of women's suffrage in Thailand', 184.

her husband and their children.[40] Conversely, it was considered shameful for a woman to continue working after marriage because this implied that her husband could not support her. By the 1920s, however, a new generation of educated women was seeking to expand their horizons beyond the domestic sphere. Around the same time, Burmese nationalists also began to highlight the educational achievements of women to justify their arguments for independence from colonial rule.

The rise of the indigenous middle-class and the 'modern' woman

As more Burmese gained a modern education and found professional employment, they gradually formed an indigenous middle class (called *asoyamin* or simply *min*).[41] Members of this emergent Burmese middle class often adopted Western customs and behaviours to display their socioeconomic status in colonial society. Upwardly mobile families purchased European household and luxury items, and the wives of government officials (*min-kadaw*) hosted English-style dinners and parties to entertain foreign guests. Wealthy parents sent their children to European schools, where they developed an interest in Western fashion, music and cinema. These overt changes were accompanied by a gradual shift in social relationships. Mi Mi Khaing, whose father was a civil servant, described how her Western-educated mother did not observe the traditional custom of serving elderly family members first at mealtimes. Mi Mi Khaing and her siblings called each other by their names instead of using deferential forms of address according to their sex and age.[42] While these changes suggest a shift towards more egalitarian gender relations, women, more so than men, were still expected to conduct themselves with restraint and modesty.

Women who embraced modern fashions and pastimes (including shopping) were criticised by nationalists for being easily seduced by the excessive materialism and consumerism associated with Western capitalism. Left-leaning nationalist writers denounced women who blindly embraced Western lifestyles and sought to live the 'high life' as

---

40   Khin Myo Chit, *Colourful Burma*, 8–10.

41   *Asoyamin* literally means 'officer of the government' and the term referred to civil servants and the officer class.

42   Mi Mi Khaing, *Burmese family*, 53, 66–67.

though they were 'the wives of British men'.[43] Chie Ikeya has pointed out that negative portrayals of 'modern' women need to be considered in the context of the political, economic and social displacement of Burmese men by British and other Asian male immigrants.[44] Increasingly, it seemed to many Burmese, the modern working woman threatened to take over men's traditional role as primary breadwinner as well. Whereas some Burmese perceived women's empowerment as a threat to men's authority, others regarded the advancement of women as an integral component of the nationalist struggle. During the 1920s and 1930s, educated women increasingly took up paid professions in areas such as public administration, law, medicine, education and journalism.[45] Burmese newspaper editors urged patriotic women to take up professional careers so that they would not fall behind women in other developed, modern and independent nations.[46] As we shall see below, educated women became some of the most influential figures in the nationalist movement against colonial rule.

Women's involvement in Buddhist-led nationalist movements

As we saw in the previous chapter, many Burmese blamed Konbaung queens for interfering in politics and causing the loss of independence. How, then, did women become involved in the political movement against colonial rule? Burmese nationalism had its beginnings in the Buddhist revival, which had been fostered by Konbaung rulers and grew in response to colonial attempts to 'civilise' the native population. In 1906, a group of young, educated Burmese Buddhist men formed the aptly-named Young Men's Buddhist Association (YMBA) in order to restore Buddhism to pre-eminence and to overcome 'the ceaseless

---

43 Amar, 'Tuí payoga' ['Our practices'], *Myanmar Alin*, New Year's special edition, 1936, p. 9, cited in Ikeya, 'The modern Burmese woman and the politics of fashion in colonial Burma', 1290. The author of this article, Daw Amar, went on to become one of Burma's most revered writers and social commentators.

44 Ikeya, 'The modern Burmese woman and the politics of fashion in colonial Burma', 1281, 1297.

45 For profiles of prominent female educators, doctors, lawyers and writers, see Saw Moun Nyin, *Myanma amyothami* [Burmese women] (Yangon: Padauk Hlaing, 1976).

46 See the 1936 New Year's edition of *Myanmar Alin* ('New Light of Myanmar'), cited in Ikeya, 'The traditional high status of women in Burma', 65.

tide of foreign civilization and learning steadily creeping over the land'.[47] Within a decade, the YMBA had become a national organisation with branches throughout the country. Male nationalist leaders began to realise the value of including women in the nationalist struggle towards the end of World War One and newspapers and magazines increasingly published articles that encouraged women to support the nationalist cause.[48] Women of all classes were eager to participate in nationalist activities following years of social, economic and legal discrimination under colonial rule. Buddhist women were particularly attracted by the religious aspect of the early nationalist movement.

YMBA leaders formed the General Council of Burmese Associations (GCBA) at the end of World War One. The well-educated GCBA leaders established *wunthanu athin* ('patriotic' organisations) throughout the country to mobilise the largely uneducated rural population in support of the nationalist movement. The GCBA's emphasis on restoring 'traditional' Buddhist values struck a chord with many village women who had lost their occupations and legal rights under colonial rule.[49] Politically-minded monks also attracted large female followings in towns and villages throughout Burma. Khin Myo Chit recalled how Buddhist women often 'went wild over some famous monk or other' during this period.[50] The

---

47   U May Oung, 'The modern Burman', *Rangoon Gazette*, 10 August 1908, reprinted, with a brief introduction by J. S. Furnivall, in *Journal of the Burma Research Society*, 33, 1 (1950): 1–7. The YMBA both imitated and rivalled the missionary-created Young Men's Christian Association (YMCA). Christian missionary activity among non-Burman indigenous populations was one of the most important factors in the development of ethnic nationalist movements during the colonial period. Under missionary and British guidance, Christian ethnic minorities were able to advance – educationally, socially and politically – to gain far greater influence than that warranted by their numbers. For example, the Christian-led Karen National Association (KNA) was formed in 1881, 25 years before the YMBA came into existence, even though less than 20 per cent of the Karen population was Christian.

48   *Thuriya* ('The Sun') and *Dagon* ('Rangoon') frequently contained articles and letters praising women's achievements and involvement in nationalist activities. During the 1920s, *Dagon* magazine published a popular series of *Yuwadi Sekku* ('Young Ladies' Papers'), which took the form of correspondence between two women who discussed a range of topics including politics. Other popular magazines also published *Yuwadi* columns. For examples of the issues raised in these columns, see Ikeya, *Reconfiguring women, colonialism and modernity in Burma*, 60–70.

49   Daw Mya Sein, 'Towards independence in Burma: the role of women', *Asian Affairs* 59, 3 (October 1972): 294.

50   Khin Myo Chit, 'Many a house of life hath held me', 28. MSS Eur D1066/1. On the political mobilisation of monks during the colonial era, see E. Michael Mendelson, *Sangha and state in Burma* (Ithaca: Cornell University Press, 1975); U Maung Maung, *From sangha to laity: nationalist movements of Burma, 1920–1940* (New Delhi: Manohar, 1990); Manuel

most infamous and influential of these monks was U Ottama, whose appeal was based on his assertion that the colonial government threatened to destroy Buddhist values and culture. U Ottama advocated the use of Ghandian non-cooperation techniques and was arrested and imprisoned on three separate occasions for inciting sedition. In 1921, a number of U Ottama's female followers gathered in Mahabandoola Garden in Rangoon to protest against his arrest until mounted police forced them to withdraw.[51] Women also joined the radical *bu athin*, whose members refused to wear foreign-made clothing, marry foreigners or pay taxes. When the government outlawed these organisations in August 1923, some female members were imprisoned for allegedly attacking police while resisting arrest.[52] The political influence of the radical *athin* was limited, however, by their small numbers.

The largest and most famous peasant uprising against colonial rule was the Saya San rebellion of 1930–32. Saya San was a charismatic peasant leader who reportedly used symbols of Burmese kingship to convince his followers that he was a *minlaung* ('imminent king') who would revitalise the Buddhist religion.[53] His use of anti-tax rhetoric, Buddhist prophecies and protective rituals appealed to disaffected peasants who were suffering as a result of increased taxation, low paddy prices and land privatisation. Operating through a network of *galon wunthanu athin*,[54] the women in 'B Galon' units provided food, shelter and logistical support for men fighting in the 'A Galon' forces. Daw Thein Nyunt, the daughter of U Aung Hla, who was hanged for his role in the rebellion, sewed uniforms for the troops and hid weapons and

Sarkisyanz, *Buddhist backgrounds of the Burmese revolution* (The Hague: Martinus Nijhoff, 1965).

51 Naing Naing Maw, 'The role of Myanmar women in the nationalist movement', 38.

52 John F. Cady, *A history of modern Burma* (Ithaca; New York: Oxford University Press, 1958), 251; Naing Naing Maw, 'The role of Myanmar women in the nationalist movement', 45.

53 Patricia Herbert has suggested, however, that the rebellion was influenced by modern education and political mobilisation tactics as much as traditionalist Buddhist beliefs. See Patricia M. Herbert, *The Hsaya San rebellion (1930–1932) reappraised* (London: Department of Oriental Manuscripts and Printed Books British Library, 1982).

54 The *galon* or *garuda* was a mythical bird that was traditionally used by Burmese royalty. In Burmese mythology, the *garuda* was often pitted against the *naga* (serpent), and British officials interpreted the rebels' use of this symbolism as evidence of their desire to defeat the British. See Maitrii Aung-Thwin, 'Genealogy of a rebellion narrative: law, ethnology and culture in colonial Burma', *Journal of Southeast Asian Studies* 34, 3 (2003): 393–419.

other supplies in her house. She was imprisoned by the authorities until her father and brother were captured.[55] The British brought the insurrection under control only after Saya San was executed, by which time 1,300 insurgents had been killed and around 9,000 had surrendered.[56]

Although women participated actively in these Buddhist-led nationalist organisations, they were restricted to supporting roles under the direction of male leaders.[57] It was difficult for women to play a more significant role because of the religious divide between monks and women and the cultural emphasis on male political authority. Towards the end of World War One, women began to form their own nationalist organisations, which allowed some women to assume greater leadership roles. The *Wunthanu Konmari Athin* (hereafter 'Konmari') was founded on 16 November 1919 as a subsidiary branch of the GCBA. Initially, the Konmari was an elite women's organisation with around 300 members led by the wives and female relatives of prominent male nationalists as well as women entrepreneurs. Konmari leaders encouraged women to support the indigenous weaving industry by wearing traditional homespun clothes, for economic as well as nationalist reasons. They used Burmese-made products wherever possible and avoided using foreign-produced food, textiles and consumer goods.[58] In 1920, the Konmari supported Rangoon University students who were protesting against the requirement for all students to reside in residential halls, which disadvantaged those from poorer families.[59] Konmari members also participated in the GCBA-led demonstration against the imprisonment of U Ottama in July 1921, when they urged Burmese women not to marry foreigners or non-Buddhists.[60]

In the early 1920s, nationalist leaders were divided over whether to support or oppose dyarchy rule and the GCBA subsequently split

55 Naing Naing Maw, 'The role of Myanmar women in the nationalist movement', 61.

56 Aung-Thwin, 'Genealogy of a rebellion narrative', 396.

57 Women did not attain prominent positions in non-Buddhist nationalist movements either, at least not during the colonial period. Christian-led nationalist movements had patriarchal ideologies and organisational structures similar to the Buddhist-led nationalist organisations, which effectively limited women's involvement to subordinate roles.

58 Mya Sein, 'Towards independence in Burma', 295; Naing Naing Maw, 'The role of Myanmar women in the nationalist movement', 40, 43.

59 Naing Naing Maw, 'The role of Myanmar women in the nationalist movement', 39.

60 Mya Sein, 'Towards independence in Burma', 295; Naing Naing Maw, 'The role of Myanmar women in the nationalist movement', 40, 43.

into two factions.[61] U Chit Hlaing's faction opposed the dyarchy system, boycotted the Legislative Council elections, and later took an anti-separationist position after the Simon Commission recommended the separation of India and Burma in 1929–30. The other faction was known as the '21 Party' after its 21 prominent leaders, who accepted the dyarchy reforms and campaigned for a separationist policy in the belief that Burma could only achieve fully representative government once free of Indian influence.[62] Konmari associations divided along similar lines as women tended to side with their husbands and male relatives. Although Konmari associations no longer presented a united front, women continued to participate in political activities under the male leadership of their respective organisations. The wives of GCBA leaders could still exercise considerable influence over their husbands. U Chit Hlaing's wife reportedly persuaded her husband to end his faction's boycott and resume his position in the Legislative Council when the family's fortune was running out.[63] U Chit Hlaing's sister, Daw Hnin Mya, became the first woman to be elected to the Legislative Council in 1929. On the whole, however, Konmari members performed supporting roles under the leadership of male nationalists.

Moderate nationalists and legislative reforms

Unlike the two GCBA factions, a third group of 'moderate nationalists' maintained close ties with the colonial elite. Daw Mya Sein, the Oxford-educated daughter of YMBA leader U May Oung, was the most prominent woman in this group. Mya Sein and her mother, Daw Hla Oung, both served as executive members of the National Council of Women in Burma, which was affiliated with the International Council of Women. The Burmese chapter was formed in 1926 by the wives of prominent officials. Most members were British, with Burmese women comprising one-fifth of the total membership. With just over 100 mem-

---

61 Under the dyarchy system, 80 members of the 130-seat Legislative Council were elected and the rest were appointed by the British. While some nationalists sought to 'change the system from within', others called for 'home rule' and campaigned for separation from India.

62 Frank N. Trager, *Burma – from kingdom to republic: a historical and political analysis* (New York: Praeger, 1966), 49–51.

63 Maung Maung, *Burma and General Ne Win* (Bombay; London; New York: Asia Publishing House, 1969), 50.

bers, the Council was also relatively small compared to most Konmari associations, whose membership often reached into the hundreds.[64]

Among the Council's affiliated associations were several Christian organisations including the Young Women's Christian Association, the Mothers' Union and the Girl Guides. These organisations were usually headed by British women and their activities formed part of the wider colonial mission of 'civilising' the local Buddhist population. British leaders of Christian women's organisations found, however, that it was easier to convert non-Buddhists, mainly Karen and Kachin women who had previously been in contact with Baptist and Catholic missionaries – who emphasised the similarities between Christian teachings and indigenous animist beliefs – as well as immigrant Indians and Chinese. According to the Council leadership, the ease with which Buddhist women could divorce under customary law made the majority of Burmans less inclined to join Christian-led women's organisations. Consequently, the reach of these organisations was limited – the Mothers' Union, for example, only had nine national branches in the late 1920s, four of which were attached to 'native' churches.[65] The National Council of Women was concerned primarily with social welfare issues and produced reports on women's working conditions and access to housing and health services.[66] Although the Council did not actively promote female participation in politics, Mya Sein's prominent position enabled her to represent Burmese women's political interests in elite colonial and international circles. In particular, she advocated legislative reforms to enable women to stand for election and to guarantee women constitutional rights of equality.

Although all Burmese men and some women were granted the right to vote in 1922, women were unable to stand for election to public office. Colonial authorities were concerned about women's involvement in the *wunthanu athin* and feared that female politicians might lend further support to the nationalist movement. In 1923, the Governor of Burma reportedly stated that '[T]he influence of women on politics in many countries

---

64   These membership figures were calculated on the basis of the List of Members for 1927. 'Introductory leaflet, setting out the aims and principles of the National Council of Women in Burma, together with lists of members, officers and affiliated bodies.' MSS Eur D 1230/1.

65   'Scripts of addresses by Mrs Bulkeley on mothering; the Christian education of children; Mrs Sumner, the founder of the National Council of Women in Burma; and the Mothers' Union in Burma.' MSS Eur D 1230/5.

66   See, for example, 'Report by the National Council of Women in Burma on conditions affecting labour in and near Rangoon. October 1929.' MSS Eur D 1230/6.

has made for nationalism, and so far as I can gather it is making for it in Burma.'[67] Since education was a requisite to women's enfranchisement, nationalist leaders became some of the strongest advocates of female education and sought to capitalise on women's 'traditional high status' to strengthen their demands for the extension of female suffrage.[68] Mya Sein was the superintendent of a national girls' high school when she began to lobby for women's political rights in the late 1920s. In February 1927, Mya Sein and other members of the Burmese Women's Association[69] organised a demonstration seeking the removal of the sex disqualification clause preventing women from standing for election to the Legislative Council. Over 100 women marched to the Legislative Council carrying banners and shouting nationalist slogans. Government supporters defeated the resolution, however, on the grounds that women were less educated than men.[70] Women were eventually granted the right to stand for government office, and in 1929 Daw Hnin Mya was elected as the first female member of the Legislative Council.

In 1931, the British government decided that Burma should be separated from India. Mya Sein pushed hard for female representation at the Burma Round Table Conference, which was convened in 1932 to resolve uncertainty over the country's future constitution. She travelled to London in June 1931 and sought support from the British press as well as academics, business leaders and politicians.[71] The Governor of Burma was reluctant to appoint Mya Sein as a delegate, even after Burmese women's groups wrote to him in support of her nomination. He believed that Mya Sein was determined to incite 'dangerous agitation [because] ... she has designs on a political career in Burma'.[72] Mya Sein was eventually invited

---

67 Cited in Mya Sein, 'Towards independence in Burma', 295.

68 For a succinct summary of the Burmese nationalists' arguments, see Ikeya, 'The "traditional" high status of women in Burma', 61–66.

69 The Burmese Women's Association was the largest women's nationalist association, which became known as the Burmese Women's National Council after 1931.

70 *Rangoon Times*, 3 February 1927. See also Daw Mya Sein, 'The women of Burma', *Perspective of Burma: An Atlantic Monthly Supplement* (June 1958): 24–27; Naing Naing Maw, 'The role of Myanmar women in the nationalist movement', 54.

71 *Manchester Guardian*, 25 and 26 June 1931. Daw Mya Sein made this trip prior to attending the League of Nations conference in Geneva as the Asian women's representative. She had been chosen as the Asian delegate for this conference after making a favourable impression at the All Asian Women's Conference in Lahore.

72 'Telegram from Governor of Burma, dated 4th October 1931 (To Viceroy, repeated to Secretary of State)', in *Burma Round Table Conference. Note on groups represented at Burma*

Figure 4.1: Daw Mya Sein (left) with a friend, Burma Round Table Conference, London, 1931 (© TopFoto UK).

to participate in the conference as the sole female delegate, after London-based women's groups and the male Burmese delegates sent letters supporting her appointment to the Secretary of State for India, Sir Samuel Hoare.[73]

At the conference, Mya Sein was primarily concerned with gaining constitutional recognition of women's rights in accordance with customary Burmese practices and law. She resisted pressure from minority group delegates who were pushing for increased communal representation, claiming that women did not need 'minority rights' because they were already respected by men:

Conference. IOR L/PO/9/3 ff. 85–86. Despite the Governor's fears, Daw Mya Sein never became a politician. In 1946, she approached Lord Pethick-Lawrence's wife about creating the post of High Commissioner of Burma. Daw Mya Sein apparently wanted to be considered for this position, but her request was declined. See 'Burma Miscellaneous. Notes dealing with points raised by Daw Mya Sein in her talk with Lady Pethick-Lawrence. Representation of Burma overseas.' IOR L/PO/9/7, ff. 150, 180, 181, 185.

73 'Burma Round Table Conference. Note on groups represented at Burma Conference.' IOR L/PO/9/3 ff. 33, 37–38, 47–49, 97.

From time immemorial, we women of Burma have held a high position in the social, economic and political life of our country ... where the women do not rule entirely, but where we manage to have a perfect balance between the sexes .... In Burma, we have always been treated as individuals, as members of the human race. We have our own rights and our own duties to perform. We contribute our own share to the general welfare of our own country. We do not desire to be made a special interest [group], nor do we wish to be classed with the children.[74]

After the conference was concluded, the Burmese legislature continued to debate the issue of constitutional reform for several more years. Dr Daw Saw Sa, a prominent female physician, was nominated to the Senate by the Governor and became a member of the Joint Committee that finalised the terms of the new constitution. Like Mya Sein, she rejected a proposal to reserve separate seats for women in the legislature, claiming that women could hold their own in elections against men.[75] Thus, the 1935 constitution contained no special provisions for women, but guaranteed equal franchise and political candidacy rights for all literate citizens aged 21 and above.

These legislative reforms may have enabled more women to vote and contest elections, but they did not lead to an increase in women's formal political representation. Hnin Mya was the only female candidate to win a seat in the new Legislative Assembly in 1936.[76] Mya Sein later insisted that women were generally content to support the male nationalist leaders, and only agitated for political rights in order to further the nationalist cause.[77] Any attempt by female nationalists to prioritise women's rights was hampered by competing loyalties based on ethnicity, religion, party, class and family. As members of the educated elite, women like Mya Sein and Saw Sa led privileged lives compared to the vast majority of women, who had limited education and involvement in formal political processes. Elite women who had close ties with the colonial authorities actually had a vested interest in maintaining the status quo.

---

74 Government of Burma, *Burma Round Table Conference, 27ᵗʰ November 1931–12ᵗʰ January 1932: Proceedings*, 54.

75 For a brief biography of Saw Sa, see Saw Moun Nyin, *Myanma amyothami*, 44–48. See also Maung Maung, *Burma and General Ne Win*, 35; John Le Roy Christian, *Burma and the Japanese invader*, foreword by Sir Reginald Hugh Dorman-Smith (Bombay: Thacker, 1945), 150–51.

76 Mi Mi Khaing, *The world of Burmese women*, 157.

77 Mya Sein, 'Towards independence in Burma', 288.

This may explain why they resisted proposals to reserve legislative seats for women, which could shift the political balance in favour of the more ardent Burman nationalists and ethnic minority groups.

Women's roles in the Thakin movement: militarism versus protectionism

While the nationalist reformers of the 1920s sought to attain self-rule through parliamentary means, a new generation of left-leaning nationalists formed the *Dobama Asiayone* ('We Burmans Association') in 1930. The male leaders of the Dobama Asiayone referred to themselves as *thakins* or 'masters', adopting the title the Burmese were required to use when addressing their colonial rulers. The thakins' wives and other women who joined the movement were known as *thakinmas*. Although these women generally assumed less prominent roles than their male counterparts, several thakinmas were key figures in the party. Emma Nyun-Han has described Daw Than Than Myint and Daw Khin Khin as 'thakinmas by conviction in the national cause, not merely because they married thakins'.[78] These two women met and married their husbands, Thakin Than and Thakin Ba Sein, only after joining the movement. The thakins and thakinmas resolved to become the masters and mistresses of their own country by bringing about 'a general and economic revolution in the country by armed conflict if necessary'.[79] Women actively participated in thakin-led strike movements during the 1930s, but the increasingly militant character of nationalist activities reinforced the view that they needed men's protection and guidance.

By the mid-1930s, thakin leaders dominated the student union at Rangoon University. On 25 February 1936, students called a strike in response to the expulsion of student union leaders, Thakin Nu and Thakin Aung San, for criticising university staff members. Female students played an important role in the success of the strike action. One university student, U Tun Ohn, described how the male students were encouraged when they heard that female students were willing to participate, and turned out in large numbers to support the motion to strike. Around 700 male students and 50 female students attended

---

78 Emma Nyun-Han, 'The socio-political roles of women in Japan and Burma' (PhD thesis, University of Colorado, 1972), 507.

79 'The Thakins', *The Burmese Review* 1, 26 (11 November 1946): 8–9, cited in Trager, *Burma – from kingdom to republic*, 54.

the meeting and many more joined the procession to the Shwedagon Pagoda.[80] Many Burmese supported the strikers, but they also expressed concern about the girls' safety. The female strikers were accommodated separately at Moulmein Zayat (pavilion) under the care of 'elder brother' Thakin Hla Maung, Daw Hnin Mya and several other women. Moulmein Zayat had water facilities which allowed the girls to prepare food for the strikers and clean up after meals. They also spent time writing articles to keep up the male students' spirits.[81] Although the female strikers were confined largely to 'traditional' tasks such as cooking and cleaning, they also gained confidence as political activists within the student-led nationalist movement. In May 1936, one of the female protestors, Ma Khin Mya, proposed a resolution that led to the formation of the All-Burma Students Union.[82]

In late 1937, thakin leaders undertook to organise the disaffected Burmese employees of the (British-owned) Burmah Oil Company in the oil-fields at Chauk and Yenangyaung. The nationalists condemned capitalists, foreigners and the government at several mass meetings before declaring an oil-field strike on 8 January 1938. Thakinmas and the strikers' female relatives collected donations for the striking workers and urged the non-strikers to support their nationalist comrades. When several thakinmas and other female picketers were arrested, male strike leaders issued pamphlets condemning the authorities, one of which pictured a woman lying on the ground and being beaten by police.[83] The strike wore on for many months before the organisers decided to march to Rangoon. As the strikers prepared to set off from Chauk, a group of thakinmas and well-wishers handed out food supplies and medicine for

---

80 'Students' Strike 1936. All Burma Youth League.' MSS Eur D 1066/2. At the time, there were 163 female students at Rangoon University College and 92 female students at Judson College.

81 *The Sun*, 27 February 1936; 'The 1936 Rangoon University Strike', Part 3, p. 3. MSS Eur D 1066/3; Maung Maung, *Burma and General Ne Win*, 46; Nyun-Han, 'The socio-political roles of women', 505–06. Thakin Hla Maung was later known as Bo Zeya and served as Chief of Staff of the Burma Independence Army during World War Two.

82 U Aye Kyaw, *The voice of young Burma* (New York: Southeast Asia Program, 1993), 74.

83 Daw Khin Yi, *The Dobama movement in Burma (1930–1938)*, with a foreword by Robert Taylor (Ithaca, New York: Southeast Asia Program, Cornell University, 1988), 70–73; Kyaw Htun, 'The road from Chauk', *The Guardian Magazine*, 14, 6 (June 1957): 17.

the long journey. The wives, children and relatives of oil-field employees formed a second line of marchers to support the strikers.[84]

Students became involved in the strike movement following the arrest of several thakin leaders. On 20 December, a group of university students, including around 50 girls, attempted to stage a protest outside the Secretariat in Rangoon. Violence erupted when the (mainly Indian) police force separated the male and female students. In their eagerness to protect the girls, the male students attacked the police and one student, Maung Aung Gyaw, was killed in the ensuing struggle. One female student, Mya Mya, gave a speech at Aung Gyaw's funeral in which she declared that his death had inspired women to join the nationalist struggle:

> We are ready to die. Our brother Ko Aung Gyaw is calling from his beautiful tomb. We are ready to follow him. Please remember that we have got to bathe our heads with blood to get independence. We don't worry about imprisonment. We are ready to use our chests as parapets. We are waiting for invitation cards from prisons. We shall rise up if we are touched and rebel if we are pressed.[85]

The revolutionary tone of this speech belies the fact that women were generally expected to confine themselves to 'feminine' supporting roles and refrain from engaging in 'masculine' militant behaviour. In both the 1936 and 1938 strikes, male nationalist and student leaders emphasised the need to protect the female participants.

In 1938, communal tensions between Burmese and Indians also revived the longstanding debate about Burmese women's marital and inheritance rights. The Burmese Legislature passed the Buddhist Women's Special Marriage and Succession Act in 1939, which protected Buddhist women's divorce, inheritance and property rights. The Burma Muslim Dissolution of Marriage Act, which enabled Burmese Muslim women to initiate divorce against their husbands, was enacted the same year. Although these laws were welcomed by many women, they reinforced the widespread belief that women needed to be protected by (and from) men.

---

84   Khin Yi, *The Dobama movement in Burma*, 100. For further details of the 1938 strike, see Burma Socialist Programme Party, *Myanma nainggan amyothamimya i naingganyei hlouqsha hmu* [Burmese women political movements] (Yangon: Sarpay Beikman, 1975), 101–23.

85   Cited in Naing Naing Maw, 'The role of Myanmar women in the nationalist movement', 88.

Experiences of female nationalist writers

Thakin leaders were heavily influenced by Marxism and other leftist political ideologies, which emphasised social egalitarianism. The issue of gender equality was never seriously addressed by male nationalist leaders, whose attention was focused on other forms of social inequality based on racial and class differences. During the 1930s, female writers, journalists and publishers emerged as some of the most articulate and influential nationalists. These women were acutely aware of persistent gender inequality in Burmese society, and their writings provide an insight into the challenges women faced as they struggled to find their place in a society undergoing great social, economic and political trans-formation.

Women had been successful publishers, editors and journalists since the 1920s, but they often disguised their identities by posing as men. *Tharrawaddy* was managed by Daw Phwa Shin under her husband's name, perhaps out of concern that her readers would regard the news-paper as inferior if they knew it was edited by a woman. Former school teacher Daw San set up her own press office and periodical, *Independent*, in 1925. The *Independent* proudly declared itself 'The Most Popular Family Paper' and Daw San used her name to appeal to a broad audience including women. Yet even Daw San wrote political articles under a male pseudonym, possibly because she was aware that politics was widely regarded as a male domain.[86] By the 1930s, however, female writers and editors were increasingly gaining a reputation for their intelligent, insightful and critical commentaries on a range of social, economic and political issues.

One of Burma's most celebrated female writers and publishers was Ma Ma Lay (1916–82). As the secretary of the Dobama Asiayone in Bogalay, Ma Ma Lay campaigned with prominent nationalist leaders. In 1938, she married fellow journalist and publisher, U Chit Maung, and continued to publish *Gyanaygyaw* ('The Weekly Thunderer') and *Pyitthu Hittaine* ('People's Forum') following his death in 1946.[87] Ma Ma

---

86 Tharaphi Than, 'Writers, fighters and prostitutes', 42–47; Naing Naing Maw, 'The role of Myanmar women in the nationalist movement', 36, 54.

87 For a brief biography of Ma Ma Lay, see Saw Moun Nyin, *Myanma amyothami*, 163–66. Burmese writers who were associated with particular newspapers or journals often incor-porated the titles of these publications into their personal names. Hence, Ma Ma Lay was commonly known as Gyanaygyaw Ma Ma Lay.

Lay publicly condemned the prevalence of male chauvinism in Burmese society. When men denounced young women who wore shorts while playing sport as 'immoral', Ma Ma Lay argued that women should not be blamed if men were unable to control their lust: 'Sirs, please do not look at things with the eyes of *kilaisa* [sensual leering] only.'[88] Ma Ma Lay also defended working women when other commentators accused them of forsaking traditional roles and culture. In an article entitled 'The deteriorating state of male mentality', she observed that some men felt threatened by women who took up paid professions outside the home:

> For some Burmese men, happiness is when their women subsist only on their [men's] earnings. To be a woman, for such men, is to be a dependant. These men cannot stomach women holding office jobs ... because they cannot bear to acknowledge that women can perform as well as men in professional careers.[89]

Anna Allott rightly describes Ma Ma Lay as 'a committed feminist',[90] although female nationalists did not usually refer to themselves as such, possibly because of the association of feminism with Western values and women's domination over men.

Ma Ma Lay later became well-known for her novels, which emphasised women's experiences in colonial society. *Mon ywe mahu* ('Not out of hate'), originally published in 1955, describes the internal conflict of a Burmese woman, Way Way, who marries a Westernised Burman, U Saw Han, and struggles to adapt to his 'foreign' lifestyle:

> He chose what she should wear .... She had to wear slippers in the house .... When they sat at the table she had to put aside her desire to mix the food and eat with her fingers as she was used to. She had to use cutlery according to another culture. As a result she never enjoyed anything she ate and always felt vaguely unsatisfied. As soon as U Saw Han left for work she ran upstairs, kicked off her shoes, and walked about the house barefooted, Burmese style, free and unhampered.[91]

---

88 '*Athinyan shi kya yan*' ('Have Wisdom'), cited in Khin Myo Chit, *Colourful Burma*, 11.

89 Ma Lay, '"Yok'yā´´ thvé raí a tve´ a khay hā aok' kya lha khye´´ ka lā´´' ['The deteriorating state of male mentality'], *Gyanaygyaw*, January 1940, 15, cited in Ikeya, 'The modern Burmese woman and the politics of fashion in colonial Burma', 1295.

90 Anna J. Allott, 'Introduction', in Ma Ma Lay, *Not out of hate*, xxvi.

91 Ma Ma Lay, *Not out of hate*, 93–94.

The above passage portrays the inner turmoil that Burmese women experienced as they grappled to find their identity in colonial society. Although many women were eager to gain the prestige associated with a modern Western lifestyle, they did not want to lose their Burmese culture and heritage.

Thway ('Blood'), first published in 1973, comments on the Japanese occupation during World War Two and the responsibilities placed on women to preserve Burmese racial purity. The novel tells the story of Yumi, a young Japanese woman who visits Burma to find her half-brother, Maung Maung, the son of a Japanese army officer and a Burmese woman, Ma Htwe Htwe. Maung Maung is teased as a child because his father was Japanese, and as a young adult he resents everything and anyone Japanese, including Yumi, who gently persists in trying to gain her brother's trust and affection. Htwe Htwe died when Maung Maung was very young, and he imagines that his mother was forced to marry his father and may even have been raped. He accuses Yumi of trying to seduce his adoptive brother, Thet Lwin, in the same way that he believes his mother was seduced by his Japanese father. Even though the novel is set more than 20 years after the war, Ma Khin Win Mu, Yumi's Burmese colleague, 'still thought very little of women who married Japanese soldiers and officers'.[92] For most of the novel, Maung Maung does not realise that his mother and father had a loving, caring relationship. He finally learns the truth when he sees their wedding photograph: Htwe Htwe is a young woman with a pretty face that 'reflected her innocence and good nature'; her husband stands by her side, 'a dignified army officer' whose '[t]enderness, kindness and love shone in his eyes'.[93] Ma Ma Lay obviously sympathises with her characters and seeks to show a more harmonious side to inter-racial relations than the one put forward by Burmese nationalists during the colonial era.

Another popular female writer, Daw Khin Myo Chit (1915–99), was working as a freelance journalist when she became involved in the nationalist movement in 1938. She was employed as a translator for Thakin Nu's *Nagani* ('Red Dragon') publishing house, which published cheap, Burmese-language editions of general political and Marxist lit-

---

92 Ma Ma Lay, *Thway* [Blood] (Yangon: Seidana Sape, 1973). *Thway* has also been translated into English as Ma Ma Lay, *Blood bond*, translated by Than Than Win (Honolulu: Center for Southeast Asian Studies, University of Hawai'i at Manoa, 2004), 21.

93 *Ibid.*, 196–97.

erature. Khin Myo Chit would later describe how her interaction with prominent thakins exposed her to new ideas about politics, religion and gender:

> I was drawn to the vibrant personality of [future communist leader] Thakin Than Tun and his crisp clear talk on political ideologies, one of his favourite subjects being the harm religion had done to Burma .... I'd seen time and again how Buddha's teachings had been twisted to suit the purpose of the older generation .... It was my karma that I should be content to stay at home like a nice young lady. But who wanted to be a nice young lady when there were so many interesting things to do such as becoming a doctor or a journalist.[94]

Her experience was probably similar to that of other young, educated women who wanted to take advantage of the new employment opportunities available to them, but struggled to overcome ingrained cultural beliefs that confined them within domestic roles. Although Khin Myo Chit was aware of gender discrimination in Burmese society, she downplayed her own importance in the nationalist movement. When asked to accompany Thakin Nu on a political tour throughout the country, she suspected that she was merely an 'added attraction' and actually spent more time running errands for her more prominent male companion than making speeches herself. Even when she was appointed to an executive position in the Dobama Sinyetha Asiayone following the outbreak of World War Two, she declared that '[N]othing could be more ridiculous than my working as an executive in a political party, for I knew nothing of politics and cared less.'[95] Khin Myo Chit's self-deprecating account of her political activities illustrates how difficult it was for women to accept that they could take on leadership roles within the nationalist movement. It was only in hindsight that she would look back on the colonial period as a time when Burmese women were restricted by nationalist ideologies and male chauvinism.[96]

Women's experiences during World War Two

The war had a dramatic impact on the lives of all Burmese women, but their wartime experiences revealed that the traditional connection be-

---

94 Khin Myo Chit, 'Many a house of life hath held me', 23.
95 *Ibid.*, 37, 77.
96 Khin Myo Chit, *Colourful Burma*, 5–7, 11–12.

tween masculinity and authority remained largely unchanged. Men assumed command over the wartime civilian and military administration, while women continued to perform supporting roles that emphasised their 'feminine' qualities and abilities. When the thakins formed an alliance with (former Premier) Dr Ba Maw to further the anti-colonial resistance, Ba Maw's wife, Kinmama Maw, fed and housed the male nationalists and helped them establish contact with the Japanese. Aung San secretly left the country in 1940, and Kinmama Maw helped his supporters, known as the 'Thirty Comrades', to plot a route across the Thai border where they were reunited with Aung San and received military training from the Japanese to form the nucleus of the Burmese Independence Army (BIA). In his memoirs of the wartime period, Ba Maw described how his wife supplied the Thirty Comrades with biscuits for their journey and sent food parcels to party members who were in prison. Ba Maw also relied on Kinmama Maw's 'quick, cat-like mind' and her ability to remain calm while secretly planning his (Ba Maw's) escape from prison.[97] While Ba Maw expressed great admiration for his wife's abilities, her influential role in the early stages of the war has been overlooked by most historians.

By mid-1942, the British had withdrawn to Simla in India and the Japanese allowed Ba Maw to form a nominally 'independent' government. For the most part, the Burmese were able to manage their own administration, economy, education and social services without much interference from the Japanese. Many Indians and Chinese had fled Burma following the outbreak of war, leaving businesses and property in the hands of their Burmese wives. Women's traditional economic roles were revived as the lack of foreign imports and labour under wartime conditions forced the Burmese to rely solely on small-scale domestic trade and production.[98] Women increasingly took up positions in the health, education and social services to compensate for the loss of foreign professionals. In particular, there was a great demand for nurses to deal with the large number of war casualties. The Japanese also established the East Asia Youth League to mobilise Burmese youth in support of the war effort. By the end of 1944, the League had more than 70,000

---

97 Ba Maw, *Breakthrough in Burma: memoirs of a revolution* (New Haven; London: Yale University Press, 1968), 69, 117–18, 131, 228–46.

98 Khin Myo Chit, *Colourful Burma*, 12–13.

members, around half of whom were young women. Although many patriotic women were eager to join the League, their tasks were limited to nursing wounded soldiers and civilians, organising fundraising activities and participating in recruitment drives. Instructional manuals for female League members reveal that women were still expected to maintain their beauty regimes, even while cleaning up the streets of Rangoon.[99]

It soon became apparent that the Japanese had no intention of granting genuine freedom to the Burmese. In August 1944, Burmese nationalists formed the Anti-Fascist Organisation (AFO), which later became known as the Anti-Fascist People's Freedom League (AFPFL), and called upon all patriotic Burmese to join the anti-Japanese resistance.[100] In October, Thakin Soe called for the establishment of a women's army to mobilise villagers in support of the resistance movement. The Women's Regiment of the BIA was subsequently formed in February 1945. Although over 100 women applied to join the regiment, only seven female soldiers were sent out with male troops. These women received training in political, military and espionage tactics, but they were not posted to frontline combat duties. Instead, the women's regiment was charged with gathering, translating and distributing intelligence information and other documents, undertaking mobilisation activities in villages, and providing food and moral support for male soldiers.[101] Tharaphi Than notes that it is unclear whether nationalist leaders believed that women were more capable of securing villagers' support than men or whether they enlisted women mainly for pragmatic reasons because men were engaged elsewhere. The fact that the women's regiment was disbanded after three months suggests that there was no significant shift in men's perception of women's (limited) capabilities.[102]

While many Burmese supported the Aung San-led BIA and AFPFL, others remained loyal to the British. Daw Mya Sein was appointed as Burmese Advisor in the Far Eastern Bureau between 1942 and 1945, prior to which she had been Director of Women's Civil Defence in Rangoon. In May 1945 she was invested with an MBE (Member of the

---

99   Tharaphi Than, 'Writers, fighters and prostitutes', 95.

100 Daw Aye Aye Mu, 'The role of Myanmar women in the anti-fascist resistance (1945)', *Myanmar Historical Research Journal* (June 2000): 63–64.

101 Tharaphi Than, 'Writers, fighters and prostitutes', 97–131; Aye Aye Mu, 'The role of Myanmar women in the anti-fascist resistance', 64–65.

102 Tharaphi Than, 'Writers, fighters and prostitutes', 105–06, 129–30.

Order of the British Empire) in recognition of her loyal service to the British.[103] Most women performed less prominent support roles in the allied war effort, however. A number of ethnic minority women, and some elite Burmans who had close ties with the colonial authorities, joined the Women's Auxiliary Service (Burma) (WAS(B)) under the honorary command of Governor Sir Reginald Dorman-Smith's wife, Lady Dorman-Smith. The 'Wasbies', as these women were commonly known, were praised as being 'the biggest single factor affecting the morale of the forward troops'.[104] The vast majority of nursing positions were filled by Christian Karen, Kachin and Chin women, whose allegiance to the British stemmed partly from long-standing tensions with Buddhist Burmans, which intensified when pro-British Karen and Kachin forces were employed against the predominantly Burman BIA troops.

Like their Burman counterparts, ethnic minority women were discouraged from taking on military roles, although some women were willing to go to great lengths to try to fight the Japanese. One article published in January 1945 in *Burma Today*, a monthly magazine issued by the (British) Government of Burma Information Office, described how a young Kachin woman disguised herself as a man so that she could enlist as a soldier in the Kachin Levies. Although she was eventually discovered and prevented from fighting, she vowed to continue resisting the Japanese.[105] This British government source was obviously intended to boost the morale of the British and allied forces, rather than encourage women to take up combat roles.

The expansion of women's horizons in post-war society

After the war, male nationalist leaders entered into negotiations with the British government with the aim of restoring independence to Burma at

---

103 'Papers and correspondence of Lady Dorman-Smith as Honorary Commander, Women's Auxiliary Service (Burma) and copies of Dorman-Smith's correspondence about the Women's Auxiliary Service (Burma), including newsletters and other items, 1944–1946.' MSS Eur E 215/51, ff. 8; 'Telegram from Sir Reginald Dorman-Smith to L.S. Amery, Simla, 22 May 1945', in Hugh Tinker (ed.), *Burma: The struggle for independence 1944–1948: documents from official and private sources*, 2 volumes (London: Her Majesty's Stationery Office, 1983–84), I, 273.

104 'Papers and correspondence of Lady Dorman-Smith', ff. 4. See also Sally Jaffe and Lucy Jaffe (eds.), *Chinthe women: Women's Auxiliary Service (Burma) 1942–46* (Chipping Norton: The Authors, 2001).

105 'The first W.A.A.C.', *Burma Today* 2, 3 (January 1945): 11. MSS Eur E 215/66.

the earliest opportunity. Many women devoted their energies to reconstruction work, mainly in the area of social services, through organisations like the Burmese Women's League and the All Burma Women's Freedom League. The members of these organisations claimed that the experience of war had awakened a 'new spirit' among many women, particularly the younger generation, who were eager to see

> ... the death of many old ideas. Among them, the notion that the sole legitimate occupation for the average woman is the care of her children and the management of her home. These are certainly important, but constitute a woman's only duty no more than they constitute her only ability. In the past five years women have proved themselves equal to almost every kind of work previously thought only capable of being done by men. Numbers of them even died in the battlefield. Now that the end has come, women must not be, cannot be, interned in their homes to look out upon the world as mere spectators. Those days are over. Even before the war, the women of the East were starting to awake to consciousness of their wider responsibilities: the war has now completed this awakening.[106]

The above passage suggests that the wartime experience had prompted a shift in women's political priorities. Before the war, women's organisations were primarily concerned with regaining independence from colonial rule rather than promoting feminist agendas. The wartime author John LeRoy Christian hinted at this when he observed that 'Burma has no women's party, no feminist movement. Women do not consider their interests as being separate to men.'[107] Throughout the colonial period, women had been constrained by cultural beliefs and political ideologies that had reinforced their maternal, nurturing roles and subordinate position relative to men. With the nationalist struggle all but achieved, women began to envisage taking on more diverse and prominent roles outside the home in an independent Burma.

Conclusions

The imposition of colonial rule presented many challenges, and some opportunities, for women. Women's ability to exert political influence

---

106 'Copies of speeches by and in honour of Lady Dorman-Smith at meetings of the Burmese Women's League and All Burma Women's Freedom League, with further material connected with the Dorman-Smiths' return to Burma. 1945.' MSS Eur E 215/55 ff. 13.

107 Christian, *Burma and the Japanese invader*, 148.

through their familial relationships with male Burmese elites was greatly reduced under the impersonalised colonial administration in which British officials held the most senior positions. Women's traditional economic influence also declined as the commercially-oriented colonial economy came to be dominated by Indian and Chinese moneylenders, traders and labourers. Access to formal education did open up new employment opportunities for women, mainly in the nursing and teaching professions, but many parents regarded female education primarily as a means to enhance their daughters' marriage prospects and only secondarily to prepare them for 'suitable' employment. The emergence of the modern female professional challenged prevailing cultural norms about gender and power and provoked opposition from men who feared that women would usurp their position of authority within the family. Although nationalist leaders encouraged women to become educated and seek employment in order to further the cause for independence, they too were highly critical of women who sought to emulate 'Western' capitalist lifestyles.

Nationalist resentment towards foreign encroachments on traditional Burmese culture was exemplified by concerted campaigns to preserve Buddhist women's marital, property and inheritance rights. In their efforts to protect women from discrimination, however, nationalists denounced Burmese women who married foreigners as immoral and unpatriotic. The religious focus of many nationalist organisations, and the protectionist attitudes of male nationalist leaders towards women, effectively reinforced the belief that women should defer to men's authority. Although female writers and journalists increasingly questioned the hypocrisy of ingrained cultural beliefs that confined women to domestic roles, women's formal political representation remained negligible and the vast majority of female nationalists performed 'traditional' supporting roles under the guidance of male nationalist leaders. The experiences of World War Two witnessed a rise in political awareness among young Burmese in particular. By the end of the war, these women looked forward to extending their roles and freedom in an independent Burma.

5

Social Workers, Beauty Queens and Insurgents: From Independence to Military Rule

*T*he Union of Burma was formally declared an independent nation on 4 January 1948. Many Burmese looked forward to the end of foreign domination and the opportunity to reassert their social, economic and political freedom, but independence also presented myriad challenges. The government made efforts to rebuild and modernise the economy, and sought to extend educational and social services, which should have increased economic opportunities for women. In many respects, however, national 'liberation' meant reverting to 'traditional' values in which women were disadvantaged economically. Women were encouraged to contribute to the national economy by entering 'appropriate' professions, mainly in education and health, but they were still expected to prioritise their domestic responsibilities. Despite constitutional guarantees of equal employment opportunities, women received less pay than men for the same work and were less likely to be appointed to senior positions in most fields, including politics. The factional nature of post-independence politics effectively limited most women's political participation to supporting, subordinate roles. Although few women were appointed to high political office, this should not be taken as a sign that women were politically apathetic. When civil war broke out soon after independence, many women joined underground communist movements which sought to 'liberate' the working class from oppression. Ethnic minority women also emerged as political and military leaders determined to protect the rights of their communities against Burman domination. The ongoing civil war contributed to the expansion of the armed forces, eventually leading to General Ne Win's seizure of power in a military coup on 2 March 1962, which signalled the end of parliamentary democracy for the next fifty years. When male politicians and insurgents were imprisoned or killed in the wake of the coup, women became some of the most outspoken opponents of military rule.

Transition to independence and the outbreak of civil war

At the end of World War Two, British and Burmese leaders entered into negotiations about how and when to hand over the reins of government, but divisions soon emerged between various political groups who sought to assert their positions. Ethnic minorities were determined to protect their political autonomy and cultural identity against Burman domination. Aung San's efforts to foster ethnic unity and his commitment to establishing a federalist state earned him the respect of many ethnic leaders and, at the Panglong Conference in February 1947, Shan, Kachin and Chin representatives agreed in principle to the formation of a Union of Burma.[1] Aung San and six of his colleagues were assassinated on 19 July 1947,[2] but progress towards independence continued under the leadership of U Nu, who served as Prime Minister for most of the parliamentary period. The new constitution that came into force later that year defined the Shan, Kachin, Karenni and Chin territorial borders, and the Shan and Karenni states were granted the right to secede from the Union by popular vote after ten years. Karen, Mon and Arakan states were eventually designated, but there was no 'Burman state', just a Burman heartland divided into seven provinces (to balance the seven ethnic states). The allocation of parliamentary seats was intended to allow ethnic minorities a significant voice in parliament, and the Shan *saopha*[3] of Yaunghwe, Sao Shwe Thaik, was appointed the first president of the Union.[4] In practice, however, the parliament was dominated by the overwhelmingly Burman AFPFL and its allies. Concerns over unre-

---

1   'Arthur Bottomley to Lord Pethick-Lawrence', Telegram, IOR:M/4/3025, Rangoon, 14 February 1947; 'Note by John Leyden on the Panglong Conference, 1947', IOR:M/4/2811, Rangoon, 20 February 1947; both reproduced in Tinker (ed.), *Burma: the struggle for independence*, II, 411–13, 423–30.

2   At the time, the pre-war Prime Minister, U Saw, was thought to have planned the assassination in an attempt to seize power. He was later tried and executed for his role in the murders, but several contemporaries claimed that British intelligence or a corrupt faction within the new Burma Army were actually behind the attack. See Martin Smith, *Burma: insurgency and the politics of ethnicity*, second edition (London; New York: Zed Books, 1999), 70–71.

3   A *saopha* (*sawbwa* in Burmese) was a Shan hereditary ruler.

4   The 125-seat Chamber of Nationalities (the upper house) was elected on a racial basis, while the 250-seat Chamber of Deputies (the lower house) was elected on a population basis.

solved constitutional matters contributed to the rise in ethnic nationalism in the years following independence.

At the same time, Burman nationalists of various, predominantly leftist, tendencies sought to gain political dominance. The AFPFL coalition broke down as U Nu and other democratic socialists became increasingly concerned about the communists' intention to gain power through revolutionary means. The Communist Party of Burma (CPB) was formally expelled from the AFPFL in October 1946. In late March 1948, following a series of communist-led labour strikes, U Nu ordered the arrest of CPB leader Thakin Than Tun, prompting the latter to take his 'White Flag' CPB underground to organise an armed struggle against the government. Thakin Soe, who had broken away from the main CPB to form his own 'Red Flag' Communist Party in March 1946, was already engaged in underground insurgent activity. The conflict soon widened when Karen, Kachin and Mon nationalists took up arms against the central government in early 1949. The political and military situation was further complicated by the arrival of Chinese nationalist Kuomintang (KMT) troops in Shan State in 1950. When the Burmese army moved to expel KMT troops from Shan territory, the violent campaign provoked insurgent activity and unrest among the Shan population. Although the government and its armed forces regained control over most areas by the late 1950s, assorted communist and ethnic insurgents remained active until well into the 1980s (and beyond, in some cases).

Amidst the political and military turmoil that marred Burma's first decade of independence, U Nu's beleaguered government struggled to revive the national economy and develop the country's social institutions with limited success. Goals of economic modernisation and the extension of educational and health services promised to open up greater employment prospects for women, but the disruptive effects of the civil war, inadequate resources, and the persistence of 'traditional' beliefs concerning women's capabilities meant that opportunities for women to expand their economic roles remained limited.

Women as social workers and bearers of tradition in the *Pyidawtha* State

Burma had been devastated by the war, and independence leaders recognised the value of harnessing women's energies to revitalise the national economy. All Burmese were expected to contribute towards building a modern, prosperous nation and it gradually became more socially acceptable for women to pursue further education and undertake paid employment. Patriotic women who had fought hard for independence were eager to make the most of the new educational and economic opportunities that became available to them with the aim of improving their own lives and those of their families and communities, and the nation as a whole. The All-Burma Women's Freedom League, led by businesswoman Kin Kin Gyi and the wives of nationalist leaders, appeared to promote equal employment opportunities for women:

> The War gave the women of this country, as it did to the women of other countries, great opportunities for service. The women of Burma were quick to seize those opportunities, and adopted careers which hitherto had been either closed to them or which they had never striven to enter. But much more remains to be done, for we are only at the beginning of our campaign for the complete enfranchisement of women. It is the purpose of our League to organise public opinion and to organise the women of Burma with a view to securing equality of opportunity with men, and contributing our proper share towards the promotion of the general welfare and progress of the nation.[5]

In reality, however, the League's focus on social welfare and the elimination of 'social evils' reinforced the belief that women's economic and social roles should reflect their 'natural' capabilities as carers and guardians of public morality:

> There are certain directions in which women are particularly fitted to tender advice and render assistance .... [T]he future of this country depends very largely upon the way and directions in which the women seize the opportunities of social service. Education, maternity welfare, vigilance societies, athletics, domestic economy, public hygiene are only some of the innumerable directions in which women can and are prepared to play their part. Further, the assistance of women would be particularly required for the suppression of the many social evils, such as public immorality and the spread of social diseases, which are the curse of modern society.[6]

---

5   Signed copy of speech to Her Excellency Lady Dorman-Smith signed by Kin Kin Gyi, President, All-Burma Women's Freedom League, 7 November 1945. 'Copies of speeches by and in honour of Lady Dorman-Smith at meetings of the Burmese Women's League and All-Burma Women's Freedom League, with further material connected with the Dorman-Smith's return to Burma. 1945.' MSS Eur E 215/55 ff. 22.

6   *Ibid.*, ff. 22–23.

The League represented the views of Burma's political elite who would assume power in post-independence society. Although the 1947 Constitution guaranteed equal opportunities for all citizens 'in matters of public employment and in the exercise of or carrying on of any occupation, trade, business or profession',[7] there was little political will to implement legislation or other measures to ensure that women's constitutional rights were upheld. Traditional ideas about gender-appropriate economic roles therefore remained largely unchanged and unchallenged.

Within the family, the husband was still expected to be the primary wage earner, while the wife provided additional income that was used to purchase household necessities (if a family was poor) or modern ameni-ties and small luxuries (in better-off families). There was little change to the traditional expectation that women should assume primary responsibility for childcare and household work, including cooking and cleaning. Only the wealthy elite could afford to employ servants to assist with these domestic tasks, and even then women were still expected to oversee their servants' duties. Women therefore had to juggle their domestic responsibilities and paid work outside the home. It is hardly surprising to find, then, that men far outnumbered women in the paid workforce. According to the 1953–54 census data, women formed 25 per cent of the total labour force in urban areas and 31.1 per cent in rural areas.[8] These census figures did not include women's casual and unpaid labour in the non-formal sector, which was significant.

When the government changed hands, the positions left vacant by departing British and Indian officials, civil servants and other profes-sionals were rapidly filled by Burmese, but the persistent belief in men's innate spiritual superiority discouraged women from seeking high-level positions in government and public administration that carried prestige and authority. Educated women tended to be appointed to lower-level clerical positions in government offices, hospitals and banks, while the majority of senior management positions went to men. The govern-ment's social goals included the provision of adequate health care and education services for the entire population, and women were encour-

---

7   See Article 14 in Constituent Assembly of Burma, *The Constitution of the Union of Burma* (Rangoon: Superintendent, Government Printing and Stationery, Burma, 1945), 3.

8   For a summary discussion and comparison of urban and rural census data, see Mi Mi Khaing, 'Burma: balance and harmony', in Barbara E. Ward (ed.), *Women in the new Asia* (Paris: UNESCO, 1963), 121–24.

aged to enter nursing and teaching professions and to participate in various social welfare organisations. This work was considered vital to the nation's development, but it was also deemed appropriate for women to take on roles that suited their 'natural' nurturing abilities.

In 1952, the government embarked on an ambitious social and economic program, known as the 'Pyidawtha Plan', which emphasised the need for citizens' voluntary contributions and cooperation in order to develop a 'Welfare State'.[9] Aung San's widow, Daw Khin Kyi, who was a trained nurse and midwife, coordinated various social services under this scheme as the Director of the Maternity and Child Welfare Board (1947–52) and chair of both the Social Services Commission (1952) and the Council of Social Services (1953–58).[10] The wives of government officials and other elite women attended planning meetings, distributed medicine and provided health advice to poor mothers in urban clinics, but the outbreak of civil war prevented the extension of these voluntary health services into rural areas.[11]

The government moved to develop a comprehensive educational policy, but it was unable to implement a nationwide education program due to the ongoing military conflict. Many families in urban areas could afford to send their daughters to primary (and increasingly secondary) school, where they would gain sufficient education to support their families and secure suitable marriages. In rural and ethnic minority areas, however, educational opportunities were limited due to inadequate resources and facilities. Traditional cultural attitudes also contributed to the low level of female education in rural areas. Poor families could only afford to send their sons to school; daughters were expected to remain at home to help with the housework, care for younger siblings and work in the fields.

In 1951, U Nu announced that the government would cover the cost of tertiary as well as primary and secondary education.[12] Female university students increasingly enrolled in traditionally male-dominated

---

9 *Pyidawtha* literally means 'sacred-pleasant-country' but it is also translated as 'happy land'. See Hugh Tinker, *The Union of Burma: a study of the first years of independence*, 4th edition (London: Oxford University Press, 1967), 104; Maung Maung, *Burma's constitution* (The Hague: Martinus Nijhoff, 1959), 111.

10 Kyaw Zwa Moe, 'The mother who was overlooked', *The Irrawaddy*, July 2006.

11 Trager, *Burma – from kingdom to republic*, 137; Maung Maung, *Burma's constitution*, 112.

12 Tinker, *The Union of Burma*, 203; Nyun-Han, 'The socio-political roles of women', 325.

subjects, but men still far outnumbered women in the fields of medicine, science and engineering. The dual impact of the loss of experienced foreign doctors and the civil war placed great strain on the nation's health services, but in 1951–52 only one third (35.5 per cent) of medical students were female.[13] According to Mi Mi Khaing, medical colleges were reluctant to admit female students because a high percentage failed to complete their studies after marriage.[14] This suggests that many women either preferred or were encouraged to prioritise childbirth and family responsibilities over their education and careers.

There was an urgent need for educated Burmese to contribute to the (re)construction and modernisation of buildings, transport and communications infrastructure following the war. University of Rangoon enrolment figures reveal that the number of undergraduate female science students increased from 417 to 1,276 between 1948 and 1958, but women still represented less than one quarter (24.66 per cent) of all undergraduate science students.[15] Women were also under-represented in the fields of transportation and engineering, which involved hard physical labour, frequent travel and close interactions with men.[16] A few female entrepreneurs successfully managed construction and mining business enterprises, but the vast majority of construction workers and miners were men.[17]

While well-educated, middle-class women living in Rangoon and other urban centres readily found employment, the vast majority of

---

13   Tharaphi Than, 'Writers, fighters and prostitutes', 3.

14   Mi Mi Khaing, 'Burma: balance and harmony', 122.

15   Mya Mya Thein, 'Women scientists and engineers in Burma', *Impact of Science on Society* 30, 1 (1980): 18.

16   Even now, limits are imposed on female enrolments in engineering courses. The Myanmar Maritime University, which opened in 2002 and provides tertiary training in maritime and electrical engineering, only began to admit female students in 2008 and caps female enrolments at 15 per cent. In an article published by the Independent Mon News Agency in 2010, a university staff member claimed that women were too 'weak in physicality' to be trained as engineers and added that the Ministry of Transport would not allow females to go to sea. A mother of two also informed the reporter that she had prevented her daughter from enrolling out of concern for her welfare. Her son, who graduated from the university, earned far more than the average Burmese. This suggests that the restrictions on female enrolments have had an adverse effect on women's potential earning power. See Kong Janoi, 'Burma's Maritime University gaining popularity', *Independent Mon News Agency*, 9 August 2010.

17   Nyun-Han, 'The socio-political roles of women', 413–14; Mi Mi Khaing, 'Burma: balance and harmony', 121–22.

working-class women experienced considerable financial hardship. Nationalist leaders blamed colonialism for the poor economic position of rural Burmese, many of whom had lost their livelihoods and land to foreign (mainly Indian) labourers and moneylenders. The new constitution vowed to protect Burmese agriculturalists and labourers 'against economic exploitation.'[18] In the mid-1950s, around two-thirds of rural women engaged in paid employment were agricultural labourers.[19] Legislation regarding land nationalisation, low-interest loans and security of land tenure offered some relief for rural families, but farmers still had to rely on private moneylenders for credit. Although rice production levels gradually increased, unstable political and military conditions and fluctuating paddy prices reduced farmers' profits. The government sought to expand the industrial sector, which opened up some opportunities for less-educated women as factory workers in textile, umbrella, soap and plastic production. These women were better paid than most agricultural workers, but on average women earned considerably less than their male counterparts, despite the fact that the constitution entitled women to the same pay as men for doing the same job.[20] The economic challenges facing women were exacerbated by ongoing debates about gender-appropriate roles in the popular media.

Tensions between embracing modernity and preserving tradition

Public debates about the benefits and challenges of modernity, which had begun during the colonial period, continued long after independence had been obtained. While it was generally accepted that economic modernisation was necessary to enable the country and its people to develop and prosper, many Burmese felt that modernity should not come at the expense of sacrificing traditional culture and values. The increase in female employment represented one of the more controversial aspects of modernisation that were discussed in the media. While some commentators advocated equal employment opportunities for women, others

---

18 Article 31 of *The Constitution of the Union of Burma*, 6.

19 Government of the Union of Burma, Central Statistical and Economics Department, Census Division, *Union of Burma second stage census 1954, Volume I: Population and housing* (Rangoon: Superintendent, Government Printing and Stationery, Burma, 1955), 11.

20 *Ibid.*, 16; Trager, *Burma – from kingdom to republic*, 151–52; Ni Ni Gyi, 'Patterns of social change in a Burmese family', 147; Maung Maung, *Burma's constitution*, 259; Nyun-Han, 'The socio-political roles of women', 407–08.

Figure 5.1: *Myawaddy* cover, August 1958 (© Pictures From History).

expressed concern that working women were encroaching on traditional male domains. In one article published in *The Guardian* in August 1963, the author urged women to prioritise their domestic responsibilities and seek temporary employment only if there was no other way to resolve financial difficulties. A successful working woman, the author argued, could potentially 'hurt her husband's feelings' and damage his 'manly ego' if he felt unable to fulfil 'his main duty as a provider'.[21] In reality, the belief that women would usurp men's role as primary breadwinner was unfounded. According to a government report published in 1958, only nine per cent of household heads who earned more than 75 per cent of the total family income were women.[22]

If some Burmese perceived modernity as a threat to traditional culture, others saw it as the means to gain social status and freedom. Advertisements

---

21 Pearl Aung, 'Working wives', *The Guardian* (Rangoon), 4 August 1963.

22 *Report on the survey of household expenditures* (Rangoon: Central Statistical and Economics Department, Government of the Union of Burma, 1958).

in newspapers and magazines encouraged young women to buy the latest fashions and consumer items. Modern women wearing high heels and makeup, smoking cigarettes, and engaging in a wide range of leisure pursuits – often in the company of men – were portrayed as wealthy, sophisticated and independent. *Myawaddy*, a monthly periodical published by the Burmese army, undercut its competitors by offering (male) readers 'better covers with prettier girls' (Figure 5.1).[23] The magazine also advertised birth control pills and 'love potions' for women, suggesting that the modern woman could enjoy sexual as well as financial freedom.[24] This sort of advertising belies the fact that women were still expected to dress and behave modestly, especially in the presence of men. The same magazine also published articles criticising women who adopted Western dress, tastes and behaviours such as dating.[25] After the 1962 coup, Ne Win banned beauty contests and *Myawaddy* covers increasingly represented women as paragons of socialist virtue (Figure 5.2).

In conservative Burmese society, 'modern' women who engaged in overt sexual behaviour and socialised freely with men (especially foreigners) represented the embodiment of lustfulness, loose morality and corruption. Independence leaders wanted to break free from foreign economic as well as cultural influences, and women who associated with foreigners were portrayed in the media either as wantonly promiscuous or victims of economic exploitation. In her doctoral thesis, Tharaphi Than critically examines cartoons published in popular newspapers and journals during the 1950s, which depict Chinese and Indian businessmen as astute, if unprincipled, opportunists who swindled money, property and women from poor and vulnerable Burmese. Several illustrations portray women cavorting with and chasing after wealthy foreigners.[26] These women invariably were young, fashionably attired and openly engaging in promiscuous behaviour, suggesting that modernity would result in the moral degeneration and corruption of women. The government sought to limit foreign ownership of economic enterprises, but women were expected to support official initiatives to keep the

---

23   Interview with *Myawaddy* founder Colonel Aung Gyi, cited in Mary Callahan, *Making enemies: war and state building in Burma* (Ithaca; London: Cornell University Press, 2003), 183.

24   *Myawaddy*, March 1956 and September 1956.

25   *Myawaddy* March 1953, November 1955, May 1957.

26   Tharaphi Than, 'Writers, fighters and prostitutes', 214–24.

Figure 5.2: *Myawaddy* cover, 1967 (© Pictures From History).

economy in native hands by not marrying foreigners who would steal the nation's wealth as well as its women.

Although many public commentators blamed foreigners for the country's poor economic performance, in reality the Pyidawtha Plan failed due to the lack of indigenous expertise, the disruption caused by the ongoing civil conflict and global economic trends.[27] Government efforts to wrest economic enterprises from foreign control and strengthen indigenous earning power were only partially successful, and the state was obliged to devote considerable resources towards suppressing insurrections. Disparities in wealth between the educated, urban elite and the majority of uneducated rural Burmese widened as the government struggled to extend its economic and social reforms throughout the countryside. The persistence of cultural beliefs concerning appropriate

---

27   For an analysis of the failure of the Pyidawtha Plan, see Mya Maung, 'The Burmese way to socialism beyond the welfare state', *Asian Survey* 10, 6 (June 1970): 533–51.

gender roles also prevented many women from taking full advantage of new economic opportunities. But if there were few avenues for women to increase their economic power, their political influence was even more circumscribed.

Women's political activism in the parliamentary era

During the colonial period, women's political activism was focused on the nationalist struggle for independence and protecting Burmese culture from foreign influences, rather than challenging indigenous beliefs that reinforced male authority and power structures. The intensely factional nature of post-independence politics also had the effect of limiting most women's political participation to subordinate roles in the male-led AFPFL, communist and ethnic organisations. The sorts of political activities that women engaged in reflected the relative power of the organisations to which they belonged. The AFPFL dominated the national parliament, and the wives of senior politicians had a vested interest in maintaining their husbands' status and power. These women supported the government by participating in fundraising activities and social welfare organisations, and exercised political power indirectly through their male relatives in high office. Women in communist and ethnic nationalist organisations were more likely to engage in direct political and military action, possibly because male leaders encouraged women's activism in order to gain greater leverage to achieve their goals. Even within communist and ethnic insurgent organisations, however, deep-rooted beliefs about appropriate gender roles made it difficult for women to achieve the same levels of authority and influence as men.

Most women who gained political prominence in the years following independence – whether they were elected to parliament or active in underground insurgent movements – were wives or relatives of male AFPFL, communist and ethnic leaders. Women's political activism was inextricably linked to their sense of family solidarity, responsibility and loyalty. This did not mean that women did not have strong political convictions of their own, however. When male politicians and insurgent leaders were imprisoned or killed, women readily assumed leadership roles in order to further their political goals.

Kinship politics and the AFPFL

AFPFL leaders became the new political elite in post-independence society. Frank Trager described Burma as a 'one-party state' during the parliamentary period because of the AFPFL's dominance both in terms of government leadership and electoral success.[28] In April 1947, when elections were held for the Constituent Assembly that would determine Burma's future course as an independent nation, 248 out of 255 seats were won by AFPFL candidates with communists taking up the remaining seven seats. The transition to independence did not see a significant increase in women's political representation; a mere five seats were won by women (all AFPFL candidates).[29] In subsequent elections held in 1951, 1956 and 1960, the AFPFL won by a convincing majority, but still only a handful of women were elected to parliament. Few women took on senior official roles within the AFPFL organisation and only one woman, Daw Sein Pyu, was elected to the Central Executive Committee (in 1958).[30]

The intense rivalry that characterised national politics, not to mention the ongoing military conflict, contributed to the perception that women would be unable to cope with the demands of a political career. Pro-AFPFL newspapers like *Bamakhit* ('New Era of Burma') actively discouraged women from engaging in high level party politics on the grounds that that it was challenging and corrupt, implying that women were too weak (both intellectually and morally/spiritually) to take on political leadership roles.[31] Burmese notions of gender-role complementarity also emphasised the importance of maintaining a clear distinction between male and female political activism. While men assumed control over political decision-making, women supported the government by participating in party fundraising and recruitment as well as social welfare activities. In addition, women were expected to take a leading role in protecting the 'purity' of the Burmese *amyo*, culture and religion.

---

28   Trager, *Burma – from kingdom to republic*, 174.

29   Tinker, *The Union of Burma*, 26.

30   A total of 18 women stood for election in the national parliament between 1948 and 1962. See Mi Mi Khaing, *The world of Burmese women*, 159; Belak, *Gathering strength*, 257.

31   *Bamakhit*'s founder, U Ohn Khin, was a close ally of U Nu. For a detailed analysis of representations of women in *Bamakhit* during the parliamentary period, see Tharaphi Than, 'Writers, fighters and prostitutes', esp. chapters 3 and 4.

In other words, women's political activities emphasised their nurturing, procreative function.

The wives of senior AFPFL politicians supported their husbands in an unofficial capacity until events obliged them to take on official political responsibilities. Following Aung San's death, his widow, Daw Khin Kyi, was offered his parliamentary seat.[32] It is highly probable that Khin Kyi was offered this role largely as a symbolic gesture and that she was expected to continue Aung San's unfinished work rather than pursue any political agenda of her own. Khin Kyi's daughter, Aung San Suu Kyi, wrote in her biography of her father that 'Aung San had married a woman who had not only the courage and warmth he needed in his life's companion but also the steadfastness and dignity to uphold his ideals after he was gone.'[33] Khin Kyi later resigned from political office, although she remained active in public life and played a leading role in the government's social welfare organisations.[34] While her resignation from parliament seemed to indicate her willingness to resume a more 'traditional' female role, Khin Kyi maintained close relationships with Aung San's political colleagues and was one of Prime Minister Nu's most prominent supporters. In 1960, he appointed Khin Kyi as the Burmese Ambassador to India and Nepal. She continued to serve in this position until 1967.

As members of the political elite, the wives of senior AFPFL politicians had a vested interest in safeguarding the reputation of the party to which their husbands belonged. Several female Burmese scholars have argued that these women had no need to run for political office themselves as long as they could take a share in political power through their male family members.[35] It was widely believed that the wives of AFPFL leaders exercised considerable political influence both through and over their husbands. When in 1958, the AFPFL cabinet split into two factions, one led by Nu and Thakin Tin and the other led by Ba Swe and

---

32 For information on Daw Khin Kyi's appointment, see 'Sir Hubert Rance to the Earl of Listowel, Telegram, Rangoon, 2 August 1947, IOR: M/4/2714', in Tinker (ed.), *Burma: the struggle for independence*, I, 482.

33 Aung San Suu Kyi, *Aung San of Burma: a biographical portrait by his daughter*, with an introduction by Roger Matthews (Edinburgh: Kiscadale, 1991), 26.

34 *The Guardian Magazine* (Rangoon), 10, 1 (January 1963): 41.

35 Ni Ni Gyi, 'Patterns of social change in a Burmese family', 148; Mi Mi Khaing, 'Burma: balance and harmony', 122; [A Retiring Civil Servant], 'The women of Burma', *New Times of Burma* (4 January 1948): 52–53, 55.

Kyaw Nyein, some Burmese blamed the politicians' wives for exacerbating the power struggles through their influence over their husbands.[36] While there may be an element of truth to these accusations, it seems more likely that the women were convenient scapegoats. In reality, a combination of personal and organisational differences eventually led to the AFPFL split. Trager likened the political situation to a marriage breaking up:

> These men and their wives – some of whom were politically and socially active in a variety of causes – had lived and worked together for almost two decades. Irritation, suspicion, and arguments frequently marked their relations. They had been together too long.[37]

Given the personalised nature of political loyalties, it is hardly surprising that women supported their husbands in an effort to maintain their hold on power. When the AFPFL split, women expressed their political allegiance through their dress: those who supported Nu's 'Clean' faction wore *htabi-wah* (yellow sarongs), while the followers of the Kyaw Nyein's 'Stable' faction wore *htabi-ni* (red sarongs).[38] Shaken by the split, Nu invited the army commander-in-chief, General Ne Win, to form an interim government and elections were deferred until 1960.

Nu had previously expressed his desire to retire from politics to pursue his religious interests. His promotion of Buddhism won Nu and the AFPFL considerable electoral support among the predominantly Buddhist population. Many women donated jewellery, money and land at party-sponsored meetings in much the same way that they supported the *sangha* financially.[39] Nu oversaw the construction of the Kaba Aye Pagoda and convened the Sixth World Buddhist Council in May 1954, which brought some 2,500 monks and Buddhist scholars to Rangoon to develop a common Theravada interpretation of Buddhist texts. The meetings were held over a two-year period and thousands of women – including Nu's wife, Daw Mya Yee, and the wives of other politicians – were involved in preparing food for the monks. During the

---

36 Frank N. Trager, 'The political split in Burma', *Far Eastern Survey* 27, 10 (1958): 148; Htin Aung, *A history of Burma*, 323.

37 Trager, *Burma – from kingdom to republic*, 175.

38 Nyun-Han, 'The socio-political roles of women', 518–19.

39 Burma Socialist Programme Party, *Myanma nainggan amyothamimya i naingganyei hlouqsha hmu*, 170.

council sessions, tensions between the wives over the organisational arrangements for the monks reflected the ongoing political power struggle between the two AFPFL factions led by Nu and Kyaw Nyein.[40] At the Council's closing session, Nu announced that measures would be taken to establish Buddhism as the state religion.[41] During the 1960 parliamentary elections, Buddhist women turned out in large numbers to vote in support of Nu and his proposal. The 'Clean' AFPFL won by a convincing majority and Nu was reinstated as Prime Minister.[42]

State promotion of Buddhism encouraged women to engage in religio-political activities in support of the AFPFL, but it also provoked strong opposition from non-Buddhist minority groups who were concerned that they would face economic and cultural discrimination.[43] Nu's attempts to promote religious tolerance failed to allay minorities' concerns, especially at a time when his government was fighting to suppress insurgencies led by Christian Karens and Kachins. Nu regarded Buddhism both as a means of restoring peace to a country divided by civil war and as a political tool to weaken popular support for the insurgencies. The government claimed that Buddhist concepts were consistent with democratic and socialist ideals and denounced its communist opponents as 'anti-Buddhists'.[44] The civil war created conditions, especially in insurgent-held areas, which provided new opportunities for women to engage in political activism.

Women in the communist movement: bold revolutionaries or bad mothers?

Whereas the AFPFL government encouraged women to focus on social welfare activities, communist leaders urged them to take up more direct political action and actively recruited female members. Party leaders claimed that communism was the only ideology that accorded women

---

40 Trager, 'The political split in Burma', 148.

41 Maung Maung, *Law and custom in Burma and the Burmese family*, 117.

42 Nyun-Han, 'The socio-political roles of women', 195–97.

43 Maung Maung, *Law and custom in Burma and the Burmese family*, 118–22.

44 The *tatmadaw*'s psychological warfare department produced and distributed over one million copies of a booklet called *Dhammarantaya* ['Buddha's teachings in danger'], which accused communist leaders of attacking Buddhism as 'the enemy of the proletariat'. See Smith, *Burma: insurgency*, 180; Callahan, *Making enemies*, 194. Both Smith and Callahan note that the effectiveness of these anti-communist campaigns was limited.

equal status with men, and promised to liberate working-class urban and rural women from economic and political oppression. Pegu Ma Khin Lay, a regular columnist for the communist party's *Pyithu* Journal, argued that the 'struggle for liberty and rights for women ... should be fought concomitantly'.[45] The party's ideological emphasis on gender equality was reflected in the term 'comrade' – female communists were known as *yebawma*, the equivalent of the male *yebaw*. Female party members received ideological and military training and some took up combat roles alongside their male comrades. Life in the underground communist movement was arduous and the image of hardened women revolutionaries traipsing through the jungle stood in stark contrast to the image of female AFPFL supporters who confined themselves to social work and fundraising. It seemed entirely fitting that communist women were known as *arzani* ('brave or daring ones').

In many respects, however, women in the communist and AFPFL parties shared similar experiences. A strong sense of familial loyalty was evident in the communist party just as it was in the AFPFL. White Flag leader Thakin Than Tun's wife, Daw Khin Khin Kyi, and Red Flag leader Thakin Soe's wife and daughter, Daw Hnin May and Ni Ni Soe, were actively involved in the armed insurgency.[46] Khin Khin Kyi had a sister, Khin Kyi, but while Khin Khin Kyi's primary political allegiance was to her husband and his party, Khin Kyi threw her support behind Nu and the AFPFL. Although elite communist women were dedicated party members, it seems unlikely that they would have remained so committed to the insurgencies without the guidance and support of their husbands and families. Women rarely attended high-level party meetings and only one woman, Daw Khin Kyi Kyi, a former BIA soldier and the wife of Thakin Thein Pe Myint, was elected to the executive committee (in July 1946). Ordinary members who initially saw communism as a means to gain equality with men later found that party leaders failed to promote women's rights outside the context of the class struggle.[47] Although female party members received military training, most were engaged in 'traditional' roles as nurses and teachers. In both the AFPFL and com-

---

45   *Pyithu Journal*, 15 April 1956, p. 15, cited in Tharaphi Than, 'Writers, fighters and prostitutes', 137.

46   Nyun-Han, 'The socio-political roles of women', 520.

47   Tharaphi Than, 'Writers, fighters and prostitutes', 156–57.

Figure 5.3: CPB meeting in Panghsang, January 1987 (© Hseng Noung Lintner).

munist parties, therefore, women's political activism was confined to supporting roles under male leadership.

Communist women were expected to balance their political and maternal roles and to raise their children to carry on the revolution. Many women gave birth in the jungle and some even took their children with them into combat.[48] Although many children joined the underground resistance, communist families were also split apart in reaction to many years spent living and fighting in harsh conditions. When forced to choose between supporting the party and providing security and stability for their children, many women chose to surrender and return to their homes. In 1960, the wives of several prominent White Flag communist leaders surrendered to government forces. They included Daw Khin Gyi, wife of CPB Politbureau leader Thakin Than Myaing, and Daw Hla May, wife of the second-most senior CPB leader Hamendranath Goshal

---

48 *The Guardian* (Rangoon), 26 February 1969; Min Zin, 'Daw Kyi Kyi passes away', *The Irrawaddy*, June 2001. Women in the Vietnamese communist movement were also expected to fulfill their traditional duties as wives and mothers. See Karen Gottschang Turner with Phan Thanh Hao, *Even the women must fight: memories of war from North Vietnam* (New York: Wiley, c1998); Sandra C. Taylor, *Vietnamese women at war: fighting for Ho Chi Minh and the revolution* (Lawrence, Kansas: University Press of Kansas, 1999).

(*yebaw* Ba Tin).[49] Daw Hnin May, the wife of Red Flag leader Thakin Soe, was arrested and imprisoned, although their daughter, Ni Ni Soe, remained in the jungle with her father for several more years.[50] While communist women from well-off families could return to the comfort of their homes, many poor women from rural backgrounds had no choice but to remain in the jungle where they and their children suffered from malnutrition and diseases like dysentery and malaria.[51]

In its campaign to weaken popular support for the insurgents, the government emphasised the damaging effects of communism on family relationships and cultural values. As the 'weaker sex', women were thought to be particularly vulnerable to 'corrupting' communist influences. Pro-government newspapers including *The Nation* and *The Guardian* denounced female communists as immoral women and bad mothers who provided poor role models for future generations of Burmese.[52] The 1949 government publication, *Burma and the insurrections*, asserted that communism, far from empowering women, actually left them open to become targets of abuse. Red Flag leader Thakin Soe was labelled a serial womaniser who had forcibly married the sister of his first wife, then deserted both sisters to marry another woman; he later abandoned this third wife in favour of a young party recruit whom he 'appropriated' from one of his lieutenants. White Flag leader Thakin Than Tun was also accused of trying to marry the relatives of prominent landowners and merchants.[53] The report further claimed that male communists molested women, including those sympathetic to their cause, citing the case of one woman who had fed and sheltered a communist leader who later raped her, which ultimately led her to commit suicide.[54] Although this document can be seen as government propa-

---

49 Trager, *Burma – From kingdom to republic*, 195.

50 Daw Hnin May was released in 1962 when the government offered a general amnesty to political prisoners.

51 Tharaphi Than, 'Writers, fighters and prostitutes', 159–60.

52 The founder of *The Nation*, Edward Yaw Lone, had numerous American contacts who provided him with a printing press and financial support. *The Guardian* was founded by Burmese army leader, Brigadier-General Aung Gyi, and the pro-military lawyer and historian Dr Maung Maung. It was funded by the army and used to convey its ideas to the public. See Bertil Lintner, *Burma in revolt: opium and insurgency since 1948* (Boulder, Colo.: Westview Press; Bangkok: White Lotus, 1994), 106–07, 141.

53 Government of the Union of Burma, *Burma and the insurrections* (Rangoon: Government of the Union of Burma, September 1949), 3.

54 *Ibid.*, 36.

ganda, Tharaphi Than's interviews with former female communists suggest that rape and sexual abuse against women was widespread in the underground communist movement, and that perpetrators were rarely punished by party leaders.[55]

Above-ground leftists were also subjected to attacks by the government and its supporters. Militant socialists raided Ma Ma Lay's editorial offices and accused her of communist leanings because her family associated with prominent Marxist leaders.[56] U Hla and his wife Daw Amar were respected leftist publishers who ran the *Ludu* ('People') Journal and *Ludu Thadinsa* ('People's Daily') newspaper. In 1949, the army destroyed the Ludu publication house on the grounds that the couple were communist sympathisers. Government troops surrounded the Ludu residence and held the family at gunpoint until locals intervened. Undaunted by these attacks, the Ludu family continued to publish from new offices. In 1953, Ludu Daw Amar was attending Soviet-sponsored peace conferences in Europe when U Hla was detained and imprisoned for three years for his involvement in CPB-inspired protests. She continued to manage the press until her husband's release, but the government temporarily closed down the paper in 1959. By then, the communist insurgency was weakening, but government troops were still struggling to suppress various ethnic opposition groups. The rise in ethnic nationalism provided opportunities for women from elite Karen and Shan families to gain prominence as members of parliament and underground organisations.

Karen insurgents and politicians

Long-standing communal tensions between Karens and Burmans were exacerbated during World War Two, when Karen villagers were subjected to atrocities at the hands of Burman BIA soldiers. In 1947, Karen nationalists formed the Karen National Union (KNU) and its defence militia, the Karen National Defence Organisation (KNDO), to push for greater political and cultural autonomy in the lead-up to independence. When the KNDO took up arms against the government in January 1949 following violent clashes with Burman military police, Karen women and girls prepared food packages and delivered supplies to the defence

---

55 Tharaphi Than, 'Writers, fighters and prostitutes', 160.

56 Lintner, *Burma in revolt*, 3.

lines where the male KNDO troops were engaged in battle. Karen nurses also left government hospitals to treat the wounded.[57] KNU leader Saw Ba U Gyi's wife established the Karen Women's Organization (KWO) in 1949 to provide financial and medical assistance for KNDO soldiers and health, education and welfare services for Karen communities. KWO members were confined to performing 'feminine' tasks, while male KNU/KNDO leaders and combat troops did most of the decision-making and fighting. The KWO's activities were also limited during the 1950s and 1960s, partly because the KNU lacked a central headquarters. It was not until the mid-1990s that the KWO would emerge as a significant political voice for Karen women.[58]

The fighting between Karen insurgents and the government forces seemed to underline religious as well as ethnic divisions, since the KNU leadership was predominantly Christian.[59] Yet some elite Christian Karens remained loyal to the government and opposed the rebellion. Ba Maung Chain, daughter of the late Karen nationalist leader Sir San Crombie Po,[60] was a member of the Protection Committee formed in 1949 to mediate between the KNU and the government.[61] The committee's attempts at negotiation failed, however, and fighting resumed. In 1953, Nu appointed Ba Maung Chain as the first minister for the newly formed Karen State; she remains the only woman to have been appointed to the national Cabinet. Ba Maung Chain struggled to convince Karens that their interests would be best served through improved education and employment opportunities, rather than armed conflict, and she resigned from office after only one year. Hugh Tinker's claim that she was unable to deal with party manoeuvres in the Karen State Council may have reflected the widespread belief that women were not tough enough to take on high-level political roles.[62] According to Josef Silverstein, however, Ba Maung Chain broke with Nu to lead an opposi-

---

57   Smith, *Burma: insurgency*, 117; Nyun-Han, 'The socio-political roles of women', 194, 519; Lintner, *Burma in revolt*, 12.

58   The politicisation of the KWO will be discussed in chapter 9.

59   Although the KNU leadership was predominantly Christian, many Karens were Buddhists or animists.

60   Sir San Crombie Po had advocated Karen independence in the 1920s, but later sought cooperation with Burman leaders.

61   Government of the Union of Burma, *Burma and the insurrections*, 52–53.

62   Tinker, *The Union of Burma*, 75–76.

tion party in Karen state, which suggests that other factors prompted her decision to resign from ministerial office.[63] In any event, we should not interpret her resignation as a sign that women were unwilling or unable to exercise political leadership. An examination of the careers of two elite Shan women reveals that they could hold their own in the male-dominated spheres of political and military action.

The 'Opium Warlady' and the Mahadevi of Yaunghwe

During the 1950s, there was an increase in nationalist and insurgent activity among sections of the Shan population who resented the continuing presence of Ne Win's *tatmadaw* (armed forces) in Shan State. The *tatmadaw* was tasked with clearing north-eastern Shan State of communist and Kuomingtang (KMT) troops who had been recruiting in the area since 1951.[64] The KMT had found a supporter in Olive Yang (Yang Kyin-hsui), the younger sister of the Kokang *saopha*. As a member of the Kokang ruling family, Olive wielded considerable political, military and economic power. In her youth, Olive had earned a reputation for her 'masculine' appearance and behaviour. Her classmates called her 'Miss Hairy Legs' and the locals joked that she carried a gun in her schoolbag. She assumed command over Kokang's militia following her father's death in 1947, her brothers having consented to her taking on this role because it suited her strong personality. As a militia leader, Olive built up an extensive patronage network as the headmen from surrounding villages sent their sons to serve under her command. She also amassed a personal fortune through her control of the cross-border opium trade, and was widely known as the 'Opium Warlady'.[65] Olive's alliance with the KMT alarmed her brothers, however, who were concerned about maintaining their positions as members of parliament.[66] In October 1952, Olive was arrested for supporting the KMT and spent five years in

---

63   Silverstein, 'Aung San Suu Kyi: Is she Burma's woman of destiny?', 270.

64   The government feared that Chinese communists might follow the KMT into Burmese territory, which would lend support to the indigenous communist movement and could potentially involve the Burmese government in a conflict with its powerful northern neighbour. The KMT's involvement in the illicit opium trade also concerned government leaders.

65   Lintner, *Burma in revolt*, 100, 186–87; Elliot, *The white umbrella*, 73, 166–68, 226–27.

66   Yang Li (Jackie Yang), *The house of Yang: guardians of an unknown frontier* (Sydney: Book Press, 1997), 71.

Mandalay prison before returning to Shan State, where she established several business enterprises.

The *tatmadaw*'s campaigns in Shan State intensified following an official Chinese protest about the continued KMT presence in Burma in 1952. Resentment against the predominantly-Burman armed forces increased as many Shan villagers were harassed, beaten and forced to act as porters for government troops; Shan women and girls were also raped and sexually abused by *tatmadaw* officers and soldiers. Sao Hearn Hkam, the Mahadevi of Yaunghwe and wife of former president Sao Shwe Thaik, spoke out against *tatmadaw* abuses when village heads came to her with grievances about the conduct of its soldiers. Her husband, who was then serving his first term as Speaker for the Chamber of Nationalities, felt obliged to remain politically neutral and was primarily concerned with modernising and facilitating the transfer of the *saophas*' powers to the state. Sao Hearn Hkam, by contrast, was a traditionalist who distrusted the Burmans and believed it was vital to protect Shan rights and independence.[67]

From 1953 onwards, Sao Shwe Thaik encouraged his wife to take on a more active, albeit unofficial, political role so that he could concentrate on religious and cultural matters. Sao Hearn Hkam met informally with the *saophas* and relayed their comments to her husband. In 1956, Sao Hearn Hkam was elected to parliament as a member of the Chamber of Deputies and also became a member of the Shan State Council. She had the support of her husband and many Shan elders who believed that her tough, forthright manner would enable her to promote Shan rights.[68] Although she now had a measure of official power, Sao Hearn Hkam was still aware of her lower status as a non-Burman woman – a minority within a minority – in the male-dominated arena of national politics. She was naturally assertive and voiced her opinions freely, but she also found that there were certain advantages to be gained when one was perceived as a 'weak' woman with 'limited' knowledge of politics. She addressed her male political opponents with deference and charm, before rebutting their arguments using her razor-sharp wit.[69] Using this

---

67   Elliott, *The white umbrella*, 237–39.

68   *Ibid.*, 242, 258–60; Chao Tzang Yawnghwe, *The Shan of Burma: memoirs of a Shan exile*, second reprint (Singapore: Institute of Southeast Asian Studies, 2010), 7.

69   Elliott, *The white umbrella*, 265.

indirect and distinctly 'feminine' approach, she appeared less threatening to male Burman politicians and gained support from Shan nationalists who were beginning to agitate for independence.

In February 1957, Shan nationalists organised mass rallies throughout the state to demand secession from the Union, but when Ne Win assumed control over the caretaker government in 1958, the *tatmadaw* stepped up its military campaigns to weaken support for the nationalist movement.[70] Nu persuaded the *saopha*s to remain part of the Union and the latter formally gave up their hereditary rights on 24 April 1959, leaving Shan State to be administered by the elected state government. Olive Yang was reappointed as head of the Kokang security forces and soon reasserted her position as the unofficial ruler of Kokang state, but her credibility was seriously weakened by persistent rumours about her lesbian affairs. She also spent much of her considerable fortune on extravagant gifts for her lover, film actress Wa Wa Win Shwe.[71] On 2 March 1962, Ne Win seized power in a military coup and dozens of male politicians were arrested including U Nu and Sao Shwe Thaik. Olive was detained in 1963 and spent five years in Insein prison, where she was abused by the male prison guards because of her sexual preferences.[72] She was released in 1968, but never regained her former political and military influence.

As members of the Shan ruling elite, Olive Yang and Sao Hearn Hkam exercised considerable political influence, but it is unlikely that they would have gained such prominence without the support of their male family members. Both women strongly opposed Burman interference in Shan affairs, which earned them support among local nationalists, although Olive appears to have been motivated more by a personal desire for wealth and status than political conviction. Neither woman was afraid to stand up to her male relatives: Sao Hearn Hkam disagreed with her husband over the issue of Shan secession, while Olive collaborated with KMT leaders against her brothers' wishes. Olive grew powerful through

---

70 Trager, *Burma – from kingdom to republic*, 195.

71 Yang Li, *The house of Yang*, 71; Lintner, *Burma in revolt*, 187.

72 Lintner, *Burma in revolt*, 187. In general, the Burmese are relatively tolerant of lesbians (*yaukkyasha*) and male homosexuals (*meinmasha*), although it is not culturally acceptable for any Burmese to engage in overt sexual behaviour in public. Women, in particular, are expected to remain modest at all times and refrain from acting in a sexually provocative manner. See Spiro, *Kinship and marriage in Burma*, 229.

her command of the Kokang militia and control over the illicit opium trade, but her deviation from culturally acceptable sexual behaviour made her the subject of public condemnation and ridicule. By contrast, Sao Hearn Hkam used her 'feminine' charms to outmanoeuvre Burman politicians as a member of parliament, although her strong personality would eventually bring her into conflict with Shan insurgent leaders in the years following the coup (as we shall see below).

Female opposition to military rule

The coup effectively brought an end to political pluralism as Ne Win and the military systematically moved to silence their opponents. Ironically, some women were able to assume greater leadership roles after male politicians and insurgent leaders were imprisoned or killed. The wives of imprisoned politicians became some of the most outspoken opponents of the military regime. Nu described his wife as a quiet woman who was 'singularly free of political opinions',[73] but after his arrest Daw Mya Yee shouted insults at prison guards until they eventually allowed her to see her husband.[74] The Austrian-born Mahadevi of Hsipaw had concentrated on raising her children and administering social welfare programs while her husband, Sao Kya Seng, served as a member of parliament.[75] She was outraged by the brutal conduct of the *tatmadaw* in Hsipaw, and felt it was her duty to take charge of her husband's affairs following his arrest.[76]

Many women felt obliged to remain in Burma while their husbands were in prison, but some chose to leave the country after their husbands 'disappeared' or died. After waiting two years for news from her husband, the Mahadevi of Hsipaw left Burma with her two daughters and

---

73 U Nu, *U Nu, Saturday's son*, translated by U Yaw Lone; edited by U Kyaw Win (New Haven: Yale University Press, 1975), 289.

74 Elliot, *The white umbrella*, 323.

75 The Mahadevi of Hsipaw was born in Austria as Inge Eberhard. She met Sao Kya Seng when they were both students at university in Denver, Colorado. The couple married in March 1953, and returned to Burma later that year. Inge was subsequently installed as Mahadevi of Hsipaw on 2 November 1957. For an autobiographical account of her life, see Inge Sargent, *Twilight over Burma: my life as a Shan princess*, with a foreword by Bertil Lintner (Honolulu: University of Hawaii Press, 1994).

76 Sargent, *Twilight over Burma*, 1, 27–28; Lintner, *Burma in revolt*, 166.

eventually resettled in the USA.[77] Sao Hearn Hkam's youngest son was killed when the family home was raided by *tatmadaw* forces during the coup; her husband died in military custody later that year. In December 1963, Sao Hearn Hkam fled to Thailand after hearing that she was about to be arrested. From there, she took on a leading role in organising Shan armed resistance against the *tatmadaw* as chair of the Shan State Army (SSA) war council. Sao Hearn Hkam's transformation from parliamentarian to insurgent leader demonstrates that women readily adjusted their political strategies in the wake of the coup. Ultimately, however, her ability to command effective leadership was hampered by internal power struggles, failed political and military alliances, limited financial resources and lack of international support. Sao Hearn Hkam's straightforward manner also increasingly brought her into conflict with the male war council members, while younger insurgents rejected what they regarded as her 'feudalistic' approach to politics.[78] Feeling that she could no longer provide effective leadership, Sao Hearn Hkam handed over most of her duties to her son, SSA commander Chao Tzang, and went to live in Canada where she remained until her death in January 2003.[79]

Another woman who defied conventional gender norms was Naw Louisa Benson,[80] who successfully combined two contrasting roles – beauty queen and insurgent leader. In many ways, Louisa represented the ideal of feminine grace and beauty to which many modern women aspired. She initially rose to fame as a film actress and was twice crowned as Miss Burma (in 1956 and 1958). As a member of Rangoon's social elite, she associated with many powerful men including Ne Win, who was reputed to have 'dated every Miss Burma.'[81] In 1964, Louisa mar-

---

77 For an account of her efforts to find out what happened to Sao Kya Seng, see Bertil Lintner, 'Burma keeps mum on the fate of the prince of Hsipaw', *Bangkok Post*, 18 August 1988. Inge later married an American, Ted Sargent, and in 1999 they established Burma Lifeline, a non-profit organisation that provides food, housing materials and health care for Burmese refugees.

78 Smith, *Burma: insurgency*, 266, 333–34; Elliott, *The white umbrella*, 347, 357, 363–64; Chao Tzang Yawnghwe, *The Shan of Burma*, 18, 20.

79 William Barnes, 'Touch of nobility dies with a Shan princess: The former first lady of Burma shattered many feudal taboos', *South China Morning Post*, 30 January 2003.

80 Louise's mother, Chit Khin, was an ethnic Karen; her father, Saw Benson, was a Portuguese Jew.

81 Elliott, *The white umbrella*, 311.

ried Brigadier Lin Tin, who was then commander of the KNDO's 5th Brigade. Lin Tin had surrendered to government forces along with other Karen insurgent leaders in 1963, but his troops remained stationed near Thaton and it was rumoured that he intended to use his wife's connections in order to assassinate Ne Win. When Lin Tin was killed in September 1965, Louisa led his troops back into the jungle to join the KNU forces on the Thai-Burma border.[82] She remained active in the Karen insurgency until 1967, before moving to the USA with her new American husband, Glen Craig. Until her death in February 2010, Louisa continued to advocate Karen rights, ethnic unity and the restoration of democracy as co-founder of the Burma Forum and board member of the US Campaign for Burma. She was also widely admired as a role model for Karen women in the exiled opposition movement.[83]

Like Nu before him, Ne Win attempted to convince the public that women's involvement in underground organisations was detrimental to family relationships. When communist leaders attended peace talks with the government in August 1963, the media paid considerable attention to the women who accompanied Red Flag leader Thakin Soe's delegation, including his daughter, Ni Ni Soe, and several 'attractive young girls in khaki uniforms'.[84] Rumours that the women were actually Thakin Soe's mistresses reinforced the government's claim that communist women engaged in immoral behaviour. *The Nation* also reported that Ni Ni Soe denounced her elder sister, who had remained in Rangoon, as a 'traitor' both to her family and the communist cause.[85] Ni Ni Soe returned to Rangoon herself in late 1964, amid reports that she had lost faith in the party and could no longer endure her father's ideological inflexibility.[86] In February 1969, *The Guardian* published a photograph of Red Flag communist Ma Zwe Myint and two other women surrendering to government forces. All three women held babies in their arms.[87] This media coverage may have been part of a deliberate government strategy

---

82 Lin Tin was shot by unknown assassins outside a cinema hall in Thaton. Bertil Lintner suggests that he may have been murdered because of his role in the alleged plot to assassinate Ne Win. Lintner, *Burma in revolt*, 181.

83 Personal interviews with KWO members, Chiang Mai, 20 June 2005.

84 *The Nation* (Rangoon), 8 August 1963.

85 *Ibid.*

86 *Eastern World* (London), 19, 1 (January 1965): 17.

87 *The Guardian* (Rangoon), 26 February 1969.

to convince female communists to surrender, but it also reflected deep-rooted beliefs about women's 'proper' role, which was in the home.

Although some families were split apart as a result of the insurrections, the military's relentless persecution of its opponents actually strengthened the political resolve of many women whose family members remained active in the underground resistance. After CPB leader Thakin Zin's death in 1975, his widow Daw Kyi Kyi held annual remembrance services in his honour until she was arrested and imprisoned in 1987.[88] Although she was briefly released in 1988, within a year she was rearrested and spent the next ten years in jail.[89] The Ludu family also faced the constant threat of arrest for their continued opposition to the military regime. Ludu Daw Amar's eldest son, Soe Win, joined the CPB in 1963 and was killed during the party purges in 1967, the year the authorities closed down the *Ludu* newspaper for good. Her second son, Than Joung, was detained from 1966 to 1972 for his involvement in the student union movement. When he went underground with the CPB to avoid rearrest in 1978, Ludu Daw Amar, U Hla and their youngest son Ko Nyein Chan were imprisoned for more than a year. Following her release, Ludu Daw Amar continued to speak out against social injustice and military oppression. Although the regime's strict censorship laws prevented her from writing about political issues, she was able to express her opinions freely via the expatriate Burmese media.[90] She was widely admired for her personal determination, courage and strength as well as her literary works, and writers and supporters from all over Burma travelled to Mandalay to celebrate her birthday from the mid-1980s until her death in 2008.

When assessing women's political influence in the parliamentary period, we need to consider several factors. Looking at the total number of women in senior positions in political organisations, women's influ-

---

88   Thakin Zin became CPB chairman following Thakin Than Tun's death in October 1968. He was killed in the Pegu Yoma (mountains) on 15 March 1975.

89   Daw Kyi Kyi was released in June 1999, but her health had suffered while in incarceration and she died in June 2001 at the age of 82. See Ma Ma Pyone, 'Spice, politics & inspiration – a tribute to Daw Kyi Kyi', in Altsean Burma, *Burma – women's voices for change*, edited by the Thanakha Team (Bangkok: Alternative Asean Network on Burma, 2002), 4–6.

90   Min Zin, 'Ludu Daw Amar: speaking truth to power', *The Irrawaddy* 10, 8 (October 2002): 25–28; 'Do or die: people power should be used if Burma junta doesn't respond to NLD call for action – respected Burmese author Ama', *Democratic Voice of Burma*, 26 April 2006; 'Burma's "mother" author Ama supports call for prisoners' release', *Democratic Voice of Burma*, 4 October 2006.

ence was negligible: a handful of women were elected to parliament, only one was appointed to the Cabinet, and very few women held senior positions in communist and ethnic parties. Most of these women initially gained prominence through their familial connections to male political and military elites. Sao Hearn Hkam and Olive Yang were born into hereditary ruling families; others, like Khin Kyi and Louisa Benson, married political and military leaders. It is highly unlikely that women like Khin Kyi and Ba Maung Chain would have been invited to assume high profile political roles – as Ambassador to India and Nepal and Minister for Karen State – were it not for their late husband's and father's reputations. To a large extent, women were expected to carry out duties on behalf of their spouses (living and deceased). Sao Hearn Hkam became a member of parliament at her husband's request, while Louisa Benson assumed command of her husband's KNDO forces after he was assassinated. Yet each of these women earned respect in her own right – Khin Kyi was widely admired for her leading role in various social welfare organisations; Ludu Daw Amar was a celebrated political and social commentator. Women demonstrated a remarkable capacity to adapt to the constantly changing political and military conditions in post-independence society. Louisa Benson made the transition from beauty queen to insurgent leader, and then to peace activist, seem effortless. Not all women were as successful in their new roles, however. As a member of parliament, Sao Hearn Hkam had the support of many Shan nationalists, but after the coup she struggled to unite the various factions in the Shan State War Council.

All Burmese who dared to oppose the government faced the threat of arrest and imprisonment, especially after Ne Win assumed power in 1962, but politically active women also faced discrimination because of their gender. Negotiating the boundaries of acceptable gender roles was challenging for all women, but particularly for those in positions of authority. A woman could be tough, but she was still expected to retain her femininity. Women in insurgent organisations could be guerrilla fighters, but they were also expected to raise children and nurse the sick. Olive Yang was a powerful military commander who inspired fear and respect in her followers, but her masculine behaviour made her the brunt of many jokes and a target of abuse. Women who chose to remain in Burma after the coup showed great courage and determination in opposing the military regime, but under constant surveillance by authorities they were unable to effect any real political or social change. Those who left Burma had greater opportunities to engage in activism in a more politically open environment, but apart from advocating on behalf of their compatriots their ability to influence affairs within Burma remained limited. In this regard, women were no more, and no less, successful than men.

Conclusions

At the end of World War Two, many Burmese women hoped that independence would provide them with greater economic, social and political opportunities. The AFPFL government initiated social and economic reforms and adopted a new constitution which, in theory, guaranteed equality for all Burmese. In reality, however, there was little change in prevailing notions of gender that both deterred women from seeking positions of public authority and confined them within domestic and nurturing roles. One reason for this was that the nationalist emphasis on preserving 'traditional' Burmese values was carried over into the independence period by the AFPFL leadership. Women were encouraged to prioritise their family duties and to enter 'suitable' professions that would not impinge on their ability to carry out their domestic roles. The process of modernisation that could have expanded women's economic roles was cut short by the outbreak of communist and ethnic insurrections.

The highly factional nature of national politics made it extremely difficult for women to gain greater access to political power. The government was dominated by conservative male elites who built up patronage networks in order to mobilise the general population in support of their policies. Politicians' wives were expected to support their husbands and only assumed official political roles when men were unable to do so. Women actively participated in the insurrections, but they too were confined to subordinate positions and only took on greater leadership roles when male leaders were imprisoned or killed. Within the communist movement, the ideological emphasis on egalitarianism did not lead to any significant increase in women's power. Although women braved the harsh jungle conditions alongside their male comrades, their primary responsibility was still caring for both children and combatants;

few women attained senior positions in the communist party structure. Despite their relatively 'traditional' roles, female communists were criticised by government supporters for their allegedly 'immoral' behaviour. Ethnic minority leaders encouraged women to assert their political rights in the fight against Burman domination, but female politicians and insurgents also faced public censure if they deviated from accepted norms of female behaviour. Prolonged insurgent activity contributed to the rise of the armed forces, most notably the *tatmadaw*, as a powerful force in Burmese politics. The next chapter will analyse the impact of military rule on women.

6

The Decline in Women's Status under Military Rule

For nearly 50 years, Burma was ruled by a series of military dictatorships – the Revolutionary Council (1962–74), Burma Socialist Programme Party (BSPP) (1974–88), State Law and Order Restoration Council (SLORC) (1988–97), and State Peace and Development Council (SPDC) (1997–March 2011). Although the SPDC has now handed over power to a nominally 'civilian' government, the military is likely to maintain a controlling influence in and over the national parliament in the immediate future.[1] This chapter examines how the increasing militarisation of Burmese society between 1962 and 1988 undermined women's ability to participate in political, economic and social life and therefore limited their access to power. As the male-dominated military extended its control over the country's political and economic institutions, women were effectively barred from attaining positions of influence in government and lost much of their former economic independence and status. The regime's educational policies disadvantaged many women, while its cultural policies were used to control women's behaviour. Ethnic minority women, in particular, faced increasing discrimination and violence as a result of the government's repressive policies, especially those living in areas of military conflict. Political repression, economic hardship, social control and increased violence were all factors that disempowered most women. Yet a minority were able to gain influence through their family relations with members either of the military elite or the leadership of resistance and opposition

---

1   Many senior military officers retired from military service in order to contest the 2010 elections. Thein Sein, former SPDC Prime Minister, is now the President of the Union and head of the Union Solidarity and Development Party (USDP) and Tin Aung Myint Oo, former SPDC Secretary-1, is one of two vice presidents. The military-backed USDP won nearly 60 per cent of seats in both houses of the national legislature and a further 25 per cent of parliamentary seats are reserved for Defence Services personnel.

movements, indicating that some women were able to negotiate alternative paths to power.

The rise of military power

The expansion of military power in Burma began soon after the country won independence. Between 1948 and 1960, the armed forces increased from 15,000 to 85,000 service personnel in response to the continuing civil war with communist and ethnically based insurgents. Military leaders largely remained outside the struggle for political power until September 1958 when U Nu, faced with the AFPFL split and security concerns, asked army chief General Ne Win to form a caretaker government. Ne Win and senior military officers took over the key administrative and policy-making positions until civilian government was restored in February 1960. After the 1962 coup, the armed forces more than doubled in size to reach 170,000 by the time of the 1988 uprising.[2] Although the armed forces represented less than five per cent of the total population, the military's power increased dramatically during this period as its (male) leaders took over and transformed existing political, economic and social institutions, cementing the *tatmadaw*'s place as the most powerful institution in the state.

The Burmese military has always been a predominantly male institution, with females representing less than one per cent of armed forces personnel during the 1970s and 1980s. Women in the military were assigned primarily to medical and lower level administrative duties; none had combat roles.[3] The low level of female recruitment reflected cultural beliefs about male superiority that discouraged most women from entering professions associated with physical strength, high prestige and authority. During the turbulent first decade of independence, many Burmese regarded the army as the only institution that was capable

---

2   After the 1988 uprisings, the government devoted considerably more resources to defence in an effort to suppress its political opponents. In 2008, the military's total strength was estimated at around 350–400,000 personnel. See Andrew Selth, *Transforming the tatmadaw: the Burmese armed forces since 1988*, Canberra Papers on Strategy and Defence No. 113 (Canberra: Strategic and Defence Studies Centre, Research School of Pacific and Asian Studies, The Australian National University, 1996), 38–39, 48–58; Sean Turnell, *Burma's economy 2008: current situation and prospects for reform* (Sydney: Burma Economic Watch/ Economics Department, Macquarie University, May 2008), 7.

3   Mills, 'Militarism, civil war and women's status', 274; Mi Mi Khaing, *The world of Burmese women*, 167–68.

of holding the country together.[4] After 1962, although the *tatmadaw*'s repressive measures and human rights abuses against civilians compromised its status and reputation, the army still offered the best means of personal security and social mobility for ordinary Burmese. Because it was almost impossible for women to ascend to senior positions in the military, its monopoly of power meant that the vast majority of women were excluded from exercising political, economic and social influence.

The decline in women's political influence under military rule

Burma's brief period of parliamentary democracy presented some elite women with opportunities to gain political office, and probably would have allowed more women greater access to political power had it been given the chance to evolve. After the coup, the authoritarian system of rule imposed by military leaders made it extremely difficult for women to gain political power or even express political views. Ne Win immediately set about dismantling the political institutions of the former democratic system and installing military authority in their place. Parliament was dissolved, civilian politicians were imprisoned, and the 1947 constitution was annulled. Ne Win established a Revolutionary Council composed entirely of male military officers to administer the country, with himself as chairman. The Revolutionary Council formed its own political party, the Burma Socialist Programme Party (BSPP) (also known as the 'Lanzin Party'), and developed an official ideology to justify its takeover. 'The Burmese way to socialism' renounced parliamentary government for failing to further socialist development, while 'The system of correlation of man and his environment' declared that the 'working people' needed a strong authority to govern them in order to create a just society free from suffering and exploitation.[5] In March 1964, the Revolutionary Council abolished all political parties except the BSPP, and Burma became a one-party state.

Despite its professed socialist ideals of equality, the BSPP was dominated by the military and, therefore, by men. During the 1960s, the BSPP was a 'Cadre Party' comprising only 24 full members at its largest, 13 of

---

4   Selth, *Transforming the tatmadaw*, 39.

5   Burma Socialist Programme Party, *The philosophy of the Burma Socialist Programme Party: the system of correlation of man and his environment* (Rangoon: Ministry of Information, 1963). This book also includes *The Burmese way to socialism*.

whom were also on the Revolutionary Council. All were men. From 1964 onwards, the government convened annual peasants' and workers' conferences in an effort to strengthen its power base and ostensibly to involve 'the people' in the socialist revolution.[6] By establishing People's Workers' and Peasants' Councils as formal state organisations (in 1968 and 1969 respectively), the government could maintain that ordinary people were allowed to participate in political and policy-making processes. In reality, however, these mass organisations were formed to mobilise popular support for the military-dominated central government.[7] Peasants' and workers' council members received education and training in BSPP ideology and 'correct attitudes', and were expected to remain 'loyal and faithful to the Lanzin'.[8] In 1971, the BSPP began to recruit mass membership in order to become a 'People's Party', still dominated, however, by the military.[9] As a military/male-dominated organisation, the BSPP provided no institutional incentive or support for female leadership, and so restricted women's access to official positions of political power.

Nonetheless, many women joined the BSPP together with their husbands in order to gain the opportunities associated with membership. By January 1981, women accounted for 15 per cent of the party membership, with 225,000 members out of a total 1.5 million.[10] Although a number of civilian women held positions of responsibility within the party, the military continued to dominate the higher echelons of the government – which were almost exclusively male.[11] Both councils at the central level were chaired by male military leaders and, although some women held executive positions in the lower-level township councils, their roles were limited to implementing the party's pre-determined policies and programs. While some women executives had relevant professional expertise, it appears that many gained their positions because they were married to senior military officers. Daw Yin Yin

---

6   *The Guardian* (Rangoon), 2–5 March 1964; S.C. Banerji, 'Burma's peasant seminars', *Far Eastern Economic Review*, 30 July 1964, pp. 204–05.

7   By 1980, the peasants' council had 7.6 million members, while the workers' council numbered 1.5 million, the difference reflecting the rural–urban distribution of the total population. These membership figures are taken from David I. Steinberg, *Burma: a socialist nation of Southeast Asia* (Boulder, Colorado: Westview Press, 1982), 80–81.

8   *The Guardian* (Rangoon), 27 February 1969.

9   Steinberg, *Burma: a socialist nation of Southeast Asia*, 79–80.

10 *Ibid.*, 103.

11 David I. Steinberg, *Burma: the state of Myanmar* (Washington: Georgetown University Press, 2001), 214; Mi Mi Khaing, *The world of Burmese women*, 160–74.

Mya, whose husband was a senior official in the Union military police, was appointed head of the Economics Department at the Institute of Education in 1970. She also served on the Council of the Central Cooperative Society, the Kamayut Township Cooperative Council, and the Kamayut Workers' Council. Daw Kyi Kyi Hla, the wife of a retired army major, became head of the Philosophy Department at Rangoon University in 1972. She undertook organisational work for the BSPP, which involved teaching party ideology courses and compiling political documents.[12] Women were only able to gain such appointments with the approval of senior party leaders.

The 1974 Constitution

In the early 1970s, BSPP leaders moved to develop a new constitution which they claimed would include socialist principles to place power in the hands of 'the people'. The 1974 Constitution declared that all citizens were equal under the law and guaranteed women's rights to political, economic and social equality as well as legal rights regarding marriage, divorce, division of property, inheritance and child custody.[13] The real purpose of the new constitution, however, was to endow the BSPP – and thus the military – with a monopoly of political power. The state was to adopt a single-party system with the BSPP as the sole political party.[14] All representatives of the unicameral People's Assembly (*Pyithu Hluttaw*) were either BSPP members or approved by party leaders. Josef Silverstein noted at the time that the new constitution, far from transferring power to the people, actually concentrated political authority in the hands of the (male) military leaders of the BSPP.[15] On 2 March 1974 the Revolutionary Council officially declared the transfer of power and the People's Assembly elected a State Council, which in turn appointed Ne

---

12 Mi Mi Khaing, *The world of Burmese women*, 160–64.

13 See Articles 22 and 154 of 'The Constitution of the Socialist Republic of the Union of Burma, 1974' in Marc Weller (ed.), *Democracy and politics in Burma: a collection of documents* (Manerplaw, Burma: Government Printing Office of the National Coalition Government of the Union of Burma, 1993), 110, 132. Daw Aye Myint, Daw Say Mya and Daw Kyu Kyu Mar were the three female members of the 97-member constitutional drafting commission: see Albert D. Moscotti, *Burma's constitution and elections of 1974*, Research notes and discussions no. 5 (Singapore: Institute of Southeast Asian Studies, September 1977), 8.

14 Article 11 of 'The Constitution of the Socialist Republic of the Union of Burma, 1974', in Weller (ed.), *Democracy and politics in Burma*, 108.

15 Josef Silverstein, 'From soldiers to civilians: the new constitution of Burma in action', in Josef Silverstein (ed.), *The future of Burma in perspective: a symposium* (Athens: Ohio University, Center for International Studies, Southeast Asia Program, 1974), 88–91.

Win as Chairman and President of the Union. The People's Assembly also elected the Council of Ministers as well as Councils of People's Justices, People's Attorneys and People's Inspectors.

Women were consistently under-represented in the national government, comprising less than three per cent of the 450-seat People's Assembly throughout the 1970s and 1980s.[16] Although more women were involved in administrative activities for lower level councils, they were essentially agents for the policies of the BSPP leadership. People's Judges, for instance, were 'chosen not for their training in the law, but are elected to serve in turn from the position of the Township Council members'.[17] Despite her recognition of this practice, Mi Mi Khaing maintained that the low level of female political representation simply reflected women's acceptance of male authority and their own reluctance to assume leadership roles.[18] This explanation, however, fails to take into account the hierarchical structure imposed by the military on the BSPP government. The military's top-down command structure reinforced existing Burmese concepts of male superiority and authority, which historically had discouraged women from pursuing political careers. Since it was almost impossible for women to ascend to high levels within the military, their influence in national politics remained negligible. Women who served as government officials were expected to defer to the decisions of male military leaders. Outside the government, fear of the military's brutal suppression of all political opposition prevented most men and women from engaging in political activities.

Restrictions on political opposition and civil society

The BSPP leadership did not tolerate public dissent or criticism from party members, let alone from anyone outside the party.[19] Peasants,

---

16   Mi Mi Khaing, *The world of Burmese women*, 150; Belak, *Gathering strength*, 257. The percentage of female politicians also remained low in other Southeast Asian countries, including Thailand where only 2.8 per cent of female members of parliament were elected between 1932 and 1991. Tamara Loos has argued that while the male leaders of the 1932 coup took steps to introduce universal suffrage, they were primarily concerned with promoting class rather than gender equality. See Loos, 'The politics of women's suffrage in Thailand', 179–82, 190n.

17   Mi Mi Khaing, *The world of Burmese women*, 172.

18   *Ibid.*, 150–59.

19   See Burma Socialist Programme Party, 'Chapter III, Code of Discipline for Party Members' in 'The Constitution of the Burma Socialist Programme Party for the transitional period of its construction,' Adopted by the Revolutionary Council, July 4, 1962.

workers and civil servants were prohibited from engaging in any political activities other than those sanctioned by the BSPP and other state-controlled mass organisations. Military authorities also imposed restrictions on civil society: independent organisations were prohibited and the few professional associations that were allowed to operate were closely monitored by the authorities. Consequently, most people were prevented from participating – or were too afraid to participate – in political processes, or express any views that were not explicitly condoned by the authorities.

A comparison between Burma and Indonesia illustrates how military rule restricted women's ability to participate in civil organisations and politics in general. Under General Suharto's 'New Order' regime, women's organisations were either disbanded or brought under government control. Wives of male civil servants and members of the police and armed forces were obliged to join one of the two mass women's organisations – the Dharma Wanita and Dharma Pertiwi – whereas female civil servants and women who were not married to government employees had to request permission to become members. The leadership of these women's organisations reflected the official centralised, hierarchical power structure. Wives of government ministers held the senior decision-making positions, while the wives of lower level government employees and ordinary members were expected to implement policies and programs in 'appropriate' areas such as social welfare and health. All members were expected to support the ruling Golkar party and were forbidden from joining other political organisations. According to Saskia Wieringa, while the wives of government ministers and senior officials gained social and political power through their leadership of women's organisations, ordinary members resented having to devote time and money to their organisational work, but feared that their husbands would lose their jobs if they did not participate.[20] The structure and policies of the Dharma Wanita and Dharma Pertiwi bore a striking resemblance to the Burmese women's organisations formed under the auspices of the SLORC government in the early 1990s, which form the subject of chapter 8. I mention them here in order to demon-

---

20   See Saskia Wieringa, 'Matrilinearity and women's interests: the Minangkabau of Western Sumatra', in Saskia Wieringa (ed.), *Subversive women: historical experiences of gender and resistance* (London; Atlantic Highlands, N. J.: Zed Books, 1995), 262–65.

strate the extent to which Burmese women were excluded from political processes during the period of BSPP rule, when there were no women's organisations at all and thus no official outlet for women's political or social aspirations.

The BSPP did face opposition from Buddhist monks, university students, intellectuals and the former political elite, who resented the military's attempts to curb their social and political influence, as well as ethnic minorities, whose hatred of the military was exacerbated by its violent campaigns against ethnic armies and civilians. With the exception of the *sangha*, women were involved in all these opposition groups. In the previous chapter, we saw how the wives of civilian politicians refused to be intimidated by military authorities when their husbands were arrested and imprisoned following the coup. Many women remained active in underground communist and ethnic organisations, which continued their armed resistance against government forces well into the 1980s (and beyond in some cases). As we shall see below, female university students and teachers were at the forefront of anti-government demonstrations in the 1960s and 1970s and, most notably, the mass popular uprisings in 1988.

Military leaders sought to extend their control over the population and silence their opponents by imposing restrictions on the press and other media. Private newspapers were either closed down or nationalised, and the government's Press Scrutiny Board expressly prohibited 'any criticism of a non-constructive type of the work of government departments',[21] which obliged publishers to practise self-censorship in order to avoid prosecution and imprisonment. After the *Ludu* newspaper was shut down in 1967, Ludu Daw Amar was no longer able to write freely about politics and turned her literary focus to history and culture, although she continued to speak out about the adverse effects of military rule including poverty, censorship and discrimination against ethnic minorities.[22] Khin Myo Chit edited the government's *Working People's Daily* newspaper during the 1960s, but she was dismissed after writing an article in which she described visiting former political prisoners with-

21 Anna Allott, *Inked over, ripped out: Burmese storytellers and the censors* (Chiang Mai: Silkworm books, 1994), esp. 5–12.

22 Her elder sons' involvement with student activists and the CPB also meant that her writing was scrutinised closely by the authorities. See Min Zin, 'Ludu Daw Amar: speaking truth to power', *The Irrawaddy* 10, 8 (October 2002): 25–28.

out fear of intimidation from military intelligence officers.[23] Despite the draconian censorship laws, some writers managed to incorporate subtle political messages into their literary outputs. Mo Cho Thinn's short story, 'Heartless Day', which describes a woman's attempts to sell her *longyi* in order to pay for her ill son's medical treatment, draws attention to the worsening socioeconomic conditions under military rule.[24] Overall, however, women who made a stand against the regime's repressive policies were unable to effect any real political or social change. The majority of women were more concerned with making ends meet in a society that was increasingly burdened by poverty and corruption as a result of military leaders' economic policies and incompetence.

Women's economic status under military rule

Military rule undermined women's status not only in the political sphere but also in the economy, where women previously had important and influential roles. The BSPP's professed goal was to construct a socialist economy that would improve the living standards of ordinary Burmese, who had been exploited under the former capitalist system.[25] In order to eliminate foreign economic influences and divest the old elite of power, the Revolutionary Council nationalised all economic enterprises, expelled foreign entrepreneurs and merchants, and discouraged international trade. Effectively this closed off the Burmese economy from the outside world and slowed the process of economic modernisation. The military personnel who were appointed to manage the nationalised businesses had little education or relevant experience, and industrial and agricultural production fell, leading to shortages of basic necessities and the emergence of a rampant black market. As prices soared, more women entered the paid workforce to supplement meagre family incomes. Female participation in the paid labour force rose from 33

---

23 Daw Khin Myo Chit, 'Dandruff in my halo', *Working People's Daily*, 21 July 1986.

24 An English translation of this story, which was originally published in 1992, can be found in Anna Allott's *Inked over, ripped out*. Mo Cho Thinn began writing after the universities were closed following the 1988 uprising. Her father, Tin Moe, a poet and prominent supporter of Aung San Suu Kyi, was arrested in 1991.

25 Burma Socialist Programme Party, Central Organization Committee, *Party Seminar 1965: speeches of General Ne Win and political report of the General-Secretary* (Rangoon: Sapay Beikman Press, 1966), 64, 101.

per cent to 36 per cent between 1973 and 1983,[26] but this increase was largely in response to deteriorating economic conditions, and so failed to give women commensurate influence in society. The vast majority of working women struggled to support themselves and their families. An important exception to the overall reduction in women's economic status was evident among women whose economic and political influence derived from their family connections to men in power.

Nationalisation of industry

Between 1963 and 1964, the Revolutionary Council nationalised all banks, private firms and retail establishments dealing in essential consumer goods. In place of the retail outlets, the government set up 'People's Stores', while private firms were replaced with 23 centrally-controlled State Corporations, all of which were managed by military personnel. Many former business owners and employees lost their livelihoods, since the military managers tended to reward their loyal subordinates with jobs. One woman, Ma Kyin Yi, later described how her ethnically Chinese father's wholesale business and rice mill were 'taken over by the Co-operatives and they had [employed] all their own people'.[27] Domestic production and distribution of food and consumer goods soon faltered under the management of inexperienced military officers. In January 1965, the *New York Times* reported that military leaders 'conceded that production had been set back because Government managers of state enterprises were mostly army officers who lacked experience .... However, this was accepted by the Government as a price worth paying for taking the nation of 24 million people down the "Burmese road to Socialism".'[28] The disruption to domestic production of consumer goods, combined with the decline in imports, led to widespread shortages of basic necessities including clothing, cooking oil, kerosene, soap and medicines, placing

---

26 'Labour Force by Sex and Residence, 1973, 1983 and 1990', in Government of the Union of Myanmar, Central Statistical Organization, *Statistical profile of children and women in Myanmar 1993* ([Yangon]: Central Statistical Organization, Government of the Union of Myanmar, [199?]), 28. Hereafter cited as '*Statistical profile of children and women in Myanmar 1993*'.

27 Mya Than Tint, *On the road to Mandalay: tales of ordinary people*, translated by Ohnmar Khin and Sein Kyaw Hlaing; illustrated by U Win Pe (Bangkok: White Orchid Press, 1996), 174.

28 'Despite shock, Burma rushes to socialism', *New York Times*, 18 January 1965.

enormous strain on ordinary women who struggled to feed, clothe and care for their families.

Military mismanagement of the nationalised State Corporations and People's Stores led to an increase in smuggling and the rapid expansion of the black market, which infamously became known as the '24th Corporation'. After her father lost his job, Ma Kyin Yi's family was reduced to selling home-made liquor on the black market because '[t]he government had its own liquor stalls [and] didn't give licences to private ones.'[29] The military's involvement in black market activities partially accounted for the government's failure to control the illicit trade in consumer goods and luxury items. Military managers of People's Stores and other state enterprises acquired goods at low prices and then sold them on the black market, thereby enriching themselves and their families and other dependents. The wives and daughters of high-ranking military officers were also heavily involved in black market trade. Ne Win apparently condoned the participation of women in this blatant corruption, noting that 'the men from our Defence Services know only how to wage war ... they ate what the wife [sic] cooked for them.'[30] Limited official efforts to control black market trade had a devastating effect on ordinary Burmese, many of whom lost their life savings when the government demonetarised 100 and 50 kyat notes in May 1964.[31] People who tried to exchange their old currency received partial compensation only from the government. One Karenni woman, Ah Mu Doe, recalled that 'Even if we gave them 10,000 or 20,000 *kyat* worth of 100 *kyat* notes, they gave back only 5,000 *kyat*. We lost so much money!'[32]

Between 1973 and 1983, the percentage of women working in manufacturing and wholesale industries fell in response to the overall decline in these sectors.[33] There was a substantial increase in the percentage of women employed in the agricultural sector over the same period. Two-

29   Mya Than Tint, *On the road to Mandalay*, 174.

30   Cited in Burma Socialist Programme Party, *Party Seminar*, 191.

31   The government's rationale for the demonetisation was described in 'The elimination of black money', *Working People's Daily*, 18 May 1964 and editorials in *The Nation* (Rangoon), 18 May 1964 and *The Guardian* (Rangoon), 19 May 1964.

32   Ah Mu Doe, 'Death threats & the disappeared duck', in Altsean Burma, *Burma – women's voices together*, 11.

33   'Distribution of employed labour force by industry and sex: Myanmar, 1973 and 1983' in M. I. Khin Maung, *The Myanmar labour force: growth and change, 1973–83*, Occasional Paper No. 94 (Singapore: Institute of Southeast Asian Studies, 1997), 63–64.

thirds of the paid female workforce engaged in agricultural and related occupations, but this figure would have increased substantially if the official statistics had included the unpaid labour performed by female relatives of male agriculturalists. The government's economic failure in the agricultural sector therefore had a devastating effect on many women and their families.

Agricultural decline

Before World War Two, Burma was recognised as 'the rice bowl of Asia' because of its productive agricultural sector, and rice exports averaged over three million tons annually. During the first 12 years of independence, annual rice exports averaged 1.5 million tons. Between 1961 and 1973, however, they dropped to less than 700,000 tons on average and plummeted to a mere 49,000 tons in 1989.[34] Although poor weather conditions and population growth provide a partial explanation for the decline in export levels, government mismanagement was the main reason for the stagnation of the rice economy. On 18 February 1963, the Revolutionary Council announced that the state would assume control over the rice trade. The government advanced loans to farmers, who were required to sell a quota of their harvested paddy to the government at fixed (below market) prices. Since the government monopolised the rice export trade, the difference between the procurement price paid to the farmer and the export price constituted an implicit tax on farmers and gave them no incentive to increase production. Farmers who failed to meet the required quotas were threatened with arrest and the seizure of their land.[35] The combined effect of the government's forced crop procurement, taxation policies and threats of land confiscation was devastating for many poor rural farmers and their families.

In urban areas, the government sold rice at subsidised prices to military personnel and civil servants, although its allocations failed to

---

34 Mya Maung, 'Military management of the Burmese economy: problems and prospects', in Josef Silverstein (ed.), *The future of Burma in perspective: a symposium* (Athens: Ohio University, Center for International Studies, Southeast Asia Program, 1974), 17–18; Jalal Alamgir, 'Against the current: the survival of authoritarianism in Burma', *Pacific Affairs* 70, 3 (Autumn 1997): 341.

35 Mya Maung, 'Burma's economic performance under military rule: an assessment', *Asian Survey* 37, 6 (June 1997): 511; Steinberg, *Burma: a socialist nation of Southeast Asia*, 91–92; Donald M. Seekins, *The disorder in order: the army-state in Burma since 1962* (Bangkok: White Lotus Press, 2002), 112.

satisfy the needs of the growing population.[36] Many ordinary people faced severe economic hardship as real incomes did not keep up with rising inflation, which was around 20 per cent in the mid-1970s.[37] The decline in living standards was evident in the rising cost of basic necessities including food. In 1961, the average urban Burmese spent nearly half his or her income on food; in 1976, they had to spend nearly 80 per cent.[38] The government's economic policies, while not gender-specific, affected women more directly than men, since women continued to bear the main or sole responsibility for putting food on the table. Under deteriorating economic conditions, exercising control over household finances was increasingly perceived by many women as a burden rather than as a privilege.[39] High inflation and widespread food shortages led to the outbreak of riots in towns and villages throughout Burma from the late 1960s onwards. These riots were brutally suppressed by the military authorities. In May 1974, workers went out on strike in Mandalay, Rangoon and other parts of the country over food shortages and the government's preferential treatment of *tatmadaw* employees. On 6 June army troops fired on the protesters, officially killing 22 and wounding 80 (although unofficially the death toll was reported to be over 100).[40] The 1974 labour unrest had a distinctly political character, which foreshadowed the more serious uprising in 1988.

Women's representation and influence in professions

Aside from agriculture, women increased their representation in professional, clerical and service employment. Growing opportunities for women in these areas reflected prevailing stereotypes about gender-appropriate work as much as they did the economic policies of the military government. While some women did hold positions of considerable status and responsibility – as doctors, lawyers and academics

---

36 Annual population growth averaged around two per cent per annum between 1963 and 1983, compared to 1.5 per cent during the 1950s. See *Statistical profile of children and women in Myanmar 1993*, 5; Khin Maung, *The Myanmar labour force*, 9.

37 'Regional statistical indicators', *Far Eastern Economic Review Yearbook 1977*, 14.

38 David I. Steinberg, *Burma's road toward development: growth and ideology under military rule* (Boulder: Westview Press, 1981), 78 and table 5.1.

39 Belak, *Gathering strength*, 157; All Burma Students' Democratic Front, *Burma and the role of women* (Bangkok: Documentation and Research Centre, All Burma Students' Democratic Front, 13 March 1997), 34–36. Hereafter cited as 'ABSDF, *Burma and the role of women*'.

40 Lintner, *Burma in revolt*, 363; Seekins, *The disorder in order*, 94.

– the percentage of women employed in managerial positions across all sectors dropped from 13 to 11 per cent between 1973 and 1983.[41] Even in female-dominated professions like teaching, only 38 to 41 per cent of senior positions were held by women.[42] Women increasingly entered the civil service, although usually at lower levels than males.[43] Those without familial connections to senior military officials found that the most prestigious and well-paid jobs were 'already "booked" by sons or daughters or close relatives of the Ministers or Generals'.[44] Most government salaries barely covered basic living costs, and many civil servants were forced to take up additional work in order to supplement their low incomes. Teachers and doctors without connections to the military elite were also more likely to be sent to work in remote areas. Since it was not culturally acceptable for women to travel or live alone, many female graduates had no choice but to take up more menial jobs.[45]

The steady deterioration of the economy under military rule increasingly drove thousands of destitute women into low-paying factory jobs, domestic slavery and prostitution. Others left Burma to seek work in neighbouring countries like Thailand, China and Bangladesh, where they were particularly vulnerable to abuse because they were not legally recognised as either refugees or migrants, and so were denied access to legal, health and educational services. The vast majority of these women came from ethnic minority areas, where employment opportunities were severely limited due to sub-standard educational, health and social services and continuing conflict between government and ethnic armies. In conflict areas, the government's policies of forced relocation and labour requisition as well as the constant threat of violence were all factors that compelled women to leave their homes and communities in search of better security and employment abroad. These issues will be explored more fully in chapter 9.

---

41   Khin Maung, *The Myanmar labour force*, 66.

42   'Percentage of female teachers by rank 1983–84 to 1992–93', in *Statistical profile of children and women in Myanmar 1993*, 41.

43   Khin Maung, *The Myanmar labour force*, 63–64, 66–67; Steinberg, *Burma: a socialist nation of Southeast Asia*, 103.

44   Young Woman from Myanmar, 'Neutral thoughts', in Altsean Burma, *Burma – women's voices for change*, 59.

45   Kalaya Nee, 'Bitter medicine' in Altsean Burma, *Burma – women's voices for change*, 73–76.

Figure 6.1: Housewives marching in Mandalay, September 1988. Photograph courtesy of Bertil Lintner.

Economic crisis and the 1988 uprising

By 1987, Burma faced a looming economic crisis due to continued rising inflation, growing foreign debt and negative GDP growth.[46] In September, Ne Win ordered the demonetisation of all 75, 35 and 25 kyat notes, which wiped out up to 80 per cent of the currency in circulation. Unlike the two previous demonetisations in 1964 and 1985, the government did not offer any compensation and panic spread throughout the population. Ah Mu Doe's sense of frustration reflected that felt by many Burmese who had lost all their savings: 'All the money we had kept for building a house, buying a garden, or sending our children to school was lost. We had nothing left and had to start again like we had just been born.'[47] By December, the economy had deteriorated to such an extent that Burma was classified as a Least Developed Country (LDC) by the United Nations.

In 1988, unrest over economic mismanagement and political oppression by the government led to widespread demonstrations throughout

---

46   Seekins, *The disorder in order*, 124–26.

47   Ah Mu Doe, 'Death threats & the disappeared duck', 11.

Figure 6.2: Women workers from North Okkalapa demonstrate. Photograph courtesy of Bertil Lintner.

the country, most notably in August, when millions of Burmese took to the streets demanding an end to military rule. Many women who participated in the demonstrations were ordinary housewives who had previously expressed little interest in politics until deteriorating economic conditions brought an end to their tolerance of the government. In July, Ne Win resigned as BSPP chairman and was replaced by Sein Lwin, known as 'The Butcher of Rangoon' because of his role in violently suppressing earlier student-led demonstrations. Popular sayings reveal that the new leader's unpopularity was also connected with economic grievances: 'If the price of one *pyi* of rice is fifteen kyat, Sein Lwin's head must be cut.'[48] Many female demonstrators carried pots and pans as they marched through the streets, which suggests that journalist Denzil Peiris's comment about the 1974 workers' strikes equally applied to the 1988 demonstrations: 'Movements to overthrow governments begin in the kitchen.'[49] The economic crisis proved to be a catalyst for

---

48 Quoted in Seekins, *The disorder in order*, 152. A *pyi* is a measure of dry volume equivalent to 4.67 lbs.

49 Denzil Peiris, 'Socialism without commitment', *Far Eastern Economic Review* 85, 36 (13 September 1974): 27.

women to participate in mass political action in a way they had never done before.

Women with connections to the military elite

Although the centralisation of economic and political power under the BSPP resulted in a decline in status for most women, those with personal and family connections to the military elite stood to gain considerable wealth and influence. A system of patronage developed between senior military officials on the one hand and lower-level military officers and soldiers, BSPP party members and civilians seeking to improve their position on the other. This military patronage network was effectively reinforced by the black market, where the wives and daughters of high-ranking government and military officials were key players. These women not only used their privileged position to accumulate wealth for themselves and their families, they also served as conduits for power relationships between men. Women 'oiled' the patronage system and enhanced their husbands' and fathers' power by facilitating the inclusion of upwardly mobile young men as loyal clients. The manoeuvrings of military leaders' wives were similar to those of elite women who facilitated royal patronage networks in pre-colonial Burma, contributing to what Robert Taylor described as the 'aura of courtly politics' that developed during Ne Win's 'reign' as BSPP leader.[50]

As the personalised nature of power relations encouraged factionalism within the senior levels of the military itself, the illegal activities of wives could be used to discredit their powerful husbands. In March 1976, General Tin U was dismissed as Defence Minister, allegedly because of his wife's black market activities.[51] The chief of the National Intelligence Bureau, Tin Oo, was also forced to resign in July 1983, ostensibly because he had misappropriated state funds in order to pay for his wife's medical treatment.[52] The real reason behind Tin U and Tin Oo's dismissals was that they had built up strong patronage networks, which Ne Win perceived as a threat to his own power.[53] Ne Win subsequently asked his

---

50 R. H. Taylor, *The state in Burma* (Honolulu: University of Hawai'i Press, 1987), 366.

51 Bertil Lintner, *Outrage: Burma's struggle for democracy*, second edition (London: White Lotus, 1990), 65.

52 Far Eastern Economic Review, *Asia 1984 Yearbook*, 137.

53 Lintner, *Outrage*, 65. Lintner suggests that Tin Oo was sacked because Ne Win's daughter, Sandar Win, did not want anyone to be closer to her father than herself. See also Frank

trusted protégé, Khin Nyunt, to overhaul the Military Intelligence Service (MIS or MI), which increasingly focused on maintaining the loyalty of the armed forces by investigating and arresting anyone suspected of political dissent.[54] In this tightly controlled environment, wives of military officials had to be discreet in their economic dealings and their ability to exercise political influence became even more heavily dependent on their husbands' loyalty to Ne Win.

Unsurprisingly, Ne Win's daughter, Sandar Win, amassed immense wealth and influence over the 26 years that her father was in power. Trained as a physician, she was one of the few women to hold a senior position in the *tatmadaw* (as an army major in the medical corps). During the BSPP period, Sandar Win exercised political influence by acting as a bridge between Ne Win and lower level military officers and BSPP officials who sought his favour. Many Burmese believed that Sandar Win also played a key role in the crackdown on pro-democracy activists during the 1988 uprising.[55] On 18 September 1988, General Saw Maung announced the establishment of a 19-member State Law and Order Restoration Council (SLORC), which dissolved the *Pyithu Hluttaw* and assumed power over all organs of the state. Ne Win continued to influence military and political matters behind the scenes after the SLORC gained power, and many government officials depended on their close ties to Sandar Win as a leverage to retain their influence, including Khin Nyunt, who was sometimes referred to as 'Ne Win's son-in-law'.[56]

SLORC leaders abandoned the 'Burmese Way to Socialism' and introduced a more open economic policy, although the military retained control of substantial economic enterprises. Women took advantage of this economic liberalisation by negotiating business deals between military leaders and their families and other economically powerful players. Female relatives of senior military officials were often granted economic concessions in return for political favours. For instance, it

---

N. Trager and William L. Scully, 'The Third Congress of the Burma Socialist Programme Party: the need to create continuity and dynamism of leadership', *Asian Survey*, 17, 9 (September 1977): 330–31.

54 Andrew Selth, *Burma's armed forces: power without glory*, foreword by David Steinberg (Norwalk, CT: EastBridge, 2002), 106.

55 Lintner, *Outrage*, 121, 123–24; Aung Zaw, 'The king who never dies: "Like father, like daughter"', *The Irrawaddy* 9, 3 (March–April 2001).

56 Seekins, *The disorder in order*, 278.

was rumoured that foreigners who sought an appointment with the Trade Minister were required to spend US$400 at one of his daughter's shops.[57] Some Burmese from modest backgrounds who worked as *pweza* (brokers) also benefited from the (relative) opening of the economy. *Pweza* acted as 'go-betweens' who approached government officials on behalf of ordinary citizens in order to expedite bureaucratic procedures and financial transactions, such as obtaining an identity card or buying a car. Successful *pweza* gained a measure of social status through their connections to *lugyi* ('big people') and their ability to assist ordinary citizens in obtaining goods and favours, but many Burmese regarded *pweza* as a 'parasitic class' that further entrenched official corruption.[58]

Although some *pweza* profited from taking bribes, the vast majority struggled to earn a living. Furthermore, *pweza* were heavily dependent on their 'patrons' and could easily lose status if the latter fell on hard times. This was increasingly the case as power struggles between senior military leaders led to a series of reshuffles in the highest levels of government, which had a ripple effect down the patron–client networks. Bénédicte Brac de la Perrière described the fate of one female *pweza* who was imprisoned in 2002 after the authorities arrested her and other *pweza* in an effort to show that they were doing something to limit corruption. As Brac de la Perrière points out, this woman's 'success' as a *pweza* 'has not given her any real empowerment [in] her own life'.[59] The ambivalent status of lower-class *pweza* was due largely to their subordinate role in the military patronage network. Female *pweza* had far less influence than women with close kinship ties to military elites, who also used their proximity to powerful men to mediate in business contexts.

As Ne Win's political influence waned during the 1990s, Sandar Win concentrated on building up her economic power through her connection to Khin Nyunt.[60] Sandar Win and her husband managed the Nawarat Hotel, Bumrungrad Hospital and an investment consultancy firm, and

---

57   See 'Rich Bitch', in Williams, *Wives, mistresses and matriarchs*, 187–88.

58   Bénédicte Brac de la Perrière, 'A woman of mediation', paper presented at Southeast Asia Session 28: Life Stories of Women in Burma as part of the Association of Asian Scholars (AAS) Annual Meeting, 26–29 March 2009, Chigago, USA. I would like to thank Bénédicte Brac de la Perrière for allowing me to cite this unpublished paper.

59   *Ibid.*

60   Aung Zaw, 'The king who never dies: 'Like father, like daughter'', *The Irrawaddy* 9, 3 (March–April 2001).

were major shareholders in the communications company Myanmar Sky-Link. Shifting power relationships between the senior SLORC/SPDC members contributed to the steady decline in Sandar Win's influence, however. In March 2002, Sandar Win was arrested along with her father, husband and sons, allegedly for plotting to kidnap the military leaders who had caused them to lose valuable economic concessions.[61] Khin Nyunt also found himself in an increasingly vulnerable position. Although he had built up a powerful support network as MI chief, Khin Nyunt's efforts to gain ceasefire-agreements with ethnic insurgents and engage in dialogue with opposition leader Aung San Suu Kyi put him at odds with SPDC chairman Than Shwe and vice chairman Maung Aye, who refused to negotiate with their military and political opponents. In May 2002, *The Irrawaddy* reported that Khin Nyunt's wife, Dr Daw Khin Win Shwe, was witnessed paying respect to Maung Aye's wife, Daw Mya Mya San, at a public ceremony celebrating the Burmese New Year (*Thingyan*). Many Burmese interpreted this as a sign that Khin Nyunt and his family were pledging their allegiance to Than Shwe and Maung Aye in an effort to retain their own hold on power.[62]

The crackdown against Sandar Win and her family can be seen as evidence of ongoing competition within the military elite between patronage networks associated with senior officers who sought to convert their political power into economic opportunities. An editorial in *The Nation* on 20 March 2002 summed up the situation in this way: '[O]ne mendacious self-serving group of generals and their relatives have simply consolidated their position and access to privilege over another one.'[63] Whoever won out, the power of the military as an institution remained unchallenged; only the personalities at the apex of the military structure changed. Although the gradual opening of the economy allowed more competition for economic wealth and power, it did not expand the political basis of that power. Economic opportunities still depended on inclusion in an influential political patronage network. Thus, while women with family connections to the military elite continued to wield

---

61   Aung Zaw, 'Junta holds second press conference', *The Irrawaddy*, 12 March 2002.

62   'Wives in the balance', *The Irrawaddy* 10, 4 (May 2002). Khin Nyunt's own arrest and subsequent fall from power will be discussed in chapter 8.

63   'Editorial 1: Little relevance in Ne Win saga', *The Nation* (Bangkok), 20 March 2002. See also Aung Zaw, 'Is Burma ready for a post Ne Win era?', *The Irrawaddy*, 13 March 2002.

considerable economic and even political influence, those without such connections benefited little from a freer market economy.

Female education under military rule

Until recently, many governments and international governing bodies accepted the view of (Western) 'developmental' theorists that economic liberalisation would inevitably raise the living standards of ordinary people, who could then use their newly acquired economic power to pressure authoritarian governments to make political and social reforms. Feminist scholars have observed, however, that such 'developmental' discourses can have negative consequences for women's status, particularly in non-Western societies.[64] In military-ruled Burma, low (and deteriorating) educational standards meant that the majority of women had few opportunities to improve their economic position, which in turn might have allowed them a greater political voice to challenge government policies that discriminated against or otherwise marginalised women. Education (in the Western 'liberal' sense) was not a priority for the military leadership because it wanted to maintain control over citizens, both male and female. Military rule also reinforced existing social and cultural barriers to female education, which adversely affected women's economic and political opportunities.

The 'Burmese Way to Socialism' set a target of achieving 'basic education for all', which did bring about some improvements in educational standards at the primary level, mainly in the Burman areas of the country. Overall female literacy increased from 61 to 73.5 per cent between 1973 and 1983 and, although the male literacy rate remained significantly higher, the gender gap narrowed considerably over the decade.[65] It is unclear whether there was any significant improvement in literacy rates in rural and remote areas, however. It is highly probable that female illiteracy was higher in ethnic minority areas where there were fewer educational facilities and where schooling was more likely to be disrupted by armed conflict. Since the government also made Burmese the official language of instruction and discouraged teaching

---

64 Mina Roces and Louise Edwards, 'Contesting gender narratives: 1970–2000', in Louise Edwards and Mina Roces (eds.), *Women in Asia: tradition, modernity and globalisation* (St Leonards: Allen & Unwin, 2000), 1–15.

65 Khin Maung, *The Myanmar labour force*, 21.

in ethnic languages, it is likely that many ethnic minority women were illiterate in their native language.

Although census data reveal that the percentage of girls in school increased significantly between 1973 and 1983, 47.4 per cent of girls still received no formal education. Boys significantly outnumbered girls at both middle and high schools.[66] The reasons behind the high drop-out rate for girls reflected cultural perceptions about the value of female education rather than official policy, although deteriorating economic conditions (which were caused by government policies) undoubtedly contributed to this trend. During periods of economic hardship, boys' education usually took precedence as they were seen as more likely to provide additional family income. Girls were more likely to be kept at home to care for younger siblings and assist with domestic work. While the government claimed that boys and girls enjoyed equal access to education, its own figures reveal that student enrolments and completions declined sharply at middle and high school levels for both sexes. Although 80 per cent of students completed primary school, only 16 per cent completed middle school and 4 per cent completed high school.[67] Disturbingly, 59 per cent of all students failed their final examinations.[68] These statistics highlight the failings of the state education system as a whole as much as the poor academic performance of students.

Government spending on education as a percentage of GDP fell over the course of BSPP rule (and continued to decline under the SLORC/SPDC). While accurate statistics are impossible to obtain, it is estimated that between 1975 and 1992 public expenditure on education fell from 15 to 2.4 per cent (whereas defence expenditure is estimated to have risen from 20 to 40 per cent, and possibly even higher).[69] The total number of schools increased, but there were fewer schools in rural and ethnic minority areas, where the need to travel longer distances prevented many girls from gaining an education. Even in urban areas, many schools

---

66 *Ibid.*, 21–22; Mi Mi Khaing, *The world of Burmese women*, 107, 160.

67 'Percentage of female students by level of education 1983–84 to 1992–93', in *Statistical profile of children and women in Myanmar 1993*, 38.

68 'Students appearing for the Basic Education High School (BEHS) Examination 1983 to 1993', in *Statistical profile of children and women in Myanmar 1993*, 45.

69 'Regional Statistical Indicators', *Far Eastern Economic Review Yearbook 1977*, 14; Mya Than, 'Recent developments in Myanmar: impact and implications of ASEAN membership and Asian crisis', in Morten B. Pederson, Emily Rudland and Ronald J. May (eds.), *Burma Myanmar: strong regime weak state?* (Adelaide: Crawford House Publishing, 2000), 150.

were overcrowded and lacked basic facilities and equipment including furniture and textbooks. The cost of education was prohibitive for many Burmese so, given existing cultural norms, poor families with several children sent their sons to school and kept their daughters at home. In addition to school fees, students were obliged to pay for extra tuition offered by teachers who sought to supplement their low salaries. Students who could not afford private tutors were disadvantaged, partly because the quality of instruction in schools was poor, but also because some teachers favoured students who attended these sessions.[70]

Student mobilisation

Educational institutions offered an opportunity to groom young Burmese into obedient supporters of the state. The BSPP established several youth organisations, which were intended to mobilise children and young adults (aged 5–25) by involving them in party-sponsored activities. Youth training, which was given to girls and boys, was introduced progressively via three organisations: *Teza Lu-Nge* ('Youth Power'), *Shay-Saung Lu-Nge* ('Youth Vanguard') and *Lanzin Lu-Nge* ('Youth Who Follow the Way'). Members received instruction in BSPP ideology and were expected to volunteer their assistance for party-sponsored projects including information-gathering for government agencies, construction work and agricultural production. According to Mi Mi Khaing, there were over 220,000 *Lanzin Lu-Nge* members in the mid-1980s, around half of whom were girls, while Steinberg reported that total membership at all three levels exceeded five million.[71] Under the SLORC/SPDC regime, students were pressured to become members of the army-sponsored Union Solidarity and Development Association (USDA).[72] Students who participated in USDA activities

---

70 All Burma Federation of Student Unions, *The current education situation in Burma: education report year 2000* (Bangkok: Foreign Affairs Committee, All Burma Federation of Student Unions, 2001), 23–24. Hereafter cited as 'ABFSU, *The current education system in Burma*'.

71 Mi Mi Khaing, *The world of Burmese women*, 110–11; Steinberg, *Burma: a socialist nation of Southeast Asia*, 80.

72 The USDA was formed in 1993 and had around 24 million members in 2007. Ostensibly a 'social' organisation, the USDA is widely regarded as a civilian front for the *tatmadaw*. SLORC-SPDC Chairman General Than Shwe was the USDA patron and all civil servants and military personnel were required to become members, while many civilians were reportedly forced to join the association. USDA members were required to undertake 'voluntary' work for various government bodies and to participate in state-sponsored rallies, including those denouncing opposition leaders and their supporters. In July 2010, the

reportedly achieved higher grades and received recommendations from their teachers, which enhanced their future educational and economic prospects.[73] Successive military governments thus adopted a 'carrot and stick' approach towards student mobilisation, offering educational, professional and even political opportunities for compliant members, while disadvantaging non-members.

Higher education and student opposition

Given the low standard of public education, parents with economic means increasingly chose to send their sons to military academies, colleges and institutes, which were considered by many Burmese to offer the best means of educational and professional advancement.[74] In a society where influence depended largely on personal relationships, contacts made in these schools drew students into influential patronage networks. During the BSPP period, therefore, as girls and women were excluded from military colleges, they were deprived of both educational opportunities and access to power through patronage. In 2000, the military opened the Defence Services Institute of Nursing, which offered a Bachelor of Science (Nursing) degree for female students. As in other military institutes, students were prohibited from engaging in political activities and were required to complete a period of military service after graduation.[75] Nursing was considered an 'appropriate' profession for women, since it did not require them to engage in armed combat; furthermore, it was also unlikely that nursing graduates would rise to senior positions within the military power structure. The government's promotion of military over non-military education contributed to the increased economic, social and political power of the military elite, while simultaneously depriving civilians, particularly women, of similar opportunities.

USDA was disbanded and many of members joined the Union Solidarity and Development Party (USDP), which won the vast majority of seats in the November general election.

73   ABFSU, *The current education system in Burma*, 23.

74   Christina Fink, *Living silence: Burma under military rule* (London; New York: Zed Books, 2001), 101–03.

75   ABFSU, *The current education system in Burma*, 70; Maung Aung Myoe, *Officer education and leadership training in the tatmadaw: a survey*, Working Paper No. 346 (Strategic and Defence Studies Centre, Australian National University, Canberra, 1999), 7–8.

University students had been at the centre of political resistance movements since the 1920s and were among the first to criticise the military
regime and its policies. In July 1962, the army fired on male and female
students demonstrating against new stringent hostel regulations at the
University of Rangoon. A number of student demonstrators were killed
and government troops later demolished the student union building
while students were still inside. Daw Hla Hla Moe, who was a second year
university student at the time, was profoundly affected by these 'heart-
wrenching events' and later became an active member of the National
League for Democracy (NLD) following the 1988 uprising.[76] Female
university students also participated in the 1974 workers' strikes and the
student-led protest over former UN Secretary-General U Thant's funeral
arrangements, both of which were violently suppressed by the authorities.
In June 1975, around 250 male and female students were arrested while
commemorating the anniversary of the 1974 workers' strike, including
Naykyi Ba Swe and Nayye Ba Swe, daughters of former Prime Minister
U Ba Swe. Both were sentenced to five years imprisonment. Nan Khin
Htwe Myint, daughter of former Minister for Karen State, Dr Saw Hla
Htun, was also arrested and jailed for three years.[77] These three women
later stood as candidates in the 1990 elections, though only Daw Hla Hla
Moe and Nan Khin Htwe Myint won seats (as the NLD representatives in
Minhla and Pa-an townships). Women were not only politicised by their
experiences as students, they often remained politically active long after
they completed their studies.

In the mid-1970s, the government reorganised the tertiary education
system, ostensibly to address development needs but also to prevent
students from organising political opposition. Military intelligence officers stepped up their surveillance in tertiary educational institutions,
often coercing or bribing staff and students to act as informers.[78] Existing
universities and colleges were restructured and dispersed throughout
Rangoon and other urban centres, and distance education was introduced for students in rural and remote areas. A subsequent increase in
overall female university enrolments was partly due to these reforms,

---

76   Daw Hla Hla Moe, 'The voices of women in our struggle', in Altsean Burma, *Burma –
      women's voices together*, 51–54.

77   ABSDF, *Burma and the role of women*, 13–14.

78   Selth, *Transforming the tatmadaw*, 108.

though it also reflected the need for women to gain further qualifications in order to find work. Differential admission policies also discriminated against women, particularly in traditionally male-dominated fields such as forestry, dentistry and engineering, where limits were imposed on female enrolments.[79] These regulations, rather than de-politicising students, contributed to growing student unrest and resentment towards the government.

Female teachers and university students were at the forefront of the 1988 anti-government demonstrations. Witnesses reported that female students were targeted by riot police and army troops sent in to suppress the protests. Some female students were stripped of their clothes and jewellery and forced into nearby lakes where they drowned; others were beaten and sexually assaulted by military officers and policemen while in custody.[80] Following the military's brutal crackdown on student demonstrators, the frequent closure of schools and universities adversely affected not only educational standards but also employment opportunities for female students. Between 1988 and 2000, non-military universities and colleges were closed for extended periods, while military academies, colleges and institutes remained open.[81] University students were also required to sign disclosure forms stating they would not participate in political activities other than those condoned by the authorities. Those whose family members were involved in opposition politics – like Sa Bae, whose father was a member of a Mon insurgent organisation – were barred from attending most tertiary educations:

> I was not able to study in a higher education institution as I belonged to a family with political convictions. The university I was allowed to attend was not only expensive but also closed most of the time. Besides, we would be pushed through the system in such a hurry that it would only take 1 year to graduate from a 4-year degree. Finally, I decided to come out to the revolutionary area with the hope of helping others with education one day.[82]

---

79 Win May, *Status of women in Myanmar* (Yangon: Sarpay Beikman Press, 1995), 30, 35; Belak, *Gathering strength*, 145.

80 Seekins, *The disorder in order*, 136; ABSDF, *Burma and the role of women*, 14–15.

81 ABFSU, *The current education system in Burma*, 37–39.

82 Sa Bae, 'Rebel's daughter', in Altsean Burma, *Burma – women's voices together*, 86.

Many educated women who participated in the 1988 uprising also fled to the jungle and into neighbouring countries like Thailand where they continued their involvement in the democratic movement and formed their own organisations to promote women's issues and rights (as we shall see in chapter 9).

Cultural 'Burmanisation' and state-sponsored violence against ethnic minority women

Burma's ethnic minorities undoubtedly experienced the worst effects of military rule including political repression, prolonged armed conflict, human rights abuses and lack of socioeconomic development. In 1962, Ne Win justified his ascension to power by claiming that a military takeover was the only way to prevent Burma from disintegrating as a result of civil war. National unity was proclaimed as the main priority in multiethnic Burma and the 1974 Constitution explicitly stated that the exercise of ethnic and cultural rights should not undermine national solidarity and security.[83] Despite constitutional guarantees of ethnic equality, there is strong evidence that military authorities actually sought to erase cultural diversity and ethnic minority rights through an unofficial policy of 'Burmanisation'. The government's promotion of 'Burmese' (read: Burman) culture consistently discriminated against ethnic minorities. Education was effectively 'Burmanised' as Burmese was made the official language of instruction in schools, and prohibitions against the use of ethnic minority languages served to discourage expressions of ethnic and cultural identity. One Shan woman, Nang Mo Ngern Hom, described her experience of discrimination as a school student in Murng Pan in southern Shan State:

> I had noticed how the teachers, who were all Burmese [Burman], were not entirely fair to the students. They did not seem interested in the Shan students and gave favours to the Burmese [Burman] students. We were not taught how to read Shan, and were not even allowed to speak Shan at school. If we were caught speaking in Shan, we were fined 25 *pyas*. We were also not allowed to study Shan outside school hours.[84]

---

83 See Article 153c of 'The Constitution of the Socialist Republic of the Union of Burma, 1974', in Weller (ed.), *Democracy and politics in Burma*, 107, 131.

84 Nang Mo Ngern Hom, 'My life as a woman soldier', in Altsean Burma, *Burma – women's voices together*, 55.

Women living in ethnic minority areas and conflict zones also suffered as a result of other government policies, including forced relocation and requisition of labour, as well as military violence including rape.

Military rule and its culture of male power exacerbated discrimination and violence against women, particularly in conflict-affected areas with large ethnic minority populations. Many civilians were subjected to human rights abuses including forced labour, summary arrest, torture and extrajudicial execution as a result of military operations and the *tatmadaw*'s policy of repression in villages frequented by ethnic armies. Women living in war-affected areas were specifically targeted by the military because of their gender. Government troops often used women as 'human minesweepers' and porters because they were more likely to accede to the *tatmadaw*'s demands, especially when threatened by violence. Paradoxically, military authorities also perceived women as a threat because they provided insurgent armies with food, shelter and intelligence information. In the mid-1960s, the *tatmadaw* adopted a policy of forcibly relocating or razing villages suspected of colluding with ethnic armies. The 'Four Cuts' (*Pya Ley Pya*) campaign aimed to cut supplies of food, funds, intelligence and recruits to insurgent armies.[85] Sometimes villagers were notified in advance and ordered to relocate to new sites near military bases, usually within a few days, but *tatmadaw* troops often entered villages without prior warning and destroyed houses, schools, churches, livestock and crops and extorted cash and valuables from villagers or fired indiscriminately at fleeing civilians. Naw Khin Mar Kyaw Zaw was 14 years old when the *tatmadaw* destroyed her village in Karen state:

> When the Na Wa Ta [SPDC] soldiers entered my village and burned down everything we were running as though the whole world was shattered and ruined. My sickly mother died when she was running from the soldiers. All our relatives and siblings were separated from each other. I have not been back to my little village since then.[86]

Communities subjected to forced relocation suffered from lack of food, public services and employment opportunities and women living under such harsh conditions struggled to care for themselves and their families. One unforeseen consequence of the *tatmadaw*'s violent campaigns

---

85 Smith, *Burma: insurgency*, 258–59.

86 Naw Khin Mar Kyaw Zaw, 'No fallen river, no fallen tree', in Altsean Burma, *Burma – women's voices together*, 4.

against ethnic minority civilians, however, was that many young ethnic minority women joined ethnically-based political organisations as a result of their experiences of military abuse.[87]

Women living in conflict zones were subjected to gender-based violence including rape and other forms of sexual abuse perpetrated by military personnel. Successive military governments consistently denied that sexual violence towards women was a problem in Burma, referring to the non-violent tenets of Buddhism and the low incidence of reported cases as evidence to support these claims.[88] While there were few reported cases of sexual assault and rape in Burma itself, this reflected the prevailing power structure rather than the low level of violence against women. Women knew that authorities would give little credence to their reports, and simply accept the denials of those military personnel who had perpetrated the crimes. Fear of reprisal undoubtedly also prevented many women and their families from reporting cases of sexual violence. Outside Burma, independent human rights groups and Burmese women's organisations have produced detailed reports to sub-stantiate their claims that rape was not incidental to armed conflict, but a deliberate tactic of war in ethnic areas.[89] Since most of these reports have been compiled since 1989, they focus on documenting cases of sexual violence committed during the SLORC/SPDC period. It is clear, however, that rape and other forms of sexual violence against women were also committed by military personnel under BSPP rule.

---

87 Nang Mo Ngern Hom, 'My life as a woman soldier', 57; Naw Khin Mar Kyaw Zaw, 'No fallen river, no fallen tree', 5. The politicisation of ethnic minority women is discussed in greater detail in chapter 9.

88 See the SPDC government's official report to the United Nations, Convention on the Elimination of All Forms of Discrimination Against Women: 'Consideration of reports pre-sented by States parties under article 18 of the Convention on the Elimination of All Forms of Discrimination against Women. Initial report of States parties. Myanmar', CEDAW/C/MMR/1 (25 June 1999), 10. Hereafter cited as 'CEDAW/C/MMR/1'.

89 Betsy Apple, *School for rape: the Burmese military and sexual violence* (Bangkok: EarthRights International, 1998); Betsy Apple and Veronika Martin, *No safe place: Burma's army and the rape of ethnic women: a report by Refugees International* (Washington: Refugees International, 2003); Shan Human Rights Foundation and Shan Women's Action Network, *Licence to rape: the Burmese military regime's use of sexual violence in the ongoing war in Shan State* (Shan Human Rights Foundation and Shan Women's Action Network, 2002) (hereafter cited as 'SHRF and SWAN, *Licence to rape*'); Karen Women's Organization, *Shattering silences: Karen women speak out about the Burmese military regime's use of rape as a strategy of war in Karen State*, with the collaboration of The Committee for Internally Displaced Karen People (CIDKP), The Karen Information Center (KIC), The Karen Human Rights Group (KHRG) and The Mergui-Tavoy District Information Department (Karen Women's Organization, April 2004).

Recent reports reveal that military personnel deliberately terrorised ethnic communities by perpetrating and condoning gross acts of violence against women. Documented cases reveal that women of all ages – including pre-pubescent girls and elderly women – were repeatedly raped and gang raped by *tatmadaw* officers and soldiers.[90] Some women who were violated with sticks, guns and knives died as a result of their injuries, or were killed to prevent them from reporting their attackers or recounting their experiences. Women whose male family members belonged to, or were believed to have connections with, ethnic armies were particularly vulnerable to sexual violence.[91] Members of the *tatmadaw* sought to demoralise ethnic armies by raping ethnic minority women in front of their husbands and children, and forcing unmarried women to marry *tatmadaw* soldiers.[92] The majority of *tatmadaw* soldiers were ethnically Burman so any children born as a result of these practices would be of mixed descent. Military rape was therefore used to bring about 'ethnic cleansing' in Burma, as it was in Bosnia. Women who became pregnant as a result of rape were often reluctant to have abortions, which were not only illegal, but were discouraged by many Burmese for religious reasons. Apart from suffering physical and psychological effects, women were sometimes shunned by husbands, families and communities who believed they had been 'spoiled' as a result of rape.[93]

Sexual violence perpetrated against Burmese women by members of the armed forces was (and remains) widespread, but it is less clear whether military rape was used as 'weapon of war' as the authors of some reports have claimed. There is no hard evidence to indicate that the central military leadership formally directed or otherwise encouraged lower level army officers to rape and sexually abuse women. It is possible that gender-based violence was initiated by local military commanders, fuelled by racial prejudice, ill-discipline, and other factors. It is clear, however, that senior military leaders knew about the widespread abuse of women by *tatmadaw* officers and soldiers, and did nothing to prevent it from occurring. Although many women suffered as victims of

---

90   SHRF and SWAN, *Licence to rape*, 11. 36, 40, 51.

91   Belak, *Gathering strength*, 61–66, 284–86.

92   Altsean Burma, *Special briefing: women's report card on Burma, April 2000* (Bangkok: Alternative ASEAN Network on Burma, 2000), 15; SHRF and SWAN, *Licence to rape*, 25, 47.

93   Apple, *School for rape*, 18–20, 94–97; Belak, *Gathering strength*, 73–78; SHRF and SWAN, *Licence to Rape*, 21–23, 34, 36, 43.

war and violence, some became more politically active in response to abuse by military personnel, especially from the mid-1990s onwards as expatriate Burmese women's organisations began to document cases of gender-based violence as part of a wider campaign to promote women's rights and empowerment.[94] The process by which these women came to view themselves as resisters rather than victims, and thereby challenge the military regime and its monopoly of power, will be examined more fully in chapter 9.

Conclusions

Women's political, economic and social status drastically declined under military rule. Ne Win created a one-party state that was dominated by the military – and, therefore, by men – and so excluded most women from senior government positions. The military regime suppressed all political opposition, although some writers, students and other activists continued to resist official encroachments on their civil liberties. The BSPP's economic policies had an adverse affect on most women, due both to the overall economic decline and the reduced economic ability of women to provide for themselves and their families. Yet economic hardship also drove many women to protest against the government and its policies. Only women with close connections to the military elite were able to enhance their economic and political influence, through the positions their male relatives held in the patronage networks of senior military officers. Under military rule, economic and educational policies were informed by a conservative, patriarchal and chauvinistic ideology, reinforcing cultural norms that had traditionally restricted women's socioeconomic progress. Many women experienced increasing discrimination and abuse under military rule, particularly ethnic minority women living in war-affected areas. While women were often regarded as victims of state-sponsored violence, some women became more politically active as a result of their experiences. By the late 1980s, public tolerance of the regime's repressive policies had reached an all-time low and in the 1988 uprising many women marched alongside men to call for an end to authoritarian rule and the restoration of democracy.

---

94 Edith T. Mirante, 'Burma's ethnic minority women: from abuse to resistance', in Marc S. Miller with the staff of Cultural Survival (eds.), *State of the peoples: a global human rights report on societies in danger* (Boston: Beacon Press, 1993), 7–14.

The next chapter will consider how one woman, Aung San Suu Kyi, came to prominence as the leader of the pro-democracy movement and, in doing so, brought a new dimension to Burmese perceptions of gender and power.

7

Aung San Suu Kyi's Political Influence and Moral Power

*A*ung San Suu Kyi has undoubtedly been the most influential figure in Burmese politics since 1988. Given the Burmese ambivalence towards female leadership and the decline in women's status under military rule, how did a woman become the most prominent and respected leader of the popular movement to restore democracy? Why does Aung San Suu Kyi still remain influential, when she has spent so many years under house arrest?[1] In considering these questions, this chapter explores how Aung San Suu Kyi successfully appropriated her father's hero status to gain legitimacy as a political leader. Furthermore, she demonstrated that she was a great leader in her own right by promoting Buddhist ideals that not only enhanced her moral power in the eyes of many Burmese, but also highlighted the moral shortcomings of the military regime. Her spiritual strength and personal charisma have given her enormous political influence, even while she has been denied access to formal political power. Yet Aung San Suu Kyi's prominence as a political leader has not translated into a significant increase in women's power within the democratic movement. Women's political activism has been constrained, not only by military crackdowns against opposition activists, but also by traditionalist understandings of women's roles espoused by democratic leaders, including Aung San Suu Kyi herself.

---

1   Aung San Suu Kyi was initially placed under house arrest on 20 July 1989 and was unable to contest the 1990 general election. She was released in July 1995, but the authorities repeatedly prevented her from meeting with her supporters. In September 2000, she was again put under house arrest. She was released in May 2002, and rearrested one year later after her convoy was attacked near Depayin village in Kachin State during her tour of upper Burma. She was released from her latest period of house arrest on 13 November 2010, six days after the general election.

Aung San Suu Kyi's early life and influences

Born in Rangoon on 19 June 1945, Aung San Suu Kyi is the only daughter of Bogyoke Aung San and Daw Khin Kyi. Aung San is still revered by many Burmese as the 'father of independence', while Khin Kyi (who died in December 1988 following a long illness) also earned widespread admiration and respect for her work in various social welfare organisations. Both parents had an enormous influence on Aung San Suu Kyi's personal and political development. Close friends claim she inherited from her parents a strong dedication to her country and the welfare of its people as well as self-discipline, courage and determination.[2] Aung San Suu Kyi was only two years old when her father died, but she would later draw on his status and ideals – particularly his desire to establish 'true' democracy,[3] improve Burman–minority relations, and create a professional army that would serve and protect the people – in order to legitimise her own political power.

Aung San Suu Kyi's political values were also shaped by her education and experiences living abroad. She accompanied her mother to India in 1960, and graduated from Lady Shri Ram College in New Delhi in 1964. Her deep respect for the Gandhian principle of non-violence can be traced to this period. She continued her education in England, obtaining a B.A. in Philosophy, Politics, and Economics from Oxford University in 1967. While in England, her informal guardian, Paul (later Lord) Gore-Booth, introduced her to many British politicians as well as her future husband, Michael Aris.[4] After graduating from university, Aung San Suu Kyi worked for the United Nations in New York for several years. U Thant, then UN Secretary-General, had been a close friend of her father's. In 1972, Aung San Suu Kyi married Michael Aris, an Englishman and scholar of Tibet. During their courtship, Aung San

---

2   Ma Than E, 'A flowering of the spirit: memories of Suu and her family', in *Aung San Suu Kyi, Freedom from fear and other writings*, 241–57.

3   Aung San distinguished between 'true' democracy – in which the state rules with the people's consent – and 'sham' democracy, where the state retains power against the people's will. See Aung San's address at the AFPFL Convention, Jubilee Hall, Rangoon, 23 May 1947, cited in Josef Silverstein, *The political legacy of Aung San*, revised edition, Southeast Asia Program Series, no. 11 (Ithaca, New York: Southeast Asia Program, Cornell University, 1993), 153.

4   At the time, Gore-Booth was permanent undersecretary at the Foreign Office in London. He had previously served as the British High Commissioner in Delhi and British Ambassador in Rangoon.

Suu Kyi expressed concern that the Burmese people might misinterpret their marriage as a 'lessening of her devotion to them' and constantly reminded Michael that she would return to Burma should her people ever need her help.[5] The couple had two sons, Alexander (Myint San Aung) and Kim (Htein Lin), born in 1973 and 1977 respectively. During the 1980s, Aung San Suu Kyi undertook academic research in Japan and India and wrote a biography of her father.[6] In March 1988, she had just commenced postgraduate study at the School of Oriental and African Studies in London when her mother's illness prompted her to return to Burma.

During her time living abroad, Aung San Suu Kyi made regular trips to Burma to visit her mother; she also sent her sons to become Buddhist novices in Rangoon monasteries. Friends and colleagues who knew her during this period have commented on her 'traditionalist' outlook, as well as her strong opinions and moralistic stance on some issues. At college, Aung San Suu Kyi wore traditional Burmese *longyi* and abstained from drinking alcohol; she also expressed disapproval when her friends discussed their sexual experiences.[7] Burma historian Michael Aung-Thwin, who knew Aung San Suu Kyi when the two were colleagues at Kyoto University's Center for Southeast Asian Studies, recalled how he once offended her by admitting that he would rather listen to the Beatles than traditional Burmese music. He also remembers having frequent 'honest disagreements' with Aung San Suu Kyi.[8]

In 2007, Aung-Thwin infamously described Aung San Suu Kyi as a 'divisive' figure who was 'always harping on about her father'.[9] Aung San Suu Kyi's open admiration for her father is hardly surprising, considering his reputation as Burma's national hero. That she should later use Aung San's 'moral capital' to enhance her own political power is also entirely understandable.[10] It is clear from Aung San Suu Kyi's academic and employment interests, as well as her discussions with her husband, that she felt a strong

---

5   Michael Aris, 'Introduction', in Aung San Suu Kyi, *Freedom from fear*, xvii.

6   Aung San Suu Kyi, *Aung San of Burma*.

7   Ann Pasternak Slater, 'Suu Burmese', in Aung San Suu Kyi, *Freedom from fear*, 258–66.

8   Nicholas Farrelly, 'Interview with Michael Aung-Thwin', *New Mandala*, 28 November 2007.

9   *Ibid.*

10   John Kane has used the phrase 'moral capital' to explain Aung San Suu Kyi's power. See John Kane, *The politics of moral capital* (Cambridge; New York: Cambridge University Press, 2001), 147–71.

sense of duty to serve the Burmese people as her father (and mother) had done. Her experiences abroad enhanced her appreciation of non-violent opposition, human rights and Western democratic principles which, together with her father's views on the importance of personal discipline, inter-ethnic cooperation and the proper role of the army, informed her political beliefs. Yet she expressed no interest in assuming a political career before the anti-government demonstrations broke out in 1988. Michael Aung-Thwin's comment takes on new meaning(s) when we focus on the development of Aung San Suu Kyi's political career. The following discussion will consider how Aung San Suu Kyi's strong will and opinions, not to mention her gender, have generated debates – both within Burma and abroad – about her effectiveness as a political leader. This chapter also examines how modern Burmese politics has been portrayed as a 'moral power struggle' between Aung San Suu Kyi and military leaders. While such portrayals undoubtedly have enhanced Aung San Suu Kyi's political and moral legitimacy, they have also impeded efforts to promote genuine and open dialogue between various political actors.

Aung San Suu Kyi's entry into politics: identification with Aung San

As early as 1974, Burma's military leaders were concerned that Aung San Suu Kyi would become involved in anti-government activities, not least because of the fact that – as Aung San's daughter – she had the potential to unite the disparate elements of the emerging political opposition. It was not until April 1988, however, that Aung San Suu Kyi witnessed the growth of a popular movement that she could wholeheartedly support.[11] Following the mass anti-government demonstrations on 8 August 1988, which the military suppressed with unprecedented brutality, she joined veteran political leaders in calling for the formation of an independent People's Consultative Committee to negotiate a peaceful solution to the country's political, social and economic problems.[12] When the authorities ignored this proposal, Aung San Suu Kyi prepared to address the people at a mass rally to be held at Shwedagon Pagoda on 26 August, the day student activists had called for a nationwide strike.

---

11   Aung San Suu Kyi, 'In the eye of the revolution', in Aung San Suu Kyi, *Freedom from fear*, 212.

12   Aung San Suu Kyi, 'The first initiative', in Aung San Suu Kyi, *Freedom from fear*, 192–97.

Before she made her first political speech, Aung San Suu Kyi was relatively unknown in her native country. Many of the thousands of people who attended the rally at Shwedagon Pagoda came out of curiosity, hoping to get a glimpse of Aung San's only daughter. Aware that she was under scrutiny, Aung San Suu Kyi explicitly linked her role in the pro-democracy movement to her personal history. Acknowledging the historical ambivalence felt by many Burmese towards women who married foreigners, she stressed that her years spent living abroad and her marriage to an Englishman 'have never interfered and will never interfere with or lessen my love and devotion for my country by any measure or degree'.[13] What Aung San Suu Kyi did not need to explain to the crowd was her karmic credentials as the daughter of Aung San, which for any Burmese went without saying. She drew on this familial connection in order to emphasise her political credentials, alluding to her family history to counter criticisms that she knew nothing of Burmese politics: 'The trouble is that I know too much. My family knows best how complicated and tricky Burmese politics can be and how much my father had to suffer on this account.'[14] She went on to say that her entry into politics was born out of a sense of duty to her father and the Burmese people: 'I could not, as my father's daughter, remain indifferent to all that was going on. This national crisis could in fact be called the second struggle for national independence.'[15] As she spoke to the crowd in fluent Burmese, standing beside a portrait of Aung San, many observers noted the strong resemblance between father and daughter. Both had a direct, honest manner and commanding presence that inspired the crowd.[16]

There were also striking similarities in their political beliefs. Like her father, Aung San Suu Kyi believed that the Burmese should embrace multi-party democracy, which she claimed was the only political ideology consistent with freedom and peace.[17] Aung San Suu Kyi's main

---

13 Aung San Suu Kyi, 'Speech to a mass rally at the Shwedagon Pagoda', in Aung San Suu Kyi, *Freedom from fear*, 199.

14 *Ibid.*

15 *Ibid.*

16 Lintner, *Aung San Suu Kyi and Burma's unfinished renaissance*, 2; 'A conversation with U Tin U: Deputy Chairman of the National League for Democracy', in Aung San Suu Kyi et al., *The voice of hope*, 269–70; Ma Than E, 'A flowering of the spirit', 242, 245, 253–57.

17 Aung San Suu Kyi, 'Speech to a mass rally at the Shwedagon Pagoda', 200.

criticism of the military government was that it turned the army into a tyrannical force used to oppress the people. Her father, she argued, had formed the army in order to serve and protect the people: 'If instead the armed forces should come to be hated by the people, then the aims with which this army has been built up would have been in vain.'[18] Both Aung San and Aung San Suu Kyi emphasised the need for the people to cultivate self-discipline and a sense of national unity in order to achieve their goals (of independence and democracy). In particular, there should be mutual trust and respect between the army and the people and among the different ethnic groups. In conclusion, Aung San Suu Kyi reiterated the protesters' demands that a multi-party system of government should be (re)established as soon as possible through the means of free and fair elections.[19]

Following her Shwedagon speech, Aung San Suu Kyi became the democracy movement's most prominent leader almost overnight. Being the daughter of Aung San established her karmic credentials, which translated into political power. Her sense of familial duty and responsibility led inevitably to her decision to become involved in national politics. She was recognised by many Burmese and foreign observers as 'her father's daughter' in terms of her appearance, personality and charisma as well as her political ideals and objectives.[20] For her Burmese supporters, Aung San Suu Kyi's struggle to restore democratic government was seen as a continuation of her father's struggle to restore independence. Her power, therefore, drew on political history and traditions that touched a chord with the vast majority of Burmese.

Several scholars have noted that women leaders in South and Southeast Asia tended to gain entry into politics through their family connections, including Begum Khaleda Zia and Sheikh Hasina Wajed in Bangladesh, Benazir Bhutto in Pakistan, Megawati Sukarnoputri in Indonesia, Wan Azizah Wan Ismail in Malaysia, Corazon C. Aquina in the Philippines, and Aung San Suu Kyi in Burma.[21] Although these women assumed leadership

---

18   *Ibid.*, 201.

19   *Ibid.*, 204.

20   Ma Than E, 'A flowering of the spirit', 242, 245, 253–57; Kane, *The politics of moral capital,* 153.

21   Andrea Fleschenberg, 'Asia's women politicians at the top: roaring tigresses or tame kittens?', in Kazuki Iwagana (ed.), *Women's political participation and representation in Asia: obstacles and challenges,* Women and Politics in Asia series, No. 2 (Copenhagen: NIAS Press, 2008),

Figure 7.1: Aung San Suu Kyi sits during an interview in front of a portrait of her father, Rangoon, 10 July 1996 (© AP via AAP [Richard Vogel]).

in countries with diverse socio-cultural and socio-political systems, they shared similar family backgrounds. All were daughters or wives of 'martyred' political leaders who had been assassinated, executed or imprisoned. This 'dynastic descent' enhanced women's political legitimacy, even though they had little or no direct political experience. These women have also been described as 'transformational leaders' since they rose to prominence when unpopular male-led political regimes were under pressure to

23–54; Rounaq Jahan, 'Women political leaders: past and present', *Third World Quarterly* 9, 3 (1987): 848–71; Linda K. Richter, 'Exploring theories of female leadership in South and Southeast Asia', *Pacific Affairs* 63, 4 (1990–91): 524–40; Mark R. Thompson, 'Female leadership of democratic transitions in Asia', *Pacific Affairs* 75, 4 (Winter 2002–03): 535–55.

reform. Under these circumstances, women's political inexperience and gender could be used to their advantage. Female political leaders could claim the moral high ground over corrupt, authoritarian, male-led regimes. Yet Andrea Fleschenberg points out that the emphasis on the way these women came to power undermines female agency: 'By narrowing down the examination to the female leaders' pathway to power, one overlooks the emancipation process undertaken throughout their political career, which is not a one-dimensional, static concept.'[22]

Aung San Suu Kyi's appropriation of her father's political beliefs and status enabled her to gain access to power through the 'family recognition factor'.[23] Burma's military leaders repeatedly asserted that Aung San Suu Kyi had no personal right to political power, and relied solely on her father's name to gain political legitimacy and support. In 1998, Tin Winn, Burma's Ambassador to the USA, declared that Aung San Suu Kyi had been 'co-opted to lead a disparate group of political activists solely on her credential as the daughter of Gen. Aung San'.[24] The regime, therefore, attempted to deny Aung San Suu Kyi's political legitimacy by downplaying her association with Aung San. Most military leaders avoided using her full name and their supporters claimed that, by marrying a foreigner, 'Mrs. Michael Aris' had 'lost her right to inherit her father's name'.[25] Aung San Suu Kyi has readily acknowledged that 'the first reason why the Burmese people trusted me was because of their love for my father .... I think a lot of that love was transferred to me. So I started off with an advantage – a ready-made fund of *metta* [loving-kindness] on which to build.'[26] Association with Aung San was undoubtedly crucial to establishing Aung San Suu Kyi's legitimacy as a political leader, but she went on to develop her own political philosophy, based on Buddhist principles of non-violence and compassion, which appealed to many Burmese who had experienced increasing violence and oppression under military rule.

---

22 Andrea Fleschenberg, 'Asia's women politicians at the top', 37.

23 The phrase 'family recognition factor' is used by Bertil Lintner in *Aung San Suu Kyi and Burma's unfinished renaissance*, 5. Gustaaf Houtman also refers to the 'Aung San recognition factor': Houtman, *Mental culture in Burmese crisis politics*, 15.

24 'Suu Kyi a "disgruntled housewife": Ambassador', *The Irrawaddy* 6, 4 (August 1998).

25 Po Yagyan, 'Adrift and washed ashore', *New Light of Myanmar*, 9 May 1997. Despite Po Yagyan's claim, Burmese women do not take on their husbands' names after marriage.

26 Aung San Suu Kyi et al., *The voice of hope*, 41.

Aung San Suu Kyi as a (woman) leader

Although her status as Aung San's daughter gave her immense popular appeal, not to mention political legitimacy, Aung San Suu Kyi was not the first choice to lead the opposition movement. Some male political veterans were reluctant to ask her to take up the role, not least because of the widespread belief that women were incapable of dealing with the harsh realities of politics.[27] It was not until Aung San Suu Kyi made her Shwedagon speech that male elites began to regard her as the strong leader they needed to unite the opposition. As Aung San's daughter, she could appeal to a broad cross-section of society, including civilians and military personnel, Burmans and ethnic minorities, students and older activists. Aung San Suu Kyi maintained that she was not interested in a political career, although she admitted that she served as 'a kind of unifying force because of my father's name'.[28] Yet, when the SLORC assumed power on 18 September 1988 and announced that it would allow political parties to form and prepare for general elections in order to establish a 'genuine democracy',[29] she declared that she was 'prepared to engage in the very kind of party politics I wish to avoid if I am convinced it is necessary to uphold the democratic system'.[30] She had already established contact with former defence minister U Tin U and other experienced leaders whom she could trust, and together they founded the National League for Democracy (NLD) on 24 September.

Aung San Suu Kyi was named the NLD's general-secretary and Tin U became chairman after Brigadier Aung Gyi stood down from this role in December 1988, allegedly because he thought Aung San Suu Kyi was being influenced by communists. This rumour was fuelled by the SLORC's unsubstantiated claims that Aung San Suu Kyi was in contact with senior CPB leaders, although she insisted that she only worked

---

27 Lintner, *Aung San Suu Kyi and Burma's unfinished renaissance*, 16. According to Lintner, many male activists secretly hoped that Aung San Suu Kyi's older brother, Aung San Oo, would return from the USA to lead the democratic movement, but he showed little interest in politics. Aung San Suu Kyi's other brother, Aung San Lin, drowned in a pond near the family home when he was a child.

28 Aung San Suu Kyi, 'The objectives', in Aung San Suu Kyi, *Freedom from fear*, 207.

29 'Announcement No 1/88 of the State Law and Order Restoration Council, 18 September 1988', in Weller (ed.), *Democracy and politics in Burma*, 142.

30 'Belief in Burma's future', *The Independent* (London), 18 September 1988. Republished as 'In the eye of the revolution', in Aung San Suu Kyi, *Freedom from fear*, 213.

with politicians who supported the democratic cause.[31] The SLORC denounced her as a communist stooge, mainly in order to discredit the NLD in the eyes of army personnel who had been fighting the CPB since 1948.[32] Following the collapse of the CPB in April 1989,[33] the SLORC switched focus and declared that Aung San Suu Kyi was being controlled by Western leaders.[34] The state-controlled media repeatedly portrayed her as a 'traitor puppet who is blatantly betraying the national cause and dancing to the delight of [Western] neo-colonialists'.[35] Even Tin U admitted that he initially thought that, as a former army officer, he could 'protect' Aung San Suu Kyi from the military.[36] Thus, there was a perception among some male leaders – including those in the NLD – that, as a woman, Aung San Suu Kyi was 'weak' and could easily be manipulated or harmed by more experienced male politicians and army officers. Following her arrest, foreign media representations of Aung San Suu Kyi also called into question the effectiveness of her political leadership by emphasising her 'feminine' qualities (such as her physical fragility) and portraying her as the powerless victim of a brutal regime who was in need of Western powers' protection.[37]

By contrast, others have argued that Aung San Suu Kyi was too strong-willed to be a mere 'figurehead' leader.[38] Her steely determination and sharp wit meant that she was not easily dominated by others. Her supporters regarded these personal qualities as political strengths. Western media representations of Aung San Suu Kyi, in particular,

---

31 Aung San Suu Kyi, 'In the eye of the revolution', 212. Some of SLORC's allegations are discussed (and then dismissed) in Fink, *Living silence*, 66–67.

32 See the speech made by military intelligence chief Khin Nyunt on 5 September 1989, published as *Burma Communist Party's conspiracy to take over state power* (Rangoon: Ministry of Information, 1989).

33 The CPB fell apart due to internal disputes between Burman leaders and lower-level ethnic minority recruits. Ethnic factions agreed to ceasefires with the central government in return for minimal interference in their affairs.

34 Lintner, *Aung San Suu Kyi and Burma's unfinished renaissance*, 24.

35 Cited in *New Light of Myanmar*, 30 June 1996.

36 Aung San Suu Kyi et al., *The voice of hope*, 270.

37 For more detailed discussion on portrayals of Aung San Suu Kyi in the Western media, see Lisa Brooten, 'The feminization of democracy under siege: the media, "the Lady" of Burma, and U.S. Foreign policy', *National Women's Studies Association (NWSA) Journal* 17, 3 (Fall 2005): 134–56; Tinzar Lwyn, 'The mission: colonial discourse on gender and the politics of Burma', *New Literatures Review* 24 (Winter South 1992): 5–22.

38 See, for instance, Kane, *The politics of moral capital*, 159.

described her determination and strong will as positive attributes that demonstrated her personal courage and commitment to the democratic cause.[39] To Burmese military leaders and their supporters, however, such personality traits only confirmed their view that Aung San Suu Kyi was an archetypal 'difficult' woman – stubborn, argumentative, irrational and (ultimately) dangerous to the state.[40] She did not know her 'proper' place (in the home or an 'appropriate' female profession), but rather involved herself in complex political affairs that – as an inferior woman – she was incapable of understanding and which should remain the exclusive domain of men. Aung San Suu Kyi remains vulnerable to such accusations, particularly since a number of commentators have argued that her insistence on economic sanctions has increased the suffering of ordinary Burmese citizens.[41] Her refusal to participate in the military-led National Convention and the 2010 general elections also prevented the NLD from participating in national political processes and decision-making, something discussed below.

Many Burmese who questioned Aung San Suu Kyi's ability to lead the opposition movement were influenced by the popular belief that women were inferior to men and, thus, incapable of effective political leadership. Given the ambivalence felt by most Burmese towards female rulers, historically, it is not surprising that many of Aung San Suu Kyi's supporters, women as well as men, downplayed the significance of her

39 Brooten, 'The feminization of democracy under siege', 134–56.

40 Maung Yin Hmaing, 'Daw Suu Kyi, the NLD Party and our ray of hope (Part 1)', in Maung Yin Hmaing et al., *'Daw Suu Kyi, NLD party and our ray of hope' and selected articles* ([Yangon]: U Soe Win, News and Periodicals Enterprise, September 2003), 1–5. After 2003, the authorities sought to justify Aung San Suu Kyi's extended detention on the grounds that she posed a threat to national stability.

41 In a recent report, the International Crisis Group claimed that while the military government's policies are largely to blame for Burma's economic crisis, sanctions imposed by the international community have adversely affected ordinary Burmese citizens. Some representatives of ethnic parties and pro-democracy activists have also called for sanctions to be reviewed or lifted altogether. See International Crisis Group, *Myanmar's post-election landscape*, Asia Briefing No. 118 (Jakarta; Brussels: International Crisis Group, 7 March 2011), 11–14. In her address to the World Economic Forum in January 2011, Aung San Suu Kyi stated that national reconciliation and political stability were necessary in order to achieve social and economic development. She acknowledged the need for economic innovation and diversification, but urged investors to put a premium on respect for the law, environmental and social factors, workers' rights, job creation and the promotion of technological skills. See 'Aung San Suu Kyi addresses the World Economic Forum in Davos', 4 February 2011. The audio message is available via the NLD website, www.nld. org, accessed 24 March 2011.

gender. They accepted her as a leader, but did not necessarily see her as a 'woman leader'.[42] For her own part, Aung San Suu Kyi refused to be drawn into a debate about the political significance of her gender. She has stated that she grew up around strong female role models (including her own mother) and, consequently, never felt oppressed as a woman. Nor did she believe, as some Western feminist scholars have argued, that she needed to 'defeminise' herself in order to gain political legitimacy: 'I don't try to make a man out of myself. I don't think that I need to develop a masculine style in order to be effective as a politician.'[43] Nonetheless, the fact that many Burmese were willing to 'overlook' Aung San Suu Kyi's gender suggests that they regarded her as an 'exceptional' woman. Moreover, by refusing to acknowledge that her gender was an issue (in terms of her ability to be an effective political leader), Aung San Suu Kyi seemed to ignore the fact that popular notions of gender impeded women's ability to access positions of political power and leadership.

The rise of the NLD and the 1990 election

Between October 1988 and July 1989, Aung San Suu Kyi and her colleagues concentrated on building up the NLD membership and support base in preparation for the general elections. Aung San Suu Kyi delivered hundreds of public speeches throughout the country, calling on people to maintain discipline and unity in order to achieve their goals of freedom and democracy. Political factionalism and power-mongering, she argued, would only weaken the democracy movement. She also emphasised her commitment to non-violence and her belief that armed struggle would only perpetuate the tradition that those who wield arms, wield power.[44] Threatened by Aung San Suu Kyi's growing influence among the electorate, the military authorities attempted to intimidate her supporters. NLD members, including many women, were specifically targeted and many were arrested and detained for their political activities. Despite these repressive measures, the NLD continued to grow

---

42   See interviews cited in Belak, *Gathering strength*, 261.

43   Cited in Judith A. White, 'Leadership through compassion and understanding', *Journal of Management Inquiry* 7, 4 (December 1998): 292. On the question of whether female politicians need to 'defeminise' themselves in order to be regarded as legitimate political leaders, see Kathleen B. Jones, *Compassionate authority: democracy and the representation of women* (New York; London: Routledge, 1993), 81.

44   Aung San Suu Kyi et al., *The voice of hope*, 25.

in size and strength. One female NLD campaigner, Daw Hla Hla Moe, later recalled how

> [a] lot of Burmese who wished for a democracy system in Burma did not even dare to attend our rallies and meetings. Often, as we made our way back to our homes, people would whisper as we passed from the roadside, 'The NLD is led by the daughter of our leader and the father of freedom, General Aung San. We will only vote for the NLD.'[45]

Apart from demonstrating that Aung San Suu Kyi's popular appeal at this time was based largely on her role as Aung San's daughter, this account supports John Kane's view that the NLD was 'an inclusive organizational vehicle that would give Aung San Suu Kyi's attractive power political effect'.[46] In other words, Aung San Suu Kyi provided a focal point around which a coherent political force (the NLD) could form.

Responding to the increasing oppression, Aung San Suu Kyi became more outspoken in her criticism of the military leadership. In July 1989, she publicly accused Ne Win of being responsible for Burma's political and economic problems and of controlling the SLORC from behind the scenes.[47] She refused to take part in the SLORC-organised ceremony to commemorate *Arzani* (Martyrs') Day and announced that she would pay respect to her father by marching with her followers instead, but the march was called off when army troops moved into Rangoon on the morning of 19 July. The authorities arrested Aung San Suu Kyi and Tin U the following day, allegedly for inciting sedition and hatred towards the armed forces. Both were detained until 1995, which prevented them from contesting the general elections held in May 1990.[48]

SLORC leaders apparently believed that, by placing Aung San Suu Kyi under house arrest, they had effectively destroyed the NLD as a political force. The government clearly underestimated the people's overwhelming desire for change: voters turned out in massive numbers to support the NLD, which won 392 of the 485 seats contested (or 80 per cent).[49] Most of the remaining seats went to ethnic parties which were allied with the

---

45 Daw Hla Hla Moe, 'The voices of women in our struggle', 52–53.

46 Kane, *The politics of moral capital*, 158.

47 'Heading for a showdown', *Asiaweek*, 14 July 1989; Aung San Suu Kyi, 'The people want freedom', in Aung San Suu Kyi, *Freedom from fear*, 233.

48 Aung San Suu Kyi was put under house arrest, but Tin U was sent to Insein Prison and placed in solitary confinement.

49 Elections were postponed in seven constituencies for security reasons.

NLD. Many ethnic minorities supported Aung San Suu Kyi because, like her father, she emphasised the need for unity and friendship between ethnic groups.[50] The National Unity Party (NUP) (formerly the BSPP) only won ten seats and NLD candidates were elected in several military-dominated districts, indicating that many *tatmadaw* personnel and their families voted for the NLD.[51] Aung San Suu Kyi later admitted that the SLORC, by harassing NLD members and placing her under house arrest, actually helped her party gain widespread support both inside Burma and in the international community.[52]

Following her arrest, opposition and foreign media organisations increasingly represented Burmese politics as an archetypal struggle between the forces of 'good' (led by Aung San Suu Kyi) and 'evil' (the military junta and its supporters). Such representations only served to enhance Aung San Suu Kyi's power in a moral, if not official, sense. As Michael Aung-Thwin observed, '[W]hen you pit a situation as good and evil only, and are given one choice, which choice will most people take?'[53] Although foreign policy makers may have encouraged such media representations for their own purposes,[54] indigenous conceptions of power have been equally important in ascribing a moral dimension to modern Burmese politics.

SLORC's structural power and Aung San Suu Kyi's personal power

In order to explain Aung San Suu Kyi's immense popularity and the NLD's electoral success, Gustaaf Houtman has drawn attention to two Burmese concepts of power – *ana* ('authority') and *awza* ('influence') – that emphasise the distinction between the military's structural power and Aung San Suu Kyi's personal power.[55] The military's power is characterised by *ana*-style authority in that it is both centralised and institutionalised.

---

50 Since the 1990 election, Aung San Suu Kyi has repeatedly called for tripartite dialogue between the military, NLD and ethnic representatives, further demonstrating her willingness to work towards genuine inter-ethnic reconciliation.

51 Lintner, *Aung San Suu Kyi and Burma's unfinished renaissance*, 25–26.

52 Aung San Suu Kyi et al., *The voice of hope*, 147. Aung San Suu Kyi was awarded the Nobel Peace Prize in 1991 in recognition of her efforts to promote peace, reconciliation and human rights in Burma.

53 Cited in Farrelly, 'Interview with Michael Aung-Thwin'.

54 Michael Aung-Thwin, 'Parochial universalism, democracy jihad and the Orientalist image of Burma: the new evangelism', *Pacific Affairs* 74, 4 (Winter 2001–02): 483–505; Brooten, 'The feminization of democracy under siege', 134–56.

55 Houtman, *Mental culture in Burmese crisis politics*, 157–76.

SLORC and SPDC leaders consistently refused to distribute power to anyone outside the military. *Ana* usually has a negative connotation, since authority is often established through the use of force. People submitted to military authority because they feared oppression, not because they respected the regime. *Azwa*, by contrast, is an inherently positive quality associated with individuals who possess great charisma, wisdom and high morality. Individuals with *awza* are influential because they are respected by the people. The Burmese have always placed great value on their leaders' personal qualities, which is why military leaders felt threatened by Aung San Suu Kyi's popular appeal.

Military authorities and their supporters portrayed Aung San Suu Kyi as a power-hungry individual who 'considers the NLD as if she owns it, and acts as the sole proprietor of the organisation, [and] is certainly not in tune with the desires of the rest of the NLD party members'.[56] She was even compared to 'evil', 'scheming' queens in Burmese history whose insatiable desire for power threatened the integrity of the state: '[Aung San Suu Kyi] would persist in attempting to break up national solidarity and jeopardise national sovereignty ... Nanmadaw Mai Nu of Konbaung Period and Supayalat of Yandabon Period might possibly have some redeeming feature but Daw Suu has none.'[57] Aung San Suu Kyi maintained that she had no desire to gain power for herself, but wished to ensure that ordinary Burmese were sufficiently empowered to participate in the governance of the country:

> We are not working to gain power [but] are working for the development of democracy because we believe that it is only a democratic government that could benefit the country. Let me make it clear that it is not because we want to be the government [but] because we believe that it is only the people that have the right to elect a government.[58]

Her statement is consistent with an *awza* model of political action in which power is distributed or dispersed among the people. Aung San Suu Kyi claimed that she was not interested in 'personality politics', although she admitted that she served as a useful focal point for the democratic

---

56 Maung Yin Hmaing, 'Daw Suu Kyi, the NLD Party and our ray of hope (Part 1)', 2.

57 *New Light of Myanmar*, 30 September, 1996.

58 Quote from Aung San Suu Kyi's statement at the closing ceremony of the 9th NLD Congress on 15 October 1997, cited in Houtman, *Mental culture in Burmese crisis politics*, 362.

movement.[59] In fact, her personal power was a crucial element in the overwhelming vote for the NLD during the 1990 election. Although Aung San Suu Kyi held no formal political office, she possessed great *awza* in terms of her personal charisma and spiritual leadership which was (and is) recognised by many Burmese. Aung San also had *awza*, but Aung San Suu Kyi's supporters believe she possesses *awza* in her own right. In the words of one female political activist whom I interviewed in 2003:

> We admire and love Aung San Suu Kyi and accept her policies because of her *awza*. I used to respect her because she was Aung San's daughter, but that is not so relevant [now] as it was ten years ago because people can see she has proven her ability as a leader .... The generals say they are Buddhists, but then they oppress the people. Aung San Suu Kyi is a true Buddhist because she treats everyone with *metta* [loving-kindness].[60]

This sentiment was echoed by other interviewees, indicating that Aung San Suu Kyi's political values, which are based largely on Buddhist principles, provide her with a source of moral power that is distinct from her role as Aung San's daughter.

Aung San Suu Kyi's use of Buddhist concepts

Aung San Suu Kyi's political principles are conceptualised in Buddhist terms, which has magnified the moral power invested in her by many Burmese.[61] Her high morality provided a stark contrast to the military generals' authoritarianism, corruption, violence and oppression. In the essay, 'In Quest of Democracy', which was published in *Freedom from fear and other writings* during her first period of house arrest, Aung San Suu Kyi described the Ten Duties of Kings as the yardstick for good government in modern Burma.[62] The ten kingly duties are liberality (*dana*), morality (*sila*), self-sacrifice (*paricagga*), integrity (*ajjava*), kindness (*maddava*), austerity (*tapa*), non-anger (*akkodha*), non-violence (*avihansa*), forbearance (*khanti*), and non-opposition to the will of the people (*avirodha*). By outlining the moral attributes of good rulers, Aung San Suu Kyi implied

---

59 Williams, *Wives, mistresses and matriarchs*, 174.

60 Personal interview, Yangon (Rangoon), 12 December 2003.

61 Some supporters have even likened her to a female *bodhisattva* – a being striving for the attainment of Buddhahood. See Houtman, *Mental culture in Burmese crisis politics*, 282–84. Aung San Suu Kyi dismisses this idea, but admits that she strives constantly for self-improvement. See Aung San Suu Kyi et al., *The voice of hope*, 28.

62 Aung San Suu Kyi, 'In quest of democracy' in Aung San Suu Kyi, *Freedom from fear*, 167–79.

that the military leaders' moral shortcomings made them unfit to rule. Furthermore, by embodying these moral qualities, she has demonstrated to the Burmese that she is capable of being a good ruler. In this way, she evokes the traditional Burmese concept of a *minlaung* ('imminent king') – one who overthrows an unjust ruler and restores benevolent rule in accordance with Buddhist precepts. According to historian Donald Seekins, many Burmese regard Aung San Suu Kyi as a (female) *minlaung*, partly because of her 'royal' heritage as the daughter of Aung San but, moreover, because of her spiritual power.[63] I have already mentioned Aung San Suu Kyi's commitment to one of the ten kingly duties (non-violence) above. Many Burmese also recognise other leadership qualities in Aung San Suu Kyi, notably her high morality, austerity, kindness and self-sacrifice.

Morality and karma

Buddhist principles form the basis of Aung San Suu Kyi's twin philosophies of 'spiritual revolution' and 'freedom from fear'. The power of the democratic movement, she has argued, derives from 'the spiritual steadiness that comes from the belief that what [we] are doing is right'.[64] For Aung San Suu Kyi, only a democratic society allows people the freedom to realise their potential. She has claimed that there is an inherent contradiction between Buddhism and dictatorship: in Buddhism, every human has the potential to create their own karma but, under authoritarian rule, the people are reduced to a 'faceless, mindless – and helpless – mass to be manipulated at will'.[65] Most Burmese are afraid to question the authorities because in doing so they risk losing their family and friends, their means of livelihood and their liberty. Military and other authoritarian leaders also operate on the basis of fear – they are afraid both of losing their power and of being held accountable for their actions. According to Aung San Suu Kyi, people can never be truly free while they live in fear: 'It is not power that corrupts, but fear. Fear of losing power corrupts those who wield it and fear of the scourge of power

---

63   Donald M. Seekins, 'Japan "Burma Lovers" and the military regime', Japan Policy Research Institute Working Paper No. 60 (Japan Policy Research Institute with University of San Francisco Center for the Pacific Rim, September 1999). See also Seekins, *The disorder in order*, 200.

64   Aung San Suu Kyi et al., *The voice of hope*, 164.

65   Aung San Suu Kyi, 'In quest of democracy', 175.

corrupts those who are subject to it.'[66] The people must, therefore, show courage and determination in opposing corruption and should not accept injustices committed by officials in the belief that the latter's bad karma will catch up with them in the end.[67] Aung San Suu Kyi believes that everyone has the power to effect change in their lives, and encourages people to question unjust laws and to educate themselves so that they will not be blinded or paralysed by fear.[68] In this sense, civil disobedience is not passive but requires positive action.

Aung San Suu Kyi's emphasis on action is directly related to the Buddhist concept of karma, which is central to how the Burmese conceive of power. On the one hand, belief in karma entails that everyone is born into the social situation that they deserve. In this sense, karma reinforces existing power structures, and military leaders used this notion of karma to claim a mandate to rule. Similarly, Aung San Suu Kyi must have gained considerable karma in previous lifetimes to be born into the family of Aung San into the first place. On the other hand, karma allows scope for personal agency: people can improve their karma, or lose it, depending on their actions in this life. By terrorising civilians through the use of violence, hatred and oppression, military leaders lost their mandate to rule. By contrast, the merit that Aung San Suu Kyi makes through conforming to Buddhist moral precepts adds to her existing karma. People who possess such merit (including senior monks and kings) have a spiritual power that enables them to do great things. Thus, Aung San Suu Kyi has the potential to lead because her moral power is recognised by the vast majority of Burmese. It is the spiritual power of her merit (*kuthou*) that the authorities fear, which is why they repeatedly extended her detention.

---

66 Aung San Suu Kyi, 'Freedom from fear', in Aung San Suu Kyi, *Freedom from fear*, 180–81. See also Josef Silverstein, 'The idea of freedom in Burma and the political thought of Daw Aung San Suu Kyi', *Pacific Affairs* 69, 2 (Summer 1996): 211–28. It is illustrative to compare the situation in Burma with that of Indonesia, where it was common for political and military leaders to accuse their opponents of involvement in corruption. Benedict Anderson noted that official corruption and the abuse of power had widespread political implications in Indonesia, since corruption was interpreted as a sign of a regime's decay. See Anderson, 'The idea of power in Javanese culture', 53.

67 Aung San Suu Kyi et al., *The voice of hope*, 169.

68 *Ibid.*, 25, 63.

Austerity

Physical confinement enhanced, rather than weakened, Aung San Suu Kyi's moral power, since it forced her to assume an ascetic lifestyle that Burmese Buddhists associate with spiritual purification. During her first period of house arrest, Aung San Suu Kyi became a dedicated practitioner of *vipassana* (insight) meditation, which many Burmese Buddhists use to cope with political crisis and confinement.[69] Vipassana meditation aims to develop wisdom or clear insight about the true nature of existence. Through meditation, it is possible to develop one's awareness of and control over fear and other emotions that stem from fear including anger and hatred: 'You cannot really be frightened of people you do not hate. Hate and fear go hand-in-hand.'[70] Aung San Suu Kyi adopted this Buddhist technique in order to overcome her own feelings of anger and frustration about the military regime's unjust policies. She even expressed gratitude to the SLORC for allowing her the opportunity to develop her spiritual strength.[71] Furthermore, through practising meditation, Aung San Suu Kyi could identify with her supporters throughout the country, including those who have been imprisoned for their political beliefs, in spirit if not in the flesh. Meditation, therefore, formed a central part of her political strategy of active resistance that enabled people to control their fear and challenge those in power.

Kindness and self-sacrifice

Aung San Suu Kyi encourages people to practise 'engaged Buddhism', which she defines as 'active compassion or active *metta* [loving-kindness]'.[72] The NLD, she argues, actively practises *metta* because 'we work like a family – we are not just colleagues. We have a real concern and affection for each other, which is the basis of our relationships.'[73] By practising *metta*, Aung San Suu Kyi demonstrates that she possesses nurturing, maternal

---

69 For a discussion on Aung San Suu Kyi and other NLD members' practice of vipassana meditation as a means of attaining personal and political awareness, see Houtman, *Mental culture in Burmese crisis politics*, 337–43. For a comprehensive study of how vipassana meditation functions as a form of popular discourse on political legitimacy and power in contemporary Burma, see Ingrid Jordt, *Burma's mass lay meditation movement: Buddhism and the cultural construction of power*, Ohio University Research in International Studies, Southeast Asia Series No. 115 (Athens: Ohio University Press, 2007).

70 Aung San Suu Kyi et al., *The voice of hope*, 35.

71 *Ibid.*, 123.

72 *Ibid.*, 37–38.

73 *Ibid.*, 158.

qualities, thereby countering claims that she is a bad wife and mother. During the mid-1990s, in particular, the state-controlled media frequently accused Aung San Suu Kyi of betraying the Burmese *amyo* by marrying a foreigner and having his children: 'Instead of preserving the race of her parents, the Myanmar race … she destroyed it by mixing blood with an Englishman.'[74] At the same time, she was accused of prostituting not only herself but also the nation as a whole. Monique Skidmore has described how the government and its supporters likened Aung San Suu Kyi to a prostitute who willingly gave up her own body and the Burmese nation to her Western 'neocolonial masters'.[75]

The SLORC also derided Aung San Suu Kyi for neglecting the needs of her own family due to her selfish desire for political power. Military leaders claimed that Aung San Suu Kyi was free to visit her husband after he was diagnosed with cancer in 1997, but the Burmese authorities refused to grant Michael a visa which would have enabled him to visit his wife. Aung San Suu Kyi chose to remain in Burma because she believed that if she left the country she would not be allowed to return. She never again saw her husband, who died in March 1999. Her sons' Burmese passports were cancelled in 1989, and she was unable to maintain regular contact with them while under house arrest as she was denied phone and internet access. Kim was finally granted a visa in November 2010 following Aung San Suu Kyi's release from house arrest, which allowed him to visit his mother for the first time in ten years.[76]

The regime's efforts to separate Aung San Suu Kyi from her family not only failed to weaken her political resolve, they also made many Burmese and foreigners more sympathetic towards her and her cause. Supporters have interpreted her political commitment as a form of personal sacrifice, demonstrating her willingness to prioritise the welfare of the Burmese in the same way that a good woman sacrifices her own needs for the well-being of her family. One female NLD member, Let Let, has described how she was 'impressed by Daw Aung San Suu Kyi's

74 Po Yaygyan, 'Adrift and washed ashore', *New Light of Myanmar*, 9 May 1997. See also Taungdwin Bo Thein, 'The US, a country surrounded by enemies', *Kyemon*, 6 July 1997; Pauk Sa, 'What do you think? The ugly American', *Kyemon*, 14 October 1996.

75 Monique Skidmore, *Karaoke fascism: Burma and the politics of fear* (Philadelphia: University of Pennsylvania Press, 2004), 133–37.

76 'Aung San Suu Kyi and son Kim reunited after 10 years', *BBC News Asia-Pacific*, 23 November 2010.

Figure 7.2: Aung San Suu Kyi and her younger son Kim visit Shwedagon Pagoda, Rangoon, 24 November 2010 (© AP via AAP [Khin Maung Win]).

courage, bravery and leadership .... Being a mother, I was even more amazed when I learned more about how she put the people of Burma above her own family life.'[77] Aung San Suu Kyi's love and concern for her fellow citizens has been likened by many Burmese to the *metta* shown by a mother towards her children. When the authorities allowed Aung San Suu Kyi to travel upcountry in 2003, thousands of supporters came out to welcome her as the 'mother' of the people.[78] During the 2007 anti-government protests, Buddhist monks marched past Aung San Suu Kyi's house while chanting the *metta* sutra, in recognition of the sacrifices she has made on behalf of ordinary Burmese.[79] Thus, Aung San Suu Kyi's

---

77   Let Let, 'We tie our hands together for strength (innocent aunty goes to prison)', in Altsean Burma, *Burma – women's voices together*, 102.

78   'Daw Aung San Suu Kyi in Phakant', *Democratic Voice of Burma*, 14 May 2003.

79   Human Rights Watch, *Crackdown: repression of the 2007 popular protests in Burma*, 19, 18(C) (December 2007), 30, 39–41.

'feminine' qualities of self-sacrifice, kindness and compassion are widely regarded as political strengths, not weaknesses.

Limitations of Aung San Suu Kyi's power

By centralising Aung San Suu Kyi's moral power, we can understand her political principles and behaviour in terms of the Burmese Buddhist concept of *awza*. Yet her *awza* presents a significant challenge in terms of how to reconcile traditional Burmese culture with the goal of achieving modern democratic rule. Although Aung San Suu Kyi stresses the importance of establishing genuine democratic institutions to empower ordinary Burmese, the NLD relies heavily on her charismatic leadership and personalised power. It is a measure of that power that the military felt it necessary to institutionalise Aung San Suu Kyi's exclusion from future political office. Following the 1990 elections, the SLORC refused to transfer power to the newly elected representatives, claiming that their task was to draft a new constitution, not to form a parliament.[80] When the military-sponsored National Convention eventually published its constitutional guidelines in September 2007, pro-democracy activists denounced them as completely unacceptable.[81] The 2008 Constitution prevents Aung San Suu Kyi (and many others) from becoming President of the Union, as presidential candidates cannot have spouses or children who are foreign citizens. Persons serving prison terms are also prevented from becoming elected representatives.[82] This provision seriously handicaps democratic activists who may wish to stand for election, since they can easily be imprisoned on trumped-up charges.

Aung San Suu Kyi's personal power and influence within the NLD are problematic for other reasons. It is extremely difficult for NLD members and other democratic actors to question or openly challenge

---

80 'Report: Khin Nyunt responds to claims about transfer of power, PRC views, prisoners, 13 July 1990', in Weller (ed.), *Democracy and politics in Burma*, 188–94; 'SLORC, Announcement No. 1/90, 27 July 1990', in *Ibid.*, 194–96.

81 'Draft constitution surfaces, stirring more debate', *The Irrawaddy*, 31 March 2008.

82 Government of the Union of Myanmar, *Constitution of the Republic of the Union of Myanmar (2008)* ([Myanmar]: Printing & Publishing Enterprise, Ministry of Information, September 2008), especially articles 59 and 121. Hereafter cited as '*Constitution of the Republic of the Union of Myanmar (2008)*'. In the wake of Cyclone Nargis in May 2008, the SPDC held a national referendum in which a reported 92.48 per cent of voters endorsed the new Constitution. Many Burmese and foreign observers denounced the referendum as a 'sham', but the constitution officially came into force on 31 January 2011 when the national legislature held its first combined session.

her views, since this can easily be interpreted as creating divisions within the party and weakening the democratic movement in general. In the lead-up to the 2010 general elections, some NLD members felt that there may be a case for participating if this would allow them a voice in parliament. The NLD planned to hold a secret ballot on the issue, but this was called off after Aung San Suu Kyi's lawyer and Central Executive Committee member Nyan Win reported that she 'would not even think about registering under these unjust [election] laws'.[83] The NLD decided not to contest the elections and the party was officially deregistered as the election laws required political parties to register for the elections by 6 May 2010. A number of NLD members broke with the main party and formed the National Democratic Force (NDF) to contest the elections, but NDF candidates only won 16 (1.4 per cent) of the elected seats in the national and regional assemblies.[84]

A report published by the International Crisis Group argues that NDF and other pro-democracy candidates suffered during the 2010 election campaign because they were perceived as going against Aung San Suu Kyi's wishes. Furthermore, the NLD's decision to boycott the elections deprived voters of an obvious pro-democratic choice.[85] As a result of this and other factors – including restrictive election laws, vote rigging and intimidation of voters by the authorities – the military-backed Union Solidarity and Development Party (USDP) won 76.6 per cent of the elected legislative seats.[86] While Aung San Suu Kyi did not openly criticise those who chose to participate in the elections, it appears that many of her supporters believed they had to show a 'united front' even if this meant ostracising those who disagreed with official NLD policy. An unintended consequence of this type of thinking is that democratic debate within the party and in the wider community is stifled.

Aung San Suu Kyi's supporters may look to her for guidance, but she has always stressed that the Burmese have the power to bring about change themselves. Decades of political oppression, media censorship and official corruption have made many Burmese reluctant to express

---

83   Ba Kaung, 'Suu Kyi against NLD joining elections', *The Irrawaddy*, 23 March 2010.

84   For a list of election results by party, see International Crisis Group, *Myanmar's post-election landscape*, 17–18.

85   International Crisis Group, *The Myanmar elections*, Asia Briefing No. 105 (Jakarta; Brussels: International Crisis Group, 27 May 2010), 11–12.

86   International Crisis Group, *Myanmar's post-election landscape*, 17–18.

their opinions freely. Since the 2010 elections, however, there have been some positive signs of a gradual opening up of political space. The government has relaxed media censorship, released some political prisoners, suspended work on an unpopular hydropower dam, and passed legislation allowing citizens to stage peaceful protests and to form unions. Aung San Suu Kyi met with President Thein Sein in August 2011, and in November the NLD decided to re-register as a political party and to contest upcoming by-elections. Aung San Suu Kyi is likely to remain a powerful political actor, but genuine democratisation should involve the strengthening of credible institutions and sources of pluralism in Burmese society which would, ultimately, dilute her personal influence.

Women's influence in the democratic movement

Aung San Suu Kyi's prominence has had a profound effect on the way women view their roles in Burmese society, particularly in terms of their political capabilities. Inspired by her courage and commitment, women became some of the most enthusiastic members and supporters of the NLD, particularly during the lead-up to the 1990 election. Some women rose to senior executive positions within the party, indicating that Aung San Suu Kyi's high profile had opened up new opportunities for women to engage in political leadership and decision-making. In total, 15 women won seats in the 1990 election. All were NLD candidates.[87] Following the election, however, the military further entrenched itself in power by expanding the capabilities of the armed forces and severely restricting the activities of NLD members and other democratic activists. The 2008 Constitution reserves one-quarter of legislative seats for appointed Defence Services personnel, ensuring that the male-dominated military will maintain a firm hold on political power in the newly formed 'civilian' government.[88] These factors reinforced the detrimental effect military rule had on women's capacity to exercise political power.

In many respects, the 1990 election marked the height of the NLD's success. After the initial elation following the party's decisive victory at the polls, many members became increasingly disillusioned due to the continued detention of Aung San Suu Kyi and other NLD leaders. The au-

---

87   The successful female candidates are listed in Belak, *Gathering strength*, 260.

88   See Articles 109(b) and 141(b) of the *Constitution of the Republic of the Union of Myanmar (2008)*.

thorities also stepped up their harassment of NLD elected representatives, members and supporters. Many female NLD members were imprisoned for extended periods. Daw San San, one of the elected representatives, was arrested in late 1990 and served a total of five years in prison. She has described how she 'felt quite demoralized living [in] prison, which is like hell. I was isolated …. I knew later that the guards had been warned by the jailer not to contact to [sic] me …. They saw and feared me as a rebel.'[89] Women were sometimes arrested simply as a warning to others not to become involved in NLD activities. One female prisoner, Thi Thi Aung, shared her cell with a woman who was 'just a sightseer, not an activist or participant in the demonstration. She was imprisoned as an example to the public of what happens to people who support Daw Aung San Suu Kyi.'[90] Thus, the regime's strategy involved punishing and demoralising NLD members, while simultaneously demonising them and Aung San Suu Kyi in the eyes of ordinary Burmese.

Political activism involved great personal sacrifices for women, since they risked imprisonment and separation from their families and children, in particular. Yet many women were prepared to endure long periods apart from their loved ones in order to further the democratic cause. When one of Aung San Suu Kyi's close colleagues, Ma Hla, was arrested, she banned her two daughters from visiting her so they would not see their mother in jail.[91] Nilar Thein, a seasoned political activist who participated in the 1988 and the 2007 anti-government protests, went into hiding after her husband was arrested in August 2007, leaving behind her four-month-old daughter whom she had been breastfeeding.[92] Relatives and friends of NLD members and other opposition activists were also subjected to discrimination and intimidation by the authorities. Daw San San's daughter, who worked in Rangoon as a public prosecutor, was reassigned to a remote post in Kachin State because of her mother's po-

---

89 Interview with Daw San San, cited in Burmese Women's Union and Assistance Association for Political Prisoners (Burma), *Women political prisoners in Burma: joint report* ([Chiang Mai; Mae Sot]: Burmese Women's Union and Assistance Association for Political Prisoners (Burma), September 2004), 127. Hereafter cited as 'BWU and AAPP, *Women political prisoners in Burma*'.

90 Interview with Thi Thi Aung, cited in BWU and AAPP, *Women political prisoners in Burma*, 145.

91 Williams, *Wives, mistresses and matriarchs*, 180.

92 Women's League of Burma, *Courage to resist: women human rights defenders in Burma* (Chiang Mai: Women's League of Burma, November 2007), 4, 10.

litical activities. Another NLD member, Daw Hman, recalled that, 'Only a few people dared to visit my house and befriend with [sic] me as the MI [military intelligence] also watched and questioned my friends and colleagues.'[93] Many opposition activists felt isolated when relatives and friends distanced themselves in an effort to avoid confrontation with the authorities. Even when family members were supportive, activists often felt guilty for endangering their safety.

The regime employed a range of strategies designed to break the spirit of democratic activists. Many political prisoners were deprived of food, medicine, clothing and water; some were beaten and tortured by military intelligence officers and prison staff. Female political prisoners were subjected to particular forms of abuse because of their gender. Many women suffered under the constant threat of sexual assault by prison guards, and some pregnant women were forced to give birth in prison without medical assistance. Christina Fink interviewed one young woman, Kyi Kyi, who was accused by intelligence officers of having affairs with her male NLD colleagues.[94] The authorities also tried to create tensions between political prisoners to destroy their morale and sense of solidarity. Ma Khin San Nwe was sent to a detention camp along with over 50 other women as part of a major military crackdown after the NLD called for the convening of a People's Parliament in 1998. Intelligence officers tried to persuade the women to resign from the party and imposed different sentences on individuals to cause divisions between them. Although Ma Khin San Nwe defiantly claimed that 'their attacks only make us stronger',[95] the NLD was seriously weakened as a result of such tactics.

By 1998, over 1,000 party members and supporters were imprisoned and 112 elected representatives were either no longer active in the party or in exile.[96] Four of the fifteen female elected representatives had been dismissed by the Electoral Commission, three were in prison, one had resigned from the NLD, and one had died.[97] Since then, many women have continued to face arrest and imprisonment for organising and par-

---

93   Daw Hman, 'True story', in Altsean Burma, *Burma – women's voices for change*, 30.

94   Fink, *Living silence*, 167.

95   Ma Khin San Nwe, 'Kha La Ya 220 anguish', in Altsean Burma, *Burma – women's voices for change*, 105.

96   Smith, *Burma: insurgency*, 436.

97   All Burma Students' Democratic Front, *To stand and be counted* (Bangkok: All Burma Students' Democratic Front, June 1998), 21.

ticipating in political activities and anti-government demonstrations. During the 'Saffron Revolution' in September 2007, in which thousands of Burmese took to the streets to protest against steep increases in fuel costs and the regime's raids on Buddhist monasteries, over 130 women were arrested. In September 2011, the Assistance Association for Political Prisoners (Burma) reported that there were 142 known female political prisoners. While many women were arrested in 2007 or later, some had been imprisoned for more than ten years.[98]

Even when women were released from prison, they were closely monitored by the authorities and threatened when they tried to resume their political activities. Daw Kyu Kyu Mar was the secretary of the NLD women's branch in North Okkapala township when she was arrested in 1998. Following her release in 2002, military intelligence officers followed her whenever she went to the NLD headquarters: 'The MI personnel were always behind us, like our shadows. If we stepped wrong, we would be [re]arrested and imprisoned.'[99] Despite obvious risks to their security, many women continued to support the NLD, but their political activities were severely circumscribed. Ah May Saw returned to her local NLD office two days after her release from prison in late 1998, only to find that her colleagues' activities were limited to 'putting [up the] party's signboards for some of our offices'.[100] Daw San San rejoined the NLD when she was released from prison in 2001 because the party's membership had been drastically depleted. She was reinstalled as vice chair of the Rangoon Division and became a leader of the NLD Women's Wing, but was forced to flee to Thailand to avoid rearrest following the assault on Aung San Suu Kyi's convoy and her supporters near Depayin on 30 May 2003, when at least ten NLD supporters were killed and many more were wounded and arrested.[101]

---

98 Assistance Association for Political Prisoners (Burma), 'Monthly Chronology September, 2011', http://www.aappb.org/chronology_2011.html. Seventeen women were released in October 2011.

99 Firsthand account of Daw Kyu Kyu Mar, cited in BWU and AAPP, *Women political prisoners in Burma*, 108.

100 Ah May Saw, 'With reminiscent images', in Altsean Burma, *Burma – women's voices for change*, 47.

101 Aung San Suu Kyi was rearrested at this time, along with many other NLD members and supporters. Daw San San had originally been sentenced to 25 years imprisonment, so her suspended sentence would have been extended if she was caught engaging in political activities. See Interview with Daw San San, cited in BWU and AAPP, *Women political*

Many women who sought to escape restrictions on their mobility went into exile or to the NLD Liberated Area (NLD–LA) on the Thai–Burma border, where the NLD–LA Women's Wing was formed in 1999. One member, Yu Yu, has described how she felt empowered working with other female NLD members and interacting with Burmese women's organisations that had been formed in exile following the 1988 uprising:

> [W]orking in a women's organization has been valuable in developing our independence and autonomy. Women's achievements are more apparent and women are central to their own capacity building. Women have something unique to offer, making them crucial to the struggle for a better Burma. When women of Burma are given the space to work abreast with men at all levels, utilizing their diverse abilities and capacities, everyone benefits.[102]

This statement implies that some female NLD members felt constrained, not only by the military's restrictions on their movement, but also by cultural perceptions about the proper role for women within the democratic movement.

The wider debate about women's rights

As indicated above, many Burmese regarded Aung San Suu Kyi as an 'exceptional' woman. Thus, it did not necessarily follow that respect and admiration for Aung San Suu Kyi would lead to an increase in women's political power in general. In reality, structural inequality within the democratic movement has limited most women's political participation to supportive roles. During the 1990 election, 84 out of 2,296 candidates were women and 15 women were elected; to put it another way, only three per cent of candidates and elected representatives were women. For many years, Aung San Suu Kyi was the only woman on the Central Executive Committee, although a number of women served in executive positions at the divisional and district levels. Aung San Suu Kyi has never explicitly addressed the issue of how gender inequality within her own party disadvantages women, although she has acknowledged that deep-rooted cultural beliefs about women's role in the family may deter many women from seeking prominent political positions:

---

prisoners in Burma, 133; Altsean Burma, *Arrested: report card on Burma, 1 Apr–30 Jun 2003* (Bangkok: Alternative ASEAN Network on Burma, November 2003), 20–21.

102 Yu Yu, 'Strength amidst tragedy', in Altsean Burma, *Burma – women's voices for change*, 51.

I think one of the things that prevents women from rising as high in politics as they ought to is the fact that they still do like to give considerable time to their families. ... Perhaps not that many women would be prepared to take so many risks if they feel they have an obligation to their family.[103]

For many years, Aung San Suu Kyi argued that it was more important to fight for human rights than women's rights because men and women were equally vulnerable to injustice and oppression under military rule.[104] Her position was similar to that taken by female nationalists of the colonial era who prioritised the nationalist struggle against British rule above everything else, including women's rights.

From the mid-1990s onwards, however, Aung San Suu Kyi began to promote women's roles within the democratic movement, possibly in response to the increased focus on women's rights and empowerment in international forums. In August 1995, she gave the keynote address at the NGO Forum as part of the UN Fourth World Conference on Women in Beijing, in which she emphasised the need to empower women and remove 'gender barriers' that discriminate against women.[105] In an article published in *The Nation* newspaper in March 2000, she stated that 'The longer I work in politics, the more I am convinced that there is a need to work for women's rights.'[106] She has also sent messages of support and encouragement to Burmese women living in exile as well as those inside the country. While recognising that many women have suffered from violence, poverty and poor education and health services, she reminds women that they also possess great courage, determination, understanding and compassion:

Women have traditionally played the role of unifier and peacemaker within the family. They instil a nurturing sense of togetherness and mutual caring. They balance love and tenderness with discipline while nurturing growth and understanding. Women have the capacity for the compassion, self-sacrifice, courage and perseverance necessary to dissipate the darkness of intolerance and hate, suffering and despair. Women

---

103 White, 'Leadership through compassion and understanding', 292.

104 Aung San Suu Kyi et al., *The voice of hope*, 159–60.

105 Having only just been released from house arrest, her speech was pre-recorded and presented at the conference as a video. A copy of her speech is published in ABSDF, *Burma and the role of women*, 55–61.

106 'Suu Kyi: a need to work for women's rights', *The Nation* (Bangkok), 14 March 2000.

have an innate talent for resolving differences and creating warmth and understanding within a framework of mutual respect and consideration. This talent should be used to address not only our individual, family and community needs, but also to contribute towards the process of reconciliation, which will make our country a democratic society that guarantees the basic rights of the people.[107]

Aung San Suu Kyi believes that women's 'innate' qualities and 'traditional' roles in the family should be regarded and respected as political strengths, not weaknesses. The above statement is consistent with her view that power should be inclusive and that genuine democratic reform and national reconciliation can only be achieved through collective effort, with everyone doing their part. Yet Aung San Suu Kyi also appears to condone cultural beliefs that emphasise the primacy of women's domestic role. She has never explicitly encouraged women to aspire to political leadership roles, particularly at the national level, possibly because she does not want to alienate supporters (including many older Burmese) who believe that politics should remain the preserve of men.

In recent years, the NLD has expanded its leadership base to address the concerns of young Burmese who felt the party's ageing leadership excluded them from decision-making processes. In this regard, female youth members experienced discrimination because of their gender as well as their age. During interviews with former NLD members now based in Thailand in June 2005, a number of young women told me that their male NLD colleagues had not allowed them to participate in decision-making.[108] In late 2008, over 100 youth members resigned from the NLD, reportedly because they felt they had no real say in determining party policy.[109] The NLD responded to these calls for more inclusive decision-making by expanding its central youth wing and women's working group. In early 2010, the NLD announced the formation of a 100-member Central Committee, which included 13 women. Daw May Win Myint, one of the 1990 elected representatives and former leader of the NLD Women's Wing, was appointed as the second woman in

---

107 Daw Aung San Suu Kyi, 'A foundation of enduring strength', in Altsean Burma, *Burma – women's voices together*, 1–2.

108 Personal interviews with former NLD members, Chiang Mai, 24 June 2005. See also Maureen Aung-Thwin, 'Burma: a disenfranchised prime minister, the myth of equality, women from heaven': 18–21.

109 Kyaw Zwa Moe, 'A house divided', *The Irrawaddy*, 17 October 2008.

the 20-member Central Executive Committee.[110] While these organisational changes appear to signal a willingness to involve more women in political leadership and decision-making, the NLD Women's Wing is primarily involved in coordinating social welfare programs, which traditionally have been regarded as 'women's work'.

Many young female activists who left Burma continue to be involved in the exiled democratic movement. For expatriate Burmese women's organisations, Aung San Suu Kyi's image serves as a unifying force. Since 1997, they have celebrated her birthday (19 June) as 'Women of Burma Day' to acknowledge women's roles in promoting peace, human rights and democracy in Burma. These organisations have publicly declared their solidarity with Aung San Suu Kyi and other female political activists inside Burma.[111] Yet many expatriate women's organisations have developed explicitly feminist objectives that Aung San Suu Kyi herself has never espoused, prompting some members to question her apparently traditionalist view of gender relations.[112] On several occasions, Aung San Suu Kyi has stated that she does not consider herself a feminist because she believes men and women are equally capable of bringing about political change.[113] While under house arrest, she was unable to clarify her position on women's rights at a time when the military government was establishing its own organisations to address – and, moreover, regulate – women's issues, the subject of the next chapter.

Conclusions

When Aung San Suu Kyi delivered her first political speech at Shwedagon Pagoda in August 1988, she offered hope to many Burmese who were desperate for change after years of oppressive military rule. Initially, some Burmese questioned whether a woman could effectively lead the opposition movement. The fact that she is Aung San's daughter undoubt-

---

110 'NLD restructures top decision-making body', *Mizzima News*, 14 January 2010; Htet Aung Kyaw and Francis Wade, 'Women included in NLD expansion', *Democratic Voice of Burma*, 15 January 2010.

111 Women's League of Burma, 'Statement on the 65th birthday of Daw Aung San Suu Kyi', 19 June 2010; 'The Women's League of Burma welcomes Daw Aung San Suu Kyi's release and demands ongoing action to ensure freedom for all of Burma', 13 November 2010. Both accessed from the WLB website, www.womenofburma.org, on 23 March 2011.

112 Interviews with members of Burmese women's organisations, Chiang Mai, 19 May 2005.

113 White, 'Leadership through compassion and understanding', 292; Aung San Suu Kyi et al., *The voice of hope*, 160.

edly raised Aung San Suu Kyi's political credibility in the eyes of many Burmese. She deliberately and explicitly invoked her father's ideals and objectives in order to emphasise her legitimacy as a political leader. Aung San Suu Kyi also demonstrated that she was a (great) leader in her own right by adhering to Buddhist principles of non-violence, compassion and kindness. The fact that she had no formal political power was largely irrelevant because it was her personal charisma and influence that attracted her followers and threatened the authorities. Yet Aung San Suu Kyi's moral approach to politics led to a political standoff with military leaders, who further entrenched themselves in power while simultaneously seeking to silence all democratic opposition. Although Aung San Suu Kyi's prominence inspired many women to join the NLD, their political roles have been constrained, not only as a result of military oppression, but also because of gender inequality within the democratic movement itself. Aung San Suu Kyi has encouraged women to use their talents and influence within their families and local communities to promote national reconciliation and democratic reform. At the central level, the NLD has included more women in its central decision-making bodies and sought to expand its reach among the female population. Yet Aung San Suu Kyi rarely challenged, and occasionally appeared to endorse, traditionalist notions of gender that limit women's political activism at a time when the military government moved to strengthen its own women's movement.

8

Women's 'Advancement' under the SLORC and SPDC

*I*n the early 1990s, the SLORC[1] began to promote itself as a government committed to 'the advancement of women'. Since the military leadership had always insisted that men and women have equal rights, this move can be seen as a response to the focus on women's rights in international forums, the political organisation of expatriate Burmese women in the borderlands, and Aung San Suu Kyi's enduring popularity inside the country. The government established its own 'national machinery' for the protection and advancement of women's rights, which actually precluded many women from participating in decision-making or forming their own independent organisations outside government control. SLORC and SPDC leaders showed little interest in addressing existing cultural discrimination against women, preferring instead to use the concept of 'traditional culture' to reinforce their own authority over women and mobilise them in support of government policies. In doing so, the regime largely ignored the socioeconomic development needs of most Burmese women, including those in ethnic and rural areas as well as pro-democracy supporters, and instead concentrated power in the hands of a few women with close connections to the military elite. Many ordinary women, in the absence of civil society, were (and are) obliged to join state-sponsored women's organisations in an effort to get ahead in life.

---

1   In November 1997, military rulers changed the name of the government from State Law and Order Restoration Council (SLORC) to State Peace and Development Council (SPDC). This name change was widely perceived as a tactical move to ameliorate a poor international image. The council leadership remained the same and there was no change in official policy regarding women's issues.

The role of the 'GONGOs'

Civil society refers to institutions and networks that operate outside the government, including religious, cultural, social, professional, educational and other community organisations. These groups provide sources of pluralism in society, potentially diffusing the power of a centralised, authoritarian state. The development of a strong civil society is widely regarded as crucial to the process of democratisation.[2] SLORC and SPDC leaders viewed civil society as a threat to their power and consequently did not allow citizens to enjoy the fundamental freedoms upon which the development and maintenance of civil society depends. Opportunities for citizens to participate in civil society remain restricted by government regulations such as the draconian Order 2/88, which prohibits unauthorised meetings of more than five persons and has not been repealed. The regime effectively co-opted civil society by creating its own organisations to mobilise support for its policies among the civilian population. Although these organisations describe themselves as 'independent', they either actively promote or indirectly support government ideology, policies and programs.[3] For this reason, critics refer to these groups as 'Government-Organised Non-Governmental Organisations' or 'GONGOs' in order to distinguish them from 'real' NGOs. I have chosen to focus on two of these organisations: the Myanmar Maternal and Child Welfare Association (MMCWA) and the Myanmar Women's Entrepreneurs' Association (MWEA).[4]

Myanmar Maternal and Child Welfare Association (MMCWA)
The MMCWA was formed in 1991 after the SLORC promulgated the Myanmar Maternal and Child Welfare Association Law 21/90.[5] The association's main objective is to promote the health and well-being of women and children with particular emphasis on maternal health. It has largely taken over the functions previously carried out by private

---

2   David I. Steinberg, 'A void in Myanmar: civil society in Burma', in Burma Center Netherlands (BCN) and Transnational Institute (TNI) (eds.), *Strengthening civil society in Burma: possibilities and dilemmas for international NGOs* (Chiang Mai: Silkworm Books, 1999), 2–3. See also Belak, *Gathering strength*, 264; Skidmore, *Karaoke fascism*, 101.

3   Belak, *Gathering strength*, 264.

4   Another 'GONGO', the Union Solidarity and Development Association (USDA), is mentioned in chapter 6.

5   *The Myanmar Maternal and Child Welfare Association Law* (The State Law and Order Restoration Council Law No. 21/90) (9 November 1990).

maternal health organisations and operates maternal shelters and outpatient clinics, which provide basic antenatal and postnatal care for pregnant women and mothers. The MMCWA also conducts educational programs on family planning, breastfeeding, nutritional needs and disease control including HIV/AIDS awareness and prevention. Childcare facilities, functional literacy programs and income generation schemes are also provided for poor women. The association works in close collaboration with related government departments and some UN agencies, notably UNICEF.

Although the MMCWA describes itself as an 'independent' NGO, many foreign and Burmese observers consider it to be indivisible from the government because all of its leaders – at national, regional and local levels – are wives of government officials. The founding chairperson, Dr Khin Win Shwe, is the wife of Khin Nyunt, who was then Secretary-1 of the SLORC.[6] The MMCWA has therefore been referred to as 'a first wives club' and 'a mirror image of the male-dominated military administration'.[7] Independent observers and opposition activists understandably have serious doubts about the MMCWA leaders' ability to communicate with and address the concerns of ordinary women, particularly in cases where violence against women is committed by military personnel.[8]

A decade after its formation, the MMCWA had 870,000 voluntary members in its 312 township and 2,030 branch associations.[9] Six years later, in September 2007, the government reported that the total membership had grown to 4.5 million members.[10] The prominence given to

---

6   Belak, *Gathering strength*, 263. The organisational structure of the MMCWA mirrored that of official women's organisations formed in Indonesia under the New Order regime. A woman's position within the Dharma Pertiwi and Dharma Wanita corresponded to the civil service or military rank of her husband. See Indra McCormick, *Women as political actors in Indonesia's New Order*, Monash Asia Institute Working Paper 123 (Clayton, Vic.: Monash Asia Institute, 2003), 5.

7   Belak, *Gathering strength*, 263; May Pyone Aung, 'Unsung heroes in an unfinished struggle', *The Nation*, 19 June 1998.

8   Interview with female opposition activist, Chiang Mai, 23 June 2005; Belak, *Gathering strength*, 30; Moe Aye, 'Women NGOs, Burma's latest propaganda tool', *The Nation*, 20 June 1999.

9   Belak, *Gathering strength*, 263.

10   United Nations, Convention on the Elimination of All Forms of Discrimination Against Women, 'Consideration of reports presented by States parties under article 18 of the Convention on the Elimination of All Forms of Discrimination against Women. Combined

the MMCWA in the official media makes it appealing to women who wish to gain social, economic and political benefits associated with membership. Burma scholar Monique Skidmore interviewed one young woman, who said that '[p]eople join the MMCWA because it is seen as elite and signifies [that members have] money left over from buying necessities, as there is a membership fee and the cost of uniforms. They are very close to the [S]LORC and it is one way of getting contacts and favours.'[11] Possible disadvantages for not joining include loss of income, lowered social prestige, children being failed in school exams, and an increased risk of political persecution.[12] The government has sought to mobilise the MMCWA to support its own political objectives. MMCWA publications have included speeches criticising 'internal destructionists', a phrase commonly used by the regime to describe NLD members and other political opponents.[13] Foreign observers have linked the MMCWA's family planning programs in Arakan State to the persecution of the ethnic Rohingya population by Burman authorities.[14] Expatriate opposition groups have also claimed that local MMCWA leaders are involved in corruption, charging women high interest on micro-credit loans and pocketing the profits.[15] It is difficult to see how the MMCWA can implement programs fairly and consistently, given that it actively discriminates against ethnic minority women and opposition activists, and exploits poor and vulnerable women.

Myanmar Women's Entrepreneurs' Association (MWEA)
The MWEA was formed in February 1995 by a group of senior business-women in order to 'organise the energies and enterprise of Myanmar women.'[16] It is a relatively small organisation with around 1,350 members

---

second and third reports of States parties. Myanmar', CEDAW/C/MMR/3 (4 September 2007), 13. Hereafter cited as 'CEDAW/C/MMR/3'.

11   Cited in Skidmore, *Karaoke fascism*, 105.

12   *Ibid.*, 106.

13   Fink, *Living silence*, 247.

14   MMCWA brochure, 'Birth spacing projects, Project to Enhance All Reproductive Lives (PEARL)', cited in Marc Purcell, '"Axe-handles or willing minions?" International NGOs in Burma', in Burma Center Netherlands (BCN) and Transnational Institute (TNI) (eds.), *Strengthening civil society in Burma*, 87, 109.

15   Women of Burma, *In the shadow of the junta: CEDAW shadow report* (Women's League of Burma: Chiang Mai, 2008), 16.

16   Myanmar Women's Entrepreneurs' Association pamphlets (Yangon: Myanmar Women's Entrepreneurs' Association, 2005).

concentrated in Yangon (Rangoon). The MWEA organises monthly meetings and regular seminars to provide members with networking opportunities and entrepreneurial and managerial skills. MWEA leaders have also implemented micro-credit and savings schemes to provide funding for poor women working in bazaars and markets.

Although the MWEA describes itself as a 'non-political' organisation, it is widely perceived as being closely associated with the government, in part because of the fact that Khin Nyunt attended a number of its early events. According to Burma scholar Christina Fink, government leaders pressured the MWEA to invite Khin Nyunt to give the keynote address at the association's first anniversary celebration.[17] MWEA founder, Daw Yi Yi Myint, who strongly denies allegations of government interference, informed me that the MWEA invited Khin Nyunt to attend its opening ceremony as part of a deliberate strategy to 'hurry along the approval process'.[18] She added that the MWEA, unlike government-initiated NGOs, did not include wives of senior generals or officials in its governing body.[19] Members of expatriate women's organisations have criticised the MWEA for not doing enough to promote women's rights: 'Although MWEA leaders say they have empowered women through job creation, in reality they have achieved very little, such as building separate toilets for women in the marketplace.'[20] Other reports claim that MWEA leaders have openly criticised Aung San Suu Kyi and the NLD at seminars and told participants that 'politics is not the business of women'.[21] Such allegations make it difficult to accept the MWEA's claims to be apolitical, since it actively discourages women from becoming involved in opposition politics.

In the absence of a strong civil society, women wishing to become involved in community issues have few outlets for participation apart from

---

17 Fink also claims that the MWEA members were pressured to join the USDA and give contributions towards the organisation: Fink, *Living silence*, 134. See also 'Perspectives – Undisputable prominent role of Myanmar women', *New Light of Myanmar*, 27 February 2006.

18 All NGOs must register under the Companies Act, a difficult and time-consuming procedure.

19 Interview with Daw Yi Yi Myint, Yangon (Rangoon), 20 December 2003.

20 Interview with member of Kachin Woman's Association (Thailand), Chiang Mai, 20 June 2005.

21 Cited in Moe Aye, 'Women NGOs, Burma's latest propaganda tool', *The Nation*, 20 June 1999.

working with government-sanctioned organisations like the MMCWA and MWEA. Women who are involved in opposition politics, or related to opposition activists, cannot join these organisations. Independent community-based organisations are closely scrutinised, and members risk arrest if the authorities believe they exceed their mandate. The government has allowed some UN agencies and international non-governmental organisations (INGOs) to set up humanitarian programs in Burma to improve women's living standards, particularly in the areas of health, education and income generation. All INGOs are required to sign a Memorandum of Understanding with the government and collaborate with state-sponsored organisations like the MMCWA, which severely circumscribes their activities. Some INGO members believe that increased dialogue and engagement with government ministries and state-sanctioned NGOs can provide opportunities to influence government policies on key women's issues.[22] Other commentators argue that cooperation with central authorities is counter-productive, since aid is allocated according to the government's agenda rather than to areas and programs where it is most needed.[23] Under the military regime, INGOs certainly could not work openly with or even be seen to engage in discussions with democratic actors, particularly Aung San Suu Kyi and the NLD. Given the restrictions placed on indigenous and international NGOs, there are few organisations capable of playing the 'watch-dog' role of effectively monitoring and evaluating government programs.[24]

Government responses to the Beijing Platform for Action

Before 1995, there were no official government bodies dealing specifically with women's issues. The main reason for this, according to government representatives, was that women already had the same legal, social,

---

22 This view was put forward in a review of the Myanmar Protection of Children and Women Cluster which was established as part of the humanitarian response following Cyclone Nargis in May 2008. See UNICEF, UNFPA and Save the Children, 'Inter-agency review of the Myanmar Protection of Children and Women Cluster response to Cyclone Nargis. External Review. Participating Agencies: UNICEF, UNFPA, Save the Children' (October 2008), 40–43. The review is available online at http://www.humanitarianreform.org/Default.aspx?tabid=720, accessed on 20 May 2011.

23 Purcell, 'Axe-handles or willing minions?', 97.

24 Belak, *Gathering strength*, 30.

economic and political rights as men.[25] Since the mid-1990s, however, Aung San Suu Kyi's enduring popularity both inside Burma and in the international community, the emergence of Burmese women's organisations in exile, and the increasing focus on women's rights in international forums, have prompted the government to make – or, at least, to be seen to make – a greater effort to promote women's rights.

In 1995, the SLORC sent a (male-led) delegation to the UN Fourth World Conference on Women, held in Beijing. The outcome of the conference was the Beijing Declaration, highlighting the Beijing Platform for Action based on 12 critical areas of concern for women's advancement. SLORC and SPDC leaders claimed they were committed to implementing the Beijing Platform for Action in accordance with the national political, economic and social objectives.[26] One of the key areas of concern outlined at Beijing related to the establishment of mechanisms to promote the advancement of women. To this end, the government formed the Myanmar National Committee for Women's Affairs (MNCWA) on 3 July 1996. The MNCWA was to be a 'high level inter-ministerial policy making committee' responsible for implementing a 'National Plan for the Advancement of Women' that would address the other critical areas of concern.[27] Khin Nyunt, then SLORC Secretary-1, was named patron and Soe Myint, Minister for Social Welfare, Relief and Resettlement, was

---

25 United Nations, Fourth World Conference on Women, 'Statement by H.E Major-General Soe Myint, Minister For Social Welfare, Relief and Resettlement and Leader of the Delegation of the Union of Myanmar to the United Nations Fourth World Conference on Women: Action for Equality, Development and Peace', Beijing, 4–15 September 1995.

26 The government identified 12 national objectives, which featured prominently in officially-sanctioned publications including the *New Light of Myanmar*. There are four political objectives: stability of the State, community peace and tranquillity, prevalence of law and order; national reconsolidation; emergence of a new enduring State Constitution; and building of a new modern developed nation in accord with the State Constitution. The four economic objectives include development of agriculture as the base and all-round development of other sectors of the economy as well; proper evolution of the market-oriented economic system; development of the economy inviting participation in terms of technical know-how and investments from sources inside the country and abroad; and the initiative to shape the national economy must be kept in the hands of the State and the national peoples. The four social objectives are to uplift the morale and morality of the entire nation; to uplift the national prestige and integrity and preservation and safeguard cultural heritage and national character; to uplift the dynamism of patriotic spirit; and to uplift the health, fitness and education standards of the entire nation.

27 United Nations, Convention on the Elimination of All Forms of Discrimination Against Women, 'Response by the Myanmar Delegation, Twenty-Second Session of the Committee on the Elimination of All Forms of Discrimination Against Women (CEDAW)', New York, 26 January 2000. Hereafter cited as 'Response by the Myanmar Delegation'.

named chair of the MNCWA. Committee members included officials from related government departments and representatives from 'notable' NGOs including the MMCWA and MWEA. Operational working committees were also established at national, state/division, district and township levels in order to implement the MNCWA's national plan. In 2000, the government stated that the ratio of female to male members on the national committees was three to one, although independent observers claimed that half the membership was male.[28]

Evaluation of the MNCWA's National Plan for the Advancement of Women
In implementing its national plan, the MNCWA chose to focus on five critical areas of concern outlined in the Beijing Platform for Action: education, health, economy, violence against women, and the 'girl-child'. The committee also added a sixth area not included in the Beijing Platform, 'Culture', in order to promote women's role in preserving and promoting 'traditional Myanmar culture'. Two further critical areas of concern were later identified before March 1999: environment and the media.[29] The government completely ignored the four other areas of critical concern – the effects of poverty on women, the effects of armed conflict on women, women's access to power-sharing and decision-making, and the promotion and protection of the human rights of women – despite their vital importance for women's advancement. The government's failure to address these issues must make us seriously question its overall commitment to promoting women's economic, social, human and political rights.

In addition to signing the Beijing Platform for Action, the government ratified the Convention on the Elimination of All Forms of Discrimination Against Women (CEDAW) in 1997. The CEDAW monitoring process aims to ensure State parties' compliance with both the Beijing Platform for Action and the CEDAW. The SPDC government submitted its initial country report to the CEDAW Committee for consideration at its 22nd Session in January 2000 and sent a high-level delegation to this session to respond to the committee's observations and questions. The government

---

28 *Ibid.*, Belak, *Gathering strength*, 29.

29 United Nations, Convention on the Elimination of All Forms of Discrimination Against Women, Office of the High Commissioner for Human Rights, 'Concluding Observations of the Committee on the Elimination of Discrimination Against Women: Myanmar', A/55/38, paras. 91–138, 4 February 2000, para. 99. Hereafter cited as 'CEDAW, "Concluding Observations"'.

delegation was led by U Win Mra, Ambassador to the Myanmar Permanent Mission at the UN, and included several women. Representatives of expatriate Burmese women's organisations also submitted a shadow, or alternative, report to the CEDAW Committee.[30] An analysis of these reports and discussions is presented below, in order to assess the effectiveness of the government's policies and programs regarding women.

General areas of concern

The MNCWA's lack of funding was a serious impediment to implementing the national plan of action. The MNCWA received no budget from the government, relying solely on donations and fundraising activities to implement its policies and programs. All committee members were expected to work on a voluntary basis. The CEDAW Committee urged the government to provide the MNCWA with sufficient financial and human resources to carry out its mandate effectively.[31] Committee members also expressed concern that the MNCWA leadership lacked relevant expertise in women's issues.[32] Brenda Belak, one of the authors of the shadow report, noted that the MNCWA leadership was predominantly male. At the national level, both the chair and the vice-chair were men and half of the remaining members were men drawn from ministries, the judiciary and the police force. At the regional and local levels, male government officials were appointed as chairs, while their wives held subordinate positions.[33] The lack of women in senior leadership positions was indicative of the government's reluctance to allow women equal access to power and decision-making. Of greatest concern was the government's commitment to the CEDAW itself. The introduction to the government's report stated that 'The status of Myanmar women is very unique as equality with men has been bestowed upon them as an

---

30 Women's Organisations of Burma's Shadow Report Writing Committee, 'Burma: the current state of women – conflict area specific. A shadow report to the 22nd session of CEDAW', January 2000, edited for *Burma Debate* 6, 4 (Winter 1999): 13 pages. Hereafter cited as 'CEDAW Shadow Report'.

31 CEDAW, 'Concluding Observations', para. 112. In its combined second and third reports submitted to the CEDAW Committee in 2008, the government reported that the MNCWA budget was provided by the Department of Social Welfare, but did not reveal how much funding was available or how it was distributed to implement programs effectively. See CEDAW/C/MMR/3, 12.

32 Belak, *Gathering strength*, 29.

33 *Ibid.*, 262–63.

inherent right.'[34] Apart from demonstrating a poor understanding of the concept of rights – natural rights are inherent and cannot be 'bestowed' – this statement revealed the government's reluctance to acknowledge that women experienced discrimination in any aspect of their lives. By taking this view, the government seemed unlikely to adopt adequate measures to improve the overall situation of women.

Education

The government's report stressed that males and females already had 'equal access to almost all levels and all forms of education', but did not provide sufficient evidence to support this assertion. Government achievements included the provision of free primary education; free school uniforms, textbooks and stationery for needy secondary students; and scholarships for outstanding students who could not afford tertiary education. Non-formal education and vocational training programs were provided for illiterate women and women from rural and border areas who could not attend school, although the reach of these programs was unclear. The government emphasised that females outnumbered males at the tertiary level (57.8 per cent of undergraduate students were females), and noted that female students were increasingly entering 'non-traditional' fields of study such as medicine and law.[35]

The CEDAW Committee noted with concern that the government provided insufficient information on girls' access to primary education, where female retention and completion rates were lower than those for males. The government merely stated that it 'hoped that dropouts at the primary level are no longer an issue',[36] and made no attempt to address the underlying reasons for girls leaving school early, which included economic hardship and the strong cultural belief that girls should assist with family duties. Furthermore, the government failed to acknowledge that there were fewer educational opportunities for girls living in rural and border areas, where cultural barriers to female education were exacerbated by inadequate school facilities, poor transport services and the effects of armed conflict.

---

34   CEDAW/C/MMR/1, 3.

35   CEDAW/C/MMR/1, 14–16.

36   *Ibid.*, 15.

Health

Although the government stressed that 'women have access to health services equal to that of men', the statistical data presented in its own report revealed that women (and men) in rural and border areas had limited access to health services. The government reported that there were 650 hospitals (roughly one per 53,000 people) and 1,140 health centres (roughly one per 24,000 people) in rural areas.[37] According to UNICEF, however, health facilities were woefully inadequate in the border areas, where there was one hospital per 132,500 people and one health centre per 221,000 people. Severe staffing and equipment shortages also negatively affected the quality of health services in these areas.[38] In terms of specialised health services for women, there were 348 maternal and child health centres in urban areas, but none in rural areas, where women's access to basic health services was already poor. The government admitted that it relied heavily on voluntary NGOs like the MMCWA to supplement existing public health care services for women in both urban and rural areas. Although the MMCWA provided some antenatal care, childcare and family planning services for women, the reach of these programs was limited. The government informed the CEDAW Committee that it sought to promote a 'holistic, life-cycle approach to health care for women' through the implementation of preventative health programs for women and girls focusing on fitness, birth spacing, reproductive health, nutritional development, immunisation, and control of sexually transmitted diseases including HIV/AIDS.[39] It was unclear how the government intended to achieve its ambitious goals, however, given the limited availability of health facilities and shortage of professionally-trained health staff.

The authors of the shadow report questioned the government's commitment to improving women's health, noting that its overall health expenditure was low (according to 1998 UN estimates, 0.5 per cent of GDP was allocated to health, compared with 7.6 per cent of GDP allocated to defence).[40] Low government spending on health and ongoing

---

37   *Ibid.*, 17–18.

38   UNICEF Myanmar, *Children and women in Myanmar: situation assessment and analysis* ([Yangon]: UNICEF Myanmar, April 2001), 82–83.

39   CEDAW, 'Concluding Observations', paras. 93–94.

40   1998 United Nations Development Programme Human Development Reports (New York: United Nations Development Programme, 1998), cited in CEDAW Shadow Report, 4, 12.

armed conflict had caused 'a crisis in the national health care system, particularly in areas populated by ethnic minority groups'.[41] Independent reports confirmed that ethnic minority women who were voluntarily or forcibly relocated as a result of military conflict often lacked sufficient access to clean water supplies, health care facilities and trained medical personnel.[42] The CEDAW Committee also noted with concern that the government failed to provide information on a woman's right to terminate pregnancy resulting from sexual violence, since induced abortion was cited as a major cause of maternal mortality.[43] The government has consistently refused to acknowledge reports that ethnic minority women have been raped by military personnel, which hinders its ability to address cases where women seek to end unwanted pregnancies resulting from rape.

Violence against women
The government did not perceive domestic and sexual violence to be significant problems in Burma. The MNCWA had conducted preliminary research only on marital violence in Yangon and concluded that, although 'marital violence exists, the magnitude is not very great'. The government also stated that there were few reported cases of rape and sexual assault, partly because Buddhists regarded these crimes as 'great sins', and partly because offenders received heavy punishments.[44] Marital rape is not recognised as a criminal offence in Burma, which may account for the low number of reported cases of domestic violence against women. Many victims of rape and other forms of violence committed by military personnel do not tell the authorities because they fear that offenders will not be prosecuted. Measures to protect women from rape by military personnel were conspicuously absent from the government's report. The CEDAW Committee expressed particular concern about state-sanctioned violence against women in conflict zones and ethnic minority areas including forced relocations, forced labour and sexual violence perpetrated by military and police person-

---

41 CEDAW Shadow Report, 3.

42 Karen Human Rights Group, *False peace: increasing SPDC military repression on Toungoo District of Northern Karen State* (Thailand: Karen Human Rights Group, March 1999); Shan Human Rights Foundation, *Displacement in Shan State* (Thailand: Shan Human Rights Foundation, April 1999).

43 CEDAW, 'Concluding Observations', para. 129.

44 CEDAW/C/MMR/1, 10.

nel. Committee members urged the government to enact legislation to protect these women as well as female prisoners who were vulnerable to abuse while in custody.

The government claimed that existing legislation protected women from violence including forced prostitution and trafficking. In some cases, however, this legislation punished, rather than protected, women. Under the Suppression of Prostitution Act (1949), which remains in force, convicted prostitutes could be imprisoned for up to three years.[45] Government-initiated measures to protect women and girls from trafficking included the establishment of a National Task Force on Trafficking in Women and Children in August 1998. Yet the government failed to acknowledge the main underlying reasons for women's involvement in prostitution and trafficking, which were lack of educational and employment opportunities. The authors of the shadow report pointed out that, under military rule, decades of economic mismanagement and armed conflict had created 'fertile conditions' for the trafficking of women, particularly in ethnic minority areas.[46] The government also prohibited women under the age of 25 from crossing national borders unless accompanied by a legal guardian. Human rights groups have noted that this regulation, which was ostensibly intended to protect women, actually impinged upon their right to travel freely.[47] Moreover, as discussed below, government-sponsored women's organisations have contravened this regulation by allowing women to cross national borders in return for payment.

Economy
The government acknowledged that female participation in the economy remained largely 'invisible', since the vast majority of work performed by women and girls was unpaid and took place in the informal, domestic sphere (including childrearing, cooking, cleaning, tending animals, collecting water and firewood, and other household duties). In addition to this informal labour, 33 per cent of women engaged in paid labour outside of the home, mainly in the agricultural, industrial and service sectors. The government estimated that 'women average 12–13 hours

---

45   *Ibid.*, 11. The maximum prison sentence was increased to five years under *The Law Amending the Suppression of Prostitution Act, 1949* (The State Peace and Development Council Law No. 7/98).

46   CEDAW Shadow Report, 8.

47   Altsean Burma, *Special briefing: women's report card on Burma, April 2000*, 16.

more "work" in a week than men.'[48] No mention was made of the need to counter prevailing gender stereotypes about work that disadvantaged women. For instance, the government noted that girls (unlike boys) were expected to help care for their younger siblings and perform household chores, but failed to acknowledge that this social expectation prevented many girls from attending or completing school. Furthermore, the government appeared to condone cultural discrimination against women by focusing on women's predominance in 'feminine' professions such as nursing and teaching, and stating that women needed to balance their career aspirations with their family duties. The CEDAW Committee urged the government to allow and encourage women to pursue professions according to their interest and ability, rather than perceived notions of gender-appropriate roles.[49]

Responding to allegations that the government authorised the use of forced labour, members of the Burmese delegation stated that existing legislation had been revised in May 1999 in order to prohibit forced labour, in accordance with recommendations made by the International Labour Organization (ILO).[50] Despite the government's claims that forced labour no longer exists in Burma, numerous reports confirm that it still condones the widespread use of compulsory labour, particularly in conflict zones and ethnic minority areas. Women are often targeted to perform forced labour because authorities consider them to be more compliant than men. Pregnant women, young girls and elderly women have been forced to perform physically demanding duties including construction work and portering for military troops. Some women have also been sexually assaulted and raped by officials while performing forced labour.[51] Women who dare to speak out against such practices risk arrest and imprisonment. In 2005, prominent labour and human rights activist Su Su Nway was sentenced to eight months in prison for

---

48   CEDAW/C/MMR/1, 16.

49   CEDAW, 'Concluding Observations', para. 126.

50   'Response by the Myanmar Delegation', January 26, 2000.

51   See, for example, Altsean Burma, *Abused bargaining chips: women's report card on Burma, March 2003* (Bangkok: Alternative ASEAN Network on Burma, February 2003), 19; Women of Burma, *In the shadow of the junta*, 50–51.

'harassing' local officials after she successfully sued the government under its own laws prohibiting the use of forced labour.[52]

The girl-child

As part of its efforts to protect girls from discrimination, the government ratified the UN Convention on the Rights of the Child (CRC) in 1991 and enacted the Child Law in 1993, which contains specific provisions intended to protect girls from exploitation and sexual abuse.[53] The government report claimed that the Burmese regarded all children as 'precious treasures, regardless of sex'. Although the birth of a daughter is not regarded as an inevitable disappointment in Burma, most Buddhists want to have at least one son because of the merit acquired though the son's novitiation ceremony.[54] Several statements in the government's report indicate that cultural acceptance of the unequal sexual division of labour disadvantages girls. For instance, the government asserted that some families prefer daughters because they were expected to 'take on more responsibilities than sons'.[55] The report made no reference to the fact that existing cultural beliefs and practices negatively affected girls' ability to gain the same educational and employment opportunities as boys. In reality, the government's policies have conditioned girls to accept constraints on their behaviour in the name of 'preserving traditional culture'.

Culture

As we have seen, Burmese governments have employed the concept of 'culture' to control women's behaviour since colonial times. SLORC and SPDC leaders drew on the racial ideology developed by nationalists during the colonial period to criticise women who 'pollute' the Burmese race by marrying foreigners, especially Aung San Suu Kyi. Ironically, given the government's view that women need to be protected from foreign influences, state-sponsored women's organisations also emphasise women's role as protectors of culture. Women are urged to uphold

---

52 Amnesty International, 'Fear of torture or ill treatment/health concern', 17 November 2007, AI Index: ASA 16/040/2007. While she was released after serving her sentence in 2006, Su Su Nway was rearrested in 2007 for taking part in pro-democracy demonstrations. In October 2011, she was released as part of a general amnesty.

53 *The Child Law* (The State Law and Order Restoration Council Law No. 9/93).

54 Ni Ni Myint, *The status of Myanmar women*, 63–64.

55 CEDAW/C/MMR/1, 9.

their 'moral character' in order to 'preserve and promote Myanmar culture and tradition.'[56] These expectations do not apply to men: for instance, it is more socially acceptable for boys to drink alcohol, smoke and have pre-marital sex than it is for girls. The MNCWA sponsors fashion shows, beauty contests and performing arts competitions for young women to promote 'traditional culture' and reward girls who conform to the government's idea of appropriate female appearance and behaviour. Winners of these competitions often receive cash prizes or scholarships.[57] Female beauty, therefore, is strongly associated with attaining social prestige as well as economic and educational benefits. In reality, these competitions perpetuate existing gender stereotypes that constrain female roles, and thus condone cultural discrimination against women. State-sponsored women's organisations devote considerable attention to women's appearance and beauty, rather than using their resources to address serious socio-economic problems that affect women.

Environment

The MNCWA encourages women to participate in 'environmental sanitation' activities to reduce air and water pollution, mainly through minimising fuel consumption and promoting safe disposal of waste. Women are also expected to engage in conservation activities, notably tree-planting ceremonies, which often take place at official government events and are publicised in the state-controlled media.[58] The government has linked women's role in environmental conservation to the Buddhist emphasis on care for all sentient beings: conservation activities provide a means of gaining and sharing merit, not only for the women involved, but also for their families and communities and the government itself.

The government emphasises its environmental credentials partly in order to deflect criticism of its controversial economic 'development' policies including large-scale extraction and exportation of teak, gas,

---

56   See 'Myanmar Women's Affairs Federation formed in order to promote wider and greater functions of Myanmar women sector: Prime Minister discusses formation of MWAF', *New Light of Myanmar*, 21 December 2003; 'Adorable customs and tradition of Myanmar women', in Myanmar Women's Affairs Federation, *Papers presented in honour of Myanmar Women's Day, 3 July 2005* (Yangon: [U Kyi Win at] Universities Press, 2005), 31–41. The formation and objectives of the Myanmar Women's Affairs Federation are discussed below.

57   CEDAW/C/MMR/1, 16.

58   *Ibid.*, 6; 'Honorary patron of Myanmar Women's Affairs Federation Daw Kyaing Kyaing attends tree planting ceremony to hail Myanmar Women's Day', *New Light of Myanmar*, 22 June 2005.

gems and other natural resources, which have contributed to massive deforestation and increased soil salinity and flooding.[59] Government-approved development projects including the Unocal/Total gas pipeline and the Salween Dam schemes were initiated without prior consultation with local populations who would be directly (and adversely) affected.[60] These projects have resulted in increased forced resettlement and forced labour in ethnic minority areas, and have deprived local populations of access to adequate land, water and fuel supplies. Women who have been forcibly displaced to make way for development projects are particularly vulnerable due to the lack of adequate reproductive health care and the expansion of the sex industry in many development zones.[61] Thus, the government's exploitation of the country's natural resources has not only increased the economic power of the military elite, which retains a controlling share in extractive industries, but has also disempowered ordinary citizens, particularly women.

Media
The government claimed that the official media promoted a 'positive image of women in [their] various roles as mother, friend and life-partner',[62] implying that these are the *only* appropriate roles for women. The activities of the MNCWA and women's NGOs are frequently reported in the state-controlled media, although critics have argued that this only reinforces how superficial their concerns actually are: 'Their main function is to go to ceremonies, opening ceremonies, closing ceremonies, ribbon-cuttings, all these things, and they shake hands with the generals and officials and present them with flowers and get their pictures taken doing it.'[63] In reality, strict censorship laws prohibited freedom of expression in the media. The authorities frequently arrested and imprisoned writers and editors who criticised the military govern-

---

59 Tun Myint, 'Implications of current development strategies for Myanmar's development: environmental governance in the SPDC's Myanmar', in Monique Skidmore and Trevor Wilson (eds.), *Myanmar: the state, community and the environment* (Canberra: Australian National University E Press, 2007), 194.

60 *Ibid.*, 192.

61 Belak, *Gathering strength*, 153; Women of Burma, *In the shadow of the junta*, 49–50; Kachin Development Networking Group, *Valley of darkness: gold mining and militarization in Burma's Hugawng valley* (Kachin Development Networking Group, 2006), 49–50.

62 Official Union of Myanmar website, http://www.myanmar.com/Women/Status.Status.html, accessed on 13 March 2002.

63 Interview cited in Belak, *Gathering strength*, 263, 265.

ment and its policies. At the same time, the government used the official media to denounce Aung San Suu Kyi and other opposition leaders. By restricting internet access and banning international news publications, the government effectively prevented ordinary men and women from exercising their right to freedom of expression and from engaging with the outside world.

The government also used the media to promote 'Myanmar Women's Day' (3 July), which was instigated by the SPDC in 1998 in an effort to present itself as a government that promoted women's issues. Since 1997, expatriate women's organisations have celebrated Aung San Suu Kyi's birthday on 19 June as 'Women of Burma Day' in order to raise international awareness about gender-based discrimination and to encourage women's participation in the struggle for peace, national reconciliation and human rights in Burma. On 26 June 1998, MNCWA leaders decided to designate the founding date of the MNCWA (3 July) as Myanmar Women's Day, presumably in an effort to counteract negative publicity concerning the government's role in condoning and perpetrating discrimination against women. Myanmar Women's Day celebrations are promoted in the official media in order to mobilise public support for government policies and programs relating to women. Officials and ordinary members of the state-sponsored and 'independent' women's organisations observe Myanmar Women's Day by attending tree-planting ceremonies, fashion shows, award ceremonies and public meetings.

Other critical areas of concern

The Burmese government focused on the above-mentioned areas of concern and largely ignored the other areas outlined in the Beijing Action Plan. The preceding discussion notes the adverse effects of poverty and armed conflict on women. Another area of particular concern was discrimination against women in political and public life. CEDAW Committee members expressed dissatisfaction with government efforts to promote women's participation in elections and in public decision-making, citing the detention of Aung San Suu Kyi, the absence of a democratic constitution, and the lack of civil society as significant barriers to achieving women's equal political participation. Although the government delegation admitted that women were under-represented at decision-making levels in the government, it suggested that this 'phenomenon could be due to culturally assigned gender roles' rather than official discrimination against women.[64] Yet the government failed to take adequate measures to eliminate existing cultural beliefs about male superiority that prevent women from attaining political power. The repeated harassment and detention of Aung San Suu Kyi and other women involved in opposition politics further demonstrated the SPDC's refusal to allow women to exercise their political rights.

The establishment of the Myanmar Women's Affairs Federation (MWAF)

Following the CEDAW Committee session in 2000, which exposed the inadequacies of the government's national plan of action, the SPDC faced increasing international pressure to do more to protect and promote women's rights. On 19 June 2002, the Shan Women's Action Network (SWAN) and the Shan Human Rights Foundation (SHRF) released a report entitled *Licence to rape: the Burmese military regime's use of sexual violence in the ongoing war in Shan State*, which presented damning evidence of the widespread use of rape and sexual violence perpetrated by military personnel against ethnic minority women.[65] After the publication of *Licence to rape*, foreign governments, the UN and international human rights organisations issued strong public statements condemning the SPDC for condoning the gross violation of women's rights. In March 2003, the Bangkok-based human rights group, Altsean Burma, published another highly critical report, *Abused bargaining chips*, which claimed that the SPDC systematically persecuted Burmese women by violating 22 of the 30 articles of the UN's Universal Declaration of Human Rights.[66] Inside Burma, the government remained concerned about Aung San Suu Kyi's undiminished popularity and influence, which became increasingly apparent after she was released from house arrest in May 2002 and allowed to travel outside Rangoon. During her subsequent tour of the country, Aung San Suu Kyi was welcomed by huge crowds of supporters before she was rearrested in mid-2003.

The SPDC took a defensive stance in response to these events, which involved denying that it tolerated or encouraged discrimination against

---

64 United Nations, Convention on the Elimination of All Forms of Discrimination Against Women, 'Press Release WOM/1166. Committee on Elimination of Discrimination Against Women concludes consideration of Myanmar report', 26 January 2000.

65 SHRF and SWAN, *Licence to rape*.

66 Altsean Burma, *Abused bargaining chips*, 2.

women. Khin Nyunt urged the MNCWA and women's NGOs to work harder to defend the government from 'slanderous' accusations made by internal and external 'destructionists' about its role in perpetrating and condoning sexual violence against ethnic women, human rights abuses and forced labour.[67] Domestic and international pressures soon forced the SPDC to re-evaluate its policies regarding women, however. In December 2003, the government formed the Myanmar Women's Affairs Federation (MWAF) in order to 'take charge' of the women's sector and to carry out the functions of the MNCWA more comprehensively and effectively.[68] The following analysis of the MWAF's leadership, membership, aims and programs demonstrates, however, that the organisation's primary function was to mobilise women in support of the government, rather than address women's real needs and aspirations.

Leadership
The government did not engage in any meaningful consultation with women before announcing the formation of the MWAF. Khin Nyunt stated that the MWAF's principles and organisational structure had already been 'laid down' by SPDC Chairman Than Shwe. The top-down structure still applied, therefore, with a central committee overseeing the organisation of various committees down to the ward and village levels. Unlike the MNCWA, however, the MWAF leadership was predominantly female. At the national level, the wives of senior SPDC leaders held the key administrative positions. Daw Kyaing Kyaing and Daw Mya Mya San, wives of SPDC Chairman Than Shwe and Vice-Chairman Maung Aye respectively, were named as 'Honorary Patrons'. Khin Nyunt's wife, Dr Daw Khin Win Shwe, was initially appointed as Chair.[69] Some women I interviewed in 2005 initially hoped that the

---

67 'Myanmar leader complains of pressures from internal, external forces', *Xinhua News Agency*, 4 April 2003; 'Burmese PM says women have full rights, dismisses "traitorous" accusations', *BBC Monitor*, 16 November 2003. In August 2003, SPDC Chairman Than Shwe ordered a cabinet reshuffle and appointed Khin Nyunt as Prime Minister. Previously, Khin Nyunt had been Secretary-1.

68 CEDAW/C/MMR/3, 8. See also 'Myanmar Women's Affairs Federation formed in order to promote wider and greater functions of Myanmar women sector: Prime Minister discusses formation of MWAF', *New Light of Myanmar*, 21 December 2003.

69 Similarly, in Indonesia, Dharma Pertiwi and Dharma Wanita leaders were inevitably wives of senior government and military officials. The organisational structure, however, was overseen by male *pembina* (guidance council advisors). See McCormick, *Women as political actors in Indonesia's New Order*, 5.

generals' wives would encourage their husbands to address women's issues more effectively than the male MNCWA leaders.[70] Kyaing Kyaing,
in particular, was widely regarded as having great influence over her
husband, Than Shwe. Other female opposition activists dismissed this
influence because it merely reinforced the perception that women must
rely on their connections to male relatives to gain power: 'Many Burmese
think that if you approach the wife you will influence the husband, but
this is not gender equality.'[71]

The fact that women were appointed to leadership positions did not
necessarily mean that they would be motivated to promote ordinary
women's rights. As members of the elite, MWAF leaders have access to
political, economic and social power that is denied to the vast majority of
women. Their privileged position limits their ability to relate to and represent the views of the vast majority of Burmese women. Furthermore,
MWAF leaders' primary loyalty is to their husbands in the government,
which prevents them from challenging official policies and programmes
that discriminate against ordinary women. In reality, some MWAF leaders actually 'cover up the sins committed by their husbands' by denying
that government policies have contributed to an increase in discrimination against women.[72] Khin Win Shwe denied that military personnel
raped and sexually abused ethnic Shan women, and reportedly warned
MMCWA members against becoming involved in opposition politics.[73]

Senior MWAF leaders have been criticised by opposition groups
and exiled media organisations for their involvement in corruption. *The
Irrawaddy* described Kyaing Kyaing as a 'corrupt first lady' who used her
influence to gain business concessions and extravagant gifts for herself
and her family.[74] When I asked some women to comment about Kyaing
Kyaing's role as an honorary patron of the MWAF, they said that she
'might appear at some public meetings and tree-planting ceremonies,
but she is more interested in making money than actually helping or-

---

70   Personal communication, Yangon (Rangoon), 22 June 2005.

71   Interview with member of the Burmese Women's Union (BWU), Chiang Mai, 19 June
     2005.

72   May Pyone Aung, 'Unsung heroes in an unfinished struggle', *The Nation*, 19 June 1998.

73   'Women and the general's wife', *Democratic Voice of Burma*, 25 January 2003.

74   Yeni, 'A blacklist goes on sale', *Irrawaddy*, 14 June 2005; 'The faces of Burma 2005', *The
     Irrawaddy*, December 2005.

How to shop without paying:

Mme Khin Nyunt demonstrates (11 April 2004, Muse)

Figure 8.1: Cartoonist Harn Lay comments on Khin Win Shwe's leadership of the MWAF and MMCWA (© Shan Herald Agency for News 2005).

dinary women'.[75] Khin Win Shwe was also believed to have built up a 'modest patronage-dispensing machine' through her leadership of the MWAF and MMCWA.[76] In August 2004, a Shan media organisation accused Khin Win Shwe and other MWAF officials of illegal profiteering by allowing young women from Shan State to travel to Thailand, despite the anti-trafficking law prohibiting women under 25 from crossing the border. The MWAF reportedly inflated prices for the 160km bus trip from Kentung to Tachilek, charging the women 150,000 kyat ($US150) instead of the usual 6,000 kyat ($US6).[77]

---

75 Personal communication, Yangon (Rangoon), 22 June 2005.

76 Bruce Hawke, 'The spook goes down', *Irrawaddy*, 12 November 2004; 'Ousted PM's wife removed as head of women organisation', *Democratic Voice of Burma*, 9 November 2004.

77 'Mme Khin Nyunt cashes in on Thai demand for young women', *Shan Herald Agency for News*, 23 August 2004; 'Underage women can pay to cross the border', *Shan Herald Agency for News*, 2 March 2006.

Leaders of official women's organisations depended on the patronage of men in power, and could easily lose their positions if they fell out of favour with senior generals. Following an SPDC leadership shake-up in October 2004, Khin Nyunt and Khin Win Shwe were arrested and detained on various corruption charges.[78] When Khin Win Shwe was subsequently dismissed as chair of the MWAF and MMCWA, members were not allowed to elect new leaders. Instead, the government appointed Daw Than Than Nwe, wife of the new Prime Minister Soe Win, as MWAF chair and Daw Khin Khin Win, wife of Secretary-1 Thein Sein, as MMCWA chair.[79] Expatriate women's organisations observed that this leadership reorganisation confirmed that state-sanctioned women's organisations were totally controlled by the government: '[The MWAF] used to be headed by Khin Nyunt's wife, and now that Khin Nyunt has been ousted, it is headed by Soe Win's wife. What kind of an independent women's organisation is that?'[80] At the grassroots level, women's involvement in decision-making remained negligible. One township MWAF official admitted that '[i]n reality we only participate in our township social activities and we do not know about the upper strata.'[81]

The MWAF leadership shuffles represented one aspect of the wider power struggle between military elites and their families to gain economic and political influence. Leadership opportunities within official women's organisations are limited to women with family connections to the ruling elite. These women can increase their wealth and influence by appropriating funds and building up patronage networks through their leadership of women's organisations, but they can easily lose their positions if their husbands fall out of favour with senior government leaders. By contrast, lower level officials and ordinary members have

---

78   'Burma probing bodies formerly led by ex-premier's wife', *BBC Monitoring Asia Pacific* (London), 2 November 2004; 'Burmese women association probed by military investigators', *Democratic Voice of Burma*, 31 October 2004.

79   'Ousted PM's wife removed as head of women organisation', *Democratic Voice of Burma*, 9 November 2004. Khin Khin Win was appointed MWAF chair in 2007 after her husband was promoted to the role of Prime Minister.

80   Cited in Subhatra Bhumiprabhas, 'Human rights award: Shan woman wins honour', *The Nation* (Bangkok), 9 March 2005.

81   'Burma probing bodies formerly led by ex-premier's wife', *BBC Monitoring Asia Pacific* (London), 2 November 2004.

little influence within these organisations and are expected to adhere to decisions made by elite leaders at the national level.

Membership

MWAF membership has grown rapidly since the organisation was formed in December 2003. In June 2005 there were one million members; by September 2007, membership had reached three million.[82] This rapid expansion was due mainly to an aggressive recruitment policy, rather than women being spontaneously motivated to become members. Wives of male government officials and military personnel are expected to join, as are female government employees.[83] MWAF leaders have denied that membership is enforced, but insufficient government funding has led some officials to coerce women into becoming members. One chairwoman of an MWAF township office in central Burma admitted that she encouraged women to join because 'rules have been laid down that we are to rely on our own funds in each township. Thus, we assume that when there are many members there will be more funds.'[84] Ethnic minority women have also been targeted *en masse* in state-sponsored membership drives. In September 2005, military commanders sought to enlist Chin women as MWAF members by coopting village leaders to distribute membership forms. Since most women could not afford the membership costs, local leaders feared they would be punished for failing to raise funds.[85] Other sources claimed that some local authorities inflated the cost of membership fees to make a profit.[86]

Aside from recruiting members to raise funds, the MWAF has actively encouraged women to become members in order to mobilise women

---

82 Clive Parker, 'Pitching Burma's women against "The Lady"', *The Irrawaddy*, 15 June 2005; CEDAW/C/MMR/3, 13.

83 A similar recruitment approach was used by official women's organisations in Indonesia's New Order. Wives of civil servants and members of the police and armed forces were obliged to join Dharma Pertiwi and Dharma Wanita. Athough the Pembinaan Kesejahteraan Keluarga (PPK) was described in official statements as a 'voluntary' movement, in reality there was significant social pressure for women to become involved in the organisation's activities. McCormick, *Women as political actors in Indonesia's New Order*, 5.

84 'Burma probing bodies formerly led by ex-premier's wife', *BBC Monitoring Asia Pacific* (London), 2 November 2004.

85 Prices for membership forms ranged from 200 to 400 kyat. See 'Move to enlist Chin women in MWAF', *Khonumthung News*, 27 September 2005.

86 'Corruption: Burmese women forced to join junta group and pay for it', *Democratic Voice of Burma*, 15 February 2006.

in support of the government.[87] All MWAF members are required to dedicate themselves to the Three National Causes – non-disintegration of the Union, non-disintegration of national solidarity, and the perpetuation of national sovereignty. Members were also expected to participate in the 'successful realisation' of the government's seven-point 'road map' for democracy, widely perceived as a stalling tactic to delay real democratic reform.[88] In March 2004, the *Democratic Voice of Burma* reported that official women's groups had undertaken mass membership drives in order to rally women's support for the government's 'road map' plan. Women who refused to join were summoned by local authorities and accused of being NLD members and supporters, and subsequently 'persecuted and prosecuted like criminals and outcasts'.[89] These reports of enforced membership suggest that many ordinary women were (and still are) required to give over what little money and independence they have in order to prevent further intimidation and harassment by the authorities.

Aims

In order to promote women's advancement, the MWAF has identified seven major objectives:

(1) To enhance the role of women in the reconstruction of a peaceful, modern and developed nation;

(2) To protect the rights of women;

(3) To ensure better economic, health, education and general welfare of women and to take measures for their life security;

(4) To instil and foster in Myanmar women a greater appreciation of their cultural heritage, traditions and customs;

(5) To systematically protect women from violence and provide means for rehabilitation where necessary;

(6) To diminish and finally eliminate trafficking in women and children as a national task;

---

87   The same can be said of 'social' women's organisations like the MMCWA. In Indonesia as well, so-called 'non-partisan' women's organisations were conscripted to support the ruling Golkar party during election campaigns and to promote government policies in general. McCormick, *Women as political actors in Indonesia's New Order*, 5.

88   Critics derided the 'road map' as 'the perfect stalling tactic of the regime: a plan to reduce international pressure while guaranteeing a pro-government outcome.' See Altsean Burma, *Arrested*, 8.

89   'Burmese women forced to join junta's organisation', *Democratic Voice of Burma*, 24 March 2004.

(7) To collaborate with international as well as local organisations, in ensuring the rights of women in accordance with the local traditions and customs.[90]

These objectives emphasise women's involvement in promoting social welfare and traditional culture, which reinforce existing gender stereotypes about the primacy of women's nurturing role. Significantly, there is no reference to women's political rights or efforts to promote female participation in decision-making processes. It is extremely difficult to assess the progress made towards achieving the above objectives because the MWAF does not publish detailed reports about its programs and activities. The government's combined second and third reports presented to the CEDAW Committee in 2008 stated that the MWAF provided vocational skills training and micro-credit programs for women, and educational subsistence allowances and mobile schools for children living in rural and remote areas.[91] In their shadow report, expatriate women's organisations pointed out that there was little information about the content, geographical scope and efficacy of these programs. They noted that most training programs focused on activities traditionally considered 'women's work', including sewing and weaving. Of greater concern was the fact that some women were forced to pay for 'free' training offered by the MWAF.[92]

The government emphasised the MWAF's role in reducing trafficking and violence against women, noting that it collaborated with government organisations in implementing awareness-raising programs and other measures that had been established to assist female victims of violence and trafficking.[93] Other sources suggest, however, that the lack of an integrated nation-wide approach prevents the MWAF from addressing the problem of trafficking effectively. In 2004, the BBC reported that some MWAF township offices did not focus on anti-trafficking measures. According to one MWAF official, this was because '[w]e do not have such cases in central Burma but at the border regions only.'[94] The decision to allocate specialised focus areas by geographic

---

90 Taken from the official MWAF website, www.mwaf.org.mm, accessed on 23 March 2011.

91 CEDAW/C/MMR/3, 9.

92 Women of Burma, *In the shadow of the junta*, 17–18.

93 CEDAW/C/MMR/3, 9.

94 'Burma probing bodies formerly led by ex-premier's wife', *BBC Monitoring Asia Pacific* (London), 2 November 2004.

region suggests that the MWAF leadership does not understand or fails to acknowledge how various aspects of women's lives are causally interconnected. For instance, many sex workers in Mon State are women from Yangon and upper Burma who have left their homes in search of work opportunities.

There is also evidence to suggest that MWAF officials fail to take adequate measures to investigate claims of gender-based violence and have even denounced victims of violence as 'immoral' women. In their 2008 CEDAW shadow report, expatriate women's organisations provided testimony from one women living in Karenni State who said, 'I have seen so many incidents of domestic violence faced by women in the area. MWAF has never come and helped the women solve such problems. Instead, they have blamed women who were battered and treated them as "bad" women.'[95] Female sex workers are particularly vulnerable to sexual violence, but some reports suggest that MWAF officials only take active measures to protect these women when they are directly affected themselves. Aye Aye Win, an MWAF official at Three Pagoda Pass in Karen State, ordered the closure of local massage parlours (brothels) only after she discovered that her husband had been visiting them.[96] The fact that many brothels are owned or patronised by state officials and others with close connections to the authorities makes it extremely difficult for women's organisations to order the closure of such businesses or protect the women working in them.[97] While the CEDAW Committee commended the government's efforts to combat trafficking of women and girls, it expressed concern about inadequate protection measures for victims of trafficking and gender-based violence. It noted that the apparent impunity of perpetrators and reports of intimidation and punishment of victims suggested that violence against women was socially legitimised. The Committee expressed further concern about the government's failure to address the root causes of trafficking and

95 Women of Burma, *In the shadow of the junta*, 54.

96 Shah Paung, 'Massage parlours closed by junta-backed women's group', *The Irrawaddy*, 12 June 2007.

97 'Women told to clear out from brothels and massage parlours in 15 days', *Independent Mon News Agency*, 10 July 2007; Women of Burma, *In the shadow of the junta*, 51; Kachin Development Networking Group, *Valley of darkness*, 49–50.

gender-based violence including poverty, armed conflict and traditional discriminatory cultural practices.[98]

Apart from the objectives outlined above, the MWAF has openly criticised democratic activists and organisations that monitor the Burmese government's compliance with international labour laws. In 2005, MWAF leaders accused Aung San Suu Kyi of 'encouraging women trafficking' through her support of economic sanctions, claiming that women who had lost their jobs as a result of factory closures were vulnerable to trafficking.[99] US officials estimate that up to 60,000 Burmese workers, including many women, were laid off as a result of garment factory closures following the US ban on the importation of Burmese textiles in mid-2003.[100] The MWAF claimed that the sanctions were imposed after expatriate and foreign organisations falsely accused the SPDC of condoning forced labour, and argued that some women subsequently became 'victims of human trafficking while struggling for their living'.[101] In 2005, the MWAF organised mass meetings attacking the ILO when the latter threatened to impose sanctions on Burma after the SPDC announced that it would prosecute anyone who made 'false complaints' about forced labour.[102] By blaming opposition activists, Western governments and the ILO for the poor economic position of women, the MWAF apparently absolves the Burmese government from taking any responsibility for improving women's economic security. Clearly, the MWAF is primarily concerned with defending the government, despite the fact that its policies have had an adverse affect on the lives of ordinary women.

---

98   United Nations, Convention on the Elimination of All Forms of Discrimination Against Women, 'Concluding observations of the Committee on the Elimination of Discrimination against Women: Myanmar', CEDAW/C/MMR/CO/3 (7 November 2008), 2, 6–8. Hereafter cited as 'CEDAW/C/MMR/CO/3'.

99   Clive Parker, 'Pitching Burma's women against "The Lady"', *The Irrawaddy*, 15 June 2005.

100 Guy Lubeight, 'Industrial zones in Burma and Burmese labour in Thailand', in Skidmore and Wilson (eds.), *Myanmar: the state, community and the environment*, 162.

101 Myanmar Women's Affairs Federation, 'Statement and background paper concerning the adverse impact on the lives of women as a consequence of the unjust allegations and sanctions against Myanmar', (Yangon, April 2005), 4–5. See MWAF website, www.mwaf.org. mm, accessed on 20 June 2008.

102 Trevor Wilson, 'Foreign policy as a political tool: Myanmar 2003–2006', in Monique Skidmore and Trevor Wilson (eds.), *Myanmar: the state, community and the environment* (Canberra: Australian National University E Press, 2007), 97.

CEDAW ten years on: re-assessing the government's commitment to women's advancement

In 2008, the CEDAW Committee considered the Burmese government's second and third reports as well as the shadow report submitted by expatriate Burmese women's organisations. The following assessment reveals that little progress had been made in the decade since the SLORC government ratified the CEDAW in 1997. The CEDAW Committee expressed deep concern about women's constitutional right to equality, noting that the 2008 Constitution reserved one quarter of parliamentary seats for the military, a predominantly male institution. Article 352 of the Constitution gives the government the right to appoint men to positions that are 'suitable for men only'. The Constitution also includes references to women as mothers, reinforcing the stereotype that this is women's primary role and that women need protection.[103] The Committee was also concerned that the MNCWA and women's NGOs lacked sufficient budgetary allocations to carry out programs effectively. Committee members described women's NGOs as 'extension-of-government' structures and questioned whether the MWAF could effectively comment on government policy and advocate change, since it relied on government funding and included ministry personnel among its members. Constraints on civil society also prevented independent community organisations from participating in activities to promote women's advancement.[104]

Budgetary allocations for health and education (totalling 1.3 per cent and 3 per cent of GDP respectively) remained woefully inadequate and the statistics provided by the government lacked detailed data disaggregated by age, ethnicity and locality, making it extremely difficult to assess the reach of health care and educational services. Although an additional 92 government hospitals and 119 rural health centres had been created between 1988 and 2006, no new maternal and child health centres had been established during this period.[105] The CEDAW Committee expressed concern about continuing high maternal and infant mortality rates as well as the high number of deaths from maternal complications, and noted that low contraceptive use increased women's vulnerability

---

103 CEDAW/C/MMR/CO/3, 2–3; Articles 352, 32(a) and 351 of the *Constitution of the Republic of the Union of Myanmar (2008)*.

104 CEDAW/C/MMR/CO/3, 5.

105 CEDAW/C/MMR/3, 33.

to HIV infection. The Committee was also concerned about the lack of education infrastructure, quality teaching materials and qualified teachers, particularly in remote and conflict affected areas.[106] The authors of the shadow report estimated that there was one school for every two villages in Burman-dominated rural areas, but only one school for every 25 villages in ethnic border areas.[107]

The Committee was particularly concerned about the disadvantaged position of women living in rural and remote areas – the majority of women in Burma – who suffered from extreme poverty and lack of access to basic health care, education and social services, and who had few opportunities to participate in community decision-making.[108] Throughout Burma, women's ability to participate in political and public life was extremely limited as evidenced by the low proportion of women in senior management positions across different sectors and the very low participation of women in government, the judiciary and the military, in particular.[109] Overall, the CEDAW monitoring process has revealed serious deficiencies in the government's national plan of action, which must be addressed in order to further women's social, economic and political advancement.

Looking forward: the new draft Plan of Action for the Advancement of Women

Although the above discussion paints a bleak picture of the situation for women in Burma, there are some signs that increased dialogue and engagement between the government and UN agencies, INGOs and community organisations have led the government to reconsider its stance on some women's issues. In the aftermath of Cyclone Nargis in May 2008, UN agencies and INGOs operating in Burma established a Protection of Women and Children Cluster in order to assess and respond to the humanitarian needs of women and children in cyclone-affected areas. Although members of the response coordination team admitted to facing challenges when working with government officials, they also claimed that increased collaboration with the Department of Social Welfare ena-

---

106 CEDAW/C/MMR/CO/3, 10–12.

107 Women of Burma, *In the shadow of the junta*, 34.

108 CEDAW/C/MMR/CO/3, 13.

109 *Ibid.*, 8.

bled them to make 'significant inroads' in influencing the government's position on key women's protection issues and specifically gender-based violence.[110] The Women's Protection Technical Working Group subsequently agreed to assist the Department of Social Welfare in developing a National Plan of Action for the Advancement of Women for 2011–15.[111]

The draft plan outlines interventions and anticipated results for the 12 priority areas delineated in the Beijing Platform for Action. Overall, the plan focuses on strengthening the capacity of government personnel to understand and mainstream gender within their own ministries and departments. Key indicators are identified for each priority area, including the percentage of the national budget allocated for gender mainstreaming and the percentage of women in senior positions in relevant government ministries. A management committee will be formed to oversee implementation, quality assurance, monitoring and reporting mechanisms. Bilateral donors, INGOs, national NGOs, UN agencies and civil society organisations will also provide financial, material and technical assistance for the implementation of the plan. While the plan appears to provide a comprehensive, accountable and transparent framework for achieving progress towards the 12 key objectives, it has not been approved by the government at the time of writing. Burmese human rights groups have also rightly expressed doubts about whether multilateral agencies can address women's concerns effectively if they rely on state-centric approaches and implementation, which potentially disempower ordinary Burmese.[112]

While the government has increased dialogue with INGOs, there is virtually no communication between state-sponsored women's organisations inside Burma and Burmese women's organisations involved in the exiled democratic movement. This poses a significant barrier to achieving real progress on women's issues in the future. Informal attempts by

---

110 Challenges included the fact that representatives of community-based NGOs were reluctant to speak freely at meetings attended by ministry and local government officials. Cluster leaders also expressed concern about government interference with the women's protection assessment. See UNICEF, UNFPA and Save the Children, 'Inter-agency review of the Myanmar Protection of Children and Women Cluster response to Cyclone Nargis', 20, 25, 32, 40–43.

111 'Draft National Plan of Action for the Advancement of Women 2011–2015', 13 May 2010, http://www.burmalibrary.org/docs09/UNCT_UNCountryTeam_Annex2-Plan%20of%20Action_eng.pdf, accessed on 11 April 2011.

112 Karen Human Rights Group, *Dignity in the shadow of oppression*, 87.

expatriate women activists to initiate dialogue with state-sanctioned women's groups have been rebuffed, partly because organisations like the MWAF are unable or unwilling to engage with women in the opposition movement. One member of an expatriate women's organisation told me that when she tried to approach the generals' wives at a CEDAW meeting, they were afraid to be seen talking to her.[113] Most expatriate women's organisations remain highly sceptical about engaging with state-sanctioned women's organisations, which to date have provided few economic, social or political opportunities for women. The following chapter will consider how Burmese women living in exile have taken steps to organise and empower themselves. In doing so, they seek to challenge persistent cultural beliefs that prevent women from participating fully in political decision-making and leadership.

Conclusions

Despite maintaining that women have the same rights as men, the military regime established its own women's organisations in order to deflect international criticism of its appalling human rights record, to counter Aung San Suu Kyi's continuing popularity and the criticisms of expatriate Burmese women's groups, and to attract foreign aid to compensate for the state's woefully inadequate social services. Notwithstanding the positive impact of some health and educational programs, state-sanctioned women's organisations have done little to empower ordinary women. The government has repeatedly denied that women suffer discrimination in any aspect of their lives, from access to health and educational services through to the ability to participate in political processes and decision-making. That much discrimination clearly does exist, however, must make us seriously question the government's commitment to the CEDAW and the Beijing Platform for Action. Official women's organisations are mostly directed either by men, or by women who owe their positions to family connections with powerful men. Instead of protecting and promoting women's rights, the government has used its control of women's organisations to limit the power of ordinary women to take control of their own affairs, from the centre all the way down to the township and village level, including ethnic minority and rural areas. Women's rights and aspirations,

---

113 Interview with member of Women's League of Burma (WLB), Chiang Mai, 23 June 2005.

whether individual or collective, are considered subordinate to government agendas, and have been sacrificed for the 'greater national interest'. Women's empowerment is encouraged only to the extent that it can be used to mobilise support for government policies, including those such as forced labour that adversely affect women. Ordinary women have few means to gain economic, social and political power other than by toeing the official line; women involved in the political opposition actually risk further discrimination and intimidation by state-sponsored women's organisations, as well as the security services. Unless affirmative measures are taken to enable ordinary women to engage in open dialogue and decision-making together with government, opposition and INGO representatives, it is difficult to see how women will be able to assert their rights and improve their condition in the future.

9

Women's Organisations in Exile: New Expressions of Female Power

*F*ollowing the 1988 uprising, thousands of women and girls seeking to escape the increasing political oppression, escalating military conflict and severe economic hardship inside Burma fled the country. Many Burmese women are still living as refugees and migrants in neighbouring countries, particularly in Thailand, India, Bangladesh and China.[1] Once outside the authoritarian confines of military-ruled Burma, women faced new challenges as refugees and migrants with limited legal, social, economic and political rights, but they were also exposed to new ideas about human rights and gender equality through the media and their interaction with international organisations. As a result, some of these women began to question and challenge traditionalist understandings of gender roles that prevented them from achieving positions of social and political power in their communities. This chapter considers how Burmese women living in exile have taken steps to organise and empower themselves with the aim of achieving greater social and political equality with men. Expatriate women's organisations have had considerable success in promoting grassroots and international support for women's rights, but their greatest challenge is how to overcome ingrained cultural beliefs and structural barriers that impede women's access to political leadership and decision-making processes.

Reasons for leaving Burma

Expatriate women's organisations were formed in different circumstances, at different times and places, and with different aims, goals and objectives. Some were established inside Burma in 'liberated areas' controlled by ethnic and communist opposition forces long before the 1988

---

1   Others have resettled in countries as far away as Canada, Norway and Australia.

uprising and subsequent military crackdown forced them further into the borderlands and, in some cases, into exile. Others have formed since 1988 in refugee camps along the Burmese border and in areas with significant Burmese populations in neighbouring countries like Thailand, India and Bangladesh. Women chose to leave Burma for various reasons related to the wider political, economic and social environment, including the ongoing civil war between the Burmese army and ethnic armed forces and the worsening economic conditions and political oppression under military rule.

Women living in conflict zones were particularly affected by relocation and displacement due to the civil war. As a result of the *tatmadaw*'s 'four cuts' campaign against ethnic armies, entire villages were destroyed or relocated, forcing thousands of displaced men, women and children to move further into the jungle along the Burmese border. Women often struggled to find adequate food, shelter and healthcare for their children and families. Ethnic minority women and girls, in particular, were vulnerable to rape and sexual abuse by Burman *tatmadaw* soldiers. Many Christian women from the Karen, Karenni and Kachin ethnic groups and Muslim Rohingya (Rakhaing) women also moved to the borderlands in order to escape discrimination and abuse by Buddhist Burman authorities. During the mid-1990s, the Burmese government escalated its military campaigns in ethnic minority areas, and many families were separated during the fighting and relocation process. Women with young children, pregnant women and young girls, who were particularly vulnerable to abuse and lacked access to food supplies and medicine, were forced to leave their male family members and seek refuge in neighbouring countries.[2] Many women and children were placed in refugee camps, but large numbers remain as unregistered ('illegal') migrants.

The exact number of Burmese refugees and migrants is unknown, but it is estimated that up to 300,000 people from Shan State alone were forced to leave their homes between 1996 and 2001, at least half of whom fled to Thailand as undocumented migrants.[3] In 1998–99, approximately

---

2   According to one report published in May 2006, up to 70 per cent of Karens fleeing Burma were women and children. See Shah Paung, 'Most Karen refugees are women and children', *The Irrawaddy*, 23 May 2006.

3   Shan Human Rights Foundation, *Charting the exodus from Shan State: patterns of Shan refugee flow into northern Chiang Mai province of Thailand* (Chiang Mai: Shan Human Rights Foundation, [200–]), 5–6, 14.

120,000 Karens were living in refugee camps along the Thai–Burma border while a further 200,000 people were internally displaced in Karen State.[4] During the same period, at least 30,000 people from Karenni State were internally displaced or living in Thai refugee camps.[5] In Arakan State, an estimated 250,000 ethnic Rohingyas fled to the Bangladesh border during 1991–92, including many women who were sexually abused by Burman military personnel and non-Muslim civilians.[6] In recent years, the flow of refugees and migrants from Burma into neighbouring countries has remained steady, although resettlement and repatriation programs have reduced refugee numbers in some countries. According to the latest UNHCR figures, there were nearly 430,000 Burmese refugees and asylum-seekers in 2009 and a further 230,000 Burmese were classified as 'internally displaced persons' (IDPs). The majority of refugees and IDPs are from the Karen, Shan, Karenni, Kachin, Chin and Mon ethnic groups. A further 750,000 Rohingyas are classified as 'stateless persons' who are not recognised as nationals by any county.[7]

Aside from military conflict, many women left Burma to escape severe economic hardship and political oppression. As the economic situation deteriorated under military rule, extreme poverty and lack of employment opportunities in their home towns and villages drove many women and girls to migrate in search of work. Following the 1988 uprising, hundreds of female democracy activists, including members of the NLD and All Burma Students' Democratic Front (ABSDF), fled with men to the jungle and border areas to avoid arrest and harassment by authorities in Rangoon and other urban centres. Many of these women were well-educated ethnic Burmans who had played important roles in the pro-democracy movement. Once in the jungle, however, they were often relegated to

---

4   Karen Women's Organization website, http://www.karenwomen.org/, accessed on 4 December 2006; Amnesty International, 'Myanmar: the Kayin (Karen) State: militarization and human rights', 1 June 1999, AI Index: ASA 16/12/99.

5   Amnesty International, 'Myanmar: aftermath: three years after dislocation in the Kayan State', 1 June 1999, AI Index: ASA 16/14/99.

6   Belak, *Gathering strength*, 68.

7   UN Statistical Online Population Database, United Nations High Commissioner for Refugees (UNHCR), Data extracted 22/05/2011, www.unhcr.org/statistics/population-database; Altsean Burma, *Burma issues & concerns vol. 4: the security dimensions* (Bangkok: Alternative ASEAN Network on Burma, April 2007), 25–36.

subordinate roles in male-dominated opposition organisations.[8] Through this experience of military repression and gender discrimination, they developed greater empathy with ethnic minority women. These different groups of women gradually began a collective push for their rights, forming their own organisations with the common goal of promoting women's social, cultural, economic and political empowerment.

Life in the borderlands

Once they were outside Burma, women faced new difficulties as migrants and refugees in neighbouring countries. Many women had limited job opportunities because they did not possess (and could not afford) identification cards or passports,[9] had little or no formal education, and spoke only Burmese or their native ethnic language. These women were obliged to take low-paid, dangerous jobs as border traders, factory workers, domestic servants and sex workers. Unregistered or 'illegal' migrants risked being arrested and repatriated to Burma if they were discovered by local authorities, so many women were reluctant to seek health or legal advice if they were ill or mistreated by their employers. Women also had to learn to negotiate with local officials and others who had their own gender-based assumptions about women, such as the perception that all female Burmese migrants were involved in the sex industry.

Women seeking asylum as refugees also had uncertain legal status and limited economic, social and political opportunities. Legal and bureaucratic definitions of 'refugee' used by governmental and UN authorities ultimately determined the status of these women, regardless of their personal situation.[10] Many Shan women were not recognised as refugees by Thai authorities who considered Shans to be ethnically related to Thais (and thus 'Thai'), while Karen and Karenni women refugees were sometimes classified as IDPs because their populations spread across the Thai–Burma border. Those women who were granted refugee status were confined to overcrowded refugee camps and were not allowed to take up

---

8   Mary O'Kane, 'Gender, borders and transversality: the emerging women's movement in the Burma-Thailand borderlands', in Navnita Chadha Behera (ed.), *Gender, conflict and migration*, Women and migration in Asia, volume 3 (New Delhi; Thousand Oaks, Calif.; London: Sage Publications, 2006), 240.

9   Although all Burmese citizens should by law be issued with national registration cards, many people in remote areas must pay bribes to local authorities in order to obtain ID cards.

10   N. Viernes, 'Shot by both sides: refugees between Burma and Thailand', *Burma Issues* 14, 7 (July 2004): 2–3.

Figure 9.1: Refugees living in Maepa Rubbish Dump, Mae Sot, Thailand (© Brenden Allen 2009). Residents of the Maepa rubbish dump gather for breakfast. These refugees from Burma spend their days searching for valuables and plastic to carry to a nearby recycling plant in return for little reward.

outside employment, despite the limited availability of shelter, food and medicine. Restrictive living conditions inside the camps increased tension and conflict within families and communities in which women suffered more than men. Domestic violence, desertion and adultery became increasingly common due to the effects of space restrictions, economic hardship and loss of personal autonomy.[11] Resistance to sex education, contraception and family planning by conservative elders and religious leaders contributed to a rise in unwanted pregnancies and sexual health problems.[12] At the same time, single mothers were regarded as promiscuous and immoral women and were often stigmatised by their families and communities; some of these women were shamed into seeking abortion services or abandoning their children.[13]

---

11 N. Ruttanasatian and S. Doherty, 'Time to face facts: a study of conflict resolution at Tham Hin', *Burma Issues* 14, 10 (October 2004): 2–3.

12 Louis Reh, 'A pregnant problem: Young women trapped by dogma and the generation gap', *The Irrawaddy*, November 2005; Saw Ehna, 'Too scared to access: HIV epidemic among Karen refugees', *Burma Issues* 14, 7 (July 2004): 5.

13 See Kevin McKenzie and Kathleen McHugh, 'An investigation into child abandonment and existing childcare options for Burmese workers in Mae Sot, Thailand' (unpublished report), 5.

Several organisations were formed to empower Burmese women living in the borderlands as refugees and migrant workers through the provision of skills acquisition, income generation and health programs. Women's Education for Advancement and Empowerment (WEAVE) was established in 1990 to assist Burmese women living in refugee camps along the Thai–Burma border, particularly Karen and Karenni women. WEAVE's health, education and income-generation projects are designed to enhance women's sense of independence, self-worth and cultural identity. Health projects include training in traditional birth attendance, while income-generating activities involve weaving and making traditional handicrafts. The education program focuses on improving literacy in women's native languages as well as English, with the aim of enhancing women's communication skills and employment opportunities.[14]

Social Action for Women (SAW) was formed in June 2000 by Burmese women living in Mae Sot on the Thai–Burma border to provide support for migrant women and their children including childcare, safe houses and education programs. With the assistance of international aid organisations and private donors, SAW established an orphanage for abandoned children and a mobile medical team that visits factories and other workplaces around Mae Sot. SAW members also offer financial support to poor women and children who need medical and legal assistance.[15] In 2006, SAW established 'Women Talk' and 'Gender-Based Violence' programs to provide safe discussion spaces, counselling and legal services for women experiencing social and economic difficulties, violence and abuse.[16]

Although these organisations' aims are primarily social, many members believe that their work is inherently political. SAW's Advisory Board and Executive Committee has included members of the NLD and other political organisations as well as teachers and health professionals. Naw Cho Cho Khaing, a volunteer teacher with SAW, has recounted how she became more aware of how the political situation in Burma had contributed to increased economic hardship for women and girls.[17]

---

14   Interviews with WEAVE Team Leaders, Chiang Mai, 20 June 2005.

15   Social Action for Women, 'Statement 1/2001', 26 November 2001 (unpublished paper).

16   Social Action for Women website, http://www.sawburma.org/, accessed on 9 March 2011.

17   Naw Cho Cho Khaing, 'University of real life', in Altsean Burma, *Burma – women's voices for change*, 62.

WEAVE leaders believe that their work is 'inevitably political given the current situation where women's rights have been overshadowed by the wider political crisis in Burma'. One team leader also described WEAVE as a feminist organisation that 'aims to redress gender balances in society and reduce structural inequality so as to improve the situation of women'.[18] In recent years, WEAVE has expanded its role to provide capacity-building training in management, organisational and advocacy skills in order to enhance women's leadership abilities. Trainers wanted to challenge prevailing concepts of authority, such as the belief that women can only take on leadership roles if they are married to male leaders, or that girls should not question their elders. They also sought to raise men's awareness of gender stereotypes that portray women as the inferior sex by producing a 'Modern Man' handbook that includes simple illustrations depicting, for example, men washing women's underwear after childbirth. These projects initially created controversy in refugee camps as some conservative elders believed they would erode 'traditional' cultural values, but they have also stimulated positive debate between men and women. WEAVE leaders reported that many women gained confidence in their abilities and received more support from their husbands as a result of such initiatives.[19]

Politicising gender in the borderlands

Women's experiences in exile had a profound and transformative impact on their capacity to organise themselves politically, and specifically to incorporate gendered perspectives and collaborative approaches while engaging in political activism. Once outside Burma, women could access information about the global women's movement and international human rights mechanisms, which provided important sources of financial, moral and political support. New spaces were created for women to promote their political aims and objectives – in refugee camps, at international conferences, and in cyberspace. Access to modern communication technologies allowed women from diverse ethnic, social and political backgrounds to share their knowledge and experiences and, ultimately, to

---

18   Interview with WEAVE Team Leader, Chiang Mai, 20 June 2005.

19   *Ibid.*

work together to achieve common goals.[20] This unity of purpose among women has empowered them to achieve increased levels of political agency through the promotion of women's rights at the grassroots level. We can distinguish between two main types of politically-oriented women's organisations operating in exile – those that are ethnically-based and those that include women from different ethnic groups.

Development of ethnic women's organisations inside Burma

Several politically-aligned ethnic women's organisations were formed inside Burma well before the 1988 uprising. The Tavoy Market Union was a nationalist organisation formed by Tavoyan women from Tenasserim Division as early as the 1930s. In 1946, this group reorganised itself as the Tavoy District Women's Union (TDWU) under the leadership of the Communist Party of Burma (CPB). The TDWU went underground with the CPB in 1948 and joined the communist rebellion against the AFPFL government. The Karen Women's Organization (KWO, founded 1949) and the Kachin Women's Association (KWA, f. 1962 or 1978)[21] were formed as 'ladies' auxiliaries' of male-dominated politico-military organisations – the Karen National Union (KNU) and the Kachin Independence Organisation (KIO) respectively – that were fighting for ethnic autonomy and rights. Initially, the KWO and KWA were primarily concerned with providing social welfare assistance to women and their families (such as basic health and education services), and preserving Karen and Kachin cultural traditions (including language, dress, skills such as weaving, and knowledge of traditional medicine). Unlike women's organisations that were formed in exile and struggled to maintain links with women inside Burma, the KWO and KWA operated in 'liberated areas' controlled by the KNU and KIO where they were ideally positioned to provide immediate assistance to women.

Karen and Kachin leaders have been fighting for greater political autonomy for decades, but the main factor inhibiting women's access to power in these communities is the persistent cultural belief that women

---

20 Yo Yo Lay, 'Women's activism in the borderlands', in Altsean Burma, *Burma – women's voices for change*, 35.

21 According to one report by Project Maje, the KWA was established in 1962: Project Maje, *This revolutionary life: women of the Kachin Liberated Area* (Cranford, NJ: Project Maje, March 1995), 3. KWA pamphlets, however, state that the KWA was formed on 19 August 1978.

should submit to male authority. The KWO and KWA explicitly linked the organisation of women to the revolutionary goals of the KNU and KIO in which the 'national liberation struggle' took precedence over anything else, including women's rights. Few women gained senior positions within the civilian or military organisations and even elite women like Ja Seng Hkawn, daughter of KIO founder Brang Seng, observed that it was extremely difficult for women to gain leadership roles because of the widespread belief that women were inherently inferior to men.[22] Although some single women took up combat roles in ethnic armies, most were limited to performing support roles as nurses in the medical corps or clerks in the civil administration. Women were expected to retire from military service once they were married, and devote themselves to raising children (with the exception of military doctors who were required to balance their medical and family duties).[23] Christian Karen and Kachin leaders also expected women and girls to preserve their 'traditional moral character' by abstaining from pre-marital sex and other 'promiscuous' behaviour and generally conducting themselves with modesty and restraint.[24]

The mid-1990s saw a shift in KWO and KWA priorities as leaders began to address cultural discrimination against women and promote gender equality as a primary goal. Encouraged by their successful organisational work in the social sector, the focus on women's rights both inside Burma and in international forums, and growing contact with other Burmese women's organisations in exile, they began to push for more significant political roles and power for women. Following the fall of Manerplaw in 1995 and subsequent shift of the KNU headquarters to the Thai border, KWO leaders expanded their efforts to promote Karen women's rights and participation in community leadership and political processes. In December 1999, the Kachin Women's Association Thailand (KWAT) was formed in Chiang Mai with similar aims of encouraging Kachin women to aspire to more leadership roles and promoting awareness of women's

---

22 Project Maje, *This revolutionary life*, 14.

23 Pippa Curwen, 'The Kawthoolei Women's Organization', *Cultural Survival Quarterly* 13, 4 (December 1989): 32–33; Project Maje, *This revolutionary life*, 2, 9–10, 15.

24 Curwen, 'The Kawthoolei Women's Organization', 33; Kachin Women's Association Thailand, *Driven away: trafficking of Kachin women on the China–Burma border* (Chiang Mai: Kachin Women's Association Thailand, May 2005), 14.

rights in Kachin communities.[25] KWAT maintains close links with the KWA through its capacity-building and knowledge-sharing programs. Shirley Seng, KWA founder and the widow of KIO founder Brang Seng, is also the KWAT coordinator. When the CPB (Tenasserim Division) dissolved in 1995, the TDWU reformed as the Tavoyan Women's Union (TWU), which now operates as an independent organisation that seeks to gain equal rights for women in all spheres of society.[26] KWO, KWAT and TWU are all founding members of the Women's League of Burma (WLB), an umbrella organisation of 12 Burmese women's groups, which was formed in Chiang Mai in 1999. The WLB's membership, objectives and programs will be discussed below.

Ethnic women's organisations formed in exile

Other ethnic women's organisations were established in exile after 1988. Many organisations grew out of informal networks created by women living in or around refugee camps and in migrant communities near the Burmese border. Most organisations are based in Thailand, including the Karenni National Women's Organization (KNWO, founded 1993), Lahu Women's Organization (LWO, f. 1997), Shan Women's Action Network (SWAN, f. 1999), Pa-O Women's Union (PWU, f. 1999), and Palaung Women's Organization (PWO, f. 2000). Other groups, such as the Rakhaing Women's Union (RWU, f. 1997) and Kuki Women's Human Rights Organization (KWHRO, f. 2000), were formed on the India–Bangladesh–Burma border.[27] Although each organisation has its own particular ethnic focus, they all share similar objectives such as promoting ethnic languages, eliminating cultural beliefs and practices that discriminate against women, enhancing women's economic op-portunities, and increasing women's participation in political processes. These are ambitious goals that raise important and complex questions. How, for example, do women's organisations define 'political participa-tion' and what constitutes 'good' and 'bad' culture? These issues will be considered below.

---

25   Interview with KWAT members, Chiang Mai, 20 June 2005.

26   'Tavoy Women's Union (TWU)', http://www.womenofburma.org, accessed on 20 June 2005.

27   For information on the establishment, aims and objectives of these organisations, see the Women's League of Burma website: http://www.womenofburma.org.

Leadership and membership

The women who established these organisations had first-hand knowledge of the issues affecting women both inside Burma and in exile; many were former refugees themselves who saw a need to support other women living in exile. Many women were very young when they formed these organisations, but this did not necessarily mean that they lacked political experience. Charm Tong, a founding member of SWAN, was sent to a refugee camp on the Thai-Burma border by her parents when she was six years old to escape the conflict in Shan State. She was educated in a Catholic orphanage and also took classes in English, Thai, Mandarin and her native Shan. As a teenager, she developed an interest in human rights and international advocacy through her work as an intern for the Shan Human Rights Foundation, Shan Herald Agency for News and Altsean-Burma. In 1999, when she was 18 years old, Charm Tong was invited to address the UNHCR in Geneva about the abuses committed by Burmese military personnel against unarmed civilians in Shan State.[28] That same year, she co-founded SWAN together with 39 other Shan women activists. Other leaders of expatriate women's organisations were previously active in political opposition groups including the NLD, ABSDF and various ethnic-based organisations.[29]

Most ethnic-based organisations are open to all women from their particular ethnic group, regardless of whether they live in exile or inside Burma. Some organisations specify that members should have a particular interest in the organisation's aims and objectives. SWAN, for example, seeks active members who are independently-minded, interested in human rights, and willing to devote time and energy to their work. The official membership of most organisations is relatively small compared to state-sponsored mass women's organisations inside Burma. KWAT only has 100 members, while the KWO is the largest organisation with around 49,000 members.[30] Some organisations are discriminating in who they want as members, but low membership numbers also reflect how deeply-rooted cultural beliefs prevent many women from becom-

---

28 Nang Charm Tong, 'A unique education', in Altsean Burma, *Burma – women's voices for change*, 83–88.

29 Interviews with members of expatriate women's organisations, Chiang Mai, 23 June 2005.

30 Personal communication with KWAT members, 24 June 2011; Karen Women's Organization, *Walking amongst sharp knives: the unsung courage of Karen women village chiefs in conflict areas of Eastern Burma* (Karen Women's Organization, February 2010), 6.

ing politically active. Fear of arrest by local authorities undoubtedly also deters many women from joining politically-aligned women's organisations. Yet membership figures do not accurately reflect the significant influence that these organisations have among women (and many men) at the grassroots level in refugee camps and ethnic communities both in exile and inside Burma. At the local community level, many people have seen concrete improvement in their living standards as a result of the education, health and income-generating programs implemented by women's organisations. Furthermore, the advocacy and networking strategies of women's organisations have raised international awareness about and support for Burma's ethnic minorities.

Multi-ethnic women's organisations: unity among diversity

Independent organisations could make only limited progress towards promoting women's social and political rights when they were geographically isolated and had questionable legal status and relatively small memberships. Individual organisations could gain strength by joining forces under larger 'umbrella' organisations that would support ethnic diversity, but also provide greater protection and bargaining power for women as a group. Such organisations could foster inter-ethnic cooperation, networking and power-sharing among women. Two multi-ethnic women's organisations were established in exile in 1995, the Women's Rights and Welfare Association of Burma (WRWAB) and the Burmese Women's Union (BWU). The WRWAB is based in New Delhi and was initially formed to provide social welfare assistance for Chin and Kuki women living near the Indian–Burmese border. It later opened membership to all Burmese women and expanded its aims to include the promotion of women's participation and leadership in all spheres of life, including politics. Members receive training in human rights, women's rights, and political and legal systems and engage in networking and advocacy activities with other expatriate and international women's organisations.[31]

The BWU was formed by a group of young female students who had fled to the Thai–Burma border following the 1988 uprising. Many founding members were well-educated Burman women who had held

---

31 'Women's Rights and Welfare Association of Burma (WRWAB)', http://www.womenof-burma.org, accessed on 20 June 2005.

senior positions within the opposition movement, only to lose their status when they moved to the border. One member told me that she had a leading role in the ABSDF inside Burma, but once she arrived in the jungle she was expected to defer to male ABSDF leaders and was no longer allowed to speak in meetings.[32] In response to this reduction in their status, these women decided to form their own organisation to promote women's rights and provide support for Burmese women living in exile. BWU membership is open to all Burmese women 'regardless of ethnicity, race, religion, marital status, sexual preference or livelihood'.[33] Since its beginnings, the BWU has expanded its reach by establishing six regional committees along the Thai, Chinese and Indian borders; there are also members in Australia, Canada, the USA, Norway and Japan. The BWU's objectives are unequivocally political: to promote women's participation in politics, to exercise and promote women's rights, to in-crease women's contribution to the struggle for democracy and human rights within a federal union, and to use women's capacity to establish long-term peace in Burma.

In November 1999, the BWU organised the first Forum of Women of Burma in Chiang Mai with the aim of strengthening relationships between expatriate women's organisations and establishing a common platform to push for gender equality in all spheres of society.[34] The Women's League of Burma (WLB) was subsequently formed on 9 December 1999. The WLB aims to promote women's empowerment and advance the status of women, to increase women's participation in all spheres of society, and to involve women in the democratic movement and national reconciliation pro-cesses through capacity building, advocacy, research and documentation. Currently, there are thirteen member organisations – eleven ethnic-based organisations and two multi-ethnic organisations: Burmese Women's Union (BWU), Kachin Women's Association Thailand (KWAT), Karen Women's Organization (KWO), Karenni National Women's Organization (KNWO), Kuki Women's Human Rights Organization (KWHRO), Lahu Women's Organization (LWO), Palaung Women's Organization (PWO),

---

32   Interview with BWU member, Chiang Mai, 19 June 2005.

33   Burmese Women's Union, *BWU activity report 1998–2001* (Mae Hong Son: Burmese Women's Union, [2002?]), 4.

34   Burmese Women's Union, *BWU activity report 1998–2001*, 11. Representatives from 14 women's organisations from Burma working on various women's issues in Thailand, Bangladesh and India attended the forum.

Pa-O Women's Union (PWU), Rakhaing Women's Union (RWU), Shan Women's Action Network (SWAN), Tavoyan Women's Union (TWU), Women's League of Chinland (WLC) and Women's Rights and Welfare Association of Burma (WRWAB).

A number of women's groups – notably the Mon Women's Organization (MWO) – have not officially joined the WLB, although some of their members attend WLB training programs and seminars and collaborate with the WLB on various projects including the CEDAW shadow report process. In my own interviews with representatives of expatriate women's organisations, members were not forthcoming about the reasons that some groups have chosen not to join the WLB. Geographical distance and limited access to communication technologies may prevent some organisations from establishing closer links with Thai-based women's organisations. The MWO, however, is based on the Thai–Burma border. Longstanding ethnic divisions may have created underlying tensions between the MWO and other ethnic-based women's organisations, including those with predominantly Burman membership. The MWO is closely aligned with the male-dominated New Mon State Party (NMSP) and the party's armed wing, the Mon National Liberation Army (MNLA), whose male leaders harbour feelings of deep mistrust towards Burmans.[35] An article published by the International Mon News Agency in October 2008 suggests that NMSP leaders are not prepared to let women take an active role in party leadership.[36] It is possible that NMSP leaders' views influenced the MWO's decision not to join the WLB, which seeks to promote women's political leadership as a primary goal.

Since 1988, negotiations between male Burman and ethnic leaders over the distribution of political power in a (future) democratic Burma have been cautious and, at times, confrontational. Multi-ethnic women's organisations like the WLB have sought to emphasise women's common experiences in order to overcome inter-ethnic tensions and to promote

---

35 The MNLA was formed in 1958 and engaged in an armed struggle against the Burmese military until an uneasy ceasefire was declared in 1995. For a comprehensive analysis of Burma's various ethnic conflicts since independence, see Smith, *Burma: insurgency*.

36 'NMSP unlikely to promote women at coming party conference', *Independent Mon News Agency*, 24 October 2008. The article quotes Mi Sar Dar, the only female on the NMSP Central Committee, as saying 'I think it is impossible to elect a woman as NMSP General Secretary like in the Karen National Union (KNU).' KWO leader Zipporah Sein was elected General-Secretary of the KNU in October 2008.

a sense of unity among women from different ethnic groups. One of the main challenges for multi-ethnic women's organisations, then, is the need to balance their acceptance and celebration of women's ethnic diversity on the one hand with their efforts to promote women's rights on the other. The WLB and its member organisations facilitate 'experiential' seminars that promote knowledge-sharing, which have enabled women to move beyond ethnic boundaries and establish common political goals. Women learn from each other's experiences and are encouraged by the knowledge that their struggle is shared by other women.[37] As one Karen woman explains,

> [W]omen understand more about women's situation [than men]. ... Whether we are born Bamar [Burman], Shan or Karen [or any nationality], we cannot separate from each other when [we] talk about women's issues because we have the same suffering. ... I believe that when we talk about women's issues, working only for Karen women is not going to benefit the whole of the woman population, and that is why I am willing to work for all women.[38]

This focus on power-sharing and promoting the rights of women collectively can help overcome differences between women from diverse ethnic backgrounds. Women are encouraged to acknowledge the damaging effects of inter-ethnic conflict, but also to commit themselves to resolving these issues with openness, flexibility and tolerance.[39] At this time, however, the collective approach to power has not been extended to include cooperation with state-sponsored women's organisations inside Burma. Many members of expatriate women's organisations do not consider the MWAF and MMCWA to be sincere about promoting women's rights because they are headed by the wives of government leaders and do not allow ordinary women to participate in decision-making processes.[40]

---

37 Interview with WLB Coordinator, Peace-Building and Reconciliation Program, Chiang Mai, 19 June 2005.

38 Naw Khin Mar Kyaw Zaw as told to Ma Ma Pyone, 'Voice for reconciliation', in Altsean Burma, *Burma – women's voices for change*, 54.

39 Ma Aye Pwint, 'Picking up the fallen rice stalks', in Altsean Burma, *Burma – women's voices for change*, 89–92.

40 Interviews with WLB, BWU and KWAT members, Chiang Mai, 19–23 June 2005; personal communication with expatriate Burmese women, May 2011.

Challenges facing women's organisations in exile

All expatriate women's organisations face considerable difficulties in achieving their goals. Individual members face personal risks to their security due to their uncertain legal status and the political nature of their work, which leaves them vulnerable to arrest and deportation by local authorities. Organisational headquarters and offices tend to operate out of residential buildings in secret locations and staff may need to relocate at short notice to avoid arrest. Lack of reliable funding makes it difficult to implement programs, which not only places serious constraints on organisations' capacities to operate effectively, but also causes members considerable anxiety. Many organisations rely heavily on financial assistance from international aid and human rights organisations and other external sources, although some have proved to be extremely resourceful in seeking new ways to generate funds. SWAN has produced several publications in collaboration with other Shan and internationally-based aid organisations, the proceeds of which are used to fund SWAN programs.[41] In 2005, SWAN and the WLB were jointly awarded the Peter Gruber Women's Rights Prize of US$200,000, which they put towards programs aimed at increasing female leadership in expatriate political organisations.[42]

Although expatriate women's organisations are based outside Burma, they aim to maintain and strengthen links between women living in exile and those who remain inside the country. Many organisations produce their own publications, ranging from training manuals and newsletters to detailed research reports on sexual violence and human trafficking, for distribution among their members and communities inside Burma as well as Burmese and non-Burmese individuals and organisations abroad. Most organisations also run training and internship programs for women covering a wide range of topics including leadership and organisational skills, constitutional and election processes, political and legal systems, human rights, gender awareness and peace-building. Once they have completed their training, women return to Burma to share

---

41 For example, SWAN has produced a children's book in collaboration with the Danish International Development Agency (DANIDA) and the Danish Burma Committee (DBC) to raise funds for SWAN's Education Program. The book features cut-out dolls dressed in the costumes of different ethnic groups in Shan State.

42 'WLB and SWAN collect Peter Gruber's Women Rights Prize', *Mizzima News*, 21 September 2005.

their knowledge and skills with others in their communities. Members of expatriate women's organisations also travel to Burma regularly, often at great personal risk, to assess the effectiveness of their programs and seek feedback from women about the issues that concern them in order to plan future initiatives.

Promoting women's rights and preserving 'traditional culture'

A major challenge facing expatriate women's organisations is how to reconcile the differences between traditionalist and egalitarian understandings of gender roles. Members of ethnic-based women's organisations, in particular, have to tread a fine line between preserving cultural traditions that form an essential component of their ethnic identity (including language, skills and knowledge) and eliminating cultural practices and beliefs that keep women in subordinate positions. The discourse of 'rights' serves a political function that can reinforce unequal power relations, since different notions of 'rights' can be used by individuals or groups to marginalise others. Male political and community leaders who invoke the concept of protecting 'cultural rights' or 'ethnic rights' can, consciously or unconsciously, undermine or deny women's rights.[43] Throughout Burma's history, male elites usually determined which cultural practices were 'good' and 'bad', while women were expected to comply. How can expatriate women's organisations challenge these definitions and reconcile their own desires to preserve cultural traditions with their goals of achieving gender equality?

For many women living in exile, the preservation of their cultural traditions is crucial to maintaining their sense of identity and self-worth. Yet appeals to 'traditional culture' can also limit women's capacities to access positions of social and political power. Although they are no longer living under authoritarian rule in Burma, many women are still influenced by 'traditional' Burmese notions of power that emphasise men's authority over women as well as the need for young people to show respect for their elders (both male and female). These beliefs make it difficult for women, particularly young women, to assume leadership roles in their communities. Women are also expected to preserve their

---

43   Maxine Molyneux and Shahra Razavi, *Gender justice, development and rights*, Democracy, Governance and Human Rights Programme Paper Number 10 (New York: United Nations Research Institute for Social Development, January 2003), 25–31.

'traditional moral character' and to place their family responsibilities above all else, which can limit their capacity to engage in political activities. One BWU leader told me that she is often criticised by men (and older women) for not conforming to appropriate standards of female behaviour because she spends a lot of time away from her husband, often travels unaccompanied to meet male opposition leaders, and has no children.[44] Expatriate women's organisations have therefore emphasised that women's political activism can enhance the lives of others in their families and communities in order to counter the common perception that women's empowerment will result in the breakdown of 'traditional' cultural values and interpersonal relationships. The KWHRO, for example, stresses that it is important for Kuki women to 'shake off their shackles and emerge out of the kitchen [so that they can] play an active and positive role in shaping the future of the Kuki nation.'[45]

It is often difficult for expatriate women's organisations to bridge the generation gap between older women who have spent most of their lives inside Burma and younger women, many of whom were born and raised in exile. Take the matter of traditional dress, for instance. Many older women take pride in wearing their traditional ethnic costumes, which serve as a visible expression of cultural identity and provide an important source of income for women who weave textiles and make and sell clothing. Girls and young women who choose to wear modern fashions are often criticised by older women who consider Western clothing to be too revealing and immodest.[46] In some cases, however, wearing traditional dress can make women vulnerable to discrimination. Young Kayan women who choose to remove the brass rings from around their necks sometimes encounter criticism from elders who claim they are forsaking tradition. Kayan girls, however, have questioned the exploitation of their people as 'tourist attractions' and believe that by removing the rings they will have greater economic opportunities.[47] Expatriate women's organisations have concentrated on developing a sense of

---

44 Interview with BWU leader, Chiang Mai, 19 June 2005.

45 'Kuki Women's Human Rights Organization (KWHRO)', http://www.womenofburma. org, accessed on 23 May 2011.

46 We will recall that young women who embraced modern fashions faced similar criticism from older generations and male elites during the colonial and early independence periods.

47 Nick Meo, 'The "giraffe" woman who cast off her brass coils', *The Times* (London), 4 November 2006.

independence among young women, but they also need to educate older Burmese about how traditional cultural practices can perpetuate gender discrimination and limit women's economic, social and political opportunities.

Members of expatriate women's organisations have also struggled to reach consensus on matters concerning female sexuality – including pre-marital sex, contraception, abortion and sexual preferences – due to different ethnic and religious beliefs about appropriate women's behaviour.[48] Tensions can arise when the religious or ethnic rights of a particular group marginalise the individual's rights to equality and fair treatment. The BWU has advocated a broad definition of equality that seeks to balance respect for ethnic and religious rights as well as the rights of the individual to free choice, expression and protection.[49] Yet, as one BWU member told me in June 2005, 'Even within our own organisation women have different views on issues like abortion. We have not begun to discuss [these issues] at this stage.'[50] Although women's organisations agree that these issues affect women's capacity to gain economic, social and political opportunities, resolving them will take time and involve considerable discussion, cooperation, negotiation and compromise by all parties.

'Empowering' women

Many expatriate women's organisations explicitly refer to the need to 'empower' women, which they interpret as the need to achieve true gender equality by promoting women's social and political rights. SWAN's objectives (in English) literally highlight the organisation's emphasis on empowering women:

> **P**romoting women's rights and the rights of children
> **O**pposing exploitation of and violence against women and children
> **W**orking together for peace and freedom
> **E**mpowering women for a better life
> **R**aising awareness to preserve natural resources and the environment.[51]

There is a strong feeling among these groups that women need to empower themselves, since most political organisations are male-dominated

---

48   Interviews with members of Burmese women's organisations, Chiang Mai, 20–23 June 2005.

49   Burmese Women's Union, *BWU activity report 1998–2001*, 23–24.

50   Interview with BWU member, Chiang Mai, 19 June 2005.

51   SWAN website, www.shanwomen.org, accessed on 22 May 2011.

with hierarchical power structures that preclude women from participating in decision-making processes. Expatriate women's organisations have focused on empowering women at the grassroots level, which differentiates them from the NLD and ethnic-based opposition groups as well as state-sponsored women's organisations like the MWAF and MMCWA.

WLB member organisations have sought to raise women's political awareness and activism through capacity-building programs at the local community level. This approach has been particularly effective because it enables organisations to identify and address ordinary women's concerns which, in turn, increases the organisations' influence among women. Many women have subsequently become members as a result of these awareness-raising campaigns, including Naw Pathi Phaw, a young Karen woman who fled to the Mae La Refugee Camp on the Thai–Burma border when the *tatmadaw* launched a major offensive against KNU-controlled areas in mid-1994. After completing the KWO's education and medical training programs, Naw Pathi Phaw joined the organisation in order to 'work for the social welfare of women refugees'. She 'continued to use every chance I could gain to get more knowledge and experience', and was elected Secretary of the KWO's 7th Brigade in 2001.[52] Through their engagement with women's organisations, women like Naw Pathi Phaw gain the experience and confidence needed to become effective community leaders and mediators who can strengthen links between women's organisations and other women living in refugee camps. Organisations like the Burma Relief Centre (BRC) aim to increase grassroots support for expatriate women's organisations and help them to extend their work inside Burma.[53] The BRC provides training in political leadership, organisational skills and gender equality for members of women's organisations, who then pass on their knowledge to others in their communities. In recent years, BRC and WLB leaders have reported that trainees and grassroots members

---

52 Naw Pathi Phaw, 'From prayer to action', in Altsean Burma, *Burma – women's voices for change*, 12–14.

53 The BRC was founded in 1988 by Pippa Curwen, a British–Shan academic who has worked closely with many expatriate women's organisations and served on the WLB executive committee.

have become increasingly involved in decision-making within expatriate women's organisations and in WLB forums.[54]

While the WLB believes that all women should have a political voice at the informal, grassroots level, it also wants to increase women's political participation, representation and leadership at the national level. According to one BWU leader, 'It's all about power .... We need to be clear about what our role is to be, at the village level as well as the national level, if we are to challenge the view that we already have power as "home ministers".'[55] As part of their strategy to promote female participation in community and political decision-making at all levels, expatriate women's organisations have sought to raise men's awareness of cultural and structural discrimination against women and to promote the concept of gender equality within the exiled democratic movement.

Building alliances with men in the democratic movement

Expatriate women's organisations and male-led opposition groups share the common goals of promoting genuine democratic reform, peace and human rights in Burma. The WLB sees the promotion and realisation of gender equality as an integral part of democratic reform and believes that women should be fully involved in political processes and decision-making at all levels. Yet some WLB members have encountered resistance from their male counterparts in the democratic movement who would prefer to 'deal with women's rights later, once we have gained democracy', or not at all.[56] Many male opposition leaders have been reluctant to allow women to participate in political decision-making at the local, let alone national, level. In public forums, expatriate women's organisations have focused on cooperation and alliance-building with men, but they are more critical of their male counterparts in informal discussions.

In interviews in June 2005, members of several expatriate organisations claimed that many men had an individual-centred view of power and wanted to retain control over decision-making, which effectively

---

54 Interview with BRC Women's Development Program Coordinator, Chiang Mai, 18 November 2003; interviews with WLB members, Chiang Mai, 23 June 2005.

55 The phrase 'home ministers' refers to the widely held belief that, since women have control over some aspects of household decision-making, they do not need to push for women's rights in other areas. Interview with BWU leader, Chiang Mai, 19 June 2005.

56 Interview with WLB and BWU member, Chiang Mai, 19 June 2005.

prevented women from participating in political processes. They noted that women have traditionally played important roles in local trade and community networks, and that women's influential role within the family provides them with negotiation, organisational and management skills. Interviewees claimed that women's communal approach to decision-making and power-sharing could help foster consensus and cooperation among different groups, which made women equally (if not more) effective as political leaders. Many women engage in informal political activities while simultaneously caring for children and other family members, managing the household and earning an income. Yet interviewees maintained that many men failed to acknowledge women's capabilities, and argued that affirmative action was required for women to gain parity with men in formal political decision-making processes.

Interviewees also believed that many men ultimately felt threatened by women's power, although they noted that men usually denied this and attempted to justify their discriminatory attitudes towards women as a form of 'protectionism'. For example, men expressed concern for women's safety when they actually wanted to prevent women from taking part in political processes. Some interviewees claimed that men were reluctant to allow their wives to become involved in politics out of fear that they would lose their authority within the family. One BWU member commented that male opposition leaders would not even let her speak to their wives for this reason: 'Whenever I meet with [the men], I always wonder what their wives are doing. Sometimes I ask them, why don't you bring your wives to see me. I would like to be able to visit them just to talk ... but I think [the men] are afraid of me.'[57] She added that when the BWU celebrated its tenth anniversary in 2004, male opposition leaders attended the event but did not bring their wives. KWAT members agreed, pointing out that women were often barred from political meetings or required to sit separately on the floor while the men took the best seats. As one interviewee put it, 'In political etiquette, it is a case of "gentlemen first, not ladies first".'[58] In an article published by *The Irrawaddy* in July 2008, BWU member Myint Myint San claimed that many men regard themselves as 'protectors' of women, and therefore as the rightful leaders of society, indicating that expatri-

---

57   Interview with BWU member, Chiang Mai, 19 June 2005.
58   Interviews with KWAT members, Chiang Mai, 20 June 2005.

Figure 9.2: 60th Karen Revolution Day, Kawthoolei, Burma (© Brenden Allen 2009). Two young Karen dancers, deep in conversation, sit behind KNLA troops on Karen Revolution Day, 31 January 2009.

ate women's organisations still have a long way to go towards changing men's perceptions about women's political abilities.[59]

Political knowledge should empower women, but interviewees expressed concern that members who undertook leadership training often experienced difficulty negotiating with their husbands and other men when they return to their homes and communities. For this reason, women's organisations have increasingly focused on raising men's awareness of women's rights and the concept of gender equality, using a 'culturally sensitive' approach that emphasises the need for social harmony and cooperation between men and women. When discussing issues such as domestic violence, for example, women's organisations stress that they want to prevent the breakdown of family and community relationships, rather than encourage women to divorce their husbands. When talking to male ethnic minority leaders, WLB members have drawn connections between the marginalisation of ethnic minorities and the marginalisation of women from mainstream political processes:

---

59   Violet Cho and Aye Aye Lae, 'Women in the movement', *The Irrawaddy*, 16, 7 (July 2008).

All of these forms of discrimination create marginalised groups that must have their rights ensured, protected, and promoted. Like ethnic or religious discrimination, gender discrimination is fundamentally unfair and deeply damaging to the democratic hopes of Burma. ... The WLB supports [special constitutional mechanisms such as quota systems] for other marginalised groups, as well as for women.[60]

In the mid-1990s, the WLB advocated the adoption of constitutional mechanisms to enhance women's participation in formal political processes and decision-making. In 2006, the WLB recommended the implementation of a quota system with an aim to achieve at least 30 per cent female representation at all levels of government.[61] The WLB position was that

[E]quality includes full empowerment to participate in all political processes. Thus, full political citizenship involves not only the right and the opportunity to vote, but the right and opportunity to participate in all levels of the state. We recognise the distinction between the formal but nominal right to hold a political position and actually exercising power and influence as a woman in that position. In order for the latter to be realized in Burma concrete action to change social and cultural norms and practices must be reinforced with appropriate legally binding measures and political will.[62]

Several ethnic minority leaders who were advocating constitutional reforms to protect the rights of ethnic minorities strongly supported the WLB's proposal. Sao Sengsuk, head of the Shan State Constitution Drafting Commission (SSCDC), even encouraged WLB representatives to push for proportional representation to ensure that 'women will be assured their rightful quota.'[63] In 2007, the Federal Constitution Drafting Committee (FCDC), comprising representatives of democratic and ethnic organisations as well as the WLB, incorporated quotas for women in the legislature in its draft Constitution for a future democratic

---

60 Women's League of Burma, *Looking through gender lenses: position paper on gender equality* (Chiang Mai: Women's League of Burma, September 2006), 1.

61 Details of the proposed quota system are outlined in *Ibid.*

62 Women's League of Burma, *Constituting our rights* (Chiang Mai: Women's League of Burma, February 2006), 4–5.

63 'Proportional representation for women: Shan charter chief', *Shan Herald Agency for News*, 28 July 2006. The SSCDC was formed at a constitutional conference in 2000 by 50 delegates representing 18 Shan State-based organisations.

Burma.[64] The subsequent adoption of the SPDC's 2008 Constitution therefore represents a huge setback for the WLB, since it contains no affirmative measures to increase women's political representation and actually reinforces male power by reserving 25 per cent of legislative seats for the armed forces.

Promoting peace and eliminating violence against women

The WLB's peace-building program forms an important component of its ongoing efforts to strengthen women's capacities to participate in and shape the national reconciliation process in Burma. The WLB and its member organisations are actively involved in promoting a 'culture of peace' both inside Burma and along its borders, which involves transforming traditional conceptions of power that marginalise women and prevent them from achieving equality with men.[65] Expatriate women's organisations seek to overcome cultural perceptions of women's traditional role as peacekeeper, where 'keeping the peace means keeping your mouth shut'. One BWU leader explains that 'women are seen as the calm, tolerant, peaceful sex, but we must also come to realise that peace-building is about raising our voices, and not keeping quiet or [being] tolerant of discrimination and violence towards women.'[66] Peace-building, therefore, involves the exercise of women's power rather than powerlessness. Violence committed by men against women involves the abuse of power, and is both condoned by existing unequal power relations and perpetuates further gender inequality in Burmese society. Expatriate women's organisations have concentrated on empowering women to speak out about their experiences of violence and actively campaign against all forms of violence against women, particularly domestic and sexual violence.

It is extremely difficult to determine the extent of domestic violence – both inside Burma and in exiled Burmese communities – due to the lack of reliable statistical data. International organisations that monitor do-

---

64 Women's League of Burma, *Building a movement within a movement: WLB marks ten years of gender activism* (Chiang Mai: Women's League of Burma, December 2009), 42.

65 Women's League of Burma and International Institute for Democracy and Electoral Assistance, 'Women and peace building. Workshops on: The role for Burmese women in developing peace building strategies', 16–17 May 2002 (New Delhi, India) and 19–21 May 2002 (Chiang Mai, Thailand) (copyright International IDEA, 2003), 3–4.

66 Interview with BWU leader, Chiang Mai, 19 June 2005.

mestic violence including the World Health Organisation (WHO) and the United Nations Development Fund for Women (UNIFEM) have so far been unable to conduct thorough investigations inside Burma. The documentation of cases of gender-based violence by expatriate women's organisations suggests that violence against women is becoming more widespread in Burma and exiled communities as a result of ongoing armed conflict, economic hardship, and the rise in drug and alcohol abuse. In these conditions men, angered and disempowered by the economic and political situation inside Burma, as well as the difficulties of life in exile, are increasingly likely to take out their frustrations on their wives and children. Reports also indicate that cultural attitudes play a significant role in perpetuating and condoning domestic violence.[67] Expatriate women's organisations argue that many Burmese tolerate domestic violence because of the widespread belief that it is a woman's duty to keep the family together, even when her husband beats or abuses her.[68] Marital rape is not regarded as a criminal offence in Burma, and many women have been socialised to accept the view that sex without consent only becomes 'rape' when the perpetrator is the 'enemy' (read *tatmadaw*).

Over the past decade, the WLB and its member organisations have produced and distributed comic books, pamphlets and posters as part of an ongoing campaign to eliminate violence against women. Multilingual posters like the one published in the Shan-language edition of the SWAN Newsletter (Figure 9.3) illustrate several ways in which men can help stop violence against women. This poster emphasises the destructive impact of violence on women and family relationships and the need for men to respect women in order to maintain domestic harmony and peace. Significantly, the poster places as much emphasis on domestic violence – including marital rape and wife beating – as it does on military rape and trafficking of women. This sends a strong message to men since it implies that if they do not treat their wives with dignity and respect, they are just as guilty of perpetrating and condoning violence against women as the Burmese authorities and *tatmadaw*.

In 2002, the WLB initiated 'Building Inner Peace' training programs which brought women together to share their experiences of violence

---

67 Women of Burma, *In the shadow of the junta*, 54.

68 Interviews with members of expatriate Burmese women's organisations, June 2005.

Figure 9.3: 'Stop! Violence Against Women' poster, in Shan Women's Action Network Newsletter, October 2003. Reproduced by permission of Shan Women's Action Network.

and to break 'the culture of silence around sexual abuse and discrimination in the different communities in Burma'.[69] Participants were encouraged to reflect critically on their own views about and prejudices against women who had been subjected to violence including rape. One female ABSDF member recounted how she had witnessed the rape of a woman who had been detained for engaging in 'suspicious behaviour':

> At the time, I was angry at the young woman, because she had been arrested for suspicious behaviour. This made it impossible for me to

---

69   Women's League of Burma, *Overcoming shadows* (Chiang Mai: Women as Peacebuilders Team, Women's League of Burma, 2004), 2.

have any consideration for her. I looked down on her and blamed her for what happened …. However, I began to wonder how many women in our society had similar experiences. A woman who is sexually abused or raped is perceived as 'bad' by her own parents, relatives and community. She is ostracized and looked down on. There are insults and some men even prey on women who have been sexually abused. There are probably many women who suffer this kind of abuse silently. After I started to ask many difficult questions about [why] sexual abuse occurs, I became able to sympathise and understand their feelings.[70]

Women were also encouraged to discuss and debate issues openly and to acknowledge and respect others with different views. As one WLB Women as Peace-builders team member explains,

[M]any people become intolerant and get offensive when others discuss, debate and disagree with their views and ideas. Sometimes, I have seen people who claim to be working for others become entirely engulfed in their own ego. This can happen due to their desire to have power and influence over others. If this desire for power and influence gets bigger, usually it does not lead to peace.[71]

Cultivating a culture of peace therefore involves fostering open and honest communication, respect and empathy for others, and critical self-analysis. Interestingly, the desire for personal power and influence over others is perceived as potentially impeding progress towards genuine peace and reconciliation.

In addition to the above initiatives, expatriate women's organisations have highlighted the use by the Burmese military of sexual violence against ethnic minority women to assert its power over ethnic insurgent organisations and force local communities into submission.[72] Out of the many reports documenting women's experiences of state-condoned violence, *Licence to rape* has had the greatest impact in terms of raising international awareness about the extent of military rape in Burma and its adverse effects on ethnic minority women, in particular. The publication of the report also raised the profile and status of expatriate women's

---

70   Ma Lay, 'Sympathy – know how now', in Women's League of Burma, *Overcoming shadows*, 13–14.

71   Naw Laydee, 'Victim of ego', in Women's League of Burma, *Overcoming shadows (2)* (Chiang Mai: Women as Peacebuilders Team, Women's League of Burma, January 2009), 85.

72   English language edition of *Shan Women's Action Network Newsletter* 3 (September 2002): 1.

Figure 9.4: WLB 'Women as Peacebuilders' training participants. Photograph courtesy of Women's League of Burma.

organisations as a powerful force within the Burmese democratic movement.

The *Licence to rape* report

Licence to rape: the Burmese military regime's use of sexual violence in the ongoing war in Shan State was jointly released by SWAN and the Shan Human Rights Foundation (SHRF) on 19 June 2002.[73] The report documents 173 incidents of rape and other forms of sexual violence against 625 women and girls committed by Burmese troops in Shan State between 1996 and 2001. The authors convincingly argued that these rapes were part of a concerted strategy by members of the Burmese army to weaken ethnic insurgent armies and their civilian supporters. Eighty-three per cent of the rapes were committed by military officers, often in front of their own troops, and only one perpetrator was punished by his commanding officer. Sixty-one per cent of the cases reported were gang-rapes and many cases involved extreme brutality including beating, mutilation and suffocation. Many women who complained to authorities about the attacks were fined, imprisoned, tortured or even

---

73   The release of *Licence to rape* was timed to coincide with the commemoration of Women of Burma Day, which is also Aung San Suu Kyi's birthday.

killed. The report also explored the psychological and social effects of rape on survivors, including discrimination from family and community members who believed women were responsible for or corrupted by rape. Women who were shamed or forced into leaving their homes often ended up as refugees or unregistered migrants in Thailand with no legal protection and limited access to humanitarian aid and counselling services. These women were particularly vulnerable to exploitation and trafficking and also faced the threat of being deported back to Burma.

The release of *Licence to rape* triggered widespread condemnation of the SPDC and Burmese military by the international community. On 18 December 2002, the UN General Assembly adopted a resolution expressing grave concern at 'rapes and other forms of sexual violence carried out by members of the armed forces' and the 'disproportionate suffering of members of ethnic minorities, women and children from such violations'.[74] Despite the international outrage, the release of the report had potentially negative consequences for women living inside Burma and in exile. The SPDC denied the allegations and denounced SWAN and SHRF as 'anti-Myanmar Government organisations' involved in terrorist activity and drug trafficking.[75] Following international pressure, the SPDC held a 'staged' investigation led by Dr Khin Win Shwe, then head of the MMCWA, which reportedly involved forcing villagers to deny that the rapes had occurred.[76] Thai authorities, fearing the report would harm bilateral ties with Burma, increased their surveillance of Thai-based women's organisations and the SWAN office was forced to close temporarily and move underground.[77]

More positively, SWAN translated *Licence to rape* into several languages and used the royalties to fund various programs including a refugee hotline, internship program, women's support centre and safe

---

74 United Nations General Assembly, 'Resolution adopted by the General Assembly [on the report of the Third committee (A/57/566/Add.3)]. 57/231. Situation of human rights in Myanmar', A/RES/57/231, 28 February 2003.

75 For details of the SPDC investigation, see Shan Women's Action Network, 'A mockery of justice: the State Peace and Development Council's investigation into the "Licence to rape" report', 24 September 2002; Altsean Burma, *Smoke screen: report card Burma, 1 July–30 Sept 2002* (Bangkok: Alternative ASEAN Network on Burma, December 2002), 48.

76 Altsean Burma, *Abused bargaining chips*, 10.

77 Shan Women's Action Network, *SWAN: a ten-year journey* (Shan Women's Action Network, March 2009), 13, 17.

house, and several clinics and schools.[78] SWAN also developed its own website which brought the report (and SWAN's other activities) to the attention of a much wider audience. The women's commitment and resourcefulness both surprised and impressed male opposition leaders, who initially thought the report would have little effect: 'Before *Licence to rape*, we thought armed struggle was the only way and these women were wasting their time and energy. Now we've learned from them, from these brave women, that there are several ways to fight the enemy.'[79] Although *Licence to rape* received a positive response from Burmese opposition groups and raised international awareness about the plight of Burmese women, the threat of violence against women remains severe. SWAN and other expatriate women's organisations continue to document and publish reports of military rape and other forms of abuse including trafficking of women and girls.[80] The WLB's Women Against Violence (WAV) program also offers practical support to women who have suffered from violence, including access to counselling services, temporary accommodation, medical assistance and legal advice.

Some commentators have criticised the way that Burmese women's experiences are reported in the exiled opposition media, noting that 'all too often, the voice that one hears is a cry of pain or anguish from the women of Burma.'[81] Communications scholar Lisa Brooten has observed that media portrayals of Burmese women as powerless victims ignore the ways in which women are active agents of change.[82] A 2006 report published by the Karen Human Rights Group describes how in many militarised and conflict zones, where men have been forced into hiding, women have taken on new roles as income earners, educators,

---

78 Patricia Elliot, 'When women stand up to tyrants', *Briarpatch* 32, 5 (2003): 14–18.

79 Shan resistance leader Sao Yord Suk quoted in Shan Women's Action Network, *SWAN: A ten-year journey*, 15.

80 See, for example, Karen Women's Organization, *Shattering silences*; Karen Women's Organization, *State of terror: the ongoing rape, murder, torture and forced labour suffered by women living under the Burmese military regime in Karen State* (Karen Women's Organization, February 2007); Karen Women's Organization, *Walking amongst sharp knives*; Kachin Women's Association Thailand, *Driven away*; Kachin Women's Association Thailand, *Eastward bound: an update on migration and trafficking of Kachin women on the China–Burma border* (Chiang Mai: Kachin Women's Association Thailand, August 2008).

81 Janis E. Nickel, 'And what about the women of Burma?', *Burma Issues*, Special Issue (August 1993): 5.

82 Lisa Brooten, 'Human rights discourse and the development of democracy in a multi-ethnic state', *Asian Journal of Communication* 14, 2 (September 2004):185–88.

medics, village heads and interlocutors with the military. Although these responsibilities place additional burdens on women, they can also empower women and promote increased recognition of women's leadership abilities.[83] Expatriate Burmese women's organisations agree that reports of discrimination against and abuse of women need to be balanced with more positive accounts of women as active leaders and role models.[84] In addition to exposing the extent of violence and abuse against women, expatriate women's organisations have demonstrated that women can be effective leaders who stand up for the rights of ordinary Burmese.

Charm Tong, one of the researchers and lead authors of *Licence to rape*, has become one of the most prominent figures in the exiled democratic movement since the report was released. She has travelled widely to speak out about women's rights in Burma and was invited to the White House in October 2005, where she discussed Burma's human rights situation with then President George W. Bush.[85] In 2005, Charm Tong was nominated for the Nobel Peace Prize along with three other Burmese women activists: Paw Paw Lu, Dr Cynthia Maung and Zipporah Sein.[86] Zipporah Sein, then KWO general-secretary, was appointed KNU general-secretary in October 2008, indicating that women's efforts to promote female leadership in the male-dominated opposition movement were beginning to bear fruit.[87] When she assumed this role, some observers did not expect her to perform as effectively as her (male) predecessor, Mahn Sha.[88] Zipporah Sein's father, General

83 Karen Human Rights Group, *Dignity in the shadow of oppression*.

84 Personal communication with members of expatriate Burmese women's organisations, May 2011.

85 Wong Kim Hoh, 'The stuff of movies', *The Straits Times* (Singapore), 8 October 2006; Clive Barker, 'Shan human rights campaigner meets US President Bush', *The Irrawaddy*, 1 November 2005; 'Meeting with a message', *The Washington Post*, 1 November 2005.

86 Shah Paung, 'Leading ladies', *The Irrawaddy*, September 2005. Paw Lu Lu runs a safe house for Burmese living on the Thai-Burma border and, among other activities, provides care for people living with HIV/AIDS. Cynthia Maung is a Karen medical doctor and founder of the renowned Mae Tao Clinic in Mae Sot on the Thai-Burma border, which provides health care and education to Burmese migrants and refugees. For a firsthand account of Cynthia Maung's work, see Dr Cynthia Maung, 'Health on the other side', in Altsean Burma, *Burma – women's voices for change*, 15–18.

87 Saw Yan Naing, 'KNU appoints Karen woman General-Secretary', *The Irrawaddy*, 20 October 2008.

88 Saw Yan Naing, 'The new KNU?–Let's wait and see', *The Irrawaddy*, 28 October 2008. Mahn Sha was assassinated in February 2008.

Tamla Baw, became KNU chairman in 2008, so her appointment could be seen as continuing the tradition of 'dynastic politics' rather than as an acknowledgement of her own leadership skills and experience. Yet Zipporah Sein has now held this position of authority for more than two years, while continuing to advocate women's rights and serving as a positive role model for young Karen women.

Other prominent female activists include Burma Campaign UK's international campaigns coordinator, Zoya Phan, daughter of the late KNU general-secretary Mahn Sha. In March 2010, Zoya Phan was recognised by the World Economic Forum as a 'Young Global Leader' for her work in highlighting human rights abuses in Karen State and promoting democratic reform in Burma. Now 31 years old, Zoya Phan is a seasoned campaigner who has addressed the European Parliament and given interviews to major media organisations, urging the international community to increase pressure on the Burmese government to end military violence against civilians, particularly ethnic minority women. Zoya Phan has also joined the WLB and the Nobel Women's Initiative in seeking to initiate a UN-led commission of inquiry into war crimes and crimes against humanity committed by the Burmese military.[89] Although some Western governments have supported this proposal, the UN recently reaffirmed its commitment to working with the Burmese government 'to advance durable peace and democracy'.[90] As the UN and other international actors seek greater engagement with the Burmese government, expatriate women's organisations will need to consider extending their collaborative strategy to political organisations and civil society groups inside Burma if they are to leverage greater political and social power for women in their home country.

Conclusions

After suffering under isolated and oppressive military rule for nearly three decades, many women who fled Burma after the 1988 uprising

---

89   Nobel Women's Initiative and Women's League of Burma, *International Tribunal on crimes against women of Burma, March 2, 2010, New York* (Women's League of Burma and Nobel Women's Initiative, 2010). The Nobel Women's Initiative was formed in 2006 by women Nobel Peace Prize Laureates to promote the work of women's rights activists, researchers and organisations worldwide.

90   'UN committed to helping Myanmar on road to peace and democracy – Ban', *UN Daily News*, 8 June 2011.

hoped that they could create a better life for themselves and their families in exile. For the first time, many women were exposed to ideas about women's rights and gender equality, which allowed them to envisage taking on greater social and political roles within their communities and in the democratic movement. Access to communication technologies and international women's forums allowed women from diverse ethnic and social backgrounds to share their common experiences of discrimination inside Burma and in exile, and to organise collectively in order to push for their political and social rights more effectively. But there were just as many challenges for women living in exile as there were inside Burma. In addition to dealing with security concerns and financial difficulties, many expatriate women's organisations have struggled to overcome persistent cultural beliefs about gender-appropriate roles that prevent women from achieving positions of social and political power. Expatriate women's organisations have sought to increase women's political awareness at the grassroots level and are working towards the greater inclusion of women in formal political processes and leadership roles. These women have earned the admiration and respect of many Burmese and others in the international community for their commitment to promoting peaceful democratic reform. There remains an urgent need for expatriate women's organisations to engage with policy makers and civil society groups inside Burma in order to address women's immediate needs and concerns, and resolve the broader political, economic and social problems that force women to leave Burma in the first place. The next and final chapter considers what prospects there are for such collaboration in the future.

Epilogue

> *World history is the progress of the consciousness of freedom –*
> *a progress whose necessity it is our business to comprehend.*
> – Georg Wilhelm Friedrich Hegel[1]

*I*f Hegel's theory of the expansion of freedom applied to the history of female power in Burma, we might expect progression from a society in which *one* has power (queens), to one in which *some* have power (as opportunities open up through colonialism and nationalism), to one in which *all* have (some) power in a modern democracy. This process of gradual 'liberation' of women that would allow them to exercise the kind of power that has taken place in the West has not occurred in Burma owing to the historical circumstances outlined earlier. This chapter reviews the main argument of the book to demonstrate how Burmese women have been empowered and disempowered over time, and considers what prospects there are for women's empowerment in the future.

Looking back into the past

The relationship of women to power in Burmese history cannot be explained without first understanding how the Burmese viewed the social world, including their conceptions of gender relations. Central to Burmese understandings of gender–power relations was the notion of *hpoun*, which legitimised the spiritual and social hierarchies in which men exercised formal authority over women. At the same time, Buddhist symbolism and rituals celebrating women's maternal, nurturing qualities enhanced women's influence within the family. The development of

---

1   Georg Wilhelm Friedrich Hegel, *Lectures on the philosophy of world history: introduction, reason in history,* translated from the German edition of Johannes Hoffmeister by H. B. Nisbet, with an introduction by Duncan Forbes (Cambridge: Cambridge University Press, 1975), 54.

the Burmese polity as a form of extended family network supported and strengthened by female royal lineages, marriage alliances and patron–client relationships enabled queens and other elite women to exercise political influence through their familial connections to male rulers. As the Burmese came into contact with Europeans from the sixteenth century onwards, some women were able to enhance their economic and social status by entering into sexual relationships with foreign male traders, and by acting as cultural power brokers between European and Burmese elites. Women who overtly challenged men's authority, however, were criticised by male elites for threatening to upset the 'natural' social order. In other words, women could exercise influence within the private domain of the family and household economy, but they could only exercise public power through men.

A decline in women's status occurred from the nineteenth century onwards. As Konbaung kings increasingly relied on the patronage networks of their ministers and alliances with leading provincial families to ensure the loyalty of their subjects, factional and succession disputes between queens, princes, and ministers competing for power became a major cause of internal political instability. At the same time, the Burmese monarchy faced an equally serious external threat in the form of British imperial aggression. Powerful queens like Me Nu and Supayalat who dominated kings and their courts were accused – rightly or wrongly – of 'interfering' in the male domains of political and military affairs and, ultimately, of causing the loss of Burmese independence. Negative portrayals of these powerful queens reinforced the view that women should not assume leadership roles – just at the time when a new nationalist movement was emerging with the aim of overthrowing colonial rule.

Colonialism provided new challenges for Burmese women seeking to exercise power. Women's ability to influence political matters through their personal relationships with male elites was limited under an impersonalised colonial administration in which British officials held the most senior positions. By prohibiting British officers from marrying 'natives', colonial rulers effectively deprived Burmese women of an important source of political power. Burmese Buddhist women who married non-Buddhist Asian immigrants also lost many of their customary marital, property and inheritance rights under the colonial legal system. Colonial policies also resulted in a severe diminution of women's traditional economic roles. Although increased educational opportunities did restore women's economic power to some extent, female education was widely perceived as an adjunct to marriage and a life of domesticity, or at most as qualification for 'appropriate' employment as nurses and teachers. Even so, educated women were among the most committed and articulate members of the nationalist movement, though the nationalist emphasis on restoring 'traditional' cultural values actually restricted women's social and political behaviour at a time when circumstances might have enabled them to assume leadership roles in the struggle for independence. As the 'weaker sex', women were perceived to be susceptible to corruption by undesirable colonial influences and in need of the protection of male nationalists: 'good' women did not liaise with foreign men or engage in 'masculine' activism. Female nationalists who agitated for women's voting and legal rights did not push for greater leadership roles for women *per se*, partly because they were constrained by the Burmese cultural values that the male-led nationalist movement promoted.

Independence promised to open up greater opportunities for women to exercise power, as the need to use cultural values as a weapon against colonial domination eased. But the departure of the British created a power vacuum, and political factionalism increased as male elites sought to assert their positions and gain popular support. Within the AFPFL, women were expected to support male political leaders and were 'invited' to assume leadership roles only when men were unavailable. Although women actively participated in the communist and ethnic insurrections that broke out soon after independence, most performed only subordinate roles within their respective organisations. Within the communist movement, the ideological emphasis on egalitarianism did not eliminate deeply engrained beliefs about the primacy of women's maternal and domestic roles. Although some female communists took up combat roles alongside their male comrades, their primary responsibility was still caring, for both children and combatants. Ethnic minority leaders engaged in the struggle against Burman domination were no more concerned with women's rights than were the male nationalists who struggled against British domination during the colonial era.

The imposition of military rule had a devastating effect on women, since it reinforced the authoritarian, hierarchical and chauvinistic values that underpinned male-dominated power structures. The government was led and dominated by the military, which was almost exclusively male. Women's economic opportunities declined as a result of the military's monopolisation and mismanagement of the economy. The government's failure to provide adequate educational and health services placed heavy burdens on women, particularly those living in rural and ethnic minority areas, who struggled to provide for themselves and their families. Like the nationalist leadership before them, male military officers also invoked the concept of 'culture' in order to control the civilian population. Ethnic minority women living in conflict zones suffered most from government policies including cultural 'Burmanisation', forced relocation, requisition of labour and rape as a means of repression. As in the past, the only women who were able to exert influence in Burmese society were those with familial connections to powerful men, including the wives of senior military leaders. The only exception was Aung San Suu Kyi, and she too initially gained political legitimacy as her father's daughter.

Aung San Suu Kyi's ability to lead the democratic movement rested in large part on her familial connection to Aung San, the martyred leader of Burmese independence, though her moral power was magnified by her commitment to the Buddhist principles of non-violence, compassion and loving-kindness. Although Aung San Suu Kyi inspired many women to become politically active, the persistence of gender inequality even within democratic parties indicates that her prominence did not translate into a significant increase in women's political power. Meanwhile, the military leadership created its own organisations to mobilise women in support of its policies, while simultaneously condemning any woman involved in opposition politics. It has principally been those women who fled Burma and established contact with the international women's movement who have sought to challenge ingrained cultural beliefs and structural barriers that prevent women in Burma from attaining positions of political power. While expatriate women's organisations have had considerable success in promoting grassroots activism and advocating women's rights in international forums, the fact remains that they have little influence over the situation inside Burma.

Looking forward to the future

Will the transition to civilian government, socioeconomic development, and increased engagement with the international community provide opportunities for Burmese women to leverage greater power in the future? In the past, international pressure has failed to prompt Burma's leadership to introduce significant political, social and economic reform. ASEAN's policy of 'constructive engagement' with Burma remains controversial and the Burmese government's poor human rights record has long been a source of embarrassment, frustration and contention for the organisation. In November 2011, ASEAN leaders announced that Burma would become chair of the regional bloc in 2014 after the Burmese government initiated talks with Aung San Suu Kyi, released some political prisoners, eased media restrictions and legalised trade unions. Critics have described ASEAN's decision as 'premature', given reports of ongoing human rights violations and the escalation of military conflict in Kachin State and eastern Burma. Others maintain that Burma's leadership should be encouraged to pursue more substantial political reform and improve its human rights standards.[2]

Political oppression, military conflict and endemic poverty inside Burma has contributed to increases in the movement of refugees, human trafficking, drug abuse and drug trafficking, and communicable diseases which pose a very real threat to regional stability and prosperity.[3] All these problems can be partially alleviated by raising the educational and living standards of ordinary Burmese, including notably women. While ASEAN leaders are eager to foster regional security, political stability and economic growth, their commitment to promoting gender equality has been less evident.[4] ASEAN's latest report on the advancement of women in the region reveals that Burma failed to provide the basic sex-aggregated data required to assess women's status and development needs.[5] The ASEAN Commission on the Promotion and Protection

---

2 BurmaNet News ASEAN archive, http://www.burmanet.org/news/category/news/asean/, accessed on 12 December 2011.

3 Altsean Burma, *Burma issues & concerns vol. 4: the security dimensions.*

4 The ASEAN Charter recognises the 'mutual interests and interdependence among the peoples and Member States of ASEAN', and affirms the organisations' commitment to promoting 'respect for and protection of human rights and fundamental freedoms', 'shared prosperity and social progress' and the 'wellbeing, livelihood and welfare of the peoples' of ASEAN. Although women's rights are implicitly acknowledged in these broad policy statements, the only explicit reference to 'gender equality' appears in relation to the appointment of executive positions to the ASEAN Secretariat. See ASEAN, *The ASEAN Charter* (Jakarta: ASEAN Secretariat, December 2007).

5 ASEAN, *Third report on the advancement of women in ASEAN* (Jakarta: ASEAN Secretariat, May 2007).

of the Rights of Women and Children (ACWC) recently announced that its first five-year work plan will focus on improving women's access to quality education and political decision-making as well as assisting victims of trafficking and violence.[6] The Burmese government could demonstrate its commitment to protecting and promoting women's rights by implementing policies and programs in line with ACWC recommendations.

The UN has welcomed Burma's recent progress towards reform, but it has also urged the government to intensify its efforts to resolve the country's serious political, development, human rights and humanitarian problems.[7] It remains extremely difficult for UN agencies working in Burma to plan, implement and monitor humanitarian aid programs effectively, though collaboration between UN agencies and government ministries in the wake of Cyclone Nargis did provide opportunities to discuss important women's protection issues. The National Plan of Action for the Advancement of Women (2011–2015), which was drafted in collaboration with the inter-agency Women's Protection Technical Working Group, provides a comprehensive framework for promoting women's social, economic and political advancement. The success of the plan will depend on whether there is genuine and sustained political will to ensure that women's issues and rights are taken seriously at the highest levels of government.

One of the most urgent tasks facing the new government is the need to raise the living standards of ordinary Burmese. In March 2011, President Thein Sein stated that economic reform would be undertaken to 'reduce the economic gap between the rich and the poor, and [the] development gap between urban and rural areas'. He also pledged to enhance the quality of education and health facilities and training for professional staff. In order to achieve these goals, the government has committed to increasing collaboration with UN agencies, INGOs and local NGOs.[8] While some Burmese and foreign analysts are cautiously

---

6   'Second press release of the ASEAN Commission on the Promotion and Protection of the Rights of Women and Children (ACWC)', Solo, Indonesia, 8 September 2011, http://www.aseansec.org/26613.htm, accessed on 12 December 2011.

7   United Nations General Assembly, 'Situation of human rights in Myanmar', A/C.3/66/L.55/Rev.1, 16 November 2011.

8   An English translation of the speech was published in the *New Light of Myanmar*, 31 March 2011.

optimistic about this policy agenda, it remains to be seen whether the government has the political will, capacity and support to follow through on these promises. The national budget for 2011–12 prioritises military expenditure over the social welfare needs of the general population. Almost 20 per cent of the total budget was allocated to the Ministry of Defence, while the ministries of Health and Education received 1.31 per cent and 4.57 per cent respectively.[9] If this disparity continues, it is difficult to see how the government will be able to implement policies and programs to address the country's serious socio-economic problems, including those that most impact on women.

State-sanctioned women's organisations like the MWAF and the MMCWA have the potential to improve women's access to health care and educational services, and provide some legal protection from violence and discrimination. To be effective, however, these organisations require greater funding and expertise to implement their programs. Measures must be taken to eliminate official corruption and to ensure that these organisations offer assistance to all women, regardless of their location, ethnicity and political beliefs. Official women's organisations can be held more accountable through publishing detailed information about the budgets, objectives and reach of their programs. Increased engagement with UN agencies could also provide much-needed training and technical assistance to government personnel and local NGO staff.

In the longer term, women's social and economic development cannot progress without increasing female participation in political policy-making and leadership. Although Burma's constitutions have all contained provisions guaranteeing women the right to vote and stand for election, none of them has resulted in more women assuming political office. In the November 2010 elections, less than eight per cent of candidates were female, and women represent only three per cent of the members elected to the National Assembly. With so few women in parliament, policy-makers are less likely to ensure that women's interests are represented. History has shown that women's rights tend to be sidelined all too easily during periods of political transition, and female activists have expressed concern that women's issues remain

---

9   Burma's state gazette titled 'The Expenditure of the Union Ministries and Union Level Organizations', reproduced in Htet Aung, 'Military security trumps human security in Burma's budget', *The Irrawaddy*, 9 March 2011.

far down the national agenda.[10] The political environment is likely to become even more complex as multiple actors seek to assert their positions and further their interests. New configurations of power are being negotiated that could potentially increase the political space available to individuals and groups who were previously excluded from power, but in the absence of strong civil society women will need to fight hard to make their voices heard.

Aung San Suu Kyi continues to command respect and influence among many Burmese and members of the international community. Thein Sein appears to be willing to include Aung San Suu Kyi and the NLD in the political process. The government recently amended controversial sections of the Political Parties Registration Law, paving the way for the NLD to re-register as a political party.[11] The NLD plans to contest upcoming by-elections, which could see Aung San Suu Kyi gain parliamentary office for the first time. Party leaders have indicated that they intend to prioritise female candidates, which would provide greater opportunities for women to engage in political processes and decision-making.[12] Aung San Suu Kyi has acknowledged that women continue to face discrimination in many aspects of their lives and stressed the need to 'empower' women and educate men in order to end violence against women, in particular.[13] With so many competing demands on her time, however, others inside and outside the country will need to push hard for women's rights, including the right to political participation, to be prioritised at the local, regional and national level.

Expatriate Burmese media organisations have long played an important role in highlighting women's achievements and condemning discrimination against women. In an article published in *The Irrawaddy* in March 2011, the prominent female writer Nu Nu Yi linked the persis-

---

10   Zoya Phan, 'Women in Burma need international support', *Mizzima News*, 8 March 2011.

11   The amendments included the removal of a clause which prohibited anyone who had been convicted of a crime from joining a political party. The amended law allows former political prisoners to become party members.

12   Myo Thant, 'NLD prepares to accept 1 million party members', *Mizzima News*, 28 November 2011.

13   Aung San Suu Kyi, Video speech delivered at the Feminist Majority Foundation's Global Women's Rights Awards Ceremony, Los Angeles, USA, 26 April 2011, http://www.youtube.com/watch?v=0PqI4zDcOJk, accessed on 19 June 2011. See also Aung San Suu Kyi, Video speech delivered at the Nobel Women's Initiative conference, 'Women Forging a New Security: Ending Sexual Violence in Conflict', 23–25 May 2011, Montebello, Canada, http://vimeo.com/nobelwomen/videos/rss, accessed on 19 June 2011.

tence of gender discrimination in Burmese society to the lack of awareness about women's rights: 'Men don't want to give important decision-
making positions to women .... If women don't know their rights, they
can't see how the way they are treated diverges from the principles of
human rights.'[14] The recent relaxation of media censorship has allowed
for increased discussion about women's rights inside the country. In
February, *The Myanmar Times* published an article acknowledging that
there is still a 'significant gap in gender matters' in Burma. Describing
the CEDAW and Beijing Platform for Action as positive developments
for securing women's rights, the author lamented the low level of female
political representation and noted that

> [W]omen are still victims of bias and discrimination rooted in cultural
> norms and values. Boys are more favoured, wives follow the husbands'
> lead, and women find it difficult to divorce because of social pressures.
> Cases of domestic violence against women are not unusual.[15]

Expatriate women's organisations have been most vocal in their
efforts to promote women's rights and their participation in political
decision-making and leadership. If the challenge of uniting the disparate
segments of the population inside the country is immense, an even
greater challenge is how to build trust and reconciliation between those
inside Burma and those living in exile. Some commentators believe that
expatriate organisations have 'lost touch' with those inside Burma who
are willing to work within the system to bring about political and social
change.[16] The Women's League of Burma may question the government's commitment to reform, but it has supported the NLD's decision
to re-register as a political party.[17] Expatriate women's organisations have
demonstrated their ability to work collaboratively with each other and
with their male colleagues in the exiled democratic movement. They
have also had considerable success in raising international awareness

---

14 Ko Htwe, 'Burmese women celebs urge struggle to close gender gap', *The Irrawaddy*, 8
    March 2011.

15 Nyunt Win, 'A long journey for women', *The Myanmar Times*, 14–20 February 2011.

16 Marie Lall, 'The 2010 Myanmar elections', Heinrich Boll Stiftung, The Green Political
    Foundation, 4 January 2011, http://www.boell.de/worldwide/asia/asia-the-2010-myan-
    mar-elections-10885.html, accessed on 20 May 2011.

17 Women's League of Burma, 'Statement on the Sixth Congress of the Women's League
    of Burma (WLB)', 27 January 2011; 'Women's League of Burma welcomes the meeting
    between two women world leaders: Daw Aung San Suu Kyi and Mrs. Hillary Clinton, 1
    December 2011.

about the effects of state-sanctioned violence against women. The real challenge facing expatriate women's organisations now and in the future is how to build on these achievements by strengthening their collaborations with political organisations and civil society groups inside Burma in order to promote women's rights and empowerment at the local and, ultimately, national levels.

In a recent interview, Aung San Suu Kyi told *Time Magazine* that her 'top priority is for people to understand that they have the power to change things themselves'.[18] If 'power' is the ability to exert influence over others, then 'empowerment' involves developing an inner awareness and strength, which enables an actor to think critically and identify solutions to problems. Burmese women have been told that they do not need to be empowered, that they already have the same rights as men. But they have been socialised to accept that men are leaders and they should be followers. Women have been taught to prioritise their families, their culture and their nation over the development of their own talents and potential. They have been encouraged to accept ideas, practices and institutions that deny them the same opportunities as men to exercise power and influence in their own society. This book has shown that Burmese women, despite many structural and cultural constraints, have proved themselves to be resourceful, engaged and influential, whether as king-makers in the past, as spiritual guides, educators, social commentators, politicians and peace activists, or as 'home-ministers'. Imagine, then, what women could achieve if they had access to quality education and health services, if they were allowed to enter occupations according to their ability and interest, if they were encouraged to participate in government policy-making, if they were taught not only to respect their cultural traditions but also to question and challenge 'traditional' beliefs and practices that discriminate against women. Burma's myriad and complex social, economic and political problems will undoubtedly take many years if not decades to resolve. The empowerment of women would not solve all these problems, but it would enable Burmese women to play an active and influential role in shaping both their own future and that of their country.

---

18   Hannah Beech, 'Aung San Suu Kyi: Burma's first lady of freedom', *Time Magazine* 177, 1 (10 January 2011).

Glossary

amhudan	people in crown service
amat	minister
ami/mi	mother
ami purā	queen; consort of the king
amyo	race; also refers to a person's lineage and class
ana	authority
arzani	'martyr'; *Arzani* Day (19 July) commemorates Aung San's death; female communist
asañ	people not legally bonded to anyone; later known as *athi*
asoyamin	middle class; refers both to civil servants and the officer class (lit. 'officer of the government')
athin	association; organisation
atwinwun	minister of the *Byedaik*
awza	influence
bhikkhuni	ordained nun
Bogyoke	general
Burman	member of Burma's largest ethnic group
Burmese	people from Burma, regardless of ethnic group; the language of the Burmans
Byedaik	crown department responsible for administration of the inner palace
cakkavatti	universal monarch in Theravada Buddhist thought
chettiar	moneylender (usually Indian)
dana	generosity, charity

315

Daw	aunt; honorific for older woman
dhammathat	civil code; compilation of customary law
Dobama Asiayone	'We Burman's Association'
eingyi	traditional blouse worn by women
einshemin	heir apparent; usually the eldest son of the king and his chief queen
galon/garuda	mythical bird associated with Burmese royalty
Hluttaw	central administrative organ of the pre-modern state administered by a council of ministers called *wungyis*
hpoun	spiritual power believed to reside in male human body (lit. 'glory')
hpoungyi	Buddhist monk (lit. 'great *hpoun*', 'great glory')
htamein	traditional Burmese sarong worn by women
kadaw	wife (especially wife of an official)
kala	foreigner (usually refers to Indians) (lit. 'caste', derived from Pali *kula*)
kan	karma; the moral law of cause and effect
karuna	compassion
Ko	older brother; honorific for a man slightly older than oneself
konmari	women's nationalist association during the colonial era
kuthou	merit
kwyan	person obligated to someone
kwyan-tō	people in crown service; same as *amhudan*
kyat	Burmese currency
longyi	traditional Burmese sarong worn by men and women
Ma	older sister; honorific for a woman slightly older than oneself
Mahadevi	wife of *sawbwa* (lit. 'great goddess')
metta	loving-kindness
mi-ba	parents (lit. 'mother-father')
mingyi	high-ranking minister; the king (lit. 'great king')

minlaung	embryo king; imminent king
mithazu	family (lit. 'mother-child-group')
Myanmar	alternative name of the country and people of Burma; language of the Burmans
myo	district or town
myoza	person to whom the crown's share of the revenue of a *myo* was assigned (lit. 'eater of *myo*')
naga	serpent; dragon
Nang	honorific used by Shan women
nat	spirit; supernatural being
Naw	honorific used by Karen women
paritta	extracts from Suttas, one part of the Buddhist scriptures, used as prayers to ward off evil
purā	Buddha, lord; also used to denote the reigning king
Pya Ley Pya	'Four Cuts'; military counter-insurgency strategy used to cut the enemy's access to food, money, recruits and intelligence
pyi	measure of dry volume equal to 4.67lbs
Pyidawtha	lit. 'sacred-pleasant-country'; AFPFL government's economic and social program during the parliamentary era
Pyithu Hluttaw	People's Assembly
sangha	order of Buddhist monks
sawbwa	hereditary ruler of Shan principality (*saopha* in Shan)
sayadaw	senior monk or (religious) teacher
setkyamin	Burmese word for *cakkavatti* ('universal monarch')
shinbyu	novitiation ceremony for Burmese Buddhist boys
tabindaing	female counterpart of the heir apparent; eldest daughter of king and chief queen
tatmadaw	Burmese armed forces
thakin	'master'; title adopted by male nationalists during the colonial era

thakinma	female *thakin*
thilashin	Buddhist nun
thingyan	Burmese new year, celebrated during mid-April
thugyi	hereditary official (female *thugyima*)
U	uncle; honorific for an older man
upasika	devout layperson who abides by Buddhist precepts
vipassana	'insight'; popular form of meditation among Burmese Buddhists
viss	measure of weight equal to 0.625kg
wun	common term denoting an appointed official
wungyi	minister of state at the *Hluttaw* in pre-modern Burma
wunthanu athin	'patriotic associations' formed during the colonial era
yebaw	'comrade'
yebawma	female *yebaw*

Bibliography

Note: Burmese personal names are cited in their full form, followed by honorifics where appropriate.

India Office Records (IOR) and British Library Oriental Manuscripts (BLOM), British Library

'A historical memorandum of royal relations of Burmah hunters family from beginning to present 1228 AD 1866. Collected from Burmah history and various parts – best corrected by various prince and Queen and old officials of this Burmah.' Yadanabhoom (Mandalay) 4th December 1866. BLOM OR 3470.

'Burma Miscellaneous. Notes dealing with points raised by Daw Mya Sein in her talk with Lady Pethick-Lawrence. Representation of Burma overseas.' IOR L/PO/9/7.

'Burma Round Table Conference. Note on groups represented at Burma Conference.' IOR L/PO/9/3.

'Burma: – treatment of the Family of ex-King Thebaw.' IOR/L/PS/10/641.

'Confidential memorandum from the Chief Secretary to the Government of Burma to the Secretary to the Government of India, Home Department, dated Rangoon, 24 January 1903. (G.B.C.P.O. – No 562, Chief Secy., 26–1–1903 – 35).' IOR/L/PJ/6/629 File 517.

'Copies of speeches by and in honour of Lady Dorman-Smith at meetings of the Burmese Women's League and All Burma Women's Freedom League, with further material connected with the Dorman-Smiths' return to Burma. 1945.' MSS Eur E 215/55.

'Extract from official report of the Legislative Assembly debates, 7 September 1925.' IOR/L/PS/10/641.

Furnivall, J. S., 'Planning for national education', 9 September 1951. MSS Eur D 1066/5.

'Government of India, Finance Department, Pensions and Gratuities, No. 458 of 1920, To The Right Honourable Edwin Montagu, His Majesty's Secretary of State for India, Simla, the 30th September 1920.' IOR/L/PS/10/641.

'Introductory leaflet, setting out the aims and principles of the National Council of Women in Burma, together with lists of members, officers and affiliated bodies. October 1929.' MSS Eur D 1230/1.

Khin Myo Chit, 'Many a house of life hath held me.' MSS Eur D 1066/1.

'Papers and correspondence of Lady Dorman-Smith as Honorary Commander, Women's Auxiliary Service (Burma) and copies of Dorman-Smith's correspondence about the Women's Auxiliary Service (Burma), including newsletters and other items. 1944–1946.' MSS Eur E 215/51.

'Parliamentary Notice, Session 1895, House of Commons.' IOR/L/PJ/6/391 File 269.

'Report by the National Council of Women in Burma on conditions affecting labour in and near Rangoon.' MSS Eur D 1230/6.

'Scripts of addresses by Mrs Bulkeley on mothering; the Christian education of children; Mrs Sumner, the founder of the National Council of Women in Burma; and the Mothers' Union in Burma.' MSS Eur D 1230/5.

'Sir Charles Bernard's letters.' MSS Eur D 912.

'Students' Strike 1936. All Burma Youth League.' MSS Eur D 1066/2.

'Telegram from Governor of Burma, dated 4th October 1931 (To Viceroy, repeated to Secretary of State)', in *Burma Round Table Conference. Note on groups represented at Burma Conference.* IOR L/PO/9/3.

'The 1936 Rangoon University Strike.' MSS Eur D 1066/3.

'The first W.A.A.C.', *Burma Today* 2, 3 (January 1945): 11. MSS Eur E 215/66.

Published and unpublished sources

Ah May Saw, 'With reminiscent images', in Altsean Burma, *Burma – women's voices for change*, edited by the Thanakha Team (Bangkok: Alternative ASEAN Network on Burma, June 2002), 44–48.

Ah Mu Doe, 'Death threats & the disappeared duck', in Altsean Burma, *Burma – women's voices together*, edited by the Thanakha Team (Bangkok: Alternative ASEAN Network on Burma, June 2003), 7–13.

Alamgir, Jalal, 'Against the current: the survival of authoritarianism in Burma', *Pacific Affairs* 70, 3 (Autumn 1997): 335–50.

All Burma Federation of Student Unions, *The current education situation in Burma: education report year 2000* (Bangkok: Foreign Affairs Committee, All Burma Federation of Student Unions, 2001).

All Burma Students Democratic Front, *Burma and the role of women* (Bangkok: Documentation and Research Centre, All Burma Students' Democratic Front, 13 March 1997).

————, *To stand and be counted* (Bangkok: All Burma Students' Democratic Front, June 1998).

Allott, Anna, 'Introduction', in Ma Ma Lay, *Not out of hate: a novel of Burma*, edited by William H. Frederick; translated by Margaret Aung-Thwin; introduced by Anna Allott; afterword by Robert E. Vore, Monographs in International Studies, Southeast Asia Series, No. 88 (Athens, Ohio: Ohio University Center for International Studies, 1991), xiii–xviii.

————, *Inked over, ripped out: Burmese storytellers and the censors* (Chiang Mai: Silkworm Books, 1994).

Altsean Burma, *Burma: voices of women in the struggle*, edited by the Thanakha Team (Bangkok: Alternative ASEAN Network on Burma, 1998).

————, *Special briefing: women's report card on Burma, April 2000* (Bangkok: Alternative ASEAN Network on Burma, 2000).

————, *Burma – women's voices for change*, edited by the Thanakha Team (Bangkok: Alternative ASEAN Network on Burma, June 2002).

————, *Smoke screen: report card Burma, 1 July–30 Sept 2002* (Bangkok: Alternative ASEAN Network on Burma, December 2002).

————, *Abused bargaining chips: women's report card on Burma, March 2003* (Bangkok: Alternative ASEAN Network on Burma, February 2003).

————, *Burma – women's voices together*, edited by the Thanakha Team (Bangkok: Alternative ASEAN Network on Burma, June 2003).

————, *Arrested: report card on Burma, 1 Apr–30 Jun 2003* (Bangkok: Alternative ASEAN Network on Burma, November 2003).

————, *Burma issues & concerns vol. 4: the security dimensions* (Bangkok: Alternative ASEAN Network on Burma, April 2007).

Amnesty International, 'Myanmar: the Kayin (Karen) State: militarization and human rights', 1 June 1999, AI Index: ASA 16/12/99.

————, 'Myanmar: aftermath: three years after dislocation in the Kayan State', 1 June 1999, AI Index: ASA 16/14/99.

————, 'Fear of torture or ill treatment/health concern', 17 November 2007, AI Index: ASA 16/040/2007.

Andaya, Barbara Watson, *To live as brothers: Southeast Sumatra in the seventeenth and eighteenth centuries* (Honolulu: University of Hawai'i Press, 1993).

————, 'From temporary wife to prostitute: sexuality and economic change in early modern Southeast Asia', *Journal of Women's History* 9, 4 (Winter 1998): 11–34.

———— (ed.), *Other pasts: women, gender and history in early modern Southeast Asia* (Honolulu: Center for Southeast Asian Studies, University of Hawai'i at Manoa, 2000).

————, 'Introduction', in Barbara Watson Andaya (ed.), *Other pasts: women, gender and history in early modern Southeast Asia* (Honolulu: Center for Southeast Asian Studies, University of Hawai'i at Manoa, 2000), 1–26.

————, 'Localising the universal: women, motherhood and the appeal of early Theravāda Buddhism', *Journal of Southeast Asian Studies* 33, 1 (February 2002): 1–30.

————, *The flaming womb: repositioning women in early modern Southeast Asia* (Honolulu: University of Hawai'i Press, 2006).

————, 'State of the field: studying women and gender in Southeast Asia', *International Journal of Asian Studies* 4, 1 (2007): 113–36.

Anderson, Benedict R. O'G., 'The idea of power in Javanese culture', in *Language and power: exploring political cultures in Indonesia* (Ithaca; London: Cornell University Press, 1990), 17–77.

Ang Chin Geok, *Aung San Suu Kyi: towards a new freedom* (Sydney: Prentice Hall, 1998).

Apple, Betsy, *School for rape: the Burmese military and sexual violence* (Bangkok: EarthRights International, 1998).

———— and Veronika Martin, *No safe place: Burma's army and the rape of ethnic women: a report by Refugees International* (Washington: Refugees International, 2003).

Aris, Michael, 'Introduction', in Aung San Suu Kyi, *Freedom from fear and other writings*, foreword by Vaclav Havel, edited and introduced by Michael Aris (Harmondsworth: Penguin Books, 1991), xv–xxviii.

ASEAN, *Third report on the advancement of women in ASEAN* (Jakarta: ASEAN Secretariat, May 2007).

————, *The ASEAN Charter* (Jakarta: ASEAN Secretariat, December 2007).

Aung San Suu Kyi, *Aung San of Burma: a biographical portrait by his daughter*, with an introduction by Roger Matthews (Edinburgh: Kiscadale, 1991).

————, *Freedom from fear and other writings*, foreword by Vaclav Havel, edited and introduced by Michael Aris (Harmondsworth: Penguin Books, 1991).

————, *Freedom from fear and other writings*, edited by Michael Aris, second edition (London: Penguin, 1995).

————, with Alan Clements, U Kyi Maung, U Tin U, *The voice of hope: Aung San Suu Kyi conversations with Alan Clements*, with contributions by U Kyi Maung and U Tin U (New York: Seven Stories Press, 1997).

————, 'A foundation of enduring strength', in Altsean Burma, *Burma – women's voices together*, edited by the Thanakha Team (Bangkok: Alternative ASEAN Network on Burma, June 2003), 1–2.

Aung-Thwin, Maitrii, 'Genealogy of a rebellion narrative: law, ethnology and culture in colonial Burma', *Journal of Southeast Asian Studies* 34, 3 (2003): 393–419.

Aung-Thwin, Maureen, 'Burma: a disenfranchised prime minister, the myth of equality, women from heaven', *Ms* (July/August 1991): 18–21.

————, 'Foreigners and females in Burmese eyes', in John J. Brandon (ed.), *Burma/Myanmar towards the twenty-first century: dynamics of continuity and change* (Bangkok: Open Society Institute, Thai Studies Section, 1997), 35–44.

Aung-Thwin, Michael, 'Prophecies, omens and dialogue: tools of the trade in Myanmar historiography', in D. Wyatt and A. Woodside (eds.), *Moral order and the question of social change: essays on Southeast Asian thought* (New Haven: Yale University Southeast Asian Studies, 1982), 78–103.

————, *Pagan: the origins of modern Burma* (Honolulu: University of Hawai'i Press, 1985).

————, *Myth and history in the historiography of early Burma: paradigms, primary sources, and prejudices* (Athens: Ohio University, Center for International Studies, 1998).

————, 'Parochial universalism, democracy jihad and the Orientalist image of Burma: the new evangelism', *Pacific Affairs* 74, 4 (Winter 2001–02): 483–505.

————, *The mists of Rāmañña: the legend that was Lower Burma* (Honolulu: University of Hawai'i Press, 2005).

Aye Aye Mu, Daw, 'The role of Myanmar women in the anti-fascist resistance (1945)', *Myanmar Historical Research Journal* 5 (June 2000): 63–72.

Aye Kyaw, U, *The voice of young Burma* (New York: Southeast Asia Program, 1993).

Aye Pwint, Ma, 'Picking up the fallen rice stalks', in Altsean Burma, *Burma – women's voices for change*, edited by the Thanakha Team (Bangkok: Alternative ASEAN Network on Burma, June 2002), 89–92.

Ba Maw, (U), *Breakthrough in Burma: memoirs of a revolution* (New Haven; London: Yale University Press, 1968).

Baird-Murray, Maureen, *A world overturned: memoirs of a Burmese childhood, 1933–1947* (Brooklyn: Interlink Books, 1998).

Belak, Brenda, *Gathering strength: women from Burma on their rights* (Chiang Mai: Images Asia, 2002).

Brac de la Perrière, Bénédicte, '"Nats' wives" or "children of nats": from spirit possession to transmission among the ritual specialists of the Cult of the Thirty-Seven Lords', *Asian Ethnology* 68, 2 (2009): 283–305.

———, 'A woman of mediation', paper presented at Southeast Asia Session 28: Life Stories of Women in Burma as part of the Association of Asian Scholars (AAS) Annual Meeting, 26–29 March 2009, Chigago, USA.

Brooten, Lisa, 'Human rights discourse and the development of democracy in a multi-ethnic state', *Asian Journal of Communication* 14, 2 (September 2004): 174–91.

———, 'The feminization of democracy under siege: the media, "the Lady" of Burma, and U.S. Foreign policy', *National Women's Studies Association (NWSA) Journal* 17, 3 (Fall 2005): 134–56.

Burma, Government of, *List of inscriptions found in Burma*, compiled and edited by Charles Duroiselle (Rangoon: Superintendent Government Printing, 1921).

———, *Burma Round Table Conference, 27th November 1931–12th January 1932: Proceedings* (Rangoon: Superintendent, Government Printing and Stationery, 1932).

———, Constituent Assembly of Burma, *The Constitution of the Union of Burma* (Rangoon: Superintendent, Government Printing and Stationery, Burma, 1945).

———, *Burma and the insurrections* (Rangoon: Government of the Union of Burma, September 1949).

————, Central Statistical and Economics Department, Census Division, *Union of Burma second stage census 1954, Volume I: Population and housing* (Rangoon: Superintendent, Government Printing and Stationery, Burma, 1955).

————, *Report on the survey of household expenditures* (Rangoon: Central Statistical and Economics Department, Government of the Union of Burma, 1958).

————, Burma Socialist Programme Party, *The philosophy of the Burma Socialist Programme Party: the system of correlation of man and his environment* (Rangoon: Ministry of Information, 1963).

————, 'The Constitution of the Burma Socialist Programme Party for the transitional period of its construction', Adopted by the Revolutionary Council, July 4, 1962.

————, Central Organization Committee, *Party Seminar 1965: speeches of General Ne Win and political report of the General-Secretary* (Rangoon: Sarpay Beikman Press, 1966).

————, *Myanma nainggan amyothamimya i naingganyei hlouqsha hmu* [Burmese women political movements] (Yangon: Sarpay Beikman, 1975).

————, *Burma Communist Party's conspiracy to take over state power* (Rangoon: Ministry of Information, 1989).

————, *The conspiracy of treasonous minions within the Myanmar naing-ngan and traitorous cohorts abroad* (Rangoon: Ministry of Information, 1989).

————, *The Myanmar Maternal and Child Welfare Association Law* (The State Law and Order Restoration Council Law No. 21/90) (9 November 1990).

————, *The Child Law* (The State Law and Order Restoration Council Law No. 9/93).

————, Central Statistical Organization, *Statistical profile of children and women in Myanmar 1993* (Yangon: Central Statistical Organization, Government of the Union of Myanmar, [199–]).

————, *The Law Amending the Suppression of Prostitution Act, 1949* (The State Peace and Development Council Law No. 7/98).

————, Central Statistical Organization, *Statistical profile of children and women in Myanmar 1997* (Yangon: Central Statistical Organization, Ministry of National Planning and Economic Development, Government of the Union of Myanmar, 1999).

————, Myanmar Women's Affairs Federation, *Papers presented in honour of Myanmar Women's Day, 3 July 2005* (Yangon: [U Kyi Win at] Universities Press, 2005).

————, 'Statement and background paper concerning the adverse impact on the lives of women as a consequence of the unjust allegations and sanctions against Myanmar', (Yangon, April 2005).

————, *Constitution of the Republic of the Union of Myanmar (2008)* ([Myanmar]: Printing & Publishing Enterprise, Ministry of Information, 2008).

————, 'Draft National Plan of Action for the Advancement of Women 2011–2015', 13 May 2010.

Burma Center Netherlands (BCN) and Transnational Institute (TNI) (eds.), *Strengthening civil society in Burma: possibilities and dilemmas for international NGOs* (Chiang Mai: Silkworm Books, 1999).

Burmese Women's Union, *BWU activity report 1998–2001* (Mae Hong Son: Burmese Women's Union, [2002?]).

———— and Assistance Association for Political Prisoners (Burma), *Women political prisoners in Burma: joint report* ([Chiang Mai; Mae Sot]: Burmese Women's Union and Assistance Association for Political Prisoners (Burma), September 2004).

Butcher, John G., *The British in Malaya, 1880–1941: the social history of a European community in colonial Southeast Asia* (Kuala Lumpur; New York: Oxford University Press, 1979).

Cady, John F., *A history of modern Burma* (Ithaca, New York: Cornell University Press, 1958).

Callahan, Mary, *Making enemies: war and state building in Burma* (Ithaca; London: Cornell University Press, 2003).

Chao Tzang Yawnghwe, *The Shan of Burma: memoirs of a Shan exile*, second reprint (Singapore: Institute of Southeast Asian Studies, 2010).

Charm Tong, Nang, 'A unique education, in Altsean Burma, *Burma – women's voices for change*, edited by the Thanakha Team (Bangkok: Alternative ASEAN Network on Burma, 2002), 83–88.

Chit Sein Lwin, *Konbaungkhit saungkyamyaing hmattan* [Notes on the Pleasure Apartment in the Konbaung Period] (Yangon: Kyonpyaw Sarpay, 1967).

Cho Cho Khaing, Naw, 'University of real life' in Altsean Burma, *Burma – women's voices for change*, edited by the Thanakha Team (Bangkok: Alternative ASEAN Network on Burma, June 2002), 62–65.

Christian, John Le Roy, *Burma and the Japanese invader*, foreword by Sir Reginald Hugh Dorman-Smith (Bombay: Thacker, 1945).

Cochrane, Henry Park, *Among the Burmans: a record of fifteen years of work and its fruitage* (New York: Fleming H. Revell Co., c.1904).

Coedès, Georges, *Histoire ancienne des états hindouisés d'Extrême-Orient* (Hanoi: Imprimerie d'Extrême-Orient, 1944).

Corfield, Justin and Ian Morson (eds.), *British Sea-Captain Alexander Hamilton's A new account of the East Indies* (17th–18th century) (Lewiston; Queenston; Lampeter: The Edwin Mellen Press, 2001). [Originally published as Alexander Hamilton, *A new account of the East Indies*, 2 volumes (Edinburgh, 1727; reprint, London: Argonaut Press, 1930).]

Cowell, E. B. (ed.), *The Jātaka: or stories of the Buddha's former births* (London: Published for the Pali Text Society by Luzac & Co., 1957).

Cox, Hiram, *Journal of a residence in the Burmhan empire*, with an introduction by D. G. E. Hall ([Farnborough]: Gregg International, 1971).

Curwen, Pippa, 'The Kawthoolei Women's Organization', *Cultural Survival Quarterly* 13, 4 (December 1989): 32–33.

Day, A. J., 'Ties that (un)bind: families and states in premodern Southeast Asia', *Journal of Asian Studies* 55, 2 (1996): 384–409.

De Mersan, Alexandra, 'A new place for Mra Swan Dewi: Changes in spirit cults in Arakan (Rakhine) State', *Asian Ethnology* 68, 2 (2009): 307–32.

Desai, Walter Sadgun, *History of the British residency in Burma, 1926–1840* (Rangoon: University of Rangoon, 1939).

Duroiselle, Charles, Taw Sein Ko, C. O. Blagden and U Mya (eds.), *Epigraphia Birmanica: being lithic and other inscriptions of Burma* (Rangoon: Superintendent, Government Printing Office, 1919–36).

Edwards, Louise and Mina Roces (eds.), *Women in Asia: tradition, modernity and globalisation* (St Leonards: Allen & Unwin, 2000).

Edwards, Penny, 'Half-caste: staging race in British Burma', *Postcolonial Studies* 5, 3 (November 2002): 279–95.

———, 'On home ground: settling land and domesticating difference in the "non-settler" colonies of Burma and Cambodia', *Journal of Colonialism and Colonial History* 4, 3 (Winter 2003) (electronic resource).

Elliot, Patricia, *The white umbrella* (Bangkok: Post Books, 1999).

———, 'When women stand up to tyrants', *Briarpatch* 32, 6 (2003): 14–18.

Elson, R. E., *The end of the peasantry in Southeast Asia: a social and economic history of peasant livelihood, 1800–1990s* (Houndmills, Basingstoke, Hampshire: Macmillan Press; New York: St. Martin's Press, 1997).

Errington, Shelley, 'Recasting sex, gender, and power: a theoretical and regional overview', in Jane Monnig Atkinson and Shelley Errington (eds.), *Power and difference: gender in island Southeast Asia* (Stanford: Stanford University Press, 1990), 1–58.

Fan Cho, *The Man Shu: Book of the Southern barbarians*, translated by Gordon H. Luce, edited by Giok-Po Oey, Data Paper Number 44 (Ithaca: Southeast Asia Program, Department of Far Eastern Studies, Cornell University, December 1961).

Fielding [Hall], H., *The soul of a people*, second edition (London: Macmillan, 1898).

———, *Thibaw's queen* (London; New York: Harper & Brothers, 1899).

———, *A people at school* (London: Macmillan, 1906).

———, 'Burmese women' ([Burma], unpublished mimeograph, [19––]).

Fink, Christina, *Living silence: Burma under military rule* (London; New York: Zed Books, 2001).

Fleschenberg, Andrea, 'Asia's women politicians at the top: roaring tigresses or tame kittens?', in Kazuki Iwagana (ed.), *Women's political participation and representation in Asia: obstacles and challenges*, Women and Politics in Asia series, No. 2 (Copenhagen: NIAS Press, 2008), 23–54.

Furnivall, J. S., 'Matriarchal vestiges in Burma', *Journal of the Burma Research Society* 1, 1 (1911): 15–30.

———, *Colonial policy and practice: a comparative study of Burma and Netherlands India* (New York: New York University Press, 1956).

Fytche, Albert, *Burma past and present, with personal reminiscences of the country* (London: C. Kegan Paul & Co, 1878).

Gaung, U, *Translation of a digest of the Burmese Buddhist law concerning inheritance and marriages: being a collection of texts from thirty-six dhammathats*, 2 volumes (Rangoon: Government Printing, Burma, 1902–09).

Gray, James, *Ancient proverbs and maxims from Burmese sources* (Trübner & Co Ltd, 1886) (reprint London: Routledge, 2000, 2001).

Guillon, Emmanuel, *The Mons: a civilisation of Southeast Asia*, translated and edited by James V. Di Crocco (Bangkok: The Siam Society under Royal Patronage, 1999).

Gutman, Pamela and Bob Hudson, 'The archaeology of Burma (Myanmar) from the Neolithic to Pagan', in Ian Glover and Peter Bellwood (eds.), *Southeast*

Asia: from prehistory to history (London; New York: RoutledgeCurzon, 2004), 149–76.

Hall, D. G. E. [Daniel George Edward] (ed.), *The Dalhousie-Phayre correspondence, 1852–56* (London: Oxford University Press, 1932).

———, *A history of South-East Asia* (London: Macmillan, 1964).

———, *Early English intercourse with Burma 1578–1743*, second edition (London: Frank Cass, 1968).

Halliday, Robert, 'Slapat rājāwan datow smin ron: a history of kings, with text, translation, and notes', *Journal of the Burma Research Society* 13, 1&2 (1923): 9–31; 33–67.

———, *The Mons of Burma and Thailand, volume 2: selected articles*, edited with a foreword and photographs by Christian Bauer (Bangkok: White Lotus, 2000).

Harvey, Godfrey Eric, *History of Burma: from the earliest times to 10 March, 1824, the beginning of the English conquest* (London: Frank Cass & Co. Ltd, 1967).

Hashim, Ruzy, 'Bringing Tun Kudu out of the shadows: interdisciplinary approaches to understanding the female presence in the Sejarah Melayu', in Barbara Watson Andaya (ed.), *Other pasts: women, gender and history in early modern Southeast Asia* (Honolulu: Center for Southeast Asian Studies, University of Hawai'i at Manoa, 2000), 105–24.

Hegel, Georg Wilhelm Friedrich, *Lectures on the philosophy of world history, introduction: reason in history*, translated from the German edition of Johannes Hoffmeister by H. B. Nisbet, with an introduction by Duncan Forbes (Cambridge: Cambridge University Press, 1975).

Herbert, Patricia, M., *The Hsaya San rebellion (1930–1932) reappraised* (London: Department of Oriental Manuscripts and Printed Books British Library, 1982).

Hla Hla Moe, Daw, 'The voices of women in our struggle', in Altsean Burma, *Burma – women's voices together*, edited by the Thanakha Team (Bangkok: Alternative ASEAN Network on Burma, June 2003), 51–54.

Hla Pe, U, *Burma: literature, historiography, scholarship, language, life and Buddhism* (Singapore: Institute of Southeast Asian Studies, 1985).

Hman, Daw, 'True story', in Altsean Burma, *Burma – women's voices for change*, edited by the Thanakha Team (Bangkok: Alternative ASEAN Network on Burma, June 2002), 30–33.

Houtman, Gustaaf, *Mental culture in Burmese crisis politics: Aung San Suu Kyi and the National League for Democracy* (Tokyo: Institute for the Study of Languages and Cultures of Asia and Africa, Tokyo University of Foreign Studies, 1999).

Hpo Hlaing, Yaw Mingyi U (Wetmasut Myoza Wungyi), *Rajadhammasangaha*, edited by U Htin Fatt (Maung Htin) (Yangon: Sape U Publishing House, 1979). [Euan Bagshawe's English translation, published in 2004, is available at http://burmalibrary.org/docs/THE_RAJADHAMMASANGAHA.pdf.]

Hta, Ma, *The education of women in Burma* (Rangoon: The Rangoon College Buddhist Association, 1914).

Htin Aung, (Maung), *Burmese drama: a study, with translations, of Burmese plays* (London: Oxford University Press, 1937).

————, *The stricken peacock: Anglo–Burmese relations, 1752–1948* (The Hague: Martinus Nijhoff, 1965).

————, *A history of Burma* (New York; London: Columbia University Press, 1967).

————, *Burmese history before 1287: a defence of the chronicles* (Oxford: The Asoka Society; London: [Distributed by] Luzac, 1970).

Human Rights Watch, *Crackdown: repression of the 2007 popular protests in Burma*, 19, 18(C) (December 2007).

Ikeya, Chie, 'The "traditional" high status of women in Burma: a historical consideration', *The Journal of Burma Studies* 10 (2005/06): 51–81.

————, 'Gender, history and modernity: representing women in twentieth century colonial Burma' (PhD thesis, Cornell University, 2006).

————, 'The modern Burmese woman and the politics of fashion in Burma', *The Journal of Asian Studies* 67,4 (November 2008): 1277–308.

————, *Refiguring women, colonialism and modernity in Burma* (Honolulu: University of Hawai'i Press, 2011).

India, Government of, *Census of India, 1931: Part One, Report*, Vol. 11, *Burma* (Rangoon: Office of the Superintendent Government Printing and Stationery, 1933).

International Crisis Group, *The Myanmar elections*, Asia Briefing No. 105 (Jakarta; Brussels: International Crisis Group, 27 May 2010).

————, *Myanmar's post-election landscape*, Asia Briefing No. 118 (Jakarta; Brussels: International Crisis Group, 7 March 2011).

Jaffe, Sally and Lucy Jaffe, (eds.), *Chinthe women: women's auxiliary service (Burma) 1942–46* (Chipping Norton: The Authors, 2001).

Jahan, Rounaq, 'Women political leaders: past and present', *Third World Quarterly* 9, 3 (1987): 848–71.

Johnston, E. H., 'Some Sanskrit inscriptions of Arakan', in Vladimir Braginsky (ed.), *Classical civilisations of South East Asia: an anthology of articles published in The Bulletin of SOAS* (London: RoutledgeCurzon, 2002), 150–78.

Jones, Kathleen B., *Compassionate authority: democracy and the representation of women* (New York; London: Routledge, 1993).

Jordt, Ingrid, *Burma's mass lay meditation movement: Buddhism and the cultural construction of power*, Ohio University Research in International Studies, Southeast Asia Series No. 115 (Athens: Ohio University Press, 2007).

Kachin Development Networking Group, *Valley of darkness: gold mining and militarization in Burma's Hugawng valley* (Kachin Development Networking Group, 2006).

Kachin Women's Association Thailand, *Driven away: trafficking of Kachin women on the China–Burma border* (Chiang Mai: Kachin Women's Association Thailand, May 2005).

———, *Eastward bound: an update on migration and trafficking of Kachin women on the China–Burma border* (Chiang Mai: Kachin Women's Association Thailand, August 2008).

Kala, U, *Maha yazawindawgyi* [The great royal chronicle], edited by Pe Maung Tin, Saya Pwa and Saya U Khin Soe, 3 volumes (Yangon: Hanthawaddy Press, 1960–61).

Kalaya Nee, 'Bitter medicine' in Altsean Burma, *Burma – women's voices for change*, edited by the Thanakha Team (Bangkok: Alternative Asean Network on Burma, 2002), 73–76.

Kane, John, *The politics of moral capital* (Cambridge; New York: Cambridge University Press, 2001).

Karen Human Rights Group, *False peace: increasing SPDC military repression on Toungoo District of Northern Karen State* (Thailand: Karen Human Rights Group, March 1999).

———, *Dignity in the shadow of oppression: the abuse and agency of Karen women under militarisation* ([Thailand]: Karen Human Rights Group, November 2006).

Karen Women's Organization, *Shattering silences: Karen women speak out about the Burmese military regime's use of rape as a strategy of war in Karen State*, with the collaboration of The Committee for Internally Displaced Karen People (CIDKP), The Karen Information Center (KIC), The Karen Human Rights Group (KHRG) and The Mergui-Tavoy District Information Department (Karen Women's Organization, April 2004).

———, *State of terror: The ongoing rape, murder, torture and forced labour suffered by women living under the Burmese military regime in Karen State* (Karen Women's Organization, February 2007).

———, *Walking amongst sharp knives: The unsung courage of Karen women village chiefs in conflict areas of Eastern Burma* (Karen Women's Organization, February 2010).

Karim, Wazir Jaham (ed.), *'Male' and 'female' in developing Southeast Asia* (Oxford; Washington: Berg Publishers, 1995).

———, 'Bilateralism and gender in Southeast Asia', in Wazir Jaham Karim (ed.), *'Male' and 'female' in developing Southeast Asia* (Oxford; Washington: Berg Publishers, 1995), 35–74.

Kawanami, Hiroko, 'Patterns of renunciation: the changing world of Buddhist nuns', in Ellison Banks Findly (ed.), *Women's Buddhism, Buddhism's women: tradition, revision, renewal* (Somerville, MA: Wisdom Publications, 2000), 159–71.

———, 'Can women be celibate? Sexuality and abstinence in Theravada Buddhism', in Elisa Jane Sobo and Sandra Bell (eds.), *Celibacy, culture and society: the anthropology of sexual abstinence* (Madison, Wisconsin: The University of Wisconsin Press, 2001), 137–56.

———, 'Monastic economy and interactions with society: the case of Buddhist nuns in Burma / Myanmar' (Lancaster University: unpublished discussion paper, 2007).

Keeler, Ward, 'Speaking of gender in Java', in Jane Monnig Atkinson and Shelley Errington (eds.), *Power and difference: gender in Southeast Asia* (Stanford: Stanford University Press, 1990), 127–52.

Keyes, Charles F., 'Mother or mistress but never a monk: Buddhist notions of female gender in rural Thailand', *American Ethnologist* 11, 2 (May 1984): 223–41.

Khin Aye, 'The role of Jātakas in Myanmar literature', in Universities Historical Research Centre, *Views and Visions, Part I, Proceedings of the Views and*

Visions Conference, 18–20 December 2000 (Yangon: Universities Historical Research Centre, 2001), 100–19.

Khin Aye Win, Dr Daw and Daw Zin Zin Naing, 'The role of Myanmar women in building a nation', in Myanmar Women's Affairs Federation, *Papers presented in honour of Myanmar Women's Day, 3 July 2005* (Yangon: [U Kyi Win at] Universities Press, 2005), 23–29.

Khin Khin Ma, Daw, 'Myanmar queens in historical and literary texts', in Universities Historical Research Centre, *Texts and Contexts in Southeast Asia, Part III, Proceedings of the Texts and Contexts in Southeast Asia Conference, 12–14 December 2001* (Yangon: Universities Historical Research Centre, 2003), 197–204.

Khin Mar Kyaw Zaw, Naw, (as told to Ma Ma Pyone), 'Voice for reconciliation', in Altsean Burma, *Burma – women's voices for change*, edited by the Thanakha Team (Bangkok: Alternative ASEAN Network on Burma, June 2002), 53–57.

———, 'No fallen river, no fallen tree', in Altsean Burma, *Burma – women's voices together*, edited by the Thanakha Team (Bangkok: Alternative ASEAN Network on Burma, June 2003), 3–6.

Khin Mar Mar Kyi, Ma, 'Race, gender and sexuality in the reconstruction of politics in 20th century Burma/Myanmar', in David S. Mathieson and R. J. May (eds.), *The illusion of progress: the political economy of reform in Burma/Myanmar* (Adelaide: Crawford House Publishing, 2004), 243–74.

Khin Maung, M. I., *The Myanmar labour force: growth and change, 1973–83*, Occasional Paper No. 94 (Singapore: Institute of Southeast Asian Studies, 1997).

Khin Myo Chit, (Daw), *Colourful Burma*, volume 2 ([Rangoon, Burma]: Daw Tin Aye [for] Paper Stationery Printed Matter and Photographic Stores Trade Corporation, BE 2500 [1988]).

Khin San Nwe, Ma, 'Kha La Ya 220 anguish', in Altsean Burma, *Burma – women's voices for change* (Bangkok: Alternative ASEAN Network on Burma, June 2002), 101–05.

Khin Thitsa, 'Nuns, mediums and prostitutes in Chiengmai: a study of some marginal categories of women', in C. W. Watson (ed.), *Women and development in South-East Asia* (Canterbury: Center of South-East Asian Studies, University of Kent at Canterbury, 1983), 4–45.

Khin Yi, Daw, *The Dobama movement in Burma (1930–1938)* (Ithaca, New York: Southeast Asia Program, Cornell University, 1988).

Kirsch, A. Thomas, 'Economy, polity, and religion in Thailand', in G. William Skinner and A. Thomas Kirsch (eds.), *Change and persistence in Thai society: essays in honour of Lauriston Sharp* (Ithaca; London: Cornell University Press, 1975), 172–96.

———, 'Buddhism, sex roles, and the Thai economy', in Penny Van Esterik (ed.), *Women of Southeast Asia*, revised edition (De Kalb, Illinois: Center for Southeast Asian Studies, Northern Illinois University, 1996), 13–32.

Koenig, William J., *The early Burmese polity, 1752–1819: politics, administration and social organization in the early Kon-baung period* ([Ann Arbor, Mich.]: Center for South and Southeast Asian Studies, The University of Michigan, 1990).

Kongres Perempuan Indonesia, *The first Indonesian Women's Congress of 1928*, translated and with an introduction by Susan Blackburn (Clayton, Vic.: Monash University, 2007).

Koop, John Clement, *The Eurasian population in Burma* (New Haven: Yale University, Southeast Asian Studies, 1960).

Kyan, Ma, 'King Mindon's councillors', *Journal of the Burma Research Society* 44, 1 (June 1961): 43–60.

Lall, Marie, 'The 2010 Myanmar elections', Heinrich Boll Stiftung, The Green Political Foundation, 4 January 2011.

Laydee, Naw, 'Victim of ego', in Women's League of Burma, *Overcoming shadows (2)* (Chiang Mai: Women as Peacebuilders Team, Women's League of Burma, January 2009), 85–87.

Langham Carter, R. R., 'Queen Me Nu and her family at Palangon', *Journal of the Burma Research Society* 19, 2 (1929): 31–35.

Lay, Ma, 'Sympathy – know how now', in Women's League of Burma, *Overcoming shadows* (Chiang Mai: Women as Peacebuilders Team, Women's League of Burma, 2004), 13–14.

Let Let, 'We tie our hands together for strength (innocent aunty goes to prison)', in Altsean Burma, *Burma – women's voices together* (Bangkok: Alternative ASEAN Network on Burma, June 2003), 101–07.

Lieberman, Victor B., 'Ethnic politics in eighteenth-century Burma', *Modern Asian Studies* 12, 3 (1978): 455–82.

———, *Burmese administrative cycles: anarchy and conquest, c. 1580–1760* (Princeton, N.J.: Princeton University Press, c1984).

———, *Strange parallels: Southeast Asia in global context, c. 800–1830, Volume 1: Integration on the Mainland* (Cambridge: Cambridge University Press, 2003).

Lintner, Bertil, *Aung San Suu Kyi and Burma's unfinished renaissance*, Working Paper 64 (Clayton, Vic.: Centre of Southeast Asian Studies, Monash University, 1990).

———, *Outrage: Burma's struggle for democracy*, second edition (London: White Lotus, 1990).

———, *Burma in revolt: opium and insurgency since 1948* (Boulder, Colo.: Westview Press; Bangkok: White Lotus, 1994).

Loos, Tamara, 'The politics of women's suffrage in Thailand', in Louise Edwards and Mina Roces (eds.), *Women's suffrage in Asia: gender, nationalism and democracy* (London; New York: Routledge, 2004), 170–94.

Low, James, Captain, 'History of Tenasserim', *Journal of the Royal Asiatic Society* 3 (1836): 287–336.

Lubeight, Guy, 'Industrial zones in Burma and Burmese labour in Thailand', in Monique Skidmore and Trevor Wilson (eds.), *Myanmar: the state, community and the environment* (Canberra: Australian National University E Press, 2007), 159–88.

Luce, G. H. [Gordon Hannington], 'The ancient Pyu', *Journal of the Burma Research Society*, 27, 3 (1937): 239–53.

———, 'Notes on the peoples of Burma in the 12th–13th century A.D.', *Journal of the Burma Research Society* 42, 1 (June 1959): 52–74.

———, 'Old Kyaukse and the coming of the Burmans', *Journal of the Burma Research Society* 42, 1 (June 1959): 75–109.

———, *Phases of Pre-Pagan Burma* (Oxford: Oxford University Press, 1985).

——— and Pe Maung Tin (eds.), *Selections from the inscriptions of Pagan* (Rangoon: British Burma Press, 1928).

———, *Inscriptions of Burma*, six volumes (Rangoon: Oriental Studies Publications, University of Rangoon, 1933–56).

McCormick, Indra, *Women as political actors in Indonesia's New Order*, Monash Asia Institute Working Paper 123 (Clayton, Vic.: Monash Asia Institute, 2003).

McKenzie, Kevin and Kathleen McHugh, 'An investigation into child abandonment and existing childcare options for Burmese workers in Mae Sot, Thailand' (unpublished report).

Ma Pyone, Ma, 'Spice, politics & inspiration – a tribute to Daw Kyi Kyi', in Altsean Burma, *Burma – women's voices for change*, edited by the Thanakha Team (Bangkok: Alternative Asean Network on Burma, 2002), 4–6.

Ma Lay, Ma, *Mon ywe mahu* [Not out of hate] (Yangon: Shumawa, 1955).

———, *Not out of hate: a novel of Burma*, edited by William H. Frederick; translated by Margaret Aung-Thwin; introduced by Anna Allott; afterword by Robert E. Vore, Monographs in International Studies, Southeast Asia Series, No. 88 (Athens, Ohio: Ohio University Center for International Studies, 1991).

———, *Thway* [Blood] (Yangon: Seidana Sape, 1973).

———, *Blood bond*, translated by Than Than Win, (Honolulu: Center for Southeast Asian Studies, University of Hawai'i at Manoa, 2004).

Maha Minhla Mingaunggyaw, *Ummadantī Pyo* (Yangon: Burma Research Society, 1964).

Mann, Michael, *The sources of social power. Vol.1. A history of power from the beginning to A.D. 1760* (Cambridge: Cambridge University Press, 1986).

———, *The sources of social power. Vol.2. The rise of classes and nation-states, 1970–1914* (Cambridge: Cambridge University Press, 1993).

Maung, Cynthia, Dr, 'Health on the other side', in Altsean Burma, *Burma – women's voices for change*, edited by the Thanakha Team (Bangkok: Alternative ASEAN Network on Burma, June 2002), 15–18.

Maung Aung Myoe, *Officer education and leadership training in the tatmadaw: a survey*, Working Paper No. 346 (Strategic and Defence Studies Centre, Australian National University, Canberra, 1999).

Maung Maung, U, *From sangha to laity: nationalist movements of Burma, 1920–1940* (New Delhi: Manohar, 1990).

Maung Maung, Dr, *Burma's Constitution* (The Hague: Martinus Nijhoff, 1959).

———, *Law and custom in Burma and the Burmese family* (The Hague: Martinus Nijhoff, 1963).

———, *Burma and General Ne Win* (Bombay; London; New York: Asia Publishing House, 1969).

Maung Yin Hmaing et al., *Daw Suu Kyi, NLD Party and our ray of hope and selected articles* ([Yangon]: U Soe Win, News and Periodicals Enterprise, 2003).

May Oung, (U), 'The modern Burman', *Rangoon Gazette*, 10 August 1908, reprinted, with a brief introduction by J. S. Furnivall, in *Journal of the Burma Research Society*, 33, 1 (1950): 1–7.

——, *Leading cases on Buddhist law* (Rangoon, 1914).

May Pwint Khaing, 'The role of Queen Supayalat during King Thibaw's reign' (MRes thesis, University of Yangon, 2001).

Mendelson, E. Michael, *Sangha and state in Burma* (Ithaca: Cornell University Press, 1975).

Mi Mi Khaing, *Burmese family* (Bloomington: Indiana University Press, 1962).

——, 'Burma: balance and harmony', in Barbara E. Ward (ed.), *Women in the new Asia: the changing social roles of men and women in South and South-East Asia* (Paris: UNESCO, 1963), 104–37.

——, *The world of Burmese women* (London: Zed Books, 1984).

Miksic, John N., 'Heroes and heroines in Bagan-period Myanmar and early classic Indonesia', in Universities Historical Research Centre, *Views and Visions, Part I, Proceedings of the Views and Visions Conference, 18–20 December 2000* (Yangon: Universities Historical Research Centre, 2001), 58–71.

Mills, Janell, 'Militarism, civil war and women's status: a Burma case study', in Louise Edwards and Mina Roces (eds.), *Women in Asia: tradition, modernity and globalisation* (St Leonards: Allen & Unwin, 2000), 265–90.

Mirante, Edith T., 'Burma's ethnic minority women: from abuse to resistance', in Marc S. Miller (ed.), *State of the peoples: a global human rights report on societies in danger* (Boston: Beacon Press, 1993), 7–14.

Mo Ngern Hom, Nang, 'My life as a woman soldier', in Altsean Burma, *Burma – women's voices together*, edited by the Thanakha Team (Bangkok: Alternative Asean Network on Burma, June 2003), 55–59.

Molyneux, Maxine and Shahra Razavi, *Gender justice, development and rights*, Democracy, Governance and Human Rights Programme Paper Number 10 (New York: United Nations Research Institute for Social Development, January 2003).

Monnig Atkinson, Jane and Shelley Errington (eds.), *Power and difference: gender in island Southeast Asia* (Stanford: Stanford University Press, 1990).

Moore, Elizabeth, 'Bronze and Iron Age sites in Upper Myanmar: Chindwin, Samon and Pyu', *SOAS Bulletin of Burma Research* 1, 1 (Spring 2003): 24–39.

———, 'Interpreting Pyu material culture: royal chronologies and finger-marked bricks', *Myanmar Historical Research Journal* 13 (June 2004): 1–57.

Moscotti, Albert D., *Burma's constitution and elections of 1974*, Research notes and discussions no. 5 (Singapore: Institute of Southeast Asian Studies, September 1977).

Mya Maung, 'The Burmese way to socialism beyond the welfare state', *Asian Survey* 10, 6 (June 1970): 533–51.

———, 'Military management of the Burmese economy: problems and prospects', in Josef Silverstein (ed.), *The future of Burma in perspective: a symposium* (Athens: Ohio University, Center for International Studies, Southeast Asia Program, 1974), 10–23.

———, 'Burma's economic performance under military rule: an assessment', *Asian Survey* 37, 6 (June 1997): 503–24.

Mya Mya Thein, 'Women scientists and engineers in Burma', *Impact of Science on Society* 30, 1 (1980): 15–22.

Mya Sein, (Daw), 'The women of Burma', *Perspective of Burma: An Atlantic Monthly Supplement* (June 1958): 24–27.

———, 'Towards independence in Burma: the role of women', *Asian Affairs* 59, 3 (October 1972): 288–300.

Mya Than, 'Recent developments in Myanmar: impact and implications of ASEAN membership and Asian crisis', in Morten B. Pederson, Emily Rudland and Ronald J. May (eds.), *Burma Myanmar: strong regime weak state?* (Adelaide: Crawford House Publishing, 2000), 138–63.

Mya Than Tint, *On the road to Mandalay: tales of ordinary people*, translated from Burmese by Ohnmar Khin and Sein Kyaw Hlaing (Bangkok: White Orchid Press, 1996).

Myo Myint, *The politics of survival in Burma: diplomacy and statecraft in the reign of King Mindon, 1853–1878* (PhD thesis, Cornell University, 1987).

Naing Naing Maw, 'The role of Myanmar women in the nationalist movement (1906–1942)' (MA thesis, Yangon University, 1999).

Ni Ni Gyi, 'Patterns of social change in a Burmese family', in Barbara E. Ward (ed.), *Women in the new Asia: the changing social roles of men and women in South and South-East Asia* (Paris: UNESCO, 1963), 138–48.

Ni Ni Myint, (Daw), *Burma's struggle against British imperialism, 1885–1895*, second edition (Rangoon: Universities Press, 1985).

———, *The status of Myanmar women* ([Kitakyushu], Japan: Kitakyushu Forum on Asian Women; [Yangon], Myanmar: Universities Historical Research Centre, September 2002).

———, 'Queen Supayalat', in Myanmar Historical Commission, Ministry of Education, Union of Myanmar, *Selected writings of Ni Ni Myint: member of the Myanmar Historical Commission* (Yangon: U Kyi Win, Manager (02384) at the Universities Press, 2004), 80–96.

———, '"Victory Land of Golden Yun" – A queen and her poem', in Myanmar Historical Commission, Ministry of Education, Union of Myanmar, *Selected writings of Ni Ni Myint: member of the Myanmar Historical Commission* (Yangon: U Kyi Win, Manager (02384) at the Universities Press, 2004), 16–26.

Nickel, Janis E., 'And what about the women of Burma?', *Burma Issues*, Special Issue (August 1993): 1–19.

Nobel Women's Initiative and Women's League of Burma, *International Tribunal on crimes against women of Burma, March 2, 2010, New York* (Women's League of Burma and Nobel Women's Initiative, 2010).

Nu, U, *U Nu, Saturday's son*, translated by U Yaw Lone; edited by U Kyaw Win (New Haven: Yale University Press, 1975).

Nyun-Han, Emma, 'The socio-political roles of women in Japan and Burma' (PhD thesis, University of Colorado, 1972).

O'Kane, Mary, 'Gender, borders and transversality: the emerging women's movement in the Burma-Thailand borderlands', in Navnita Chadha Behera (ed.), *Gender, conflict and migration*, Women and migration in Asia, volume 3 (New Delhi; Thousand Oaks, Calif.; London: Sage Publications, 2006), 227–54.

Okell, John, '"Translation" and "embellishment" in an early Burmese *Jātaka* poem', *Journal of the Royal Asiatic Society* 3/4 (October 1967): 133–47.

Orwell, George, *Burmese days* (London: The Camelot Press, 1935).

Pandita, Sayadaw U, *In this very life: the liberation teachings of the Buddha*, foreword by Joseph Goldstein; edited by Kate Wheeler (Somerville, MA: Wisdom Publications, 1992).

Parsons, Talcott, *The social system* (Glencoe, Illinois: Free Press, 1951).

———— and Edward A. Shils (eds.), *Toward a general theory of action* (Cambridge, Mass.: Harvard University Press, 1951). [Harper Torchbook edition reprinted and published by Harper & Row, New York, 1962.]

————, *Structure and process in modern societies* (Glencoe, Illinois: Free Press, 1960).

Pasternak Slater, Ann, 'Suu Burmese', in Aung San Suu Kyi, *Freedom from fear and other writings* (Harmondsworth: Penguin Books, 1991), 258–66.

Pathi Phaw, Naw, 'From prayer to action', in Altsean Burma, *Burma – women's voices for change*, edited by the Thanakha Team (Bangkok: Alternative ASEAN Network on Burma, June 2002), 12–14.

Pe Maung Tin, 'Women in the inscriptions of Pagan', in Burma Research Society, Fiftieth Anniversary Publications No. 2, Selections of articles from the *Journal of the Burma Research Society* (History and Literature) (Rangoon, 1960), 411–21. [Originally published in the *Journal of the Burma Research Society* 35, 3 (1935): 149–59.]

Phayre, Arthur Purves, *History of Burma, including Burma proper, Pegu, Taungu, Tenasserim, and Arakan: from the earliest time to the end of the first war with British India*, second edition (London: Susil Gupta, 1967).

Po Ka, U, *The citizen of Burma* (Rangoon: British Burma Press, 1914).

Pollack, Oliver B., *Empires in collision: Anglo–Burmese relations in the mid-nineteenth century* (Westport; London: Greenwood Press, 1979).

Pon Nya, U, *Paduma Pyazat*, Buddha's birth story no. 193 (Rangoon, 1927).

Project Maje, *This revolutionary life: women of the Kachin Liberated Area* (Cranford, N.J.: Project Maje, March 1995).

Pu Gale, *Kabya pyatthana* [The half-caste problem] (Yangon: Kyi Pwa Yei, 1939).

Purcell, Marc, '"Axe-handles or willing minions?" International NGOs in Burma', in Burma Center Netherlands (BCN) and Transnational Institute (TNI) (eds.), *Strengthening civil society in Burma: possibilities and dilemmas for international NGOs* (Chiang Mai: Silkworm Books, 1999), 69–109.

Pye, Lucian W., *Politics, personality, and nation building: Burma's search for identity* (New Haven; London: Yale University Press, 1962).

Pyone Yin, 'Women in the Bagan period' (MRes thesis, University of Yangon, 2001).

Ratthasara, Shin Maha, *Catudhammasara Kogan Pyo* (Rangoon: Buddha Sasana Council, 1959).

Reid, Anthony, 'Female roles in pre-colonial Southeast Asia', *Modern Asian Studies* 22, 3 (1988): 629–45.

———, *Southeast Asia in the age of commerce 1450–1680. Vol. 1: The lands below the winds; Vol. 2: Expansion and crisis* (New Haven; London: Yale University Press, c1988–93).

Richter, Linda K., 'Exploring theories of female leadership in South and Southeast Asia', *Pacific Affairs* 63, 4 (1990–91): 524–40.

Roces, Mina, *Women, power, and kinship politics: female power in post-war Philippines* (Westport, Connecticut: Praeger, 1998).

——— and Louise Edwards, 'Contesting gender narratives: 1970–2000', in Louise Edwards and Mina Roces (eds.), *Women in Asia: tradition, modernity and globalisation* (St Leonards: Allen & Unwin, 2000), 1–15.

Sa Bae, 'Rebel's daughter', in Altsean Burma, *Burma – women's voices together*, edited by the Thanakha Team (Bangkok: Alternative ASEAN Network on Burma, June 2003), 85–87.

Sai Aung Tun, U, 'Shan-Myanmar relations as found in the Hsipaw Chronicle', in Universities Historical Research Centre, *Texts and Contexts in Southeast Asia, Part III, Proceedings of the Texts and Contexts in Southeast Asia Conference, 12–14 December 2001* (Yangon: Universities Historical Research Centre, 2003), 248–78.

Sangermano, Vicentius, *A description of the Burmese empire*, compiled chiefly from Burmese documents by Father Sangermano; translated from his manuscript by William Tandy; with a preface and note by John Jardine (London; Santiago de Compostela: Susil Gupta, 1966).

Sargent, Inge, *Twilight over Burma: my life as a Shan princess*, foreword by Bertil Lintner (Honolulu: University of Hawai'i Press, 1994).

Sarkisyanz, Manuel, *Buddhist backgrounds of the Burmese revolution* (The Hague: Martinus Nijhoff, 1965).

Saw Moun Nyin, *Myanma amyothami* [Burmese women] (Yangon: Padauk Hlaing, 1976).

Schober, Juliane, 'Colonial knowledge and Buddhist education in Burma', in Ian Harris (ed.), *Buddhism, power and political order* (London; New York: Routledge, 2007), 52–70.

Schreurs, Peter, *Caraga Antigua, 1521–1910: the hispanization and christianization of Agusan, Surigao, and East Davao*, second edition (Manila: Republic of the Philippines, National Commission for Culture and the Arts, National Historical Institute, [2000]).

Scott, Sir James George, 'The position of women in Burma', *The Sociological Review* 6, 2 (1913): 139–46.

Seekins, Donald M., 'Japan "Burma Lovers" and the military regime', Japan Policy Research Institute Working Paper No. 60 (Japan Policy Research Institute with University of San Fransisco Center for the Pacific Rim, September 1999).

———, *The disorder in order: the army-state in Burma since 1962* (Bangkok: White Lotus Press, 2002).

Sein Sein, Daw, 'The position of women in Hinyana Buddhist countries (Burma, Ceylon and Thailand)' (MA thesis, University of London, 1958).

Selth, Andrew, *Transforming the tatmadaw: the Burmese armed forces since 1988*, Canberra Papers on Strategy and Defence No. 113 (Canberra: Strategic and Defence Studies Centre, Research School of Pacific and Asian Studies, Australian National University, 1996).

———, *Burma's armed forces: power without glory*, foreword by David Steinberg, Norwalk, CT: EastBridge, 2002).

Shan Human Rights Foundation, *Displacement in Shan State* (Thailand: Shan Human Rights Foundation, April 1999).

———, *Charting the exodus from Shan State: patterns of Shan refugee flow into northern Chiang Mai province of Thailand* (Chiang Mai: Shan Human Rights Foundation, [200–]).

——— and Shan Women's Action Network, *Licence to rape: the Burmese military regime's use of sexual violence in the ongoing war in Shan State* (Shan Human Rights Foundation and Shan Women's Action Network, May 2002).

Shan Women's Action Network, 'A mockery of justice: the State Peace and Development Council's investigation into the 'Licence to rape' report', 24 September 2002.

———, *SWAN: a ten-year journey* (Shan Women's Action Network, March 2009).

Shway Yoe, *The Burman: his life and notions*, with an introduction by John K. Musgrave (New York: W. W. Norton & Company, Inc., 1963).

Silverstein, Josef (ed.), *The future of Burma in perspective: a symposium* (Athens: Ohio University, Center for International Studies, Southeast Asia Program, 1974).

————, 'From soldiers to civilians: the new constitution of Burma in action', in Josef Silverstein (ed.), *The future of Burma in perspective: a symposium* (Athens: Ohio University, Center for International Studies, Southeast Asia Program, 1974), 80–92.

————, 'Aung San Suu Kyi: Is she Burma's woman of destiny?', in Aung San Suu Kyi, *Freedom from fear and other writings*, forward by Vaclav Havel, edited and with an introduction by Michael Aris (Harmondsworth: Penguin Books, 1991), 267–83.

————, *The political legacy of Aung San*, revised edition, Southeast Asia Program Series, no. 11 (Ithaca, New York.: Southeast Asia Program, Cornell University, 1993).

————, 'The idea of freedom in Burma and the political thought of Daw Aung San Suu Kyi', *Pacific Affairs* 69, 2 (Summer 1996): 211–28.

Singer, Noel F., 'The golden relics of Bana Thau', *Arts of Asia* 22, 5 (September–October, 1992): 75–84.

Skidmore, Monique, *Karaoke fascism: Burma and the politics of fear* (Philadelphia: University of Pennsylvania Press, 2004).

———— and Trevor Wilson (eds.), *Myanmar: the state, community and the environment* (Canberra: Australian National University E Press, 2007).

Smith, Martin, *Burma: insurgency and the politics of ethnicity*, second edition (London; New York: Zed Books, 1999).

Social Action for Women, 'Statement 1/2001', 26 November 2001 (unpublished paper).

Spiro, Melford E., *Buddhism and society: a great tradition and its Burmese vicissitudes* (New York; London: Harper and Row, 1972).

————, *Kinship and marriage in Burma: a cultural and psychodynamic analysis* (Berkeley: University of California Press, 1977).

————, 'Gender hierarchy in Burma: cultural, social, and psychological dimensions', in Barbara Diane Miller (ed.), *Sex and gender hierarchies* (Cambridge; New York; Oakleigh, Vic.: Cambridge University Press, 1993), 316–33.

Stargardt, Janice, 'The great silver reliquary from Sri Ksetra: the oldest Buddhist art in Burma and one of the world's oldest Pali inscriptions', in Marijke J. Klokke and Karel R. van Kooij (eds.), *Fruits of inspiration: studies in honour of Prof. J. G. de Casparis, retired Professor of the early history and archaeology of South and Southeast Asia at the University of Leiden, the Netherlands, on the occasion of his 85th birthday* (Groningen: Egbert Forsten, 2001), 487–517.

Steinberg, David I., *Burma's road toward development: growth and ideology under military rule* (Boulder: Westview Press, 1981).

———, *Burma: a socialist nation of Southeast Asia* (Boulder, Colorado: Westview Press, 1982).

———, 'A void in Myanmar: civil society in Burma', in Burma Center Netherlands (BCN) and Transnational Institute (TNI) (eds.), *Strengthening civil society in Burma: Possibilities and dilemmas for international NGOs* (Chiang Mai: Silkworm Books, 1999), 1–14.

———, *Burma: the state of Myanmar* (Washington: Georgetown University Press, 2001).

Stivens, Maila (ed.), *Why gender matters in Southeast Asian politics* (Clayton, Vic.: Centre of Southeast Asian Studies, Monash University, 1991).

———, 'Why gender matters in Southeast Asian politics', in Maila Stivens (ed.), *Why gender matters in Southeast Asian politics* (Clayton, Vic.: Centre of Southeast Asian Studies, Monash University, 1991), 9–24.

Stuart-Fox, Martin, 'Who was Maha Thevi?', *Journal of the Siam Society* 81, 1 (1993): 63–72.

Sykes, Colonel, 'Account of some Golden relics discovered at Rangoon, and exhibited at a Meeting of the Society on the 6th June, 1857, by permission of the Court of Directors of the East India Company', *Journal of the Royal Asiatic Society of Great Britain & Ireland* 17 (1860): 298–308.

Symes, Michael, *An account of an embassy to the Kingdom of Ava, sent by the Governor-General of India in the year 1795* (London: W. Blumer and Co., 1800; republished Westmead, Farnborough, Hants., England: Gregg International Publishers Limited, 1969).

———, *Journal of his second embassy to the Court of Ava in 1802*, edited with an introduction and notes by D. G. E. Hall (London: Allen & Unwin, 1955).

Taw Sein Ko, *Burmese sketches* (Rangoon: British Burma Press, 1913).

Taylor, Jean Gelman, *The social world of Batavia: European and Eurasian in Dutch Asia* (Madison, Wis.: University of Wisconsin Press, 1983).

Taylor, Robert H., *The state in Burma* (Honolulu: University of Hawai'i Press, 1987).

Taylor, Sandra C., *Vietnamese women at war: fighting for Ho Chi Minh and the revolution* (Lawrence, Kansas: University Press of Kansas, 1999).

Tennyson Jesse, Fryn, *The lacquer lady* (London: William Heinemann Ltd., 1929).

Than E, Ma, 'A flowering of the spirit: memories of Suu and her family', in Aung San Suu Kyi, *Freedom from fear and other writings* (Harmondsworth: Penguin Books, 1991), 241–57.

Than Tun (ed.), *The Royal Orders of Burma, A.D. 1598–1888*, edited with an introduction, notes and summary in English of each order by Than Tun (Kyoto: Center for Southeast Asian Studies, Kyoto University, 1983–90).

———, 'History of Burma 1000–1300', in Paul Strachan (ed.), *Essays on the history and Buddhism of Burma by Professor Than Tun* (Whiting Bay: Kiscadale Publications, 1988), 3–21.

———, 'Religion in Burma 1000–1300', in Paul Strachan (ed.), *Essays on the history and Buddhism of Burma by Professor Than Tun* (Whiting Bay: Kiscadale Publications, 1988), 23–45.

———, 'Social life in Burma 1044–1287', in Paul Strachan (ed.), *Essays on the history and Buddhism of Burma by Professor Than Tun* (Whiting Bay: Kiscadale Publications, 1988), 47–56.

———, 'The legal system in Burma 1000–1300', in Paul Strachan (ed.), *Essays on the history and Buddhism of Burma by Professor Than Tun* (Whiting Bay: Kiscadale Publications, 1988), 69–82.

Thant Myint-U, *The making of modern Burma* (New York: Cambridge University Press, c2001).

Tharaphi Than, 'Writers, fighters and prostitutes: women and Burma's modernity, 1942–1962' (PhD thesis, University of London, School of Oriental and African Studies, 2010).

The Glass Palace Chronicle of the kings of Burma, translated by Pe Maung Tin and G. H. Luce (London Oxford University Press, 1923; Rangoon: Rangoon University Press, 1960).

Thein, Saya, 'Shin Sawbu', *Journal of the Burma Research Society* 1, 2 (December 1911): 10–12.

Thet Htoot, 'The nature of the Burmese chronicles', in D. G. E. Hall (ed.), *Historians of Southeast Asia* (Oxford: Oxford University Press, 1961), 50–62.

Thompson, Mark R., 'Female leadership of democratic transitions in Asia', *Pacific Affairs* 75, 4 (Winter 2002–03): 535–55.

Tin (of Mandalay), *Konbaungzet maha yazawindawgyi* [Great royal chronicle of the Konbaung Dynasty], 3 volumes (Yangon: Ledimandaing, 1967–68).

Tin (of Pagan), *Myanma min okchokpon sadan* [Documents relating to the administration of Burmese kings], 5 volumes (Yangon, 1931–33).

Tinker, Hugh, *The Union of Burma: a study of the first years of independence*, 4th edition (London: Oxford University Press, 1967).

— (ed.), *Burma: The struggle for independence 1944–1948: documents from official and private sources*, 2 volumes (London: Her Majesty's Stationery Office, 1983–84).

Tinzar Lwyn, 'The mission: colonial discourse on gender and the politics of Burma', *New Literatures Review* 24 (Winter South 1992): 5–22.

———, 'Stories of gender and ethnicity: discourses of colonialism and resistance in Burma', *The Australian Journal of Anthropology* 5, 1&2 (1994): 60–85.

Tosa, Keiko, 'The chicken and the scorpion: rumour, counternarratives, and the political uses of Buddhism', in Monique Skidmore (ed.), *Burma at the turn of the 21st century* (Honolulu: University of Hawai'i Press, 2005), 154–73.

Trager, Frank N., 'The political split in Burma', *Far Eastern Survey* 27, 10 (October 1958): 145–55.

———, *Burma – from kingdom to republic: a historical and political analysis* (New York: Praeger, 1966).

— and William L. Scully, 'The Third Congress of the Burma Socialist Programme Party: the need to create continuity and dynamism of leadership', *Asian Survey*, 17, 9 (September 1977): 330–38.

— and William J. Koenig, *Burmese sit-tàns, 1764–1826: records of rural life and administration* (Tucson: University of Arizona Press, 1979).

Trench Gascoigne, Gwendolen, *Among pagodas and fair ladies: an account of a tour through Burma* (London: A. D. Innes, 1896).

Tun Aung Chain (Mingyinyo), 'Women in the statecraft of the Awa kingdom (1365–1555)', in *Essays given to Than Tun on his 75th birthday: studies in Myanma history, volume 1* (Yangon: Than Tun Diamond Jubilee Publication Committee, 1999), 107–20.

———, 'Pegu in politics and trade, ninth to seventeenth centuries', in Sunait Chutintaranond and Chris Baker (eds.), *Recalling local pasts: autonomous history in Southeast Asia* (Chiang Mai: Silkworm Books, 2002), 25–52.

Tun Myint, 'Implications of current development strategies for Myanmar's development: environmental governance in the SPDC's Myanmar', in Monique Skidmore and Trevor Wilson (eds.), *Myanmar: the state, community and the environment* (Canberra: Australian National University E Press, 2007), 190–217.

Turnell, Sean, *Burma's economy 2008: current situation and prospects for reform* (Sydney: Burma Economic Watch/Economics Department, Macquarie University, May 2008).

Turner-Gottschang, Karen and Phan Thanh Hao, *Even the women must fight: memories of war from North Vietnam* (New York: Wiley, c1998).

United Nations, Fourth World Conference on Women, 'Statement by H.E. Major-General Soe Myint, Minister For Social Welfare, Relief and Resettlement and Leader of the Delegation of the Union of Myanmar to the United Nations Fourth World Conference on Women: Action for Equality, Development and Peace', Beijing, 4–15 September 1995.

———, Convention on the Elimination of All Forms of Discrimination Against Women, 'Consideration of reports presented by States parties under article 18 of the Convention on the Elimination of All Forms of Discrimination against Women. Initial report of States parties. Myanmar', CEDAW/C/MMR/1, 25 June 1999.

———, 'Press Release WOM/1166. Committee on Elimination of Discrimination Against Women concludes consideration of Myanmar report', 26 January 2000.

———, 'Response by the Myanmar Delegation, Twenty-Second Session of the Committee on the Elimination of All Forms of Discrimination Against Women (CEDAW)', New York, 26 January 2000.

———, Office of the High Commissioner for Human Rights, 'Concluding Observations of the Committee on the Elimination of Discrimination Against Women: Myanmar', A/55/38, paras. 91–138, 4 February 2000.

———, 'Consideration of reports presented by States parties under article 18 of the Convention on the Elimination of All Forms of Discrimination against Women. Combined second and third reports of States parties. Myanmar', CEDAW/C/MMR/3, 4 September 2007.

———, 'Concluding observations of the Committee on the Elimination of Discrimination against Women: Myanmar', CEDAW/C/MMR/CO/3, 7 November 2008.

———, General Assembly, 'Resolution adopted by the General Assembly [on the report of the Third Committee (A/57/566/Add.3)]. 57/231. Situation of human rights in Myanmar', A/RES/57/231, 28 February 2003.

————, 'Situation of human rights in Myanmar', A/C.3/66/L.55/Rev.1, 16 November 2011.

UNICEF Myanmar, *Children and women in Myanmar: situation assessment and analysis* ([Yangon]: UNICEF Myanmar, April 2001).

[UNICEF, UNFPA and Save the Children], 'Inter-agency review of the Myanmar Protection of Children and Women Cluster response to Cyclone Nargis. External Review. Participating Agencies: UNICEF, UNFPA, Save the Children' (October 2008).

Van Esterik, Penny (ed.), *Women of Southeast Asia*, revised edition (De Kalb, IL: Center for Southeast Asian Studies, Northern Illinois University, 1996).

————, 'Lay women in Theravada Buddhism', in Penny Van Esterik (ed.), *Women of Southeast Asia*, revised edition (De Kalb, IL: Center for Southeast Asian Studies, Northern Illinois University, 1996), 42–61.

Ward, Barbara E. (ed.), *Women in the new Asia: the changing social roles of men and women in South and South-East Asia* (Paris: UNESCO, 1963).

Weber, Max, *Economy and society: an outline of interpretive sociology*, edited by Guenther Roth and Claus Wittich, 3 volumes (New York: Bedminster Press, 1968).

Weller, Marc (ed.), *Democracy and politics in Burma: a collection of documents* (Manerplaw, Burma: Government Printing Office of the National Coalition Government of the Union of Burma, 1993).

White, John, *A voyage to Cochin China*, introduced by Milton Osborne (London: Longman, Hurst, Rees, Orme, Brown and Green, 1824; reprinted in Kuala Lumpur; New York: Oxford University Press, 1972).

White, Judith A., 'Leadership through compassion and understanding', *Journal of Management Inquiry* 7, 4 (December 1998): 286–93.

Wieringa, Saskia, 'Aborted feminism in Indonesia: a history of Indonesian socialist feminism', in Saskia Wieringa (ed.), *Women's struggles and strategies* (Aldershot, Hants, England; Brookfield, Vt.: Gower, c1988), 69–89.

————, 'Matrilinearity and women's interests: the Minangkabau of Western Sumatra', in Saskia Wieringa (ed.), *Subversive women: historical experiences of gender and resistance* (London; Atlantic Highlands, N. J.: Zed Books, 1995), 241–68.

Williams, Louise, *Wives, mistresses and matriarchs: Asian women today* (London: Phoenix Press, 2001).

Wilson, Trevor, 'Foreign policy as a political tool: Myanmar 2003–2006', in Monique Skidmore and Trevor Wilson (eds.), *Myanmar: the state, community and the environment* (Canberra: Australian National University E Press, 2007), 82–107.

Win May, *Status of women in Myanmar* (Yangon: Sarpay Beikman Press, 1995).

Wolters, O. W., *History, culture, and region in Southeast Asian perspectives*, revised edition, Studies on Southeast Asia No. 26 (Ithaca, New York: Southeast Asia Program, Cornell University in association with the Institute of Southeast Asian Studies, Singapore, 1999).

Women of Burma, *In the shadow of the junta: CEDAW shadow report* (Chiang Mai: Women's League of Burma, 2008).

Women's League of Burma, *Overcoming shadows* (Chiang Mai: Women as Peacebuilders Team, Women's League of Burma, 2004).

———, *Constituting our rights* (Chiang Mai: Women's League of Burma, February 2006).

———, *Looking through gender lenses: position paper on gender equality* (Chiang Mai: Women's League of Burma, September 2006).

———, *Courage to resist: women human rights defenders in Burma* (Chiang Mai: Women's League of Burma, November 2007).

———, *Overcoming shadows (2)* (Chiang Mai: Women as Peacebuilders Team, Women's League of Burma, January 2009).

———, *Building a movement within a movement: WLB marks ten years of gender activism* (Chiang Mai: Women's League of Burma, December 2009).

———, 'Statement on the Sixth Congress of the Women's League of Burma (WLB)', 27 January 2011.

——— and International Institute for Democracy and Electoral Assistance, 'Women and peace building. Workshops on: the role for Burmese women in developing peace building strategies', 16–17 May 2002 (New Delhi, India) and 19–21 May 2002 (Chiang Mai, Thailand) (copyright International IDEA, 2003).

Women's Organisations of Burma's Shadow Report Writing Committee, 'Burma: the current state of women – conflict area specific. A shadow report to the 22nd Session of CEDAW', January 2000, edited for *Burma Debate* 6, 4 (Winter 1999): 13 pages.

Woodman, Dorothy, *The making of Burma* (London: The Cresset Press, 1962).

Yang Li (Jackie Yang), *The house of Yang: guardians of an unknown frontier* (Sydney: Book press, 1997).

Yi Yi, 'Life at the Burmese court under the Konbaung kings', *Journal of the Burma Research Society* 44, 1 (June 1961): 85–129.

Yo Yo Lay, 'Women's activism in the borderlands', in Altsean Burma, *Burma – women's voices for change*, edited by the Thanakha Team (Bangkok: Alternative ASEAN Network on Burma, June 2002), 34–39.

Young Woman from Myanmar, 'Neutral thoughts', in Altsean Burma, *Burma – women's voices for change*, edited by the Thanakha Team (Bangkok: Alternative Asean Network on Burma, June 2002), 58–61.

Yu Yu, 'Strength amidst tragedy', in Altsean Burma, *Burma – women's voices for change* (Bangkok: Alternative ASEAN Network on Burma, June 2002), 50–52.

Yule, Henry (comp.), *A narrative of the mission to the Court of Ava in 1855*; together with The journal of Arthur Phayre, Envoy to the Court of Ava, and additional illustrations by Colesworthy Grant and Linnaeus Tripe; with an introduction by Hugh Tinker (London, 1857; reprinted in Kuala Lumpur; London; New York: Oxford University Press, 1968).

Newspapers and periodicals

Asiaweek

Bamakhit [New Era of Burma]

Burma Issues

Burmanet News (news archive on Burma issues)

Dagon [Rangoon]

Eastern World (London)

Far Eastern Economic Review

Far Eastern Economic Review Yearbook

The Guardian (Rangoon)

The Guardian Magazine (Rangoon)

The Irrawaddy

The Irrawaddy Magazine

Manchester Guardian

Maulmain Chronicle

Myawaddy

The Nation (Rangoon)

New Light of Myanmar

New Mandala

New Times of Burma

Rangoon Times

Shan Women's Action Network Newsletter

Thuriya [Sun]

Time Magazine

Working People's Daily

Index

*Note: Page numbers in **bold** type refer to illustrations*